Enlightened Mind, Divine Mind

THE NOTEBOOKS OF PAUL BRUNTON
(VOLUME 16)

ENLIGHTENED MIND, DIVINE MIND

PAUL BRUNTON
(1898–1981)

An in-depth study of
the final four categories
from the notebooks

Published for the
PAUL BRUNTON PHILOSOPHIC FOUNDATION
by Larson Publications

International Standard Book Number (cloth) 0-943914-44-2
International Standard Book Number (paper) 0-943914-46-9
International Standard Book Number (series, cloth) 0-943914-17-5
International Standard Book Number (series, paper) 0-943914-23-X
Library of Congress Catalog Card Number: 84-47752

Manufactured in the United States of America

Published for the
Paul Brunton Philosophic Foundation
by
Larson Publications
4936 Route 414
Burdett, New York 14818

2   4   6   8   10   9   7   5   3

The works of Paul Brunton

A Search in Secret India
The Secret Path
A Search in Secret Egypt
A Message from Arunachala
A Hermit in the Himalayas
The Quest of the Overself
The Inner Reality
(*also titled* Discover Yourself)
Indian Philosophy and Modern Culture
The Hidden Teaching Beyond Yoga
The Wisdom of the Overself
The Spiritual Crisis of Man

Published posthumously

Essays on the Quest

(continued next page)

CONTENTS

EDITORS' INTRODUCTION

This culminating volume in *The Notebooks of Paul Brunton* gives a definitive account of "Enlightenment" and explores the principles underlying it. Treating with unprecedented clarity the distinctions between inspired-human and divine identity, it intimately illustrates the stable goal of spiritual development and provides a standard by which to evaluate claims of "union with God."

Enlightened Mind, Divine Mind is our composite title for the final four categories of Paul Brunton's twenty-eightfold "Ideas" schemata. It completes this first cycle of publications drawn from the richly varied personal notebooks Paul Brunton (1898–1981) reserved for posthumous publication.

Part 1, *World-Mind in Individual Mind*, brings us nearly full-circle from our starting point in the introduction to volume one, *Perspectives*. Here we get the details of what we there spoke of as "a condition of mind and heart which is rare in any century." Here we get what cannot fail to be recognized as a firsthand, "insider's" account of that goal which makes sense of spiritual aspiration and inspires continued rational effort, day by day, toward stable and honest self-realization. Here we see a wisdom nourished, rather than challenged, by facts; a serenity comprehending, rather than oblivious of, events; a spiritual maturity fulfilled in, rather than at odds with, efficient practicality. Here, in short, the reader can see clearly why we felt a need to attribute such unusual importance to the then-forthcoming late writings of P.B. Other reliable accounts of lasting, complete enlightenment are either deliberately incomplete or expressed in language appropriate to other times or other cultures than our own. Here is a vivid updating, for modern mentalities, of what a mind continually attuned to God is like and offers its society, a convincing testimony that much of what appears in these *Notebooks* expresses such a mind.

As to the editorial structure of the remainder of this volume, a few remarks may clarify a number of reasonable questions that will arise. A significant amount of the material in each of the three remaining sections—Part 2, *World-Idea*; Part 3, *World-Mind*; Part 4, *The Alone*—could almost equally be placed in either or both of the others. We have tried to place such paras according to their primary emphasis. We approached individual paras that speak of all three—Mind, World-Mind, and World-Idea—for example, with the questions, "Which of them is this para telling us the *most* about; which does it discuss most definitively; what is its emphasis?" Likewise, we asked the same questions of paras addressing only two of the three terms. Nonetheless, there remain paras whose placement is still not obvious. In such cases, we have placed the paras where we hope they will be most useful to the reader's increasingly subtle understanding of P.B.'s thought. Because of the subtlety in many of the sections, we have done a much more extensive job of sequencing paras in general than on previous volumes. On some of the placements, we still have friendly disagreement and look forward to responses from readers.

Three subthemes within Part 2, *World-Idea*, likewise contain thematically similar material to one another. The subtheme "evolution's goal is not merger" focuses on the problem, "Can there be an understandable purpose to evolution if it leads ultimately to annihilation or its equivalent, featureless merger?" Although many paras that deal with evolution in general are related to this question, only those paras directly stating or answering it have been placed in the "no merger" theme—which emphasizes realization of the World-Idea as the *goal* of evolution. The subtheme "World-Idea guides evolution" contains most of the paras dealing with the *process* of evolution, with the World-Idea as the underlying *propulsive force* guaranteeing that evolution's goals will be achieved. The theme "purpose of human life" deals with issues common to these prior two, but separates out the paras emphasizing the World-Idea as the only structure within which human life can have significance.

Because of the thematic similarities running through Parts 2, 3, and 4 (*World-Idea, World-Mind, The Alone*), we have provided a composite index for these three sections at the back of the book. Other editorial conventions with regard to quantity of material, spelling, capitalization, and related copy-editing practices for this volume are the same as have been outlined in earlier introductions. As in earlier volumes, (P) at the end of a para indicates that the para also appears in *Perspectives*, volume one of *The Notebooks* series.

This final volume in the twenty-eightfold "Ideas" section of *The Notebooks* seems an appropriate place for us to express our profound gratitude for the opportunity of working so extensively with the material in this series. While we find ourselves, as stated earlier, having come something like full-circle from volume one, the pattern is more appropriately described as a spiral or helix. Having lived for most of the past seven years with these notes, having had the good fortune of being able to invest thousands of hours learning to appreciate more clearly the subtleties of P.B.'s thought through the effort of evolving a structure for publication, having enjoyed the cooperation of a steadily increasing network of supportive and remarkably helpful friends—without whom publication of this series would still be far from complete, if not impossible—our understanding and appreciation of P.B.'s monumental work have grown in ways we could not have anticipated in 1981. We are grateful to more people than it is feasible to name here. We are profoundly grateful to Anthony Damiani, founder of Wisdom's Goldenrod and lifelong student of P.B., for inspiring dozens of others along with ourselves to hold nothing back in getting these notes out to readers, but even more so for introducing each of us to P.B. Finally, we are inexpressibly grateful to P.B., for being what he was, for writing this goldmine of notes, and for giving us the opportunity both of knowing him and of growing closer to ourselves through this communal labor of love.

Part 1:
WORLD-MIND IN INDIVIDUAL MIND

The highest attainment in philosophy, that of the sage, comes from a union of the sharpest, subtlest thinking and the capacity to enter the thought-free state—a combination of real knowledge and felt peace—balanced, united, yielding truth. This is what makes the sage, whose understanding and peace are his own, who does not depend upon any outside person. Yet it is not the little ego's emotion nor its intellectuality which has brought him to this truth. It is the highest human mind, the finest human feeling. The total man cannot lose what he has attained. It is the higher power working inside the human being.

He does not regard greatness to be in him but only behind him. Neither vain ambition nor false egoism can deceive him about the inner reality of his psychological situation. He understands and feels that a power not his own and not human is using him as its human instrument, that a larger mind is overshadowing his ego.

1

THEIR MEETING AND INTERCHANGE

God is in Man

"The God in the sun is the 'I' in me"—this put tersely is the essence of man's relationship to divinity. A whole book may be needed to explain it, a whole lifetime to get direct experience of its truth as insight.

2

We see plenty of evidence that the universe is not mindless, and therefore that there is a Universal Mind related to it—that is to say, related to us, who are parts of the whole.

3

It might well be said that I am connected with God on the one hand, with the world on the other hand, but both connections are highly ingenious inventions. God is literally in me. His "I" makes my "I" possible. My own sense of being is immersed in God's archetypal thought.

4

The individual mind not only exists within the World-Mind, it is born *of* the World-Mind.

5

Jesus' use of the metaphor, the Son and the Father, was intended to point out that man, in his inner self, was born of, and is still in relation to, the Higher power, God.

6

The innermost being of man and the cosmos is ever at rest, and single. The incarnate being of both is ever in movement, and dual. The inner is the Real, Changeless; the other is the Appearance, and subject to the play of two opposed but interpenetrating active forces. Because it is the quintessence of consciousness and intelligence, I call the first Mind. It is without shape, infinite and untouchable by man, but because it *is*, universes are able to appear, expand, disintegrate, and reincarnate. This activity is directly due to the agency of the first entity to appear, which I call World-Mind. From the latter flows ceaselessly the energy which is at the heart of every atom, the life-force which is at the heart of every man. World-Mind and Mind are for us the twin sides—a crude but simple, understandable metaphor—of God. The human being draws breath, exists, and thinks with awareness only because of this relationship. If he declares himself an atheist, sees himself only as an animal, rejects any divine basis to his mind, he testifies thereby to a failure on his own part: he has failed to seek and find, or because of prejudice—that is, of prejudgement—has sought wrongly. Jesus gave two helps in this matter: seek the kingdom of heaven *first*, and seek it *within*. It is open to anyone to test this truth that he is related to God. But if he does not bring certain qualities into the work, such as patience and humility, the going may be too hard, the result disappointing.

7

Something of that Mind is in us, as a parent has left some legacy in the child, but at the same time we are also in that Mind.

8

Gospel of John, chapter 17, verse 21: "As thou, Father, art in me, and I in thee."

9

An ever-active Mind within an ever-still Mind—that is the real truth, not only about God but also about man.

10

The World-Mind reproduces something of itself in each individual entity we call the Soul, or Overself.

11

The soul in man, the Overself, is linked with, or rooted in, the soul in the universe, the World-Mind.(P)

12

The Infinite Mind is centered within its finited expression, the human ego.

13

Because we have all—yes! sinners as well as saints—come forth from the divine substance in our bodies and from the divine mind in our entities, there is something god-like in each of us.

14

How can a man escape from the World-Mind since he is indissolubly united with it? Through the Overself he is a very part of it, his consciousness could not work without it.

15

The Godlike deepest Self in us knows and feels on its own level; therefore the intellect's reasonings and the aesthetic feelings are reflections on a lower level of spiritual activities.

16

So many human sufferings are the consequences of human errors, and so many of these errors arise from human ignorance. The supreme ignorance of all which leads to the greatest sins and sufferings is that he does not know he is an individualized part of a greater consciousness. Although this consciousness shines through his ego it is apart from the ego, for it stands in its own right and exists as an entity by itself. It is this consciousness which enables a man to act and think in the physical body and it is his diviner part. Blinded by the error of materialism, he identifies it with the body itself.

17

The self of every creature is divine Being, the ultimate Consciousness, but only when evolution brings it to the human level does it have the possibility of discovering this fact.

18

It is true that the mind makes its own world of experience, but it is not true that it makes it by itself; for behind the individual mind is the Cosmic Mind.

19

If the world is but an idea there must be a mind which conceived it. Although my individual mind has so largely contributed to its making, it has not contributed to its original conception. Such a mind must be an undivided universal one in which my own is rooted. It must indeed be what men commonly call God.

20

Thus the World-Mind originates our experience for us but we ourselves mold it. It supplies the karmic-forces material and we as individuals supply the space-time shape which this material takes. Thus there is a union of the individual with the universal.

21

Whether we think of this mysterious origin as manifesting itself in waves of energy or in particles of the same force, it is and must be there for the deeply reflective atomic scientist. Whether we think of it as God the

Creative Universal Mind or as God the inaccessible all-transcending Mind remote from human communion, it is and must be there for the intuitive. But in both cases this entire universe is but a thought in the Universal Mind. Every object and every creature is simultaneously included in this thought: therefore every human being too. Through this relationship it is possible for a man to attain some kind of communion with IT. This is what the quest is all about.

22

The ultimate Knower is supra-personal, divine pure consciousness, the knowing and understanding Self, Saint Thomas Aquinas' "God Himself who is the Soul's Creator and only Beatitude." All this is higher than the ego, the person, the individuality, the man himself.

23

The omnipresence of the Infinite Mind carries great meaning for us individually. For it signifies that this Mind is not less present and not less active in us too.

24

The World-Mind cannot be separated from any point of the world. It is present in every point, every creature, now, at this very moment. There is no need for anyone to think himself cut off or apart or remote from this divine source of his being. This is just as true in his sorrowful hours as in his joyful ones.

25

It is because the World-Mind supports man, gives him consciousness and energy, that he is a sharer in divine existence.

26

If there were any part of the universe, or any thing in the universe, or any creature in the universe, without God in its essence, then the universe could not have been manifested by God. The essential self of man must be divine.

27

Wang Yang-ming's disciples often remarked, "The streets are full of enlightened men!" By this they reiterated their Master's teaching that all men have the possibility of attaining enlightenment because all have the divine self hidden under their egoism.

28

Each of us is linked with that Being, the Mover of all this moving universe. This link must be brought into our field of awareness. There lies the highest fulfilment of our lives.

29

The individual consciousness is not alone. It is fathered by a universal consciousness. Between the two there is this link. To awaken one day and discover (in several cases, rediscover) it will be a man's most satisfying experience.

30

The World-Mind is omnipresent. There is a point where every man touches it. When he attains awareness of this point, he is at last attending the true Holy Communion service.

31

The little centre of consciousness that is myself rests in and lives by the infinite ocean of consciousness that is God. The first momentary discovery of this relationship constitutes a genuine religious experience, and its expansion into a final, full disclosure constitutes a philosophic one.

32

If God is everywhere, as He must be, then He is in man too. This fact makes possible his discovery, under certain conditions, of a diviner element in his being which is ordinarily obscured.

33

In the end, no man can miss being in the presence of, or confronted by, the divine power. It is a fact which, whether he accepts or denies the idea of its existence, he must one day reckon with. This is because he has never really been separated from it, never been aware of any thing or thought except by virtue of consciousness derived from it.

34

What we know through the senses as forms points to the existence of the mind. What we know through the intellect as thoughts points to the mind. What does the individual mind itself point to? We can find the answer by plunging deep into its core, deeper and ever deeper in the practice of contemplation until we come to its ultimate source. There, where the world vanishes and the ego is stilled, we become one with the infinite and eternal Mind behind the universe.

35

Ordinarily man cannot directly penetrate that layer of the mind which is continuous with, and contiguous to, the Overself. But during the deepest state of meditation he may do so.

36

The human mind, finite and limited though it be, can become an inlet to the universal Mind. Such a happening is attended by blissful yet tranquil feelings. This little being that is *me* merges into larger consciousness that is pure infinite *Being*—until the body calls me back.

37

There is something deeper than our ordinary thoughts and feelings, something that is our inmost essential self. It is the soul. It is here, if we can reach to it, that we may meet in fellowship with the Divine. Through it the World-Mind reveals something of its own mysterious nature.

38

He has come far when he has come to *feel* not only that divinity truly is but also that it is as near as his own being.

39

He discovers that Consciousness, the very nature of mind under all its aspects, the very essence of be-ing under the personal selfhood, is where man and God finally meet. He knows that God indisputably exists, not because some religious dogma avers it but because his own experience proves it.

40

There is a vital and definite connection between every man's mind and the Universal Mind, between his individual existence and Its existence. Because of this connection he is called upon to worship It to commune with It and to love It.

41

Only as a result of being liberated from himself, taken out of himself, can he find the universal being.

42

The illuminated men of earlier generations, who usually appeared at the beginning of each historical epoch and from whose ranks the great social lawgivers and religion-founders were drawn, had no personal master for none was available at the time. Who taught them? It was none other than the World-Mind, operating directly through each man's Overself and within his human consciousness. Whoever is unable to find an outward master in our own times may still find, when he has worked on himself sufficiently to be ready for it, this same direct inward help (grace) from the World-Mind if he turns to that Mind.

43

Through the power of the God within the seeker can be led to a higher truth, or what the Greek thinkers called the *Logos* can help him to find for himself.

44

If he refuses to seek and cling to the human personality of any master but resolves to keep all the strength of his devotion for the divine impersonal Self back of his own, that will not bar his further progress. It, too, is a way whereby the goal can be successfully reached. But it is a harder way.

45

Socrates got his wisdom from within himself. He had no master.

46

The teachings of Jesus were not based on any of the ancient doctrines—that is, those of the Jews, Egyptians, or Indians. They were entirely Self-inspired.

47

The human mind is fortunate in this, that it has a connection with the Divine Mind. It can become his spiritual teacher and moral guide. But he must be careful: first, not to mix his own opinion with what he receives; second, and not less but more important, to put himself through a preparatory and purificatory discipline to make the connection vitalized.

48

After all, it is the Overself which was the real Teacher of all the teachers themselves.

49

No geographical limits ought to be set for the sources whence a man draws spiritual sustenance. Why exclude other lands and remain shut in with India alone? Nor should any temporal limits be set for it. Why exclude the modern world and remain shut in with the ancient one alone? Enlightened individuals have been born all through history, have contributed their ideas beliefs experiences and revelations, and all through the social scales. This is so, must be so, because Truth, Reality, Goodness, and Beauty, in their best sense, are in the end *got from within*.

50

God is in your very being. To know him as something apart or far-away in time and distance or as an object outside yourself, separate from you—that is not the Way—impossible. Jesus gave away the secret: *he is within you.*

51

It is surprising how widely people have ignored Jesus' message ("The kingdom of heaven is within you") when its meaning is so clear, its phrasing so strong.

52

If a man lives in harmony with the divine World-Idea, he may also live in trust that he will receive that which belongs to him. This will be brought about either by guiding him to it or guiding it to him.

53

"All things whatsoever the Father hath are mine." That which you need is yours now—if only you could raise yourself to the recognition of your true relation to your Overself.

54

Emerson: "The heart, which abandons itself to the Supreme Mind, finds itself related to all its works, and will travel a royal road to particular knowledges and powers . . ."

Man is not, does not become, God

55

We may dwell in mystical inner fellowship with God but we may not become as God. Those who proclaim such false self-deification needlessly make a grotesquely exaggerated statement of what is already by itself a sufficiently tremendous truth.

56

It would be a grave error to believe that when philosophy says that the divine dwells in everything, it dwells equally in everything.

57

Man is not God. Yet he can approach God so intimately, be suffused by His presence so completely, that the first mystics to call this state "union with God" may be excused. The telepathic closeness which sometimes exists between two separated lovers, relatives, or friends is a slight hint of the telepathic closeness which exists between the harmonized human ego and its divine soul.

58

In my alleged claim that every human being can develop the divinity within himself, I do not mean that we poor mortals can ever rise to the stature of the Almighty, and I completely concur with the warning of Baha'u'llah against man's attempting to "join partners with God." I mean only that we have within us something that is linked with and related to God: it is our higher self, the discovery of and union with which represents the limit of our possible attainment.

59

If it is wiser and humbler to leave some mystery at the bottom of all our intellectual understanding of life than to indulge in self-deceiving finality about it, then it is no less wiser and humbler to acknowledge the ultimate mystery at the heart of all our immediate mystical experience of life. The mystic's claim to know God when he knows only the deepest part of his own self, is his particular kind of vanity. Whatever terminous and transcendental consciousness he may discover there, something ever remains beyond it lost in utter inscrutability. The World-Mind is impenetrable by human power. This agnostic conclusion does not, however, touch the validity of the mystic's more legitimate claim, that the human soul *is* knowable and that an unshakeable union with it is attainable.

60

The mystic may indeed feel the very stuff of God in his rapture but this does not supply him with the whole content of God's knowledge. If therefore he claims not only to be one with God but also to be one with God's entire consciousness, it is sheer presumption.(P)

61

The mystical union with God can never be a union of nature and substances, can never achieve a complete identity of the atom with the Infinite.

62

What is possible of achievement is, to speak in terms of spatial symbolism which is the only satisfactory way of treating such a transcendental subject, to unite with a single *point* within the immeasurable infinity of God.

63

Anon: "Ruysbroeck gives a description of the Beghards, which corresponds generally with that of the Papal Bull. He divides them into four classes, and accuses them all of the fundamental error of making man's unity with God to be *a unity of nature and not of Grace*. The Godly man, he admitted, is united to God, not however in virtue of his essences but by a process of re-creation and regeneration. Ruysbroeck was obviously hidebound by the dictates of theology, and to that extent his mystical knowledge was suppressed. He accused the first class of heresy against the Holy Spirit, because they claimed a perfect identity with the Absolute, which reposes in itself and is without act or operation. They said that they themselves were the divine essence, above the persons of the Godhead, and in as absolute a state of repose as if they did not at all exist; inasmuch as the Godhead itself does not act, the Holy Spirit being the sole operative power in it. The second class were considered heretics against the Father, because they placed themselves simply and directly on an equality with God; contemplated the 'I' as entirely one with the divinity so that from them all things proceeded, and being themselves by nature God, they had come into existence of their own free will. 'If I had not so willed,' one of them said, 'neither I or any other creature would be.'"

64

Much grotesque misconception exists among the mystics about this claim to have united with God. Not having passed through the metaphysical discipline and consequently having only a confused notion of what God is, they do not comprehend how exaggerated their claim is. For if they were really united with God, they should have the power of God too. They would be able to set up as creators of entire universes, of suns, stars, and cosmic systems. This feat is plainly beyond them. Let us hear no more of such babble and let them confine their strivings to realizable aims.

65

The mystic who talks vaguely of being one with God must surely know that the experience has not put him in personal management of the universe.

66

If the mystic really attains a complete identity with the World-Mind, then all the latter's evolutionary and dissolutionary powers and especially its all-pervading all-knowing character would become the common property of both. But even the most fully perfected mystic has no such powers and no such character.

67

The frontiers between God and man cannot be obliterated although the affinity between them can be established.

68

If a man really appreciated his own finite littleness and the higher power's sublime infinity, he would never have the impertinence to claim the attainment of "union with God." All such talk is irresponsible babble, the careless use of words without semantic awareness of what is being said. No human mind can capture the One Life-Power in all its magnitude, and its understanding of itself and its universe. All it can do is to act as a mirror, in the deepest recesses of its own being, and in its own humble way, of the attributes which it confers on the Absolute from its own limited human point of view. The rest is silence.

69

Although God is inaccessible to man, man is not inaccessible to God. (Note attached to para reads, PB: Use above as the basic principle of Agnostic Mysticism in former class XIII.)

70

It would be sheer arrogance were it not mere ignorance to believe that because we can go beyond the limited ego, therefore we can go beyond the divine soul and encompass the World-Mind itself in all its entirety.

71

No mortal may penetrate the mystery of the ultimate mind in its own nature—which means in its static inactive being. The Godhead is not only beyond human conception but also beyond mystic perception. But Mind in its active dynamic state, that is, the World-Mind, and rather its ray in us called the Overself, *is* within range of human perception, communion, and even union. It is this that the mystic really finds when be believes that he has found God.(P)

72

This condition is commonly said to be nothing less than "union with God." What is really attained is the higher self, the ray of the divine sun reflected in man, the immortal soul in fact—God Himself being forever utterly beyond man's finite capacity to comprehend. However the mystical experience is an authentic one and the conflict between interpretations does not dissolve its authenticity.(P)

73

We exist always in utter dependence on the Universal Mind. Man and God may meet and mingle in his periods of supreme exaltation, he may feel the sacred presence within himself to the utmost degree, but he does not thereby abolish all the distinctions between them absolutely. For he arrives at the knowledge of the timeless spaceless divine infinitude after a process of graded personal effort, whereas the World-Mind's knowledge of itself has forever been what it was is and shall be, above all processes and beyond all efforts.(P)

74

God, the World-Mind, knows all things in an eternal present at once. No mystic has ever claimed, no mystic has ever dared to claim, such total knowledge. Most mystics have, however, claimed union with God. If this be true, then quite clearly they can have had only a fragmentary, not a full union.

Philosophy, being more precise in its statements, avers that they have really achieved union not with God, but with something Godlike—the soul.(P)

75

It is quite inevitable for the mystic, overwhelmed by this tremendous experience, to say "I am God!" But once he has entered philosophy and passed through semantic discipline and cross-examined his use of words in thinking and speech, he will know that this term "God" is too extravagant to use in such an unqualified way. For if he means by that the World-Mind, then he lacks Its powers and knowledge.

76

There is a type of mysticism calling for criticism. It is uncritically pantheistic and says it is "the conception of God in Man." An instance of this type is Al Bistami's utterance, "Beneath my cloak there is naught else than God." Another is Al Hallaj's words, "I am the Divine Reality." My view of this type, which may be called self-deificatory, coincides with that of Al Ghazzali, who is no pantheist, and who teaches that there is a spark of the Divine in man's soul and that man can know and recognize it. The correct type may be designated as agnostic mysticism. This asserts man's inability to unite with the Absolute, his incapacity to attain the Godhead because it is unknowable.

77

A peril in all self-deificatory teachings is that they so easily induce the man, who attains a degree of success with meditation and who believes in them, to clothe himself in a disguised arrogance of the ego and a deceptive communication or union with God. In *The Spiritual Crisis of Man*, I briefly mentioned the Muhammedan mystic Al Hallaj who had fallen into this peril. I could have added that an Egyptian master in the same Sufi Order, Abu Al Mawahib, who lived in the fifteenth century, passed the following comment upon him: "Had Al Hallaj attained the reality of self-annihilation (*fana*) *and the fullness of its meaning* he would have been saved from the error he incurred through saying, 'I am He!'"

78

The Sufi term "companionship with God" is more accurate than the Christian-Hindu "union with God."

79

Omar Khayyam's agnostic position is perfectly in accord with philosophy's position. Both his school of Sufism and our teaching declare the impossibility of man knowing God. We can discover only that God exists and that the Soul exists but not go farther.

80

Agnostic Mysticism—This teaching refuses to regard the human spirit as divine but only as having attributes that relate it to the divine.

81

Vedantic claims which equate the self with God lead only to moral self-deception and intellectual confusion. For a god can do no wrong and a human loses his identity, his significance, and his spiritual obligation to the quest if he thinks himself a god already.

82

The danger of anarchic mysticism is not only metaphysical fallacy but also moral foolishness. For if I am God, I cannot sin, cannot even be touched by evil.

83

The mystic who claims to have achieved absolute identity with God is either speaking quite loosely or taking something to be God which is not.

84

What the mystic does attain is the feeling of being possessed by the Overself. Just as there is such a thing as demoniac obsession, so there is such a thing as divine possession. But this does not entitle him to proclaim himself God.

85

This claim could not arise if the word "God" had been subjected to semantic analysis, so that he knew what he was talking about.

86

Few individuals are properly qualified to form a correct conception of the successful mystic's experience. If in the joy of his ecstasy he chooses to call it "the union with God," he does so because preconceived belief leads him to expect such "union." But when scientifically examined from inside no less than from outside—which means that the examiner can thoroughly know what he is talking about and appraise it at its true worth only if he has been both a practising mystic and, above all, an initiated philosopher himself—it will be found that the ecstasy mingles personal and emotional reaction to the awareness of the divine presence with the presence itself.

87

Philosophy is more modest in its claim than mysticism. It makes no arrogant claim to lead man to identify himself with God. If the identity is a complete one, then reason alone tells us that an absurd situation will immediately arise. If it is only a partial one, then no mystic has ever been specific enough to tell us which part of God he has become nor competent enough to distinguish the parts. The fact is that no man has ever done so, no man could ever do so.

88

Those mystics who talk of becoming united with God have fallen into the dualistic fallacy. They talk as though God were separate and apart from themselves. The truth is that they already exist within God and do not need to become united with Him. What they need is to become conscious of Him—which is a different matter.

89

Man is not God, God is not man, despite all Vedantic self-drugging; but there exists an unbreakable relation between the two.

90

Vedanta is unsatisfying partly because it is too jerky. It jumps abruptly from the finite and physical individual to the ineffable and unutterable Absolute Itself. It swings from one extreme to another. It fails to recognize that there is and must be an intermediary—the Overself.

91

The pantheist who is so intoxicated by his discovery of the truth that God is everywhere present and consequently in himself too, that he goes on to the pseudo-discovery that he and God are one, is simply a man who is too vain to acquiesce in his own limitations.

92

This danger of misinterpreting his own experience besets the mystic at this stage. Because he feels himself to be in the presence of Deity, he believes that he is Deity. But the finite can never contain the Infinite. Deity transcends man.

93

The danger of men's deifying themselves afflicts the mystic path. This mind-madness must first be frankly admitted as a danger, for then only can it be guarded against.(P)

94

Agnostic Mysticism—The error of pantheism is so common in the Orient only because there is a base of truth in it. It regards a part of man as divine when it is only linked with the divine.

95

An error of mysticism which must make the penetrative seeker turn to philosophy was the deification of man implicit in its claim that the mystic can attain to union with God. There was some truth in this claim but there was also some falsehood and certainly much confusion.

96

When they speak of "union with God," it would be useful if they defined their conception of what they mean by such a union.

97

Man is but a small token of the greater Mind which spawned him. He is but the merest hint of That which is behind him in the present, was in the past, and shall be in the future.

98

The true explanation of mystical ecstasy is not union with God but union with the Soul.

99

When consciousness is successfully turned in on its own deepest state, which is serene, impersonal, and unchanging, it receives the experience of the divine Soul, not of the Godhead. It brings us nearer to the Godhead but does not transform us into it. We discover the divine ray within, we do not become the sun itself.

100

The mystic attains knowledge and experience of his own soul. This is not the same as knowledge of the ultimate Reality. The two are akin, of course—much more closely than the little ego and the Real are akin. But the Godhead is the Flame of which the soul is only a spark; to claim complete union with it seems blasphemous.

101

When a man says that he has communed with God, be he a great prophet in trance or a humble layman in prayer, the truth is that he has really communed with something within himself which is so closely related to God that he may perhaps be pardoned for his error. But still it is not God. It is his soul, the Overself.

102

When he believes he is communing with God he is actually communing with his own inner reality. The enlightenment that seems to come from outside actually comes from inside himself.

103

In his great ecstasy he feels himself to be a supernormal, super-powerful, and super-wise being. He is to be pardoned if he rashly declares that he is God.

104

The human being cannot go farther in its pilgrimage than the discovery of his own origin, his Overself.

105

The soul constitutes both the connection between man and God and the ultimate attainment of man.

106

The best a man can hope for, in rising above the ego and the world, is to rise into awareness of his true soul. This is valuable enough but it is not the same as looking into God's mind or becoming united with God's being. Those theologians who describe the mind merely show us the capacity or quality of their speculations and imaginations. Those mystics who describe the being, really describe their own souls.

107

The realization of the Overself enables us to taste something of the flavour of World-Mind's life but it is only the flavour, not the full life itself. Flint says, "Man is made in the image of God, but man is not the measure of God."

108

His discovery of being born out of, and still remaining rooted in, the Infinite Mind of God, is a tremendous one but it does not make him identical with God.

109

It makes the mystic a channel only for the cosmic mind, not one with it. He touches the cosmic and does not become entirely transformed into it.

110

Human beings can only hope to realize the Overself which is a ray or intermediary, but not the World-Mind itself. For the latter is too vast and infinite and remote. Hence when mystics talk of knowing God or feeling God, this is only partly true for they can never know or feel God in his fullness.

111

The soul is as close as we can approach to that Mind, but surely it is enough. For it reflects something of the Mind's nature. This is why the seers who wrote the Hindu bible called it a "Spark of the One Divine Flame" and the prophets who wrote the Christian bible declared it to be "created in the image of God."

112

The finite minds which are the offspring of the One Mind may not hope to rise in power or understanding to its attitude. Nevertheless, because they are inseparable from it, they may find hints of both these attributes within themselves. The Divine Essence is undiscoverable by human sense and intellect but not by human intuition and insight.

113

We may, however, attain to partial knowledge of the transcendent Absolute by and through its emanation in us, the higher self.

114

The Real is wholly nothing to the five senses and wholly unthinkable to the human intellect. Therefore and to this extent only it is also called the Unknowable. But there is a faculty latent in man which is subtler than the senses, more penetrative than the intellect. If he succeeds in evoking it, the Real, the unknowable, will then come within the range of his perception, knowledge, and experience.

115

But although the Absolute in its passive state is unknowable, the Overself as representative of its active aspect, of the World-Mind, *is* knowable.

116

If the pure essence of Godhead is too inaccessible for man, nevertheless he has not been left bereft of all divine communion. For there is a hidden element within himself which has emanated from the Godhead. It is really his higher, better self, his soul.

117

The Infinite Mind is beyond human perception but its presence and operation are not. The point in human consciousness where these become known is the Overself.

118

But although the Absolute is imperceptible to human powers, It has not left us utterly bereft of all means of communion. We are linked to It by something that lies hidden in the very deeps of our own being, by Its deputy to man, the divine Overself. Human power can penetrate to those deeps and discover the hidden treasure.

119

This higher self is what the successful mystics of all religions have really achieved union with, despite the widely different names, from "God" downwards, which they have given it.

120

We cannot ever know the Divine which is Transcendent but we can acknowledge that it IS. We may however know the Divine which is Immanent, recognize, perceive, and feel its presence.

121

He may know that God is here even though he is incapable of knowing what God is like.

122

If we cannot know the all of God because we do not have the equipment of God, we can at least know something of God and the way we are related through the Overself.

123

An important warning is needed here. Wherever the idea of agnostic mysticism has been supported, the idea that there is no possibility of knowing the Absolute and so no communication of such knowledge, the reference is to ordinary human intellect. No positive result can come of its investigation into that which transcends it. But what intellect unaided cannot know, intuition—a higher faculty—can. It can discover its point of contact with the Absolute—its higher individuality, the Overself, even though it can go no farther and penetrate the Absolute. When intuition becomes active in this matter, it may or may not take the shape of a mystical experience. When it is developed by philosophic training, it expands into insight.

124

Agnosticism, the belief that we cannot know ultimate truth, applies only to the attempts of the intellectual faculty. It does not apply to those of the intuitive faculty. But even then limitations are imposed upon us. No man can come to know God as God is in Himself, for that is impossible, but all men can come to know God as He is in relation to man. This is because the Overself is all men's contact-point with the World-Mind.

125

I am not God but rather an emanation from God. I am still a man but there is something Godlike in the centre of my being. The Deity is inaccessible but that centre is not.

126

When it is said that the Infinite Being cannot be known by the finite mind it is not meant that the Infinite Being is forever unknowable by human beings. For there is in every one of us a link between the two, and if a man is willing to let go of his worldly concerns long enough to find his way to that link—whether by reflection or by meditation—he will discover that this link—intuition—can lead him into the Infinite Presence. At that sacred moment he becomes IT because he forgets the personal self. It exists whether he exists or not, but he exists only in dependence upon it. If the very interesting question be asked, "How did the first man come to discover this Presence?" I suggest that the questioner read a little book, quite a short book called *The Awakening of the Soul*, written some hundreds of years ago in Arabic and translated first by an Englishman, Edward Pococke. (Since then there has been a better and fuller translation made by Dr. Paul Bronnle, published in the *Wisdom of the East* series.) The author of the book was called Ibn Tufail. It is in the nature of a story, a sort of Robinson Crusoe story, but it is much more than that. I ought to mention that Pococke's translation, made in the seventeenth century, was from the Latin into which the Arabic itself had been translated.

127

We may draw near to the holy of Holies yet never enter it, feel its eternal atmosphere yet never understand it.

128

God alone knows why this manifestation should be. Even the mystic never attains God in its fullness but only that ray of God within himself, which is the soul. Although such an attainment is imperfect in the conventional mystic, the philosophic one can hope to attain perfection. However, neither can cross the Overself's farthest boundary—but that is another matter.

129

That which he finds deep within himself is, he understands intuitively, a reflected ray from that which exists behind the whole universe but it is still only a ray.

130

Men may know the soul but not God. They may not see the face, or understand the nature, of the final essential reality—and live. He who claims such experience practises self-deception and is caught in illusion.

131

When they assert that they have united with God, they have, if truly attained, united with God's deputy, their higher self, their own divine soul—which is not the same. And if they have deceived themselves then they have united only with their conception of God. That is, they have never gone outside the enclosing circle of their own thought.

132

The five senses cannot perceive It and the thinking faculties cannot conceive It. It cannot be brought down to the level of man nor can man raise himself to its height. Whoever believes that he experiences the Absolute at any time, experiences only an imagination of his own brain.

133

The Overself is so close to God, so akin to the World-Mind, that no man need look farther, or aspire higher.

134

Our finite minds cannot lift more than the smallest corner of the smallest corner of the infinite veil behind which the Ultimate Mind eludes us.

135

No one overwhelmed by the experience of Enlightenment has yet said the last word about Absolute Truth; for no words can either exhaust it or even touch it.

136

No teaching can be a final complete and exhaustive one. The universe may yield its secret but man's mind is not the World-Mind; it cannot put into finite words what is greater than itself.

137

If a man claims to know what God is in the same way that God knows it, he is talking nonsense, and falling into the sin of spiritual pride. No one can penetrate this irreducible mystery except in his own imagination, speculation, or psychic fantasy. No human effort can plumb the depth of the ultimate power. No human being has found the truth in all its angles, nor uttered the last word upon it.

138

Whatever knowledge a mystic may acquire through trance or intuition, it will always be limited. The World-Mind's knowledge is always absolute. The circumferences of these two circles can never coincide.

139

The *statement* of high truth made by any prophet or sage will always remain an individual interpretation—this is a point that is too often unnoticed or unknown or unacceptable. All history authenticates it.

140

The highest authority by which any mystic can speak is really his higher self's. His revelation and communication cannot therefore be valid for, or binding upon, other men. If, however, they do accept his pronouncements as such, they do so as a venture of faith. When a mystic takes his inner voice to be nothing less than God's, his inner experience to be nothing else than the uttermost union with God, and then proceeds to use them as justification for imposing his commands on other men, he is no longer a true mystic. He has introduced an "other." He no longer touches the perfect unity of his own innermost being but has returned to the world of duality. And because no finite man can really become the infinite God, that "other" reduces itself to being a figment of his imagination at best or a lying, possessing spirit at worst.

141

Full enlightenment is not attainable, except in the exuberant emotional fancy of over-enthused followers, for the gulf between man and God is too deep and too wide to be crossed. But partial enlightenment is attainable, for something godlike has been *reflected* into the human being's heart.

142

But if it is impossible to become a part of God, it *is* possible to become a "son of God"—that is, a man inspired and guided by God.

143

In time his relation to the higher self becomes more intimate than any earthly friendship, closer than any human union could ever be. Yet it always remains a relation, never becomes an absorption; always a nearness, never a merger.(P)

144

We never become God. We only become a channel for *part* of God's light, wisdom, and power.

145

If perfect union, in the Indian sense, is not attainable, what is attainable is the intimate presence of, and mental communion with, God in our heart, which brings peace and truth.

146

Is a tiny spark the same as a great fire? Can it destroy a house as a fire can? No—although the two are of the same nature, they are not of the same identity. For any man to say "I am God" is incorrect, unless he understands the statement to refer only to the nature of his innermost being and only in this way, that he is but an insignificant spark of God, with all the limitations that belong to a spark.

147

We have to find our own self before we can find that of God's. Hence there is real need of the higher self tenet.(P)

148

We are not entitled to aspire towards union with the wholeness of God so long as we still have not attained union with the godlikeness in man.

149

Agnostic Mysticism—The mystical quest does not open the inner mysteries of God to our gaze. It opens the inner mysteries of man. It leads him to his own divinity, not to God's.

150

Philosophy rejects decisively all those Vedantic pantheistic notions and Western mystical naïveties which would deify man and identify him with God. It asserts that the phrases in which these beliefs are embodied, such as the Indian "That thou art," the Persian "I am God," and the medieval European "union with God," are exaggerations of the truth, which is that God is immanent in us, that through realization of our higher self we become more *like* God, but that God never ceases to be the Unattainable, the Incomprehensible.(P)

151

The individual is as inseparable from the Infinite as the ray from the Sun. Nevertheless he differs from it in degree and in attribute.

152

Just as a little child may be closely intimate with its mother but not with its mother's mind, so the human being may be closely intimate with the World-Mind but not with Its full consciousness.

153

The higher kingdoms of Nature cannot be understood by denizens of lower ones. Just as a plant can grow but cannot move about, just as an animal can both grow and move but cannot reflect hence cannot enter into human consciousness, so man can grow move and reflect but cannot enter into God's infinitely mysterious consciousness.

154

The mystic's endeavour to unite with God—much more his claim to achieve it—is without meaning if God is the Ultimate and the Unique. No finite limited human intelligence could ever directly communicate with the infinite and illimitable Mystery or give and receive love from it. All this has meaning only when the concept of the Overself is introduced.

155

The teaching of a higher individuality needs to be correctly understood. It is not that a separate one exists for each physical body. The consciousness which normally identifies itself with the body—that is, the ego—when looking upward in highest devotion or inward in deepest meditation, comes to the point of contact with universal being, World-Mind. This point is its own higher self, the divine deputy within its own being. But if devotion or meditation is carried still further, to the very utmost possible stretch of consciousness, the point itself merges into its source. At this moment the man is his source. But—"Man shall not see My face and live!" He returns eventually to earth-consciousness, where he must follow out its requirements. Yet the knowledge of what he is *in essence* remains. The presence of the deputy is always there meanwhile, always felt. It may fittingly be called his higher individuality.(P)

156

Being itself infinite, the World-Mind is able to express itself in an infinite number of individual souls.

157

The uniqueness of each person, his difference from every other person, may be metaphysically explained as due to the effort of Infinite Mind to express itself infinitely within the finite limitation of time and space, form and appearance.

158

Whenever I have written that the higher individuality is a part of the divine World-Mind, this is so only from the ordinary human standpoint looking upwards. But from the ultimate one, it is not so, for the World-Mind is not the sum total of a number of parts. It cannot be divided into them. This is why I prefer to use the phrase "rooted in the World-Mind."

159

It is true that the subject in consciousness cannot make an object of itself, cannot perceive itself, but there is in man another self which knows the subject, is aware of the subject although the subject is not aware of it. But there is an important difference to be noted here. First, the transcendental self does not know in the same way that the thinking self knows (by thinking self I mean the subject) for its knowledge is immediate, swifter than the swiftest computing machine. Secondly, it is part of the universal mind, the World Mind, yet mysteriously connected with a limited human mind.

160

Union with the Overself is not the ultimate end but a penultimate one. What we look up to as the Overself looks up in its own turn to another and higher entity.(P)

161

An illumined being would better describe his inner status by the phrase "God am I" than by "I am God," as his first thought is not "I" but "THAT."

162

Agnostic Mysticism: Let us not match our petty and limited minds against the infinite and incomprehensible World-Mind, and let us not say with some foolish mystic that we are God. Let us say rather what we can truly say, which is that there is something of God in us.

163

It is not for the philosopher to inflate himself with the arrogance of such pompous self-deification. He remains always the humble adorer, the meek suppliant.

164

It is humbly truer to admit, with Muhammed, "I am the servant of God, I am but a man like you," than arrogantly to assert with the Advaitin, "I am the infinite Brahman!" It is better to say modestly with Jesus, "The father is greater than I," than to announce with the Sufi Mansur: "I am God."

165

The declaration "I am God" is true in a certain qualified sense but false in a literal one. The declaration "God within me" is true in every sense.

166

Although the mystic's claim to become one with God is, in the full sense of the term, an unquestionable exaggeration, a splendid illusion, he can certainly claim to have entered into a conscious relationship with God.

167

The mystic proudly declares, "I have attained union with God." The philosopher mostly says, "I have obtained union with my soul and to that extent drawn nearer to God."

168

The falsity of claims of self-deification: Jami, the Sufi, very beautifully distinguishes the doctrine of annihilation in God from that of identification with God in the following verse:

> So tread this path that duality may disappear,
> For if there be duality in the path, falsity will arise:
> Thou wilt not become He; but, if thou strivest,
> Thou wilt reach a place where thou-ness shall depart from thee.

Fallacy of "Divine Incarnation"

169

Philosophy displaces the belief in Divine Incarnations by belief in divinely inspired men. Although it refuses to deify any man into being fully representative of the Infinite Consciousness, it affirms that any man may approach nearer to and be uplifted by that Consciousness.

170

God is never identified with any man, nor incarnated in him. For God alone is uniquely the Unindividuated whereas all men are individualized creatures. Even the highest type of man, the sage-saviour, is a particular light, whereas God is the light itself.

171

That the Divine has descended into a holy man's mind and heart is philosophically tenable. That the Divine has actually and specifically incarnated in him is not.

172

The belief among Christians and Hindus that God incarnates in human form through Christ or Krishna is not held by Muhammedans or Buddhists. That God may *use* a human channel at times is more rational. But this God is World-Mind, not the Unapproachable.

173

The popular Hindu belief that God reincarnates himself periodically as an Avatar is a Puranic one, which means that taken literally it is sheer superstition. If it is to be correctly understood, it must be taken as really being an oversimplification of psychological truth for the benefit of simple minds. Hence it is inevitably misleading if its surface interpretation is taken to exhaust its entire significance.

174

There is a danger to truth and a fanaticism of mind in the belief that only some one historic person, whether dead or alive, some particular man, was or is the only true Guide, the only Sufficient Helper.

175

To say that God was more incarnate in any one man than all others since the human race began, is to say that God was less infinitely active at that time than at any other—which contradicts the meaning of the word God. Such deification of any mortal is always exploited by the vested interests of religions because it appeals to the superstitious.

176

If the Divine Essence could really subject itself to the limitations of human existence, this could only be achieved at the cost of impairing its own infinitude and absoluteness. But even to comprehend the hint of a hint about it, which is all that we may hope to do, is enough to show how utterly impossible such subjection would be. The notion that the infinitude of Deity can be compressed and contained within a special human organism is unphilosophical. Whether such an avatar be Krishna in India, Horus in Egypt, or Jesus in Palestine, there has never been any ground for raising one above the others, for the simple reason that there have never been any avatars at all. And if the doctrine of divine incarnations is irrational, the sister doctrine of predicted and messianic second advent is partly a wish-fulfilment and partly a miscomprehension. If a divinely inspired being first appears visibly in the flesh of his own body, his second appearance is invisibly in the heart of his own worshippers.

177

The downfall of every faith began when the worship of God as Spirit was displaced by the worship of Man as God. No visible prophet, saint, or saviour has the right to demand that which should be offered to the Unseen alone. It is not true reverence but ignorant blasphemy which could believe that the unattainable Absolute has put itself into mortal human form however beneficent the purpose may be. The idea that God can enter the flesh as a man was originally given to most religions as a chief feature for the benefit of the populace. It was very helpful both in their mental and in their practical life. But it was true only on the religious level, which after all is the elementary one. It was not quite true on the philosophical level. Those few who were initiated into the advanced teaching were able to interpret this notion in a mystical or metaphysical way which, whilst remote from popular comprehension, was closer to divine actuality. They will never degrade the Godhead in their thought of it by accepting the popular belief in personification, incarnation, or avatarhood. It is a sign of primitive ignorance when the humanity of these inspired men is unrecognized or even denied, when they are put on a pedestal of special deification. The teaching that Godhead can voluntarily descend into man's body is a misunderstanding of truth. The irony is that those who try to displace the gross misunderstanding by the pure truth itself are called blasphemous. The real blasphemy is to lower the infinite Godhead to being directly an active agent in the finite world.

Nothing can contain the divine essence although everything can be and is permeated by it. No one can personify it, although every man bears its ray within him. To place a limitation upon it is to utter a blasphemy against it. The infinite Mind cannot be localized to take birth in any particular land. The absolute existence cannot be personified in a human form. The eternal Godhead cannot be identified with a special fleshly body. The inscrutable Reality has no name and address. It cannot be turned into an historical person, however exalted, with a body of bones nerves muscle and skin. To think otherwise is to think materialistically. The notion which would place the Deity as a human colossus amongst millions of human midgets and billions of lesser creatures shows little true reverence and less critical intelligence.

We must acknowledge the ever-existence of Absolute mind, even though it is incomprehensible to the senses and inconceivable to the thoughts. We must deny that it can ever manifest itself within time and space and consequently deny also that it can ever show itself under a human form. We must deny that any man is right in arrogating to himself the sole channel through whom worship must be performed, communion achieved, or belief given.

The time has come to repudiate all this foolish worship of human beings and to transfer our reverence and obedience to the pure divine Being alone. The more metaphysical comprehension we develop, the less we shall look to the person of a teacher. We shall then regard the Teaching itself as the essential thing.(P)

178
It was always a profitable game for the priesthood of various religions to maintain superstitions like that of a chosen race or fallacies like that of a divine incarnation.

179
This wrong idea of incarnate Godhood is, however, not a smoke without some fire within it. For it is the corruption of a true idea.

180
The REAL is unique and indivisible, sole and unadulterable. It never becomes less than it is, never descends to become human, never mixes with what is mere phenomena.

181
The theological dogma that God can take on the nature of man con-

stitutes a mystery beyond human understanding. It is unintelligible and unacceptable to philosophy, which can limit God's unbounded being to no particular place, no "here" or "there."

182

The moment we give to finite human beings that which we should give to infinite God alone, in that moment we place earthen idols in the sacred shrine.

183

We must not give to any individual man the attributes of Divinity as we must not give to Divinity the attributes of individual men.

184

There is metaphysically no such thing as a human appearance of God, as the Infinite Mind brought down into finite flesh. This error is taught as a sacred truth by the Bahais in their Manifestation doctrine, by the Christians in the Incarnation doctrine, and by the Hindus in their Avatar doctrine. God cannot be born in the flesh, cannot take a human incarnation. If He could so confine Himself, He would cease to be God. For how could the Perfect, the Incomprehensible, and the Inconceivable become the imperfect, the comprehensible, and the conceivable?

Yet there is some fire behind this smoke. From time to time, someone is born predestined to give a spiritual impulse to a particular people, area, or age. He is charged with a special mission of teaching and redemption and is imbued with special power from the universal intelligence to enable him to carry it out. He must plant seeds which grow slowly into trees to carry fruit that will feed millions of unborn people. In this sense he is different from and, if you like, superior to anyone else who is also inspired by the Overself. But this difference or superiority does not alter his human status, does not make him more than a man still, however divinely used and power-charged he may be. Such a man will claim no essential superiority over other men; on the contrary, he will plainly admit that they, too, may attain the same state of inspiration which he possesses. Hence Muhammed confessed, repeatedly: "I am only a human being like unto yourselves. But revelations are made to me." And the tenth Sikh guru declared, "Those who call me the Supreme Lord, will go to hell." No human temple can receive the Infinite Essence within its confining walls. No mortal man has ever been or could ever be the Incarnation of the all-transcending Godhead. No earthly flesh or human intelligence has the right to identify itself with the unknowable principle. Only minds untrained in the metaphysics of truth could accept the contrary belief. The widespread character of this belief evidences how few have ever had such a training, and the widespread character of the corruptions and troubles which have always followed in the train of such man-worship, evidences it as a fallacy.(P)

185

To turn any man of uncommon spiritual insight into the Deity is neither really to honour nor rightly to revere him. On the contrary, it is to misunderstand him and blaspheme against Deity. But those who do this do so in ignorance and are not to blame. Those alone are blameworthy who have become their spiritual guides without having become qualified by divine inspirations, rather than human institutions, to lead them aright.

186

Such a one is not God incarnate. He is a man still, but a man with unusual awakening to his higher consciousness, unusual intimacy with the Source.

2

ENLIGHTENMENT WHICH STAYS

Hitherto we have been considering the state of the man who is seeking enlightenment. But what is the state of the man who has attained it? This is also worthwhile for our closest study. For after all, he is the type we are one day destined to become, the type we are being shaped into by life itself.

2

An utterly honest appraisal of what enlightenment and liberation really are both in experience and idea is still needed.

3

Is it given to any human being to express his higher self constantly and without interruption by his ego?

4

This is a sphere about which the most confused ideas exist or else it has been entirely misunderstood.

5

It is needful to distinguish between the imagined joy of spiritual self-realization and the Reality itself. The first is largely current in the circles of sectarian mysticism, but the second is rarely found and only there where the larger freedom is gained by bridling imagination and surrendering to the calm, silent Mind.

6

After we have separated the fantastic myths and fabulous marvels which have been woven around the simple achievement of soul-knowledge, we reach the residue of plain and pregnant truth.

7

Enlightenment is both a bestowal by grace and achievement by self.

8

Enlightenment, philosophically found, is both an experience and an understanding.

9

It is a state attained by very few and only after a great struggle.

10

"Awareness" is not enough to describe full enlightenment. "Knowing-ness" includes it but goes farther and is hence a better term.

11

There is in him now a translucency of mind which gives all things, all persons, all events, a deeper diviner significance. Life henceforth has a wonderful and beautiful meaning.

12

Although the higher consciousness may vary in vividness, before settling down to a fixed evenness of quality, it remains permanent at this stage.

13

All problems vanish from his mind as though they had never been. He is under no necessity to concern himself about anything or anyone. "God's in his heaven and all's well with the world." There is no tormenting situation to be cleared up, no difficult decision to be made, no quest to be followed through drawn-out struggles and personal self-disciplines, and inevitable disappointments. He now has the secret of it all, the blissful state of enlightenment.

14

Hitherto he has been only partially himself. Now, with this radiant entry into the eternal, he is completely himself. Now he can speak to others, move in the world, and work out relationships, solely from his centre, straight from his core: no distortions, no hypocrisies, no insincerities.

15

Here at last is true normality, existence as it was meant to be but is never found to be.

16

He has attained the delight and freedom of spontaneous living. The savage may have it, too, but on an altogether lower level.

17

When the knowledge of the soul is not merely intellectual, however convincing, not only a matter of belief, however firm, but an unchangeable awareness of its ever-present existence, it is true knowledge, authentic revelation, and blissful salvation.

18

We move up from being to Being.

19

It is a state which has been attained *in its fullness* by only a few persons during each century but which has been glimpsed at least once in a lifetime by many more.

Glimpses and permanent realization

20

Glimpses have been had more often than most people believe but enlightenment that is continuous and always present is rare.

21

To have the intermittent experience of the inner self is one thing, but to have the continuous experience of it is quite another.

22

Emotional union with the Overself is insufficient, fugitive ecstasies are not the final accomplishment. Better than both is the unshakeable serenity of the sage.

23

The glimpse, in anticipation and retrospect, as well as when it first happens, is abnormal and extraordinary. But in the sage the divine presence is always available, and the awareness of it comes effortlessly, naturally, and easily to him.

24

When the mystery of it all is solved, not merely intellectually but in experience, not only in the person himself but in transcending it, not only in the depth of meditation but in the world of activity; when this answer is richly felt as Presence and God, clearly known as Meaning and Mind, then, if he were to speak he would exclaim: "Thus It Is!" But this is not the beginner's glimpse: it is the sage's settled insight.

25

Too often beginners regard lofty emotions or extraordinary powers or ecstatic rapture as the measure of attainment, when the only genuine measure is "awareness."

26

As the human mind develops, it forms higher and higher conceptions of the deity until, finally, it is lifted above itself into a tremendous experience. It loses itself in the deity itself, and when it returns to normal living, it does not need to seek further. I do not refer here to the experience which several mystics have had called "the glimpse," but something which is of a once-and-for-all nature and which does not, in its essence, ever leave him.

27

The glimpse, because it is situated between the mental conditions which exist before and afterwards, necessarily involves striking—even dramatic—contrast with their ordinariness. It seems to open on to the ultimate light-bathed height of human existence. But this experience necessarily provokes a human reaction to it, which is incorporated into the glimpse itself, becomes part of it. The permanent and truly ultimate enlightenment is pure, free from any admixture of reaction, since it is calm, balanced, and informed.

28

The Glimpse, even at its fullest extent, as in the Hindu *nirvikalpa* and the Japanese *satori*, is only intermittent. If it becomes continuous, an established fact during the working and resting states, *both*, only then is it completed.

29

The awareness of Truth is constant and perennial. It cannot be merely glimpsed; one must be born into it, in Jesus' words, again and again, and perceive it permanently. One must be identified with it.

30

Quite a number of men have experienced a Glimpse like an eruption that begins and soon ends, but few are the men who have experienced a settled enlightenment of their being like a plateau that continues at a great height for a great distance.

31

The *realization* of truth is one thing; the *inspiration* to seek truth is another. The first is being, the second is experience. The first abides for life; the second is only a glimpse, hence passes and returns intermittently.

32

Many readers of *The Hidden Teaching Beyond Yoga* became both concerned and critical when I pointed out the limited nature of the mystical states. What they did not know is that this was part of the esoteric doctrine given to the few students of the higher philosophy both in India and in several other Asiatic countries. This was confirmed in my meeting with Professor A.J. Arberry (of Cambridge), who translated some of the Islamic mystical works into English. He quoted the tenth-century mystic and philosopher Gunaid of Iraq, "Truth comes *after* states and ecstasies and then takes its place." Swami Siddheswarananda of the Ramakrishna Mission and a lecturer at the Sorbonne in Paris also told me before he passed away that V. Subrahmanya Iyer of Mysore, who had been one of his teachers, had been initiated into the traditional esoteric doctrine of the original Sri Shankaracharya and that it was not written in the books, but taught privately only.

33

It is easier to glimpse the truth than to stay in it. For the first, it is often enough to win a single battle; for the second, it is necessary to win a whole war.

34

I tried to make it quite clear in *The Hidden Teaching Beyond Yoga* that just as psychic experiences were not to be sought for their own sake, so even mystical experiences were not the highest goal. It was only when their intermittent nature became obvious, however remarkable and uplifting they may have seemed, that one who experienced them was ready to seek for the higher Truth. This was not only a matter of personal feeling, but also of impersonal intuitive knowledge confirmed by reason and experience.

35

"Not everyone that saith 'Lord, Lord' shall enter into the kingdom of heaven," Jesus declared. Only to a very few is it given to enter and remain stabilized in the kingdom; many more must be content with glimpses only.

36

The belief is all too common that "union with God" is experienced as a tremendous uprush of ecstatic emotion. This is true in several cases but not in all. In any case, only after the excitement has abated and calm has descended on the man will he be able to see whether this is merely another of those temporary glimpses or whether it is really a lasting discovery of his divine identity. For the truth is that such a durable discovery, such an ever-present fulfilment of his highest possibilities, comprises much more than this inspired, but still personal, excitement.

37

It is true that our sins and faults are automatically dispersed by the inrush of Enlightenment, but it is equally true that they will return if we have not prepared ourselves to be able to stay in the Light.

38

To gaze upon this great light without sufficient previous training of the inward life is ordinarily not possible for more than a short time. The few exceptions who were able to stay in the light unbrokenly were men of special genius and special destiny.

39

The difference between the two states has been symbolically stated by Al Hujwari, the eleventh-century Sufi writer. Those who have attained the abiding state are, he says, "in the sanctuary, but those who have attained the transient one are only at the gate."

40

Visions, mental states, and experiences may succeed each other progressively or otherwise as they do with the yogis, but they are not the same as a continuous stabilized awareness of that which is behind all these temporary states.

41

When the glimpse experience has been repeated many times it will come to be looked upon as a natural experience. The state it induces will seem to be a normal one. The miracle which the beginner makes of it will seem an unnecessary exaggeration to the matured proficient man.

42

The difference between the intermediate and the final state is the difference between feeling the Overself to be a distinct and separate entity and feeling it to be the very essence of oneself, between temporary experience of it and enduring union with it.(P)

43

Whereas the glimpse may be a dramatic experience when it first occurs, being "established" is natural, simple, pleasant but not rapturous, and continuously aware.

44

We must learn to differentiate between the partial attainment of the mystic who stops short at passive enjoyment of ecstatic states and the perfect attainment of the sage who does not depend on any particular states but dwells in the unbroken calm of the unconditioned Overself. From his high point of view all such states are necessarily illusory, however personally satisfying at the time, inasmuch as they are transient conditions and do not pertain to the final result.(P)

45

All aspects of human nature need to be illumined and equably balanced if the illumination itself is to be total, pure, and reliable. This statement is no more, and no less, than the truth. Yet ignorance of it is widespread among would-be mystics and even among real mystics. If there is contradiction between their results, it is because they too often experience the illumination fully through their feelings, to a limited extent through their wills, and hardly at all through their intellects.

46

Illumination is not a result which follows moral purification and emotional discipline. These things are necessary but only preparatory. It is a result which follows conscious attempts to seek the Real and discard the illusory. This discrimination will show itself in the kind of values that are attached to the world, in the thinking reflections that are made about the world, and in the deliberate rejection of ego that takes place during meditation. It begins with either the intellect as enquiry, or the feelings as world-weariness, but it passes gradually into the whole life of the individual.

47

If the enlightenment is to be continuous and the self-conquest completed, the technique which is to achieve them must be a sufficiently adequate one.

48

To become established in the Reality is to give up seeking all those transient and temporary experiences which come by pursuing particular techniques, whether they be techniques of yoga or techniques of taking drugs, and take to philosophy.

49

We must carefully qualify by such words as "intermittent," "partial," and "temporary," the attainments to which exercises lead. This is because the full and permanent attainment cannot emerge out of meditation alone. It is a fruit of the threefold planting of meditation and reflection and action combined. Hence although the foregoing exercises will bring the student considerably nearer it, it must not be thought that any mystical exercise of itself can confer ultimate enlightenment. The path to this exalted result must traverse all three fields of yoga, metaphysics, and self-abnegating activity.

50

Somewhere beyond meditation with its starts and stops, its ecstasies and drynesses, beyond yoga, lies the permanent ever-enduring be-ness. It is therein he must be established.

51

We need to know the truth, the wisdom-knowledge, but it is not enough. We need to have the living mystic experience, the vital feeling of what I am, but it is not enough. For we need to synthesize the two in a full actual intuitive realization, conferred by the Overself. This is Grace. This is to emerge finally—born again!

52

Let meditation stay as a beautiful, peace-bestowing, and calming exercise. If it does, it need not limit you to getting stuck with "Experience" as a final attainment. It is a felt experience, but one which must be accompanied by the knowledge that the entire universe is a form of knowledge. The two together complete the meditation experience. Thus you learn to understand that you must advance beyond meditation to this goal of Being, to become established in it, in this stillness, ever-present and ever-proven. So do as you wish in this matter, do not deprive yourself of the occasional or even regular practice of meditation, should you be inclined toward it, so long as you comprehend that though it has its very important place in the Quest, it is not essential to attainment of the ultimate goal itself.

Sudden or gradual?

53

Does enlightenment come all of a sudden? Or do we have to work slowly for it by degrees? The answer varies with the case concerned. Most need time to fit and equip themselves for the glorious moment of insight, but a few receive it in a day. It must be remembered that it does not actually happen in time but out of it, in the great Stillness. The man does not *know* the absolute final truth a second before—and then it is all there. How soon it can settle down in him will also vary with different persons— it was a few hours in one case but three years in another.

54

Whether enlightenment is reached by steps as an outcome of practice unremittingly done, or that it comes suddenly all at once, it must be a concept-free phenomenon, a dogma-less understanding, and a recognition of what always was, is, and will be.

55

Is insight achieved gradually or suddenly, as the Zen Buddhists claim? Here again both claims are correct, if taken together as parts of a larger and fuller view. We have to begin by cultivating intuitive feelings. These come to us infrequently at first and so the process is a gradual and long one. Eventually, we reach a point, a very advanced point, where the ego sees its own limitation, perceives its helplessness and dependence, realizes that it cannot lift itself up into the final illuminations. It should then surrender itself wholly to the Overself and cast its further development on the mercy and Grace of the power beyond it. It will then have to go through a waiting period of seeming inactivity, spiritual stagnation, and inability to feel the fervour of devotion which it formally felt. This is a kind of dark night of the soul. Then, slowly, it begins to come out of this phase, which is often accompanied by mental depression and emotional frustration, into a higher phase where it feels utterly resigned to the will of God or destiny, calm and peaceful in the sense of accepting that higher will and not in any joyous sense, patiently waiting for the time when the infinite wisdom will bring it what it once sought so ardently but what it is now as detached from as it is detached from worldly ambitions. After this phase there will come suddenly unexpectedly and in the dead of night, as it were, a tremendous Realization of the egoless state, a tremendous feeling of liberation from itself as it has known itself, a tremendous awareness of the infinitude, universality, and intelligence of life. With that, new perceptions into the Laws of the cosmos will suddenly unfold themselves. The seeker must thus pass from intuition into insight.

56

It is the making the man ready, the preparation of his mind and heart, which takes so much time, so many years even in many cases; but the enlightenment itself is a single short happening: the effect remains permanently.

57

When all illusory ideas are discarded, he will be able to see directly into the truth, and to see it without delay. For what need could there then be to pass through progressive stages?

58

The name "lightning flash of insight" should not be allowed to give the impression that its swiftness is its most important attribute. That is merely incidental. What constitutes its essential attribute is its introducing an entirely different state of mind, an entirely new kind of perception, within us so that we are transformed in ourselves along with the world with which we are in relation.

59

When the ego finally falls out of the picture, it does so with the swiftness of a flash of lightning.

60

The story of King Janaka's initiation by the Sage Ashtavakra illustrates a condition similar to that of Socrates' being caught by the flash during a military campaign and standing still throughout a day and night in its spell. Ashtavakra took Janaka to a forest for this initiation, Janaka riding horseback and Ashtavakra walking alongside. When they reached the spot selected, Ashtavakra told Janaka to dismount. Janaka began to do so. When halfway through the act of dismounting, he was caught by the flash. One leg was raised above the horse's back, while the other rested in the stirrup. So he remained for some days. His Queen sent attendants to search for him, and they brought him home to the palace—still transfixed in the same attitude. He was put in bed still in the same posture. Ashtavakra was called and he bade Janaka to awaken, which he did, becoming bodily normal again. Thereafter he was a fully enlightened rishee. This does not mean that everyone who once glimpses the flash thereafter becomes permanently enlightened. Most do not, for it depends partly on their previous karma and present tendencies whether they can remain permanently in the light or drop out of it again. But it illustrates the swiftness with which it dawns and the need of recognition, surrender, and union with it.

61

Enlightenment seldom comes all at once. But in the case of rare geniuses or of those with rare good karma, the possibility is certainly there.

62

That illumination can be quite instantaneous in some cases, only gradual in others, and entirely absent in most, need not be an enigma. The workings of the law of recompense are still the same even when they are beneath the surface.

63

Wu Men said: "Even though Chao Chou became enlightened, he should continue to work for thirty years more to graduate."

64

When enlightenment comes through philosophic preparation for it, the experience is sudden, direct, unexpected, and spontaneous.

65

It comes to some minds with the force of a Himalayan mountain torrent rushing out from a narrow gorge.

66

Enlightenment may come slowly or suddenly but in the second case it has the effect of sunlight bursting through the sky.

67

The impossibility of such instantaneous illumination being permanent without due preparation and purification was taught by the Buddha: "If the cloth be dirty, however much the dyer might dip it into blue, yellow, red, or lilac dye, its colour will be ugly and unclear—Why? Because of the dirt in the cloth. If the heart is impure one must expect the same sad result."

68

Those geniuses who get a lasting illumination by direct gift of Grace without having worked, studied, prepared, or trained for it, are rare. A Saint Francis or a Ramana Maharshi is an exceptional phenomenon to gaze at, not a model whose life may be closely imitated with the assurance of being able to produce a like result. Everyone else has to undergo the gradual development and patient ripening that a flowering bush has to undergo.

69

The calmness which he carries inside himself, and which is apparent in all his bearing, has not arisen out of nothing. It has come to him out of long struggle and after varied suffering.

70

Not all persons come into this desirable state through formal methods of meditation and regular practice of them. Some attain it through adopting a higher attitude to the happenings, situations, impressions, and emotions which each day's course presents to them.

71

Lao Tzu was a librarian by profession, Janaka a king, and Brother Lawrence a kitchen menial. Yet all had this same wonderful experience of peaceful communion with Overself, proving that one's antecedents, or work, or position are neither helps nor handicaps.

72

It is true that illumination is itself an instantaneous experience, since we pass into it from one moment to the next, and since the Real is timeless. But to hold this illumination against the intrusions of negative personal habits and negative personal characteristics is another matter and success in it is quite rare.

73

When conditions are ripe and prerequisite qualifications fulfilled, the truth spontaneously shows its self-revealing character.

74

It may come as an instantaneous flash of understanding or as a vision of the cosmic drama, but most often it comes quite slowly in bits and pieces.

75

The holy joy may visit you but cannot stay in you if both the animal and the ego are staying in you. Purify yourself of the one and empty yourself of the other, if you would convert a passing glimpse into the permanent union.

Enlightenment comes quietly

76

He will find that the onset of insight will not be at all like the picture of it which he had previously and erroneously formed.

77

When you awaken to truth as it really is, you will have no occult vision, you will have no "astral" experience, no ravishing ecstasy. You will awaken to it in a state of utter stillness, and you will realize that truth was *always* there within you and that reality was always there around you. Truth is not something which has grown and developed through your efforts. It is not something which has been achieved or attained by laboriously adding up those efforts. It is not something which has to be made more and more perfect each year. And once your mental eyes are opened to truth they can never be closed again.(P)

78

The discovery of his true being is not outwardly dramatic, and for a long time no one may know of it, except himself. The world may not honour him for it: he may die as obscure as he lived. But the purpose of his life has been fulfilled; and God's will has been done.

79

There is nothing melodramatic about realization of Truth. Those who look for marvels look in vain, unless indeed its bestowal of singular serenity is a marvel.

80

It is extraordinary how the same experience may produce the same metaphoric sentences used to describe it, although the speakers belong to lands thousands of miles apart and use utterly different languages. A South Indian illumined mystic, telling me of the moment when illumination dawned on him, said that it was all as simple as seeing a fruit held in the palm of one's hand. A Chinese mystic of the same high status said that it was as obvious as seeing a pearl in the palm of one's hand!

81

Chuang Tzu wrote: "From wholeness one comprehends; from comprehension one comes near to Tao. There one stops. To stop without knowing how one stops—this is Tao."

82

No one really knows how this enlightenment first dawns on him. One moment it was not there, the next moment he was somehow in it.

83

No announcements tell the world that he has come into enlightenment. No heralds blow the trumpets proclaiming man's greatest victory—over himself. This is in fact the quietest moment of his whole life.(P)

Naturalness of the attainment

84

He who has attained the consciousness of Overself puts in no claim to the attainment. He accepts it in so utterly natural and completely humble a manner that most people are deceived into regarding him as ordinary.

85

He has not attained who is conscious that he has attained, for this very consciousness cunningly hides the ego and delivers him into its power. That alone is attainment which is natural, spontaneous, unforced, unaware, and unadvertised, whether to the man himself or to others.

86

At this stage there is no struggle for further growth; it comes as softly and as naturally as a flower's. There is no sacrifice of things the ego desires or clutches to itself, for there is such insight as to their worth or worthlessness that they stay or fall away of themselves.

87

It is better to attain such high status without knowing it. For this absence of pride and presence of humility keeps the ego from threatening it.

88

The actions of a man who has attained this degree are inspired directly by his Overself, and consequently are not dictated by personal wishes, purposes, passions, or desires. They are not initiated by his ego's will but by a will higher than his own.

Since there is no consciously deliberate thinking, no attempt at ordered logical formulation of ideas, there is also no hesitation, no broken trends. There is only spontaneous thought, feeling, and action, all being directed by intuition.

89

Plotinus even made the point that it is better for a man *not* to be aware that he is acting virtuously, courageously, wisely, or practising contemplation beautifully, free from interfering mental images or thoughts. For then, if he does not know that he—*the person*—is doing so, no egoism will taint his consciousness. It will be pure being. He will do whatever has to be done by him as a human creature—whether it be a physical act or a mental one, he will respond to all situations that call for a human response, but neither the act nor the response will be accompanied by the personal ego. This does not mean that his worldly life or he himself will suffer loss of identity—only that he will be isolated from the worldly self-centered thought, desire, and motive which prompts the existence of the mass of people.

90

He feels no need—so conspicuous in neurotics with a message—to call attention to himself. Rather does he seek to keep it away.

91

Chuang Tzu: "Unawareness of one's feet is the mark of shoes that fit, unawareness of right and wrong is the mark of a mind at ease. . . . The moment a centipede becomes conscious of his seventeenth or twenty-third pair of legs he cannot move any more. . . . As fish forget themselves in water, so should men forget themselves in Tao."

92

It is then as natural as breathing. The sage does not have to be self-conscious about his sagehood, as if it were a quality apart but added to his other qualities.

Degrees of enlightenment

93

The strength of the enlightenment will determine the extent of its effects.

94

An illumination may be permanent but at the same time it may be only partial. Not until it is complete and lasting is it really philosophic.

95

It is not only true that there is variety in the types of illumination but also true that there is a scale of degrees in the illumination itself.

96

Until he is established permanently, although not necessarily at the very highest level, the consciousness can become corrupted, the man himself can fall back.

97

There are varying degrees of spiritual illumination, which accounts both for the varying outlooks to be found among mystics and for the different kinds of Glimpse among aspirants. All illuminations and all Glimpses free the man from his negative qualities and base nature, but in the latter case only temporarily. He is able, as a result, to see into his higher nature. In the first degree, it is as if a window covered with dirt were cleaned enough to reveal a beautiful garden outside it. He is still subject to the activity of thinking, the emotion of joy, and the discrimination between X and Y. In the next and higher degree, it is as if the window were still more cleaned so that still more beauty is revealed beyond it. Here there are no thoughts to intervene between the seer and the seen. In the third degree, the discrimination is no longer present. In the fourth degree, it is as if the window were thoroughly cleaned. Here there is no longer even a rapturous emotion but only a balanced happiness, a steady tranquillity which, being beyond the intellect, cannot properly be described by the intellect.

Again, mental peace is a fruit of the first and lowest degree of illumination, although thoughts will continue to arise although gently, and thinking in the discursive manner will continue to be active although slowly. But concentration will be sufficiently strong to detach him from the world and, as a consequence, to yield the happiness which accompanies such detachment. Only those who have attained to this degree can correctly be regarded as "saved" as only they alone are unable to fall back into illusion, error, sin, greed, or sensuality.

In the second degree, there will be more inward absorption and cerebral processes will entirely fade out.

Freedom from all possibility of anger is a fruit of the third and higher degree.(P)

98

The Witness is both an abstract metaphysical concept and a concrete mystical experience. It is not an ultimate one, yielding pure Being, the unsplit Consciousness, but a provisional one.(P)

99

The Witness itself, while witnessing, is being witnessed.

100

To be the witness is the first stage; to be Witness of the witness is the next; but to BE is the final one. For consciousness lets go of the witness in the end. Consciousness alone is itself the real experience.(P)

101

He discovers the presence of this link with World-Mind by a wonderful experience, brief and passing though it be. It is felt intensely and known intuitively. That the divinity is within him is thenceforth his certainty even at the times when awareness is absent. But eventually, if mind develops, he has to ask the question, "What of the world outside?"

102

Human thought can rise to levels of godliness until it takes the final leap and transcends itself.

103

We may reasonably hope to see God one day but not to be God. The Cosmic Vision of the World-Mind at work which Arjuna had may be ours too but not the complete union with the World-Mind Itself.

104

Although there are certain similarities between the experiences of Adepts and that of Saint Paul, the nature and ultimate aim of the trance which they underwent was different from those of Saint Paul. There are various degrees and kinds of trance, ranging from mere oblivion to psychical visions and mental travelling, and higher still to a complete immersion of the ego in cosmic Divinity.

105

A rare but complete illumination must not only pass from the first to the final degree of intensity, but must also contain a picture of the cosmic order. That is to say, it must be a revelation. It must explain the profounder nature of the universe, the inner meaning of individual existence, and the hidden relationship between the two.(P)

106

Two factors account for the differences between individual cosmic illumination. First, there is the human contribution made by the mind itself; second, there are ascending stages in the Illumination or rather in the receptivity to it.

107

Cosmic Vision is of two kinds: (a) seeing the forms and objects around and feeling one with them, (b) seeing only the Idea of the universe. This is called identifying through worship with Hiranyagarbha. It is the subtle universe. It is an advanced experience, not the ultimate: "So one ought not to stop there," said the Professor.

108

There is some confusion on this point in the minds of many students. On attaining enlightenment a man does not attain omniscience. At most, he may receive a revelation of the inner operations of life and Nature, of the higher laws governing life and man. That is, he may also become a seer and find a cosmogony presented to his gaze. But the actuality in a majority of cases is that he attains enlightenment only, not cosmogonical seership.(P)

109

The deeper one penetrates into the Void the more he is purified of the illusions of personality, time, matter, space, and causality. Between the second and third stages of insight's unfoldment there are really two further subsidiary stages which are wrapped in the greatest mystery and are rarely touched by the average mystic or yogi. For both of them are stages which lead further downwards into the Void. The yogi touches the edge of the Void, as it were, but not its centre. These two stages are purificatory ones and utterly annihilate the last illusions and the last egoisms of the seeker. They are dissolved forever and cannot revive again. Nothing more useful can and may be said about it here. *For this is the innermost holy of holies, the most sacred sanctuary accessible to man.* He who touches this grade touches what may not be spoken aloud for sneering ears, nor written down for sneering eyes. Consequently none has ever ventured to explain publicly what must not be so explained.(P)

110

All human beings on this planet are imperfect. Perfection is not fully attainable here. But when a man has striven for it and advanced near to it, he will attain it automatically as soon as he is freed from the body.

111

So long as man is immured in this earth plane, so long must the enlightenment he attains be an imperfect one, or the fulfilment he experiences a limited one.

112

The liberation from further reincarnations can be attained while still here in the flesh, but the full completion of its consequent inner peace can come only after final exit from the body.

113

So long as he is held by the finite flesh, so long as existence in the inner human body is continued, the perfect and complete merger of his individuality in the cosmic mind is impossible. But once through the portals of so-called death, it becomes an actuality.

114

It is not that philosophy denies the possibility of escaping from personal consciousness into the universal one; on the contrary, it well admits it. But it declares that the journey is still not finished.

Nonduality, sahaja, insight

115

The illuminate is conscious of both the ultimate unity and the immediate multiplicity of the world. This is a paradox. But his permanent resting place while he is dealing with others is at the junction-point of duality and unity so that he is ready at any moment to absorb his attention in either phase.

116

The understanding that everything is illusive is not the final one. It is an essential stage but only a stage. Ultimately you will understand that the form and separateness of a thing are illusory, but the thing-in-itself is not. *That* out of which these forms appear is not different from them, hence Reality is one and the same in all things. This is the paradox of life and a sharp mind is needed to perceive it. However, to bring beginners out of their earthly attachments, we have to teach first the illusoriness of the world, and then raise them to a higher level of understanding and show that the world is not apart from the Real. *That Thou Art* unifies everything in essence. But this final realization cannot be got by stilling the mind, only by awakening it into full vigour again after yogic peace has been attained and then letting its activity cease of its own accord when thought merges voluntarily into insight. When that is done, you know the limitations of both yoga and enquiry as successive stages. Whoever realizes this truth does not divorce from matter—as most yogis do—but realizes non-difference from it. Hence we call this highest path the "yoga of non-duality." But to reach it one has to pass through the "yoga of philosophical knowledge." Christian Science caught glimpses of the higher truth but Mrs. Eddy got her facts and fancies confused together.

117

The knowledge of Allah follows upon the dissolving of the ego, *fana*, says Sufism. But some Sufi masters go even farther and assert that it follows only on the dissolving of this dissolving (*fana-el-fana*). What does this strange statement mean? The answer is nonduality. What nonduality itself means is to be gleaned from another Sufi declaration: "The outer path: I and Thou. The inner path: I am Thou and Thou are I. The final insight: neither I nor Thou."

118

The expression used by some Buddhists, "the Undivided Mind," has the same meaning as "the Oneness with all things" used by many mystics—that is, a permanent knowledge got in a *single* glimpse, a great nondual truth.

119

In this high state his own mind is consciously connected with the divine Mind. The result can scarcely be understood by the uninitiated.

120

When the masculine and feminine temperaments within us are united, completed, and balanced, when masculine power and feminine passivity are brought together *inside* the person and knowledge and reverence encircle them both, then wisdom begins to dawn in the soul. The ineffable reality and the mentalist universe are then understood to be non-different from one another.

121

Where both unity and diversity are experienced and the individual is able to attain both these levels, he is surely gifted with insight. However, if diversity has to be blotted out before becoming aware of unity, this may be regarded as a penultimate faculty; that is, the insight is genuine but is still not fully mature. Everything depends on the capacity of the individual.

122

When his mind moves entirely and wholly into the One Infinite Presence, and when it settles permanently there, the divided existence of glimpse and darkness, of Spirit and matter, of Overself and ego, of heaven and earth, will vanish. The crossing over to a unified existence will happen.

123

When duality is blended with, *and within*, unity it is the true *jivanmukta* realization. The One is then experienced as the Two but *known* to be really the One.(P)

124

The state of nonduality is a state of intense peace and perfect balance. It is so peaceful because everything is seen as it belongs—to the eternal order of cosmic evolution; hence, all is accepted, all reconciled.

125

That which is called duality in Oriental metaphysics, the related two, self and non-self, self and universe, self and its experience, is transcended.

126

Quoted from Advaitin John Levy's *Immediate Knowledge and Happiness*: ". . . although outwardly something of duality appears to still remain, he is nevertheless established in nonduality." Ramakrishna admitted that a slight bit of ego still is left over to continue functioning in the physical body.

127

A twelfth-century Japanese scroll at Museum Rietberg, Zurich, is inscribed with verse by Monk Saih-len: "For the heart in inner harmony and for which everything is one, no difference exists between this and that."

128

To such a man, the here and there become as one.

129

Paras on *sahaja*: It is *wrong* to use the illustration of a camera shutter—the image getting larger or vaguer or smaller and sharper as it opens or closes—for attention focused on *nirvikalpa* in meditation or spread out in *sahaja* in the wakeful state. The correct illustration is this: the stillness is being experienced at the centre of a circle, the thoughts revolve around it at the circumference. But the degree of Stillness remains just as much in outer activity as in meditation.

130

There are two different ways to realization: (a) The path of yoga meditation whose goal is *nirvikalpa samadhi*. (b) *Gnana* whose goal is *sahaja samadhi*. This looks on the world as being only a picture, unreal. Both seek and reach the same Brahman, the world disappearing for both.

131

The concept of *Nirvana* has often been miscomprehended in the Occident. Because the name itself is derived from the Sanskrit word (*Nirva*) "to extinguish," the earliest translators of Buddhist texts took *Nirvana* as being the extinction of being, the annihilation of man, self completely ceasing to exist.

132

It is the difference between visiting a palace (the glimpse) and coming to live permanently in one (*Sahaja*).

133

Ramana Maharshi often used the term *sahaja samadhi* to describe what he regarded as the best state. Although the word *samadhi* is too often associated with yogic trance, there is nothing of the kind in his use of this term. He said it was the best state because it was quite natural, nothing forced, artificial, or temporary. We may equate it with Zen's "This life is very life" and "Walk On!"

134

The only worthwhile enlightenment is the one which lasts all through the year and every year. The Zen flash is not the same.

135

Sahaja: This is "natural" as contrasted with "artificial" spirituality, "spontaneous" as against "cultivated," and "unconscious" by comparison alongside "professionally conscious," with its narrow limits.

136

With all the other *samadhis* the yogi goes in or comes out; whereas with *sahaja* he stays permanently.

137

The constant application of meditation to the activity of knowledge, to behaviour, thought, and feeling, eventually brings about a continuous awareness. This is called *Sahaja*.

138

Sahaja samadhi is not broken into intervals, is permanent, and involves no special effort. Its arisal is instantaneous and without progressive stages. It can accompany daily activity without interfering with it. It is a settled calm and complete inner quiet.

There are no distinguishing marks that an outside observer can use to identify a *sahaja*-conscious man because *sahaja* represents consciousness itself rather than its transitory states.

Sahaja has been called the lightning flash. Philosophy considers it to be the most desirable goal.

This is illustrated with a classic instance of Indian spirituality involving a king named Janaka. One day he was about to mount his horse and put one foot into the stirrup which hung from the saddle. As he was about to lift himself upwards into the saddle the "lightning flash" struck his consciousness. He was instantly carried away and concentrated so deeply that he failed for some time to lift himself up any higher. From that day onwards he lived in *sahaja samadhi* which was always present within him.

Those at the state of achieved *sahaja* are under no compulsion to continue to meditate any more or to practise yoga. They often do—either because of inclinations produced by past habits or as a means of helping other persons. In either case it is experienced as a pleasure. Because this consciousness is permanent, the experiencer does not need to go into meditation. This is despite the outward appearance of a person who places himself in the posture of meditation in order to achieve something.

When you are engaged in outward activity it is not the same as when you are in a trance. This is true for both the beginner and the adept. The adept, however, does not lose the *sahaja* awareness which he has achieved and can withdraw into the depths of consciousness which the ordinary cannot do.(P)

139

What is the difference between the state of deepest contemplation, which the Hindus call *nirvikalpa samadhi*, and that which they call *sahaja samadhi*? The first is only a temporary experience, that is it begins and ends but the man actually experiences an uplift of consciousness, he gains a new and higher outlook. But *sahaja* is continuous unbroken realization that as Overself he always was, is, and shall be. It is not a feeling that something new and higher has been gained. What is the absolute test which distinguishes one condition from the other, since both are awareness of the Overself? In *nirvikalpa* the ego vanishes but reappears when the ordinary state is resumed: hence it has only been lulled, even though it has been slightly weakened by the process. In *sahaja* the ego is rooted out once and for all! It not only vanishes, but it cannot reappear.

140

Sahaja samadhi is the awareness of Awareness, whether appearing as thoughts or not, whether accompanied by bodily activities or not. But *nirvikalpa samadhi* is solely the awareness of Awareness.

141

I am an Advaitin on the fundamental point of nonduality of the Real, but I am unable to limit myself to most Advaitins' practical view of *samadhi* and *sahaja*. Here I stand with Chinese Zen (*Ch'an*), especially as I was taught and as explained by the Sixth Patriarch, Hui Neng. He warns against turning meditation into a narcotic, resulting in a pleasant passivity. He went so far as to declare: "It is quite unnecessary to stay in monasteries. Only let your mind . . . function in freedom . . . let it abide nowhere." And in this connection he later explains: "To be free from attachment to all outer objects is true meditation. To meditate means to realize thus tranquillity of Essence of Mind."

On *samadhi*, he defines it as a mind self-trained to be unattached amid objects, resting in tranquillity and peace. On *sahaja*, it is thorough understanding of the truth about reality and a penetration into and through delusion, to one's Essence of Mind. The Indian notion of *sahaja* makes it the extension of *nirvikalpa samadhi* into the active everyday state. But the *Ch'an* conception of *nirvikalpa samadhi* differs from this; it does not seek deliberately to eliminate thoughts, although that may often happen of its own accord through identification with the true Mind, but to eliminate the personal feelings usually attached to them, that is, to remain unaffected by them because of this identification.

Ch'an does not consider *sahaja* to be the fruit of yoga meditation alone, nor of understanding alone, but of a combination seemingly of both. It is a union of reason and intuition. It is an awakening once and for all. It is not attained in *nirvikalpa* and then to be held as long as possible. It is not something, a state alternately gained and lost on numerous occasions, but gradually expanded as it is clung to. It is a single awakening that enlightens the man so that he never returns to ignorance again. He has awakened to his divine essence, his source in Mind, as an all day and every day self-identification. It has come by itself, effortlessly.

142

This is as high as human consciousness can possibly go while yet encased in the flesh.

143

I do not claim that sahaja yields ultimate reality: I only claim that it yields the ultimate so far *known to man*.(P)

144

It is as present to him as his clothes, yet it exists through a sixth sense. He lives simultaneously aware of both worlds of being. And he knows which is the eternal one.

145

When *sahaja* is established in a man, when it stays with him for the remainder of his years, he is truly blessed.

146

This state is paradoxical for the very name is really wrong, since it implies something that can be different later or was different earlier, something that is in *time*. But what is being here described is not of that kind. Time flows out from it, there is no change yet to come that will better it or bring it any gain. It still is what it always was. Why, then, is the word "state" used at all? Partly, of course, through the poverty of human language in describing what is trans-human and partly because there is a state but it is in us, the change which brings us into it being in our minds.

147

The general idea in the popular and religious circles of India is that the highest state of illumination is attained during a trance condition (*samadhi*). This is not the teaching in the highest philosophic circles of India. There is another condition, *sahaja samadhi*, which is described in a few little-known texts and which is regarded as superior. It is esteemed because no trance is necessary and because it is a continuous state. The inferior state is one which is intermittently entered and left: it cannot be retained without returning to trance. The philosophic "fourth state," by contrast, remains unbroken even when active and awake in the busy world.(P)

148

When body is still and ego-mind is at rest, there is peace, sometimes even ecstasy. But when both are active but I am not, when there is neither questing nor non-questing, there is unchanging stability. That is realization.

149

When the sense of this presence is a continuous one, when the knowledge of the mentalness of this world-experience is an abiding one, and when the calm which comes as a result is an unshakeable one, it may be said that he is established in the Truth and in the Real.

150

He does not have to enter into formal meditation to find his soul. It is an ever-present reality for him, not merely an intellectual conception or emotional belief.

151

If he has no need to sit down specially for an arranged period of meditation, it is only because he has successfully gone through all three stages of the practice.

152

In the world you will find only two kinds of people—the unconscious and the conscious. The first kind know only their own little egos and their own large desires. The second kind know continually that they are in the presence of the Overself, and enjoy its great peace.

153

The consciousness of Consciousness never deserts him. It remains somewhere on the outer periphery of the mind all the time and expands to its fullness at special times—that is, when withdrawn from all activities for a few minutes.

154

He lives in inwardly silent thought-free awareness of whatever is presented to him, whether it be the body in which he must live or the environments in which he finds himself. He enjoys a supernal calm, being indeed "free while living," as the ancient Indian phrase describes the state.

155

The true deathlessness must be a changeless one. Consequently it must be an eventless one. But this does not necessarily mean a boring one. For if we realize our higher individuality, we shall be able to hold consciously and unaffected such an immortal life within our hearts whilst entering into relations with a changeful world process without them. And this will be true whether the world be on our present physical level of perception or not, whether in the flesh or out of it.

156

He who has reached this degree will be always poised in the Overself, always aware of his identity with its inimitable nature yet also conscious of his limitations as an ego. This may seem queer and contradictory yet the man will never feel himself pulled in different directions but, on the contrary, will feel a perfect harmony between the human and the divine.

157

This, once established, will remain when all else is but a heap of ashes.

158

Insight always remains with its possessor whereas intuition only comes and goes. Insight deals solely with the Real whereas intuition deals with the phenomenal. Amid all this variegated world-activity, the Real remains unchanged and unchangeable just as the dream-world which is emanated from the mind of a dreamer leaves his mind unaffected and unaltered. It never changes. Hence the first characteristic of insight—that faculty in man which can perceive this reality—is likewise that it never changes.

159

While still continuing to feel the presence and enjoy the peace of the

Infinite, he attends to ordinary everyday affairs. But it is inevitable that the attention demanded by the latter forces some reduction in awareness of the former.

160
His work in the world, his life in the home, and even his pleasures in society will not at any moment stray outside his divinized consciousness but will always be held within it.

161
He will remain in relation with the mystical part of him, the part that is forever alone.

162
The Buddhists call lasting enlightenment by the name of *Nirvana*.

163
Because the fourth state is a thought-free, passion-free state, it is also a steady and unaltering one. Yet it is so delightful that there is no monotony, no boredom in it.

164
To attain this advanced stage is to attain the capacity to enter directly and immediately into meditation, not merely at a special time or in a particular place, but always and everywhere.

165
Once this stage is attained, neither the knowledge of reality nor the feeling of serenity will ever leave him again. He has found them not for a few hours but forever.

166
Therefore the man who perceives this naturally, perceives the ultimate reality everywhere. He does not need to meditate or to go into a trance to find it.

167
His whole nature has come completely to rest in the Overself.

168
The *disciple* is aware of the Overself at some times but not at other times. The *adept*, however, always has this awareness in an unbroken flow.

169
Inner strength, divine joy, deep understanding, and unspeakable tranquillity will pervade him always and not be limited to the hours of solitary meditation. This is so because the Overself whence these things come is always with all men. Only, they know it not, whereas he has awakened to its abiding presence.

170

At this stage his mind never loses its magnificent poise but remains always fixed on its own deepest level.

171

When this has been fully achieved without fluctuations or breaks, when the mind is always established in this lofty state, it is characterized by a beautiful peace.

172

He sits, poised in this great Mind.

Conscious transcendental sleep

173

He may be said to have entered and settled in the fourth state when he is conscious of its purity egolessness and freedom at all times, and even during the torpor of sleep or the activity of work.

174

When this awareness is so stabilized that it maintains itself at all times awake or asleep, he is at the end of the quest.

175

The divine presence does not leave the enlightened man when he goes to sleep and return to him when he awakes, nor does it leave him when he enters the state of dream and return to him when he leaves it; it is in truth something which is ever present. If he enters the sleeping state, he enters it while in the light of knowledge, and the same applies if he enters the dream state.

176

The sage does not retire at night in the darkness, the ignorance of ordinary sleep, but in the light of the Consciousness, the ever-unbroken Transcendence.

177

His sleep is a suspended state, with his awareness never fully lost but retracted into a pin-point.

178

There are no breaks in the awareness of his higher nature. There is no loss of continuity in the consciousness of his immortal spirit. Therefore he is not illumined at some hour of the day and unillumined at another hour, nor illumined while he is awake and unillumined while he is asleep.

179

That alone is the final attainment which can remain with him through all the three states—waking, dream, and deep sleep—and through all the day's activities.

180

What is ordinarily known during deep sleep is the veil of ignorance which covers the Real. That is, the knowing faculty, the awareness, is still present, but caught in the ignorance, the veiling, and knowing nothing else. The sage, however, carries into sleep the awareness he had in wakefulness. He may let it dim down to a glimmer, but it is always there.

181

This state of conscious transcendental sleep is symbolized in some mystical figures of antiquity by forming or painting them without eyelids.

182

Sleep is a condition which nature imposes on man. No one, not even the sage, can alter its general course and therefore even the sage has to accept this condition as an inevitable part of his own human lot. But if he is to attain full self-realization, this must eventually pertain to his sleeping state as much as to his waking state, else it will not be what its name suggests.

183

If the sage's sleep is wholly without those varied mental experiences of persons and places which manifest as dreams, then it will pass so swiftly that an entire night's sleep will take no longer than a few seconds of wakeful time.

184

Although the sage withdraws with the onset of sleep from wakeful awareness, he does not withdraw from all awareness. A pleasurable and peaceful sense of impersonal being is left over. In this he rests throughout the night.

Individuality remains

185

They are still debating in India, as they debated hundreds of years ago, whether the soul will always preserve its individuality or whether it will eventually merge and vanish into the One.

186

After this passing-over into the Overself's rule, does he carry a loss of identity? Is he no more aware that he is the named person of the past? Were this so he could not exist in human society or attend to his duties. No!—outwardly he is more or less the same, although his pattern of behaviour betrays recognizable signs of superiority over the past man which he was. Inwardly, there is total revolution.

187

What or who is using the body and mind of a self-realized person? Is it God or man who acts, works, speaks, or writes then? Is it true that the ego is kept but subordinated by him? Or does it vanish altogether and only seem present to the outer observer?

188

We do not accept that interpretation of mystic experience which proclaims it to be an extinction of human personality in God's being.

189

The differences between human beings still remain after illumination. The variations which make each one a unique specimen and the individual that he is, still continue to exist. But the Oneness behind human beings powerfully counterbalances.

190

When it is said that we lose our individuality on entering Nirvana, words are being used loosely and faultily. So long as a man, whether he be Buddha or Hitler, has to walk, eat, and work, he must use his individuality. What *is* lost by the sage is his *attachment* to individuality with its desires, hates, angers, and passions.

191

The line of demarcation between man and the World-Mind can be attenuated but not obliterated.

192

It is perfectly possible to become impersonal in attitude and yet remain individual in consciousness. The winning of the one condition does not mean the losing of the other.

193

We humans recoil from the bleak picture of an impersonality without feeling, a life without passion, or survival without ego. Yet it seems bleak because it is rarely known or seen in experience, and also because it is unfamiliar and unrealized.

194

Freed at last from this ever-whirling wheel of birth and death to which he was tied by his own desire-nature, what happens to him can only be an opening up to a new better and indescribable state, and it is so. He as he was vanishes, not into complete annihilation and certainly not into the heaven of a perpetuated ego, but into a higher kind of life shrouded in mystery.

195

They must face this dilemma in their thinking, that if their absolutist "realization" is a fixed and finished state there is no room for an ego in it, however sublimated, refined, and purged the ego may be. The end, then, can only be a merger, a dissolution into Nirvana and a total disappearance of the conscious self. This is a kind of death. But there is another kind of salvation, a *living* one where unfoldment and growth still continue, albeit on higher levels than any which we now know.

196

The gap between the finite human mind and the infinite World-Mind is absolute. A union between them is not possible unless the first merges and disappears into the second.(P)

197

Will he have to surrender all conscious life and get in return the problematical advantage of a merger indistinguishable from complete annihilation? True, the possibility of further suffering will then be entirely eliminated. But so will the possibility of further joy.

198

It is a fallacy to think that this displacement of the lower self brings about its complete substitution by the infinite and absolute Deity. This fallacy is an ancient and common one in mystical circles and leads to fantastic declarations of self-deification. If the lower self is displaced, it is not destroyed. It lives on but in strict subordination to the higher one, the Overself, the divine soul of man; and it is this latter, not the divine world-principle, which is the true displacing element.(P)

199

He is united with, but not absorbed by, the infinite Overself. He is a part of it, but only individually so. This is his highest condition while still in the flesh.

200

There is some kind of a distinction between his higher individuality and the Universal Infinite out of which it is rayed, whatever the Vedantins may say. And this distinction remains in his highest mystical state, which is not one of total absorption and utter destruction of this individuality but the mergence of its own will in the universal will, the closest intimacy of its own being with the universal being.(P)

201

The Overself is one with the World-Mind without however being lost in it.

202

There is no final absorption; the individual continues to exist somehow in the Supreme. The fact that he can pass away into it at will and yet return again, proves this.

203

Something is there, something must take the place of the absent ego to perform its function and do in the world what needs to be done.

204

The unit of mind is differentiated out and undergoes its long evolution through numerous changes of state, not to merge so utterly in its source again as to be virtually annihilated, but to be consciously harmonized with that source whilst yet retaining its individuality.(P)

205

If on the one hand he is conscious of himself in the divine being, on the other he is conscious of himself in the human ego. The two can coexist, and at this stage of advance, do. But the ego must knit itself to the higher self until they become like a single entity. When his mind is immovably fixed in this state, his personal will permanently directed by the higher one, he is said to have attained the true mystical life.

206

What he has to do in the world as a human being is henceforth to be done not really by his ordinary personal self but by the Presence which, shapeless and silent though it be, is the vital living essence of what connects him with God. If this seems to deprive him of the attributes which make a man *man*, I can reply only that we are here back with the Sphinx. Yes, the enigma is great; but the realized understanding and experience is immeasurably greater in its blessedness.

207

His life becomes a lengthened awareness of this Presence. He is never lonely because he is never encased in the belittling thought that this narrow personal self-consciousness is the totality of his "I."

208

He lives every moment in the awareness of his higher self. Yet this does not oppose nor interfere with the awareness of his lower one.

209

Everything he then does is done by the ordinary personal self alone, out of and in harmony with the Overself, or his higher individuality. In thus working together, the divine presence supports the ego's presence, but the ego is put in its place and kept in harmony with the higher individuality. If this is what people mean by killing out the ego (which is really killing out its tyranny), there could be no objection to the statement. But to assert that it is not functioning at all is silly.

210

If the claim of complete merger is valid, if the individual self really disappears in the attainment of Divine Consciousness, of whom then was this same self aware in the experience of attainment? No—it is only the lower personal self that is transcended; the higher spiritual individuality is not.(P)

211

When the universe itself runs down and disintegrates given enough time, how can this little and limited being of man hope to preserve his personal consciousness, his personality, his character just as it is today? Any belief fostered by any kind of authority—religious or metaphysical or any other—which fosters this illusion is a false one. But, this said, let it be countered by that other truth which is needed to complete the thought. If the individualized being must one day part with its limited consciousness, this is only in order to return to its origin in the universal consciousness, for consciousness cannot come out of nothing. It came from and goes back to the universal mind. Therefore, if a man loses the little and temporary immortality of the ego, it will only be to gain the greater and true immortality of that mind.

212

The higher individuality is preserved, but the lower personality, with its miserable limitations, is not.

213

The difference between the individual and the universal self persists throughout the incarnations and no mystical emotionalism or metaphysical jugglery can end it. It will end indeed not by the individual transforming himself into the greater being but by his merging himself into it, that is, by the disappearance of his separate consciousness in the pure essence of all consciousness. But it need not so end unless he wants it.

214

Jew and Christian alike have honoured Martin Buber. If his views are examined and appraised, it will be found that two tenets received his weightiest emphasis. In his early period it was the mystical feeling and mystical experience. In his later period, it was the application of truth to everyday living, the immersion of routine physical existence in spiritual influence that came to matter most to him, or in short, the non-separation of the Overself from the body. The appeal of both these tenets to the Western mind, starved as it was, and is, of deeper inner experience and fearful of being sucked into monastic flight from the world as the only answer to the question "How shall I fulfil my duty as a spiritual being?" is quite obvious, understandable and natural. But there was a metaphysical error in this second phase, expressed in his claim that the ego persists even in the state of alleged union with God, and therefore in his denial that such a union is really what it purports to be. Albert Schweitzer fell into the same error. The only way to expose such an error is to pass through the tremendous and transforming experience itself; but then its validity will exist only for oneself, not for others, unfortunately. What happens then is that the feeling of a personal separate "I" vanishes during the short period of profound inward absorption when "I" is absent, Overself is present. There is really no ego because the mind is not at work producing thoughts. But when the meditation ends, and the ordinary life is resumed, the "I" necessarily is resumed too. In the case of a philosopher—that is, one who has thoroughly understood the nature of the ego—the relationship with this "I" is no longer complete immersion and identification. It is there, yes, but he is detached from it, a witness of it. His world-experience does not contradict his inner experience, hence the latter fulfils the test of ultimate reality.

215

It is impossible to put into sharply precise statements any positive definition or description of Mind that would be quite satisfactory. It is just as hard to put into proper words what the resultant is when ego vanishes, when the No-thing reigns in the consciousness. To assert that there is non-existence would be as misleading as to assert that there is existence, even if it were of a higher kind. For if the ego is gone, what is it that activates the body in its dealings with the world, or even with itself? Because the topic is incomprehensible, the answer to this question must itself be either incomprehensible or wholly phrased in negative terms. But to say what IT is not, does not make very lucid what it is.

216

His individual characteristics still remain and make him outwardly different from other men. No inward unity can obliterate them. So it would be correct to say that it is his egoism rather than his ego which disappears.

217

There is no reason why he should not preserve his individuality even if he should surrender it to God.

218

The goal is achieved when the higher self encloses and absorbs the ego.

219

Though he has been caught up into something immensely greater than himself, he still remains an individual—albeit a loosely held one.

220

Nirvana is never achieved, never attained, never realized. For if that were possible then the achiever, the attainer, the realizer—that is, the ego—would be on the same unchanging level, would itself be Ultimate!

221

If there is no such entity as a "me," an ego, you are entitled to ask *who* then has this enlightenment? And the answer is the only possible one: it is the Void having the experience of itself: or rediscovering itself as it does in each person who attains this level.

222

In such a person, the Impersonal becomes the individual, the Relationless enters into a duality of "I" and the "Not-self."

223

With one's own being, "I" as person expands through knowledge into "It" as universal Self. When? Never. For now I perceive all this as a dream. "It" alone IS on awakening; "It" alone was then.

224

The idea of a higher individuality was more acceptable to Western mentality than the Brahmanic one of total dissolution in a single mass consciousness. It was also more understandable. The lesser self finds its transcendental goal in submission to this higher individuality. Here is the highest form of duality.

225

The "I" has been transformed into the "I Am."

226

His further life will be a record of discovery rather than speculation, of insights rather than intellections.

World continues

227

What will happen to his environment after illumination? Nothing. It will not be miraculously transformed so that he sees auras, ghosts, and atoms mixed up with its ordinary appearance. It will still look as it did before. The grass will have the same shapes and colour.

228

Some—especially Indians—imagine that a fully attained man lives only in a state of abstraction, as if he were in a prolonged half-dream. They confuse a stage on the way up with the end itself.

229

The mind passes through a stage when, seeking after truth, it finds out that the world is other than it seems to be, and that its material substance is not matter at all but energy: its form is illusory. But this is not the end. For the seeker does not stop there; if he proceeds farther, he may find that illusion is itself an illusion. It is next found to be derived from reality and to be a form assumed by reality. This is the sage's enlightenment, this is his experience.

230

The ordinary man is aware of his surroundings, first, by naming and labelling them; second, by linking them with past memory of them; and third, by relating them to his own personal self. The illumined egoless man is simply aware of them, without any of these other added activities.

231

Whether in the sage or the simpleton the thought of the world, as well as of all that the man has to do in the world, is inescapable if he is to remain in it. The difference between them is that the ignorant one is held captive by what *appears* to him whereas the enlightened one knows also its inner reality. Whoever believes that he is the body alone cannot escape the name materialist. The other man reverses this belief, regards himself as distinct from and possessor of the body. His is not just a belief, however, but a piece of knowledge. It has the certitude which follows being freed from all doubt. Why then should he be afraid of acknowledging his personal-impersonal existence in, and awareness of, the world?

232

Japanese Zen Master Dogen: "Unwise people think that in the world of essence there should be no bloom of flowers and no fall of leaves." The Master here shows that in the mind of the enlightened man the external world appears as for the ordinary man and remains a mere mentation for the mentalist.

233

The permanence which ordinary normal people seem to find in merely living does not exist for him. He finds only transience. This affects both the bright and dark sides of existence, the good fortune and ill fortune. All is unstable and subject to change.

234

The enlightened man has the same kind of body and the same five senses as unenlightened men have. His experience of the world must be the same, too. But—and this is a vast difference—he experiences it along with the Overself.

235

For incarnate man the cosmic dream is always going on. This is also the case for the sage. But he has the *knowledge* of what is happening and the power to intromit it one step further back.

We are all in this dream which is itself the product of, and hidden within, a greater dream. Is God, the Dreamer, then asleep? This is the mystery: that he is both awake and asleep *at the same time.* How can man's tiny mind understand such a thing? Of course not. Let him be still and seek not to carry his profane curiosity into the Holy of Holies. In the end it shall be as if he were never existent, but this cannot be the same as death. For the dream—of which he is a part—goes back into the Dreamer, into the Living God.

236

If the illuminate detaches himself from the world because of its immediate transiency, he re-attaches himself to it again because of its ultimate unity with his own innermost being.

237

He lives in the knowledge of the World-Idea—not in its fullness of detail but in its general outline—which is fulfilling itself in the whole universe and with which he tries to co-operate according to his knowledge. This it is which supports his inner being, counters his everyday experience of human weakness and evil, and transfigures him when leaving the hour of communion to resume that experience.

238

Is such a statement that the sage sees no world because no world exists to be taken literally? Does it really mean what it says? If so, the sage is squatting in complete isolation, not even seeing a single sage existent anywhere in space now, or in time earlier, and who hears or records this statement, since all others are non-existent along with the world.

239

Philosophic discipline relates at every point to the act of living. For once insight has been unfolded, the philosopher is continuously aware of the oneness of the stuff of the world existence—which includes his own existence, too.

240

How does the illuminate react to his own *karma*? "Even after knowledge of the self has been awakened, *Prarabdha* (the portion of past *karma* now being enjoyed) does not leave him but he does not feel *Prarabdha* after the dawning of the knowledge of the truth because the body and other things are unreal like the things seen in a dream to one on awakening from it," replies *Nadabindu Upanishad*. That is, he treats his karmic suffering as being but ideas.

241

The contradictory attitudes involved in satisfying physical need and submitting to spiritual detachment are united and resolved by the sage into a single harmonious insight.

242

The man who has this higher consciousness permanently will see and experience the outer world like other men, but he will understand the relation between what he sees and the Real world which is behind it. In the same way, anyone can understand the relation between his body and its shadows; but whereas unenlightened men see the shadow alone, the enlightened one sees both.

243

Of little use are explanations which befog truth and bewilder understanding. To inform a Western reader that an enlightened man sees only "Brahman" is to imply that he does not see forms, that is, the world. But the fact is that he *does* see what unenlightened men see—the physical objects and creatures around him—or he could not attend to the simplest little necessity or duty of which all humans have to take care. But he sees things without being limited to their physical appearance—he knows their inner reality too.(P)

General effects of enlightenment

244

As man grows in true understanding, he moves from mere existence to authentic essence.

245

When the wall between his little ego and the infinite Being collapses, he is said by some Orientals to have entered Nirvana, the Void, and by others to have joined his soul to God.

246

This disclosure that the whole universe exists in the mind comes with Reality's revelation.

247

This is the spiritual climax of one's life, this dramatic moment when consciousness comes to recognize and understand itself.

248

He will be conscious that inwardly he has been born utterly and unmistakably anew, that not only has the old self passed away but also the belief in the existence and reality of self has passed with it.

249

What does it give to the dignity of man? It provides a rare link with the Absolute, an answer to What am I? and a touch of the Untouch.

250

It is the gift of an inner security, the blessing of a peace which comes to stay.

251

The Overself will overshadow him. It will take possession of his body. There will be a mystical union of its mind with his body. The ego will become entirely subordinate to it.

252

Whoever attains this inner liberation rarely finds it reflected in the outer world of human societies. Only by going to the lonely places of nature, to forests and fields, deserted shores and unbuilt-on hills can he match the freedom felt. If he ventures into an ashram—however reputed—the sense of entering a cage is produced. It could be that this is partly caused by the mental pressure of its authorities or inmates, by the smug if unexpressed exclusiveness. If he enters a church, he is at ease only if he is the only worshipper; otherwise sectarian pressure comes to awareness.

253

From the time that this great shift of consciousness has taken place, the event itself as well as its tremendous effects ought to be wrapped in secrecy and revealed only under authentic higher guidance.

254

If he has become enlightened, a discerning eye may note the fact by his body and his actions, by his silences and his utterances. But an ignorant eye may note nothing at all.

255

The effects of enlightenment include: an imperturbable detachment from outer possessions, rank, honours, and persons; an overwhelming certainty about truth; a carefree, heavenly peace above all disturbances and vicissitudes; an acceptance of the general rightness of the universal situation, with each entity and each event playing its role; and impeccable sincerity which says what it means, means what it says.(P)

256

He cannot dwell in that magical state without transforming his experience in the world so that in some way or other it serves God's purpose, thus turning even outer defeats to inner victory.

257

He understands then what it means to do nothing of himself, for he feels clearly that the higher power is doing through him whatever has to be done, is doing it rightly, while he himself is merely watching what is happening.

258

The experience of enlightenment brings a tremendous feeling of well-being.

259

It is in his attitude toward himself particularly that we see the immense advance he has made beyond ordinary men.

260

Just as the Illumined State does not prevent him from receiving physical impressions from the world around him, so it does not prevent him from receiving psychic impressions from the people around him. But he does not cling to any of these impressions, nor does he let his emotions get entwined with them.

261

For him there is no split between spiritual and secular, nothing done that is not done in holy meditation.

262

The serenity of his life is a hidden one. It does not depend on fortune's halting course.

263

The feeling nature of one who attains enlightenment opens itself to purely impersonal reactions.

264

It is a state of tranquil feeling, not of emotional feeling.

265

Both opposites find their place in existence for the unenlightened, the masses, the narrow-horizoned. The tension between them contributes toward development, the conciliation of extremes broadens views. With enlightenment comes equilibrium, harmony, balance, the larger outlook, piercing insight.

266

In that universal Mind wherein he now dwells, he can find no man to be called his enemy, no man to be hated or despised. He is friendly to all men, not as a deliberately cultivated attitude but as a natural compulsion he may not resist.

267

When this consciousness of the Overself is attained *and maintained*, his mind becomes perfectly equable and his moral character perfectly unblemished.

268

The tremendous tension of effort which makes the quest, with all the evanescent elations and despairs which it involves, comes at last to a welcome end.

269

His submission to the divine will is henceforth spontaneous and innate; it is no longer the end product of a painful struggle.

270

He is no longer able to will for himself for the simple reason that some other entity has begun to will for him. Egoism in the human sense, sensualism in the animal sense, have both been eliminated from his heart.

271

Selflessness of purpose is said to follow attainment of this high spiritual status. On this point there is some misrepresentation so that beginners get half-false, half-true notions. It does not mean that, as against other men, an enlightened person must surrender his possessions, his position, or his services to them. He has his own rights still and does not automatically have to abandon them.

272

A man may attain this union with the Overself and yet produce no great work of art, no inspired piece of literature as a result. This is because the union does not bestow technical gifts. It bestows inspiration but not the aesthetic talent which produces a painting or the intellectual talent which produces a book.

273

Henceforth he is to work knowingly and lovingly with the power behind his life.

274

Henceforth he functions as the human instrument of a trans-human power.

275

One result then comes, that what he does by instinct and what he does by choice are henceforth one and the same.

276

These finer qualities will no longer appear only in momentary impulses. They will possess his whole character.

277

One of the foremost features of enlightenment is the clarity it gives to the mind, the lucidity of understanding and luminosity which surrounds all problems.

278

He who understands the Truth at long last, does so only because he becomes the Truth.

279

All that he knows will be intensely lived, for he knows it with his whole being.

280

He has come to the end of this quest. His discovery of truth has released the power of truth and conferred the peace of truth.

281

The pieces of life's mosaic are at last fitted neatly into place. He has attained complete understanding.

282

The intellectual faculties will not be extinguished by this radiant exalta- tion, but their work will henceforth be passively receptive of intuitive direction.

283

Freed from obsession with the past as well as anticipation of the future, he will regard each day as unique and live through it as if he were here for the first time.

284

Changes in the functioning of man's mind could bring about such complete changes in his sense of time that he could veritably find himself imbued with the sense of eternity. This continuous flux of time which to us seems to go on forever, to them is but an illusion produced by the succession of our thoughts. For them, there is only the Eternal Now, never-ending.

285

The realized man does not look back constantly for memories of the past and does not consider them worth recapitulating, for they belong to the ego and they are blotted out with the blotting out of the ego's tyranny. The only exception would be where he has to draw upon them to instruct others to help them profit by his experiences.

286

Only what the mind gives him *now* is alive and real for him.

287

He is not afraid to be outside the current of his time. This is because inwardly he is inside the Timeless.

288

It is one sign of the sage who lives in perfect detachment that he does not miss an enjoyable experience which has passed away, and another sign that he is not afraid of this passing while he is enjoying it.

289

What happened in all those earlier years is now veiled history to the enlightened man; what happens now, in the Eternal Now, is the important significant matter. Thus his mind is free from old burdens and errors. Yet, if needed, dead events can be resuscitated by intense concentration.

290

The background of his mind is far away from everyday consciousness as if invisible, but it can spring instantly forward if needed. There is no split between higher and lower mind: they are in harmony but the kind of activity is different.

291

It would not be correct to say that his consciousness splits itself into two.

292

The proficient can mentally turn inside from the busyness of his environment and within a few moments find the divine presence there.

293

One part of him can enter frequently into cerebral thinking but another part can drop out of this into celestial experience.

294

Our work remains active in the foreground of consciousness, while our wisdom remains in the background as its inspirer.

295

He moves in the world of bodily senses and their surrounding objects without losing the Presence, being held by it rather than holding on to it.

296

Illumination and the Illumined Life [Essay]

"Thou art a Man, God is no more,
"Thy own humanity learn to adore,
"For that is my Spirit of Life.
"Awake, arise to spiritual strife.
—William Blake

One day the mysterious event called by Jesus being "born again" will occur. There will be a serene displacement of the lower self by the higher one. It will come in the secrecy of the disciple's heart and it will come with an overwhelming power which the intellect, the ego, and the animal in him may resist, but resist in vain. He is brought to this experience by the Overself as soon as he is himself able to penetrate to the deeper regions of his heart.

Only when the disciple has given up all the earthly attractions and wishes, expectations and desires that previously sustained him, only when he has had the courage to pluck them out by the roots and throw them aside forever, only then does he find the mysterious unearthly compensation for all this terrible sacrifice. For he is anointed with the sacred oil of a new and higher life. Henceforth he is truly saved, redeemed, illumined. The lower self has died only to give birth to a divine successor.

He will know that this is the day of his spiritual rebirth, that struggle is to be replaced henceforth by serenity, that self-reproach is to yield to self-assurance, and that life in appearance is transformed into life in reality. At last he has emerged from confusion and floundering and bewilderment. At last he is able to experience the blessed satisfaction, the joyous serenity of an integrated attitude wholly based on the highest truth. The capacities which have been incubating slowly and explosively during all the years of his quest will erupt suddenly into consciousness at the same moment that the higher self takes possession of him. What was formerly an occasional glimpse will now become a permanent sight. The intermittent intuition of a guardian presence will now become the constantly established experience of it. The divine presence has now become to him an immediate and intimate one. Its reality and vitality are no longer matters for argument or dispute, but matters of settled experience.

When a man has reached this state of inward detachment, when he has withdrawn from passion and hate, prejudice and anger, all human experience—including his own—becomes for him a subject for meditation, a theme for analysis, and a dream bereft of reality. His reflection about other men's experiences is not less important than about his own. From this standpoint nothing that happens in the lives of those around him can be without interest, but everything will provide material for detached observation and thoughtful analysis.

He who has attained the state of desirelessness has liberated himself from the need to court, flatter, or deceive others, from the temptation to prostitute his powers at the behest of ambition or Mammon, from the compulsion to drag himself servilely after conventional public opinion. He neither inwardly desires nor outwardly requires any public attestation to the sincerity of his services or the integrity of his character. The quiet approval of his own conscience is enough.

Although he holds to the apex of all human points of view to which philosophy brings him, he keeps open the doors of his mind to all sincere writers, to all good people, and to all lower points of view. To him every day is a school day and every meeting with other persons a class lesson, since everyone has something to teach—even if it is only what not to do, how not to think or to behave.

When the ego willingly retires from all its worldly concerns or intellectual preoccupations to the sanctuary of the heart to be alone with the Overself, it becomes not only wiser but more powerful. At moments when the divine influx blissfully invades a man, it will not be out of his ordinary self that he will speak or act, but out of his higher self.

It is natural as well as inevitable that one who has entered into the larger life of the Overself should show forth some of its higher powers. Such an individual's thoughts are informed by a subtler force, invested with a diviner element, pointed by a sharper concentration, and sustained by a superior will than are those of the average person. They are in consequence exceedingly powerful, creative, and effective.

That which the sage bears in his heart is for all men alike. If few are willing to receive it, the fault does not lie with him. He rejects none, is prejudiced against none. It is the others who reject him, who are prejudiced against him.

297

Outwardly he appears to act as intensely or as vigorously as other men. But inwardly he will really be at rest in the Overself, which will lead him like a child into performing necessary actions. His mind is still, even though his body is busy. And because of this leading, his actions will be right and even inspired ones, his personal will will be expressive of a higher one.

298

So wherever the illuminate goes, he is immovably centered in truth. He may descend into the noisy maelstrom of metropolitan life. He may retire to the green quietudes of the countryside. He may meet in his wanderings with violence and accident or with flattery and fortune. Yet always and alike, he remains self-composed, calm, and king-like in his mental grandeur.

299

At long last, when the union of self with Overself is total and complete, some part of his consciousness will remain unmoving in infinity, unending in eternity. There, in that sacred glory, he will be preoccupied with his divine identity, held to it by irresistible magnetism, gladly, lovingly.(P)

300

The sage is a man who lives in constant truth-remembrance. He has realized the existence of the Overself, he knows that he partakes of Its life, immortal and infinite. He has made the pilgrimage to essential being and returned again to walk amongst men, to speak their language, and to bear witness, by his life amongst them, to Truth.

301

His relationship to the Overself is one of direct awareness of its presence—not as a separate being but as his own essence.

302

Intimate communion and personal converse with the higher self remain delightful facts. The Beloved ever companions him and never deserts him. He can never again be lonely.

303

There is a feeling of living in a self other than the ego, although that also is present but subdued and submissive.

304

The awareness will be with him at all times, a part of all his actions and feelings. It will indeed be the essence of every experience and enable him to pass through it more happily.

305

He has no fixed abode, no permanent address, for like the wind he comes and goes from nowhere to anywhere. Destiny or service may keep his body in one place for a time, or for a lifetime, but it will not keep *him*.

306

For the person who has come to this understanding, who continually feels that IT IS, who is ever in remembrance of It, rituals, ceremonies, mantras, and prayers are not only unnecessary but are a waste of time.

307

The owl, which sees clearly at midnight, is an old and good symbol of the sage whose mind is ever at rest in, and lighted by, the Infinite Mind.

308

Because this Mind is common to all men, it is an inevitable and inescapable consequence of awakening to its existence that the initiate rises above a merely personal outlook and maintains a sympathetic attitude towards all men.

309

At this level, he is beyond bothering to listen to the discordant sounds of competing sects and cults: he is uninterested in the claims made for different teachings. He has only one concern: direct communion with the God within him as a felt, grace-giving Presence.

310

At this point all written doctrines, however ancient revered and established they may be, can be thrown away. His further needs can be satisfied only from within himself.

311

Henceforth he is able to return his consciousness and retract his attention from the ego—and this, not only at will, but throughout his lifetime.

312

The mind emptied of all the activity of ordinary thoughts and filled with the beauty of this presence is a divinely sustained mind.

313

He will be surrounded by an Overself-conscious atmosphere even in the midst of social functions. His inward repose will be no less evident there than in solitude.

314

He may be most intensely occupied with his worldly affairs, but he will remain fixed in the holy presence.

315

The illuminate stands in the centre of the world-movement, himself unmoving and unmoved.

316

The liberated person is liberated from all intellectual dogmas, perplexities, and questionings—whether they concern the present past or future, whether they relate to himself personally or to the universe abstractly. For all these can interest only a limited egoistic consciousness.

317

At last he has not only peace of mind—a philosophic attitude toward the events of his personal life—but also peace *in* the mind, a freedom from the struggle against baser impulses and ignoble tendencies.

318

The momentous results of this inner change will naturally reflect themselves in his outer life as a general nonattachment to the world. And because he has become free even of intellectual possessions, he is able to enter with full sympathy into the views and ideas of every other person— although this does not prevent his deeper wisdom from calmly noting at the same time the defects and errors of those views and ideas. To himself the practical value of this attainment is its conferment of freedom, but to humanity the practical value is his resulting dedication to service.

319

The sense of strain which accompanies present-day living vanishes. The peace of being relaxed in thought and feeling, nerve and muscle, replaces it.

320
He becomes a focus where persons, utterly incompatible and totally diverse otherwise, are able to meet.

321
The sense of a divine presence will be with him, the conviction of its supreme reality will grip him, and the feeling of an indescribable serenity will suffuse him.

322
The Master necessarily lives in an inner world of his own, immeasurably remote from some of those environments in which he is plunged. Nevertheless, he possesses the power to recall himself freely and instantly from one to the other, and in either direction.

323
It is one sign of this attainment that a man becomes less critical of other persons. Yet this does not mean he understands them less accurately.

324
A fulfilment such as this must bring joy to the heart and peace to the mind.

325
He may remain human in several ways—but not too human.

326
Penetrated by the feeling of a divine presence as he daily is, his life becomes a truly inspired one.

327
His first reliance will be on the soul. His last reliance will be on the soul.

328
His life silently becomes a witness to the fact of the Overself's continuous presence.

3

THE SAGE

There is a wide confusion in religio-mystic circles, both of the Orient and of the Occident, as to what a sage is really like, what a spiritually enlightened master really experiences, what both say and do when living in the world of ordinary people, how they behave and appear. On these points truth is inextricably bound up with superstition, fact with exaggeration, and wisdom with sentimentality. There is also a wide confusion of the Real with its attributes and aspects, that is to say, with human reactions, interpretations, and experiences of IT.

2
The conventional picture of what a man attuned to God is like needs to be revised.

3
It is not the invisible imprimatur of any pontifical canonization that really makes a man one of God's saints but the invisible imprimatur of his Overself.

4
There is no higher point in human existence.

5
Without direct experience of the inner nature of things, without personal revelation from the Overself, the only kind of knowledge men can possess is obtained by the use of logical thinking aided by memory. The cosmogony of a sage is truly scientific, for it is exactly descriptive of what really exists whereas the other kind of knowledge is merely argumentative.

6
Philosophy uses the attained man not as a god for grovelling worship and blind obedience, but as an ideal for effectual admiration and reverent analysis.(P)

7
To worship him as a god, to put him beyond all possible criticism, will only confuse our thought about him and obstruct our understanding of him.

8

He not only has developed all his forces to their highest degree of maturity but also has attained a perfect equilibrium of them.

9

The masses who turn such a figure into an idol to be worshipped and the few who turn it into an inspiration to be received, are not functioning on the same level.

10

He is one whose psyche is ruled by reality.

11

Because some holy men have been uncouth, unkempt, uncivilized, uneducated, and unmannerly, it is foolish to connect this with holiness. They were simply barbarians.

12

He is an ambassador from the infinite, an envoy to all men from the higher plane of their own being.

13

Such an individual is a link between the commonplace world of ordinary living and the sublime world of mystical being.

14

The illuminate is the conscious embodiment of the Overself, whereas the ordinary man is ignorant of that which his heart enshrines. Hence, the Chinese say that the illuminate is the "Complete Man." He is the rare flower of an age.

15

The sage is only a man, not a God. He is limited in power, being, knowledge. But behind him, even in him—yet not of him—there is unlimited power, being, knowledge. Therefore we revere and worship not the man himself, but what he represents.

16

For practical purposes he is an emissary of the Deity, even though in theoretical truth no one is sent out because everyone has his or her roots in the Deity already.

17

His utterances should be closely studied, his behaviour minutely analysed.

18

The disillusionments brought by protracted experience have compelled me to distinguish between adepts by name, who are amusing, and adepts by nature, who are amazing.

19

The outside observer will not be able to see what is happening to him, and to that extent will not be able to share in it. But he will be able secretly to affect the subconscious mind of the observer, if the latter is associated with him in some way and is at all sensitive.

20

The name "Rishee" was bestowed in ancient, as well as modern, India on the man who had reached the peak of spiritual knowledge; literally it means "seer." What is it that he sees? He is a see-er of reality, and through illusion.

21

People form quaint and queer notions of what constitutes an illuminate. They would divest him of all human attributes, make him a man who never even sneezes or yawns!

22

In him the higher power manifests itself and through him it flows for the inspiring of others.

The race of sages

23

We imagine that the thought of the Sage is too far behind us; we left all that when we left the primitive and medieval ages. The philosophic quest is apparently something quite obnoxious to the modern matter-of-fact spirit. The reality is that the thought of the Sage is too far ahead of us, and leaves the plain man panting.

24

The Masters exist, not as a special community in far-off Tibet, but as scattered individuals in different parts of the world. They have their strange powers and enigmatic secrets, but these are not the theatrical and sensational things that imaginative occultists would have us believe.

25

The spiritually stronger a man becomes, the less he needs to lean on other men. Consequently advanced mystics have little or no need of joining any society, fraternity, or community. All talk of the adepts and masters themselves being members of such associations, living together in Tibet or elsewhere, is nonsensical fantasy.

26

It is an invisible spiritual order to which they belong, one which needs no visible organization because that could never express it but only limit its universality and falsify its insights.

27

There is an aristocracy of time in a truer sense than that which we in the West usually give the word. It is formed from the aristocrats of the mind; a superior caste of men which was founded hundreds of thousands of years before our first European noble was given his accolade. Their breeding is not based on fleeting codes, but on the eternal laws of life. What is ethical to meaner mortals is aesthetical to them.

28

I sought to track down the truth about Mahatmas, to determine whether they were pure myth or whether they were human beings. Here was a subject engulfed in superstition, misinformation, and wishful thinking—not only in the distant West but also in its own Oriental homelands. After I discovered it, I then discovered that people did not know the most elementary facts about Mahatmas but preferred, in their mental picture, either to deprive them of all humanity or to turn them into overly sentimental all-too-human creatures.

29

The rarity of such men among us shows what anyone can quickly see—that their attainment is hard to realize. But it also shows that most of them do not return to this earth again. They pass on. But the tradition is that they do not pass without initiating one other person at least.

30

Such men and women are indeed the spiritual vanguard of the human race.

31

In one sense, he is the loneliest of men, for he rarely meets with others of his kind inhabiting the planet. But in another sense he is not, for the extent and depth of the affection which he receives are out of the ordinary.

32

Such men are so few, their worth to society so great, the darkness around us gathering so thickly, that their presence among us is the greatest blessing.

33

According to our traditions the history of the world does not contain any period where there were not men who had realized their higher nature. But they were very very few.

34

Is there anyone among those you know today, as well as all those you have known in the past, to whom you can point as a fully enlightened man, as one conscious of his Overself? Your answer will reveal how rare this attainment is.

35

The succession of saviours has existed as long as the human race itself has existed. The infinite power which shepherds its evolution can always be trusted to send these illumined men as and when its own laws and human needs call for them.

36

Men who have entered into the full glory of spiritual illumination, who have realized to the utmost their diviner possibilities, are rare in any age, rarer still in our own materialistic one.

37

This deep union with the Overself occurs in the greatest secrecy. Nobody else knows what has happened to the man, much less understands. Nor will he let anyone know. Except in the case of a prophet sent on a public mission to mankind, people will have to discover it for themselves. The greater the man, the more he shrinks from being made a show. The race of sages is nearly dead. There may be some hiding in the monasteries of Tibet or in the penthouses of New York City.

38

It remains what it always was—a very small inconspicuous minority although some individuals among it, gifted with talent or singled out by destiny, have become personally conspicuous at times.

39

Why are they so few, these sages, these serene and urbane self-realized ones? Nature works very hard and only attains her aim once in a multitude of throws. In mankind she may well be contented if she creates one sage in a hundred million people.

40

It is indeed difficult to find men whose lives are thus touched with Truth. They stand supreme but solitary in the mystic battlefield of life, but when they enter the public arena the world becomes aware that a star of unwonted brilliance is blazing in its firmament.

41

There was either a longer past or a loftier planet than our own behind these great masters.

42

It is true that most people believe that they cannot think like the sages or live like the saints and that it is useless to entertain any further thought about them. They look at the world around them and see the events which are taking place or read about them and they believe that this is not the kind of world with which sages and saints could cope and that therefore they have little value for us today. But here they are not altogether right. A study of history from the earliest times will show that whenever sages and saints have appeared there were great evils in the world of their time and they were always exceptional figures among their peoples. The memories of them have remained carefully kept and guarded by those who know the importance of right values. That importance remains today and what these figures of eminent wisdom and holiness have to tell us about the higher laws of life and the higher nature of man is still as true as ever it was.

43

There is no democratic equality here. If such a man speaks, others are entitled only to whisper!

44

There never yet has been a time, however thinned out their ranks may be, when those who know have faded out from this world—and there never will be such a time. For it is an inexorable duty laid upon them to hand down the light to posterity. And thus a chain of teacher and taught has been flung down to us from the dimmest epochs of antiquity right into this noisy, muddled twentieth century of ours.

45

Through such illumined men there has been constant expression of truth, and through this individual expression it has been able to survive socially.

46

Those who are "out of centre," eccentric and different from others because they are unbalanced mentally and uncontrolled emotionally, will not heed what conventional society demands from them. But there exists a second group of persons who are likewise "different" and heedless of conventions, although often in other ways. This group is what it is by reason of its being a pioneer one which has advanced farther along the road of evolution than the herd behind. From it are drawn the great reformers and their followers, those who stand firmly by moral principle and factual truth. It is they who try to lift up society and put right its abuses and cruelties, its wrongs and superstitions. They are daring champions who do not stop to count the cost of their service but, enduring ridicule, persecution, or even crucifixion, go ahead unfalteringly where others draw back.

47

Whoever will take the trouble to search for them, as I once did, may find that several records have been left behind for posterity by men who successfully penetrated to the inside of Truth and made themselves at home there. The lands in which they lived were wide apart and included England, France, Germany, Denmark, Greece, Palestine, Iraq, Persia, India, China, Japan, Vietnam, and even Australia. For such men Truth was not a theory but a living experience.

48

There has not yet manifested itself one outstanding personality who merges the simple mystic in the wise sage, who speaks the mind of truth for our time, and who is willing to enlighten or lead us without reference to local or traditional beliefs. Such a man will certainly be heard; he may even be heeded.

49

There is a tradition in Siam, Burma, and Ceylon that Nirvana is no longer attainable in our decadent times. The Buddha himself predicted this decline, they say. But statistics about the number of sages are not available. One can give only the unpromising results of a fairly wide and fairly constant search. Nor is it likely that they will ever be available, for those who attain Nirvana do not broadcast the news of their attainment and do not parade their knowledge. There are numbers of so-called sages, adepts, Mahatmas, Gurus, masters, and saints in India and Tibet who do not fail to find fairly extensive followings. But then, the criterion set up by these masses is not the loftiest.

50

Include the name of Akhnaton as an illumined mahatma when quoting Jesus, Buddha, etc., as examples.

51

It may be that such men are vanishing from the world scene, that their successors today are second and third rate, possessors of a shallower enlightenment and a narrower perception.

52

These men are not just abnormal variations of the human species but glorious harbingers of its future development when its own time arrives.

53

It is quite comical to read so often that "modern" historians, solemnly applying their scientific methods, doubt whether certain celebrated figures of the B.C. period were real persons or not, just as many "modern" religious critics even doubt whether Jesus himself was more than a fancy. What does it matter if Lycurgus, Krishna, and Jesus never existed? Would not someone else have existed who had enough wisdom to write down the precepts, counsel, and teachings which, for reasons of his own, he attributed to the other person?

54

It is a blessed historic fact that divine life and light came to the world through these men. But now what is more important is that it shall come to us today too.

55

These great historic prophets, sages, and teachers were not the first discoverers of this secret consciousness, nor will they be its last.

56

Such a circle, with its esoteric doctrines and exclusive membership, cannot be understood properly by those who stand outside it and who therefore do not know its informing spirit.

57

Some German mystic, whose name and period I do not remember, spoke of the seven mysterious sages hidden under the earth and directing the world's evolution.

58

One may quote Jesus, Krishna, and the *Upanishads* for the rarity of the self-realized man, but most people will be astonished that I should quote such a shrewd, practical, worldly man as Cicero who wrote: "I think it oftener happens that a meal brings forth a cold than that Nature produces a sage." But Cicero himself writes somewhere that he believes profoundly in God.

59

The existence of the sage as a type is hard to prove simply because the existence of the sage as an individual is hard to confirm. He is almost unique on this planet. He is, for practical purposes, an Ideal rather than an ACTUALITY.

Remarks on specific illuminates

60

Pythagoras divided his students into two classes, the "probationers" and the "mathematicians." But the latter term signified more to him than it means to us. For him it meant those devoted to advanced thinking and it embraced those who studied philosophy and science as well as mathematics. For Pythagoras regarded the rational disciple as essential to the higher quest.

61

We are told that Jesus was a man of sorrows. But was he not also a man of joys? The joy of bearing a divine message, the joy of bringing light into a darkened world, and the joy of helping men find their own soul.

62

If Jesus wept over the folly of cities, he was also glad over the Presence and Providence of God. If he was a man of sorrow at some times, he was also a man of joy at all times. For the sorrow was merely transient, outward, superficial, and for others whereas the joy was everlasting, inward, deep, and his own. No man can come into the Father's kingdom, as he came, without feeling its happiness and enjoying its ecstasy.

63

Socrates used to listen to an inner voice, his daimon, warning him against false decisions. While so doing, he would sink into deep meditations where he would commune with the divine in order to receive the power to instruct men in Truth.

64

Socrates possessed an absolutely original intellect; he took nothing for granted but probed and penetrated into every subject which came under discussion. He struck out a new path in the philosophy of his time and so well was it made that it can still be trodden today with profit.

65

It is a profound error to include Buddha among the founders of religion. He was a sage and taught philosophy only, never a theological teaching, a religious doctrine. The word "God" had no meaning in his system. The Buddhist religion arose later and was founded by men who lived long after Buddha died. It represented a degradation of his philosophy, a dereliction of his teaching, and an adoption of rites and practices which he would not have permitted in his own lifetime.

66

It is a fact that Jesus wrote nothing and that he never asked his apostles to write anything. Why? What he had to give directly or through them was no message to or argument with the intellect. It was an evocation of the intuition. It had to be transferred to each man psychically.

67

The benign figure and still meditative face of Gautama, sitting in his thrice-folded yellow garment and penetrating into the deep secret chambers of mind, offers an inspiring spectacle. The solid strength and paradisaic calm stabilized in his person have helped millions of people in the Asiatic lands. Yet there were fateful moments when Gautama refused to appear in public to tell others what he knew, when the peaceful life of utter anonymity was his reasoned preference.

68
Sri Ramakrishna came to his illumination without practising any systematic discipline in yoga and after only six months of passionate prayer, whereas it took Buddha six years of arduous disciplined effort to attain his illumination. The difference of the two accounts and the difference of efforts explains why Ramakrishna attained the high stage of mysticism whereas Buddha attained the high stage of philosophy. The longer the road, the loftier is the attainment, and only those who take the time and trouble to traverse the whole length of the way may expect to gain all the fruits. He who stops part of the way may only expect to gain part of the result.

69
Jesus and Buddha inspired their immediate disciples with something of their own spiritual vitality.

70
Porphyry's statement that Plotinus achieved union with God four times may be misleading. For he qualified it with the words "during the period I passed with him." Now Plotinus was fifty-nine years old when Porphyry first met him, and died at sixty-six. So seven years is the length of the period referred to. Against this must be set the forty earlier years of spiritual seeking and teaching during which Plotinus must have had other illuminations.

71
John Burroughs: "With Emerson dead, it seems folly to be alive. No man of just his type and quality has ever before appeared upon the earth. He looked like a god. That wise, serene, pure, inscrutable look was without parallel in any human face I ever saw. Such an unimpeachable look! The subtle, half-defined smile of his soul. It was not a propitiatory smile, or a smirk of acquiescence, but the reassuring smile of the doctor when he takes out his lance; it was the sheath of that trenchant blade of his. Behind it lurked some test question, or pregnant saying. It was the foil of his frank, unwounding wit, like Carlyle's laugh. It was an arch, winning, half-playful look, the expression of a soul that did not want to wound you, and yet that must speak the truth. And Emerson's frank speech never did wound. It was so evident that it was not meant to wound, and that it was so true to himself, that you treasured it as rare wisdom."

72
It is a mistake to imagine the sage as a weakling. The Buddha delivered his lectures in such a strong voice that it was likened to the roar of a lion; hence he was called "Simha" (The Lion). Swami Vivekananda was equally powerful in his public addresses as well as in private capacity. When hostile

critics of his own race slandered him behind his back, he likened himself to an elephant treading down worms in its path.

73

As part of his program of secrecy, Pythagoras got into the habit of casting much of his teaching into symbolic and figurative form—into parables, metaphors, and enigmas. What happened to his teachings is what happened to the teachings of many mystics and religious prophets in other lands. The literal form tended to be taken as the whole of the truth and the inner reality was missed.

74

The sayings of Jesus cannot be authenticated by anyone as being historically true. But every illumined man can authenticate them as being mystically true.

75

Those who can understand the mystery of what is called by theologians (not by philosophers) the Incarnation, will understand also that the crucifixion of Jesus did not last a mere six hours. It lasted for a whole thirty-three years. His sufferings were primarily mental, not physical. They were caused, not by the nails driven into his flesh at the end of his life, but by the evil thoughts and materialistic emotions impinging on his mind from his environment during the whole course of his life.

76

Ramana Maharshi had no Long Path experience at all; he practised no techniques; yet he was permanently enlightened at an early age. There are two lessons in this event. First, without either a Long or Short Path previous history a man may still find himself in the higher consciousness. This shows that Grace alone is a sufficient cause. Second, aside from the feeling of disgust with the world through failure to pass his school examinations, the only preparation which Maharshi underwent was falling involuntarily and profoundly into the trance state for three days. Here he was "pulled in" away from the senses and outer awareness by a strong force. This shows that *depth* of inner penetration of the mind's layers and *length* of period that contact is held with the Overself are the two important governors of the result attained. Go as deep as you can; stay there as long as you can; this seems to be the silent message of the Maharshi's own experience.

77

When I first met the Indian woman saint, Ananda Mayee, in 1936, she spent much time in withdrawn states of *samadhi*. When I last saw her, nearly twenty years later, she did not any longer pass into such states except for days of special public celebrations—at the most, a few times a year. She had become famous, and visited centres scattered around India and bearing her name. This means that she had by then developed to the grade where temporary *samadhis* were no longer either necessary or to be regarded as the goal as they are with developing yogis.

78

Socrates was an awakener of men. He tried to stir their minds by questions, and their conscience by revealing fresh points of view.

79

This man who came among them to tell of a deeper kind of life that would give them unearthly peace, who sought to bless them by removing an ancient curse from their history, was rejected, yet Jesus had to do what he did, to say what he said.

80

Whenever he could, Lao Tzu went to the mountains and there—sitting alone and looking down from a height—he put human beings and their worldly existences into the proper proportion. As he was also a human being, he was able to reduce his own egoism and tranquillize his own desires and recast his sense of values until the great peace came over him and he was enlightened.

81

After a certain day when she underwent an experience wherein God seemed to take out her heart and carry it away, Saint Catherine of Siena remained peaceful and contented for the rest of her life. She could not describe that inner experience but said that in it she had tasted a sweetness which made earthly pleasures seem like mud and even spiritual pleasures seem far inferior.

82

The miracles of Christ were an expression of special power manifested by Him in virtue of His special mission to humanity.

83

Meister Eckhart, the German mystic, has written or said some quite incomprehensible things. But he has also written or said many clear things. There is, however, one statement he makes which belongs to neither category, but which is exceedingly interesting. He says, "A man should be so disinterested that he does not know what God is doing in him." This appears in his sermon entitled, "Blessed Are the Poor." A similar obscure but interesting statement is, "Man's highest and last parting occurs when for God's sake he takes leave of God." I shall at some later time add a commentary to these mysterious statements of Eckhart.

3: The Sage / 89

84

Where Socrates was moralist and ascetic, Plato was metaphysician and artistic. Socrates kept his independence and freedom by a monk-like bareness of living but Plato, worshipping beauty, required aristocratic luxury in living.

85

Socrates put his questions to professional teachers and public men in such a manner that he forced them to reveal their ignorance.

86

Jesus opened up the Mysteries to the masses of the Western continent and gave to the many what had hitherto been given only to the chosen few. Buddha did precisely the same for the masses of the Asiatic continent.

87

This does not mean that Jesus himself ever taught philosophy to his immediate circle; nobody has yet found evidence that he ever did so. Where, for instance, will the reader find in his sayings any explanation of the nature of truth or discussion of the nature of ultimate reality? The period of three years from the beginning of his mission till his death was too short to raise such simple folk as had gathered around him into mastery of both the second and third degrees.

88

The sage is indistinguishable from the multitude. He bears no external signs. He is modest to the point of self-effacement. Buddha interdicted the use of his portrait during his own lifetime, and so great was the force of his interdiction that two hundred years passed before the Buddhists dared to carve his face in sculptured decorations. He did this to direct attention to truth, and away from his own personality.

89

Brother Nikolaus, also called Bruder Klausens, Klaus von Alve, rose to the highest place in his community, both in position and prestige; for the first fifty years he remained in the world, had ten children, but got increasingly disgusted and sickened by it, especially by political life. From youth he was attracted to unworldly things. A spiritual friend, Pastor von Stans, Heimoam Grund, initiated him into the secrets of mysticism. At fifty he took leave of wife and children, became a pilgrim, and never returned. On the Alps, in Melchtal, a hunting area, he settled for the next nineteen years in strongest asceticism. From far and near, pilgrims streamed to him, "the living saint," to get advice and consolation. However he was not set free from political life; it returned to him within a few years after his resignation of all official posts, in the form of Counsellor and Peacemaker between cantons and cities, and between Switzerland and other countries. Embassies came to him from Germany, Austria, Venice, etc., so that he became very influential in diplomatic life. His 500th jubilee anniversary was celebrated throughout Switzerland with bell-ringing, for his "great patriotic beneficial influence over the land." He is the actual National Saint of Switzerland.

Differences in attainment, expression

90
Although philosophy rejects the theory of Divine Incarnations in favour of the truth of divinely inspired human beings, it does not say that all the latter are of the same kind or importance or that their inspiration manifests in the same way and to the same degree. It admits differences here.

91
The five principal types of illumined individuals are: (a) the Teacher, (b) the Messenger, (c) the Saint, (d) the Reformer, (e) the Prophet.

92
The originality and individuality which are proofs of the prophet's creativity will define themselves by his differences from other seers, even though some have drawn from one and the same MIND. These differences are inevitable and must appear. No two humans are completely alike.

93
These men do not find a higher truth: they reaffirm the ancient and eternal truth. It could not be that if it were subject to change. But each reaffirms it in his own way, according to his own perception and as his environment requires. This accounts for part of the differences in its presentation, where it has been really attained. The other part is accounted for by there being varying degrees of attainment.

94
It is a mistake to believe that the mystical adepts all possess the same unvarying supernormal powers. On the contrary, they manifest such power or powers as are in consonance with their previous line of development and aspiration. One who has come along an intellectual line of development, for instance, would most naturally manifest exceptional intellectual powers. The situation has been well put by Saint Paul in the First Epistle to the Corinthians: "Now there are diversities of graces, but the same Spirit. And there are diversities of ministries but the same Lord. And there are diversities of workings but the same God who worketh all in all." When the Overself activates the newly made adept's psyche, the effect

shows itself in some part or faculty; in another adept it produces a different effect. Thus the source is always the same but the manifestation is different.(P)

95

The undiscerning often believe that because some great saints have been fools in worldly affairs, a saint who is always clever cannot be great. Yet the spiritual aspirations which diminish a man's desire for worldly activities do not therefore diminish his competence for them. He who is born a fool usually remains so; he who is born clever usually stays so; and both cases are unaffected by the attachment of the heart to God.

96

We must not think that every mystic who has been blessed with the light of the Overself stands on the same spiritual peak of vision and consciousness, of being and knowledge. Some are still only on the way to the summit of this peak. There are definite differences between them. If they all share alike the consciousness of a higher Self, they do not share it in the same way or to the same degree.

97

The saints and mystics serve a high purpose in *reminding* humanity of that diviner life which must one day flower in human evolution, but they do not serve as perfect exemplars of its final growth. The sages alone can do that.

98

Why did Ramana Maharshi and Ramakrishna refuse to heal themselves? One possible explanation is that healing powers are like intellectual powers. One may be a realized person and yet not possess much intellect. Similarly, one may not possess healing power. Realization does not endow one with encyclopaedic knowledge or with all the talents.

99

We must make a difference between the Messenger, who is sent to communicate a teaching through writing or speech, and the Master, who comes to embody the teaching and who alone possesses the power to bless others with his Grace. This difference is not so clearly understood among the yogis as it is among the lamas and Sufis, a lack which leads to confused ideas and unjustified customs.

100

Having reached this stage he is free to continue his personal life as before, to accept the load of new responsibilities on his shoulders, or to retire wholly from the world. To work for humanity in public is one thing, to work for it in secrecy is another, while to enjoy the freedom and privacy of complete retirement is a third and very different thing. Naturally and inevitably any public appearance will soon turn him into a lightning rod, attracting the aspirations and yearnings of many spiritual seekers.

101

If he has really found his inner freedom, he must necessarily be free to stay in the world and do the world's work. He does not have to retire into isolation, although he is free to do that. But whatever he decides to do, he will henceforth be an impersonal channel for higher forces, which he will obey, and whose directions he will follow, whether he remains in the world or not.

102

It is necessary to give certain terms often but wrongly used interchangeably, and hence confusedly, a sharper definition. The *Saint* has successfully carried out ascetic disciplines and purificatory regimes for devotional purposes. The *Prophet* has listened for God's voice, heard and communicated God's message of prediction, warning, or counsel. The *Mystic* has intimately experienced God's presence while inwardly rapt in contemplation or has seen a vision of God's cosmogony while concentrated in meditation. The *Sage* has attained the same results as all these three, has added a knowledge of infinite and eternal reality thereto, and has brought the whole into balanced union. The *Philosopher* is a sage who has also engaged in the spiritual education of others.

103

There is a third type of illumined man, besides the Teacher and the Saint. He is the Messenger. He renders service not by dealing with persons and their problems but by stating truths and principles in general.

104

From *Tripura Rahasya*, an ancient Sanskrit work: "Some [realized] *jnanis* are active; some teach scriptures; some worship deities; some abstract themselves into *Samadhi*; some lead an austere life and emaciate themselves; some give clear instructions to their disciples; some rule kingdoms quite justly and rightly; some openly hold disputations with other schools of thought; some write down their teachings and experiences; others simulate ignorance; a few do even reprehensible actions; but all these are famous as wise men in the world."

105

Some of the enlightened ones sit as recluses in meditation, others travel and preach, still others create centres where they teach, a fourth class heal the sick, and a fifth write. Each does what his tendency or mission dictates.

106

The sage may sit under a village tree, head an ashram, or live as a sequestered hermit. He may also live in a luxurious palace, head a business organization, or farm land. These things are not the point, which is his consciousness of divine presence. The world, its pleasures and treasures, does not deceive him: he sees through its values even if he is active in the midst of it.

107

He may move obscurely through the world an unrecognized solitary, or he may declaim publicly to the crowd. He may teach only the few what he will not tell the many, or he may shed his light freely on all. In either case, his own disposition and destiny will shape the result.

108

The man who had attained some measure of knowledge was not bound to serve his epoch in any particular rigid way. He would carry out his task according to no rules and regulations but according to his personal circumstances and opportunities, and relate it as he could to the needs of his environment. He was free to choose his manner of his service, just as he was at liberty to select those whom he would personally help. Therefore, he was fully justified in devising his own method of working and not blindly following that which critics foisted upon him.

109

The sage is as much the creature of his epoch, the inheritor of its historical heritage as others, for he must express himself in a tongue they can understand.

110

The wise do not make invidious comparisons between the great Prophets of God. Only the ignorant attempt to show that one ranks higher than another in ethical reach. Such do not know that the teachers who give out a religion to a people or race always consider the circumstances and mentality of the people before preaching their new doctrine. What is *not* revealed or taught is kept back because it is not needed at the time, never because it is unknown.

111

If some enlightened souls are given a mission to stir the world to higher ideals, others feel no such duty and remain quiescent or even saturninely secluded.

112

There is no obligation on a sage to sit stationary in one place or to travel, perpetually, from city to city. His inner guidance alone decides the matter, as his personal karma also makes its contribution toward that decision.

113

If some acknowledge and accept the responsibility which accompanies their spiritual eminence, others prefer to leave mankind in God's keeping and keep to themselves!

114

Some illuminates are willing, even eager, to get involved with individuals but others are not. If they prefer to live quietly, unnoticed, this does not make them more selfish and less holy.

115

The illumined men wrote either out of their intellect or their intuition, sometimes for scrupulous academic scholars and sometimes for simple persons. A sage like Lao Tzu wrote for neither the one class or the other, for he put forward the deep paradoxes of life; but another man not less illumined may have provided footnotes on nearly every page.

116

It is not possible to predict with precision what a man would do if he attains enlightenment. With some persons, force of habit or innate tendencies may lead to the continuance of the same *outer* life which he led before enlightenment. So a monk or hermit leading a solitary withdrawn life may still do so whereas another may start a preaching crusade to the mass of people. For, with the personal self subdued by the Overself, the latter is then the operative factor. And the spirit is like "the wind which bloweth as it listeth."

117

Confucius showed men the way to behave outwardly, Lao Tzu the way to be merged in the stillness inwardly. Despite the seeming difference both were remarkable sages.

118

Communicators of the Doctrine, Prophets of the Deity, Transmitters of healing—all these have their place.

119

He who has realized truth according to the Secret Doctrine may continue to follow the same vocation which he was practising before. That is, a king may remain a king and a carpenter may continue his carpentering. There is no law or rule which may be laid down as to the kind of work an illuminate may perform or abstain from performing. Similarly, the illuminate is not to be judged by his practice of or his omission to practise asceticism. If people say, as they say in India, that he will give up his wife on attaining realization, they thereby merely reveal their ignorance of truth. The continuance of his state of realization has nothing whatever to do with the possession or nonpossession of a wife, any more than it has to do with his possession or nonpossession of one or two legs.

120
These are the true Olympians, not the mythic beings of human creation. They may dwell apart on their mountain—like Sengai, the Japanese—or in the city with its crowds—like A.E., the Irishman.

121
The Sufi masters fall into two groups, the Mudzubs who are outwardly childish, fanatics, fools, extremists, or even insane, and the Saliks who are outwardly normal, balanced, and adult.

122
In the harmless studies of a scholar, the peaceful activities of a writer, the quiet life of a mystic, and the deep reflections of a philosopher, he may pass his days.

123
To be constantly subject in every action and movement to the watchful gaze of others—critical on the part of the world, adulatory on the part of followers—is a life-experience to which prophets and saints submit but to which others refuse to submit. They accept no personal disciples and remain obscurely in the world. Some are sages, all are enlightened.

124
The sage includes the saint, but is not limited by him. The sage possesses qualities and attributes which may be missing in the saint.

125
Not until the light he has received becomes stabilized as a permanent thing can he be regarded as a master, and not until it is also full and complete can he be regarded as a sage.(P)

Wisdom beyond bliss

126
By the term "sage" it has been traditional to mean someone who is not only wise and dispassionate but who is also ready to proffer counsel out of his superior wisdom. He may dwell apart from humanity, if he chooses, but his Olympian aloofness will not be such that you cannot get a word of guidance out of his shy shut lips. Somehow we feel, and rightly, that the anchorite who has lost compassion or grown wholly self-centered may be pure and peaceful—but he cannot be a sage.

127

No man who is sensitive to the sufferings of humanity can really enjoy "divine bliss" or unmitigated ecstasy. Therefore the sage is quite different from the mystic. The latter revels in emotional joyfulness, whereas the former maintains a quiet exalted peace. His power lies in keeping this self busy with constant service of humanity. The bliss of the mystic belongs to the realm of his personal feeling and signifies his indifference towards suffering humanity; the wisdom of the sage belongs to the realm of his realization of oneness, which is incompatible with indifference to others.

128

It is not a state of dreamy futility but one of intense usefulness.

129

There is some confusion, at least in India, but also in the West, about the kind of life an enlightened man will live. It is popularly believed, especially in the Orient, that he sits in his cave or his hut or his ashram sunk continually in meditation. The idea that he can be active in the world is not often accepted, especially by the masses who have not been properly instructed in these matters and who do not know differences between religion and mysticism and between mysticism and philosophy. The truth is that the enlightened man may or may not practise meditation; but he has no dependence upon it, because his enlightenment being fully established will not be increased by further meditation. Whenever he does meditate, it is either for the purpose of withdrawing from the world totally for short periods, at intervals, either for his own satisfaction or to recuperate his energies, or to benefit others by telepathy. When it is said "for his own satisfaction," what is meant is that meditation in seclusion may have become a way of life in his previous incarnation. This generates a karmic tendency which reappears in this life and the satisfaction of this tendency pleases him, but it is not absolutely essential for him. He can dispense with it when needful to do so, whereas the unenlightened man is too often at the mercy of his tendencies and propensities.(P)

130

There is no classification into matter and spirit for the Sage. There is only one life for him. If a man can find reality only in trance, if he says that the objective world is unreal, he is not a Sage, he is a Yogi.(P)

131

The mystic who becomes immobilized by his inheritance of asceticism and escapism will also become indifferent to the sorrows of a mankind whom he regards as materialistic. The sage, self-disciplined to live in the world with his heart and thought molded after his own fashion, will not turn in contempt or helplessness from the so-called materialistic but, on the contrary, will find in their ignorance the motive for his incessant service of enlightenment to them. The stultified stony apathy of the first is shamed by the courageous acceptance of life as a whole of the second.

132

The saint is satisfied to attain freedom from his lower self but the Master does not stop there. He seeks also to carry enlightenment to others, remove their misery, and save them from the illusion in which they are involved.

133

His attainments in the mental, ethical, and philosophic spheres must take concrete shape in the disinterested service of humanity, or he is no illuminate.

134

The mystic would certainly wish that all others might attain to his own inner peace. But because he has not himself realized this higher unity (which is all-embracing) he does not feel that he bears any personal responsibility for their uplift. On the contrary while the ascetic, under the illusion that worldly life is a snare set by Satan, sits smugly in his retreat, the illuminate knows that *all* life is divinely born, never relaxes his efforts for the enlightenment of mankind.

135

Judge the sage if you must by the profound impress he makes on the soul of his age or by the service which he incessantly renders to the utmost limit of his strength.

136

The inutility of many monks is in striking contrast to the worth and activity of the sages. Thus, the Buddha worked unceasingly for fifty years to remove spiritual ignorance from the minds of men and death caught him trudging unweariedly on foot, an old man over eighty, trying to reach the next place where he was due to teach others and thus serve them in the best way of which he was capable. He was no idler. Jesus, too, moved unweariedly and incessantly trying to awaken the hearts of men to their true goal and giving to those who approached him with faith the benediction of his grace. Death caught him in the midst of so much of this activity that it aroused the hostility of professional religionists whose vested interests were in danger and who to save their own purses put Jesus on the cross.

137

He alone may rightly be called a sage who not only has attained the highest mystical stage but has also found a new meaning in the finite world and the finite human life. He does not need to run away from the familiar world, for he sees it by a diviner light. He experiences not only its obvious transiency and multiplicity but also its hidden eternality and unity.

138

If the so-called practical persons and the self-confessed materialistic ones only knew how much nearer to realities the sage is than they think, how much more "practical" he is, they would be very much surprised.

139

The sage's personality is a fully integrated one. He does not seek to be unnatural or abnormal, whereas the mystic may. Aurobindo Ghose's silence and retreat, Ramana Maharshi's ashram couch and non-handling of money, are abnormalities.

140

The sage is not a frustrated visionary who hides himself in disappointment and looks down with superior disdain upon the world.

141

The man who has attained Truth is not faced with the problem which faces the man who attains success in yoga; the latter's first impulse is to desert the world, the former's to convert the world.

142

Two Christian mystics who felt they were in close intimacy with God— Saint Catherine of Siena and Ignatius Loyola—felt also the urge to spend most of their years in great activity and outgoing work.

143

Even Emerson did not live always in transcendental ideas and dreams. He took his share in the anti-slavery agitation, bought railway and bank shares, married twice, and often travelled the rough pioneering West on lecture tours. Was he any less spiritual than the saintly or the sequestered ascetics of Asia Minor, or of Hindustan?

144

The earthly troubles of mankind *are* the concern of the true sage, and indifference to them is a mark of the mere mystic, that is, one who has mistaken his partial attainment for a complete realization.

Qualities, characteristics of the sage

145

Where is the man who is free of the ego? To him we must bow in deep reverence, in wondering admiration, in enforced humility. Here is one who has found his true self, his personal independence, his own being. Here at last is a free man, someone who has found his real worth in a world of false values. Here at last is a truly great man and truly sincere man.(P)

146

Whosoever enters into this realization becomes a human sun who sheds enlightenment, radiates strength, and emanates love to all beings.

147

His serenity is alive and buoyant, not lethargic and dull.

148

To comprehend the mysterious side of an adept's personality correctly, we must comprehend its twofold nature.

149

He is worthy to be called a sage who unites in his person mature judgement and experience, prudent speech and conduct, correct reasoning and adequate knowledge, humanized sanctity and spiritual enlightenment.

150

In the loneliness of the divine presence he is always unutterably humble. In the presence of his fellow men he is incomparably self-possessed, quietly dignified, and subtly armed with authority.

151

The wearing of a halo would not make him any happier; he is not interested in being marked out as a "spiritual" person; spirituality is not a separate special feature for him but something that ought to be the natural state of a human being. Consequently he finds the thought of being singled out for this quality, or becoming conspicuous for it, uninteresting to him.

152

This paradox is the extraordinary situation of such a man. He accepts the ego but he also repudiates it at the same time.

153

Although he has reached a Godlike level, he is never arrogant, never pretentious, yet always keeps a simple natural dignity.

154

Just as there is no special virtue in going to sleep, nothing to be proud of, so the sage regards his being in Being as no less natural, nothing to vaunt before other men. This seems undue humility to the world but it seems ordinary to him.

155

It is a matter of complete assurance and scientific observation for the sage that God exists, that man has a soul, that he is here on earth to become united with this soul, and that he can attain true happiness only by following good and avoiding evil.

156

The sage is not a quester after saintly prestige: he will not outwardly try to present himself as a holy man.

157

He could never make a commercial business out of spiritual uplift, nor even turn it into a paid professional career. How different from those ambitious leaders whose pretended motive of serving humanity is really a cover for service of their own ego.

158

People think a sage exercises infinite tolerance and patience. This is because they have no standard by which to measure the qualities of his rhythm of consciousness. Tolerance and patience imply their opposites. The sage's reactions conform to neither. He literally lives where they do not apply. The set of conditions which for the ordinary man gives rise to the possibility of tolerance and patience or their opposites is for the sage an opportunity for reflection.

159

Such a man has no enemies, although he may have those who regard him as their enemy. For hate cannot enter his heart; goodwill towards all is its fragrant atmosphere.

160

In all relations, whether as friend or lover or husband, he is unpossessing, but he requires in return to be unpossessed.

161

The adept has no indispensable need to *know*. *He is being*, which is his foundational consciousness—pure, unmixed with mental images or thoughts, and not dispersed in the existence of the five senses.

162

He does not seek and will not accept those who are already members of any society or group which provides them with instruction, for he will not interfere between the teacher and the taught. Truth must be sought in its fullness, not as a supplement to the teaching of others. For the sage will not adulterate truth. The truth he has to give is *not* the same as that taught by them and he does not want to distort it to fit such misconceptions.

163

He who has found his genuine self does not need to pose for the benefit of gushing disciples. He obtains the deepest satisfaction merely from being himself. What others may say about him in praise cannot bring him anything like the pleasure which his own higher consciousness brings him.

164
His ever-present calmness is not a mask for secretive emotions, inner conflicts, mental tensions, or explosive passions.

165
He has paid a high price for this serenity. He has accepted the necessity of walking alone, the shattering of all illusions, the denudation of human desire, and the funeral of animal passion.

166
The illuminated man's conduct in this world is a guided one. His senses tell him what is happening in the world about him, but his soul guides him to a proper evaluation of those sense reports. In this way he lives in the world, but is not of it. Of him alone is it true to say that his is a spiritual life.

167
He possesses a largeness of heart at all times, an immense tolerance towards the frailty of faulty men and women.

168
When he has fully accomplished this passing-over, all the elements of his lower nature will then have been fully eliminated. The ego will be destroyed. Instead of being enslaved by its own senses and passions, blinded by its own thoughts and ignorance, his mind will be inspired, enlightened, and liberated by the Overself. Yet life in the human self will not be destroyed because he has entered life in the divine Overself. But neither will it continue in the old and lower way. That self will henceforth function as a perfectly obedient instrument of the soul and no longer of the animal body or intellectual nature. No evil thought and no animal passion can ever again take hold of his mind. What remains of his character is therefore the incorruptible part and the immortal part. Death may rob him of lesser things, but not of the thing which he cherishes most. Having already parted in his heart with what is perishable, he can await it without perturbation and with sublime resignation.(P)

169
When we comprehend what it is that must go into the making of a sage, how many and how diverse the experiences through which he has passed in former incarnations, we realize that such a man's wisdom is part of his bloodstream.(P)

170

There are noteworthy differences between the genuine illuminate and the false one. But I shall indicate only a few of the points one may observe in the man who is truly self-realized. First of all, he does not desire to become the leader of a new cult; therefore, he does not indulge in any of the attempts to draw publicity or notice which mark our modern saviours. He never seeks to arouse attention by oddity of teaching, talk, dress, or manner. In fact, he does not even desire to appear as a teacher, seeks no adherents, and asks no pupils to join him. Though he possesses immense spiritual power which may irresistibly influence your life, he will seem quite unconscious of it. He makes no claim to the possession of peculiar powers. He is completely without pose or pretense. The things which arouse passion or love or hatred in men do not seem to touch him; he is indifferent to them as Nature is to our comments when we praise her sunshine or revile her storms. For in him, we have to recognize a man freed, loosed from every limit which desire and emotion can place upon us. He walks detached from the anxious thoughts or seductive passions which eat out the hearts of men. Though he behaves and lives simply and naturally, we are aware that there is a mystery within that man. We are unable to avoid the impression that because his understanding has plumbed life deeper than other men's, we are compelled to call a halt when we would attempt to comprehend him.(P)

171

Despite all his psychical knowledge and personal attainment, the sage never loses his deep sense of the mystery which is at the heart of existence, which is God.(P)

172

Passion of any kind, whether angry or sexual, cannot touch this man. Those writers and preachers who portray a wrathful and indignant Jesus attacking the temple moneychangers are mere sentimentalists, projecting their own limited characteristics, their own narrow conception of virtue, on a man whose state of consciousness they are unable even to approach. They might as well attribute repressed sexual urges to the Buddha as expressed angry ones to Jesus. It is all their theory and speculation based on ignorance.

173

He is not grieved when past or present history brings to his notice the fact that human nature is less than perfect, nor is he disillusioned when he himself is made to suffer personally from this imperfection. He knows men as they are, as well as what they will one day become, and has a tolerant attitude toward their frailties. Nothing that any of them may do can embitter him, or weaken his confidence in the higher laws, or deter him from abiding by the higher principles, or blur his insight into the ultimate greatness of every human being.

174

Without pretension or affectation, neither seeking to draw attention nor seeking to impress others, he is truly humble in his greatness.

175

Anyone who has this awakened consciousness at all times will be radiant at all times. He will make the best of things and things will be for the best with him.

176

Peace is perpetually within him.

177

It is *not* the humility of an inferiority-complexed person but of a man who communes with the higher power. It is not the equanimity of stupid empty-mindedness but of one who feels deep spiritual peace. It is not the dignity of self-conceit but of profound respect for the God within him.

178

A man finds his greatest fulfilment of life, his greatest joy and happiness, in spirit, so that in reducing lower things he misses nothing at all, for he has outgrown them. This was the belief, feeling, and practice of one man who became a veritable sage—Plotinus!

179

So much intuition, like dream, gets lost in the passage to verbal expression or even mental formulation. In earlier years, questions peppered his mind. Now they have ceased to do so. Not only because he does not want to disturb the peace he now enjoys; nor because his intellect has decayed; but because he knows that behind it all is Mystery: that one man cannot play the role of omniscient God, that he may well leave to God the endless questions that arise.

180

A peace pervades him, gathered from deep thought and, much more, from the stillness which transcends all thought.

181

The peace fills him with amiability, like warm sunshine, and makes ill will impossible. The sensitive benefit, momentarily or permanently, by the contact, although they may not feel the peace till afterwards; the insensitive, well!—they may shrug their shoulders in wonder at what others see and find in him.

182

His varied experience of human beings makes him familiar with the heights and depths of human nature, its saintly possibilities and its sinful actualities. This knowledge does not make him more cynical, only more patient. His patience is the outcome of his understanding, his tolerance the outcome of his knowledge. The cosmic plan of evolution through birth after birth illuminates many situations for him.

183

He neither hopes for the best nor fears the worst, for he lives in perfect serenity.

184

He stands out in moral grandeur.

185

His voice seems to speak not merely with utter conviction but with absolute authority. His knowledge seems to come from a very deep level.

186

There is the supreme relaxation of one who keeps certain resources—the most hidden, the most powerful—always in reserve.

187

He is not good because of imposed rules or prescribed regulations. He is good because it is impossible for him to be anything else.

188

He will find his proper place in the cosmic order, neither too low nor too high, and know his proper relationship to the divine intelligence behind that order, the World-Mind.

189

The enlightened man can "establish" truth gleaned by insight, not put together by intellect through any organized institution or printed publication.

190

A man who is in this state automatically repels negative thoughts and effortlessly wards off destructive ones. They cannot live in his atmosphere.

191

The serenity is not something which has been added to him. It has been integrated as a part of his being.

192

Although he is forced, like all humans, to take cognizance of the world around him, of its horrors and squalors, its evils and vilenesses, the gate leading out of it all can be opened at will, and quickly. The way back into the ethereal world, with its beauty and peace, is always existent for him.

193

That certitude which comes to him is not merely the kind which opposes the meaning of hesitance, but also the kind which is the opposite of mere belief, which is born of complete understanding, perfect knowledge, and direct experience.

194

Ashtavakra Samhita: "The sage of vacant mind knows not the conflict of contemplation and non-contemplation, good and evil. He abides, as it were, in the state of Absoluteness. Devoid of the feeling of 'mine-ness' and 'I-ness', knowing for certain that nothing is, and with all his desires set at rest within, the man of knowledge does not act though he may be acting."

195

The adept is marked off from his fellows by the aura of controlled emotion and calm sureness which he carries with him. He does not fear his fellow men however evil they be, for he does not depend upon his own personal strength alone but also upon the Higher Self and its boundless power.

196

One feels that such an adept is in mind the oldest man one knows and yet in heart the youngest.

197

The sage is not less practical for all his transcendental consciousness and mystical experience. He understands as well as any cynic the low depths on which so many human relations function. He sees quite clearly the greeds, the pettinesses, and the rancours that fill the air of human society. But he also sees beyond and above them.

198

Whether he is alone in the privacy of his room or in public being watched by others, whether performing routine actions or entirely new ones, he will attain unified conduct because he has attained conscious unity of being.

199

Do not be deceived by his modesty, his freedom from any of the varied forms of personal vanity, for beneath the surface there is ironclad assurance.

200

A man of his status is able to scatter light in so many different types of mind because he is free from inflexible standpoints.

201

So completely has he freed himself from the tyrannic sway of egoism that he can enter, through emotive thought, into another man's personality, however offensive or antipathetic that man might ordinarily be to him.

202

He can project his empathic imagination into another person's mind to such a degree that he can identify himself with that person.

203

The Sphinx is a perfect image of the adept in whom the man controls the animal. The attainment is a rare one—too many are satisfied to remain hardly more than animal, with a few human traits.

204

There is no patronizing condescension in his attitude toward those who are less evolved, no spiritual snobbery towards the masses.

205

He cannot possibly suffer from the gloomy disappointment which those suffer who, believing that they have a clear mission in life, sadly find that they cannot establish their ideas or gather a following. Either they have not freed themselves sufficiently from clinging emotional desires— whether to be applauded by others or to reform them—or they have not freed themselves from identification with the personal ego.

206

It is not only a matter of having more goodness than ordinary people that distinguishes him. It is primarily his contact with a higher dimension of being altogether.

207

The sage has achieved perfect obedience to this fundamental Law of Balance in himself, in his life, and in the universe.

208

The sage will not be an adherent of martyristic ideology. He will make no pretense and set up no pose of exaggerated altruism. He will do what needs to be done for his own self. But at the same time he will also do what needs to be done for others. It is not altruistic folly but altruistic wisdom that he seeks to practise. Hence he prefers to be a live servant of the good in mankind than a dead martyr to the evil in mankind. He will not swing from the extreme of utter selfishness to the extreme of unbalanced selfless- ness. He will not ignore his own needs or fail to work for his own better- ment even while he is attending to the needs of others and working for their betterment. He can well serve individual ends alongside his service of social ones.

209

He does not dwell in his own heart on his spiritual usefulness to other people. If ever he were to do so that would only be the ego wallowing in its vanity. And it is precisely because his ego has been cast down that he has such usefulness at all.

210

If men do not care for his own road but set their feet on other roads to the soul's finding, he will feel no disappointment and express no criticism. Rather will he rejoice that they have entered on the quest, even though it be in a different way from his. He is too large in mind and heart to wish that it were otherwise.

211

He does not need to ask others for help of any kind for they usually offer it spontaneously and unasked. There is some quality in him which arouses in them the strong desire to serve him.

212

He will not seek any public acknowledgment of his services. If it does come, he will not be unduly elated; if it does not come, he will not be particularly discontented.

213

When such a man hears from time to time of the far-reaching results of his work, he feels afresh the need of a great humility. For if it has achieved anything at all, it has not been achieved by any other power than that of Grace—which moves so mysteriously and so silently and so effectively.

214

His is a disciplined freedom, without the hardness of the rigid moralist or the license of the flabby hedonist.

215

Whatever sin is committed against him, or wrong done to him, his forgiveness is available to the sinner immediately and completely. This is not an attitude he has to bring himself to create but one which is natural and easy.

216

The master is free, totally free, from the greeds and lusts of ordinary men. In this he is a forerunner of the men who are to appear later.

217

He need assume no oracular air, no conceited manner. The simple expression of what he is suffices to impress others of its own accord.

218

In him, perception and volition are fused and not, as in ordinary men, separated and discordant. That which he sees ought to be done, is accepted and executed by the will.

219

Such a man will spontaneously love the Ideal, practise virtue, and promote the spread of Truth.

220

The glowing warmth of his goodwill is natural, sincere.

221

The practice of goodness is as natural with such a man as the act of breathing.

222

A heart filled with peace and love will be felt through a radiant countenance and poised bearing.

223

He will always show forth a courtesy that comes from the heart rather than from the dictates of formality.

224

If the adepts appear to stand aloof, it is not because they feel proudly superior but because they feel humbly incapable of bettering the work being done on humanity by Nature (God) in her long-range evolutionary plan. They could never have become what they are if they had held illusions of personal grandeur.

225

He makes no pretense of omniscience.

226

The simple and modest outward bearing of an illuminate frequently belies the infinite subtlety of his intelligence.

227

The illuminate is a man at peace with himself, able to stand emotionally aside from his affairs but unable to surrender to transient defeats. He knows when he is defeated; he never knows such a thing as failure. His life is a consecrated one. It has an impressive value. There is a timeless flavour about it. That is why he can work quietly not only for the immediate moment but even for results which he knows he will not live to witness.

228

"The adept appears without exposing his head" is the Chinese esoteric description. It means that he makes no outward demonstration of his adeptship, behaves unostentatiously and modestly, and is acted through rather than acting with his egoistic will.

229

While worldly men strain their heads and knit their brows, the sage sits quietly or works unhurriedly, self-absent, unutterably wise in the Infinite. In a world half given over to despair, he dwells with an intrinsic power that all feel who contact him, or he moves radiating a calm strength to every environment.

3: The Sage / 109

230

He is detached, watching the passing show go by, but not so detached as if he were far away. For his interest in the world's affairs is vivid; his intelligence is active, seeing the interplay of cyclic impetus and karmic results.

231

His wonderful calmness does not make him utterly impervious to all the happenings of his era, nor callous to all the turns of national fortune or disaster.

232

There is such a perfect harmony of his faculties that although each still continues to exist autonomously, all work together like a single faculty.

233

There is profound power, there is ample security in this presence. The sage alone may dare to be himself, may live unrelated to the fads and fashions around him.

234

The sage tries to make all his acts tend toward harmony but he does not mistake uniformity for unity. Differences there will be.

235

He possesses the ability to produce peace within himself and to radiate it outside himself.

236

He is sufficient, himself and not anyone else, an original and not a copy, music and not its echo—in short, a true individual.

237

It is a fact that in such a man these three passions—anger, lust, and hatred—are stilled forever. There is no temptation which can now have any power over him, no fear which can overcome him, no frustration which can depress him.

238

There will be an air of settled conviction, of inward assurance about his speech and writing.

239

The aura of peace and wisdom and power that emanates from his person is the best testimonial to the value of his ideas.

240

This superb poise is not an act, put on for the benefit of onlookers; it is real.

241

He may be poor outwardly but he will be rich inwardly. He may have to endure troubles but he will endure them without worry.

242

He will show this high degree of advancement by the assured direction of his efforts, the unflinching strength of his purpose, and the effective results of his work.

243

When the sage undertakes a public task or mission he will neither over nor under do his work. He will do exactly what is required.

244

The sage expresses self without selfishness, individuality without individualism.

245

He possesses a sense of infinite leisure, a manner devoid of all haste, a willingness to achieve his ends little by little.

246

Although fully deserving it, he is too humble to demand and always too embarrassed when offered any special reverence.

247

His personality is one with his teaching: his life incarnates, practises, and actualizes it.

248

He is content to let them attribute to others the help they are getting from him. His ego needs no gratitude and no recognition and would not know what to do with them if they came. He rejoices in their progress as the chief thing.

249

What he gives he gives freely and asks for no requital.

250

Since his life itself is not fixed but moves incessantly, he cannot congeal his thought into fixed dogmas or his character into fixed attitudes. He will put forth whatever wisdom indicates in any situation and to any question, not solely what the past indicates—which is what accumulated knowledge or a lined-up character really does. His mind is free, his policies always fresh. He is neither orthodox nor unorthodox. Naturally such a fluid standpoint will not find approval from the many who have to wear a partisan or fanatic label.

251

The self-renounced illuminate sits beside the gleaming river of life and dips his pitcher like others into those troubled waters of passion or pain.

Yet he wears an inscrutable smile which perhaps says: "I see all and know all. If I drink with you, it is to be you. If I remain with you, it is to help you. For paradoxically, I sit also at this river's source."

252

The illuminate stands on the very apex of the pyramid of knowledge. That is why he can understand the position of all others and sympathize with them, too. But alas, that is also why they cannot understand him. Hence the plaint of Buddha: "I do not quarrel, O Bhikkus, with the people, but it is the people who quarrel with me. One, O Bhikkus, who speaks the Truth, does not quarrel with anyone."

253

"There were four things from which the Master was entirely free. He had no foregone conclusions, no arbitrary pre-determinations, no obstinacy, and no egoism."—*Confucian Analects*

254

A real maharishee has no preconceived ideas as to what he is going to do.

255

No cult can claim him and no organization can label him, for he will be too aware of the limitations of all cults and organizations.

256

He is not working for this generation, nor for this country, nor for any millenium, but for an infinite duration of time. Therefore he is, he must be, infinitely patient.

257

The plane of negative thoughts, emotions, and behaviour does not exist for him. His only awareness of it is as it exists in others. Otherwise there is no contact with it within himself.

258

He alone can afford to be as boundlessly patient as Nature is. He alone can rightly be lavish with time.

259

The true sage seeks to lead men into a life that is noble, beautiful, and intelligent, and to save them from their sins of self-exhaustion through febrile and foolish conflicts. The sage has lifted his thinking above the level of both free will and fate, matters which concern the ego. He lives in the Witness Self. The practical result is that he does not feel the caress of pleasure or the sting of pain so keenly as others. He exemplifies the truth of Nature's dictate, "To him who asks nothing everything is given."

260
Whatever greatness the world looks up to him for possessing, vanishes utterly from his mind in the presence of this infinite greatness.

261
Modest and unassuming, as Lao Tzu makes the sage appear, his realization of the truth does not weigh down on him. He finds it natural and does not feel it to be exceptional, although others do.

262
He is no propagandist, never aggressively intrudes his views in conversation nor forces his conclusions on others in an argumentative manner. He accepts people as they mentally are.

263
He enters the inner stillness as a learner, as one who is sensitive to the Interior Word and capable of responding to it. Such response is as far beyond the guidance of the good religious man by moral conscience as that in turn is beyond the primitive man's instincts, appetites, and desires.

264
If in some ways he is as human as everyone else, in other ways he is unlike other men. This is inevitable because he has gone ahead and surpassed his fellows.

265
Insofar as he is aware of other men and of the objects which surround him, he expresses the Mind which is the Real. And insofar as he may be either lifted at times out of his little ego, or endowed with insight which sees beyond that ego, does he express it further still.

266
The intellectual argues where the sage announces.

267
It is the difference between arguing from theory and announcing from experience.

268
To live in lonely contemplation of the secrets deep down in the heart, to place all ambitions and restless desires on a funeral pyre and burn them up in a heap—these things demand the highest courage possible to man. Those who would denominate one who has achieved them as a coward, because he does not run with the crowd who fight for pelf and self, make a ghastly mistake.

269
He will bear witness in thought and speech to the joy of this awakened consciousness.

270

If a man deserts blood relations, it is only to take on spiritual ones. If he leaves his earthly house, it is only to enter the monastery, a spiritual one. If he forsakes the society of wife and children, it is only to enjoy that of teacher and students. Thus absolute escape is a mirage and cannot be found. The kind and quality of his bonds can be changed and transformed but not really severed. The only attainable freedom lies deep within. It is invisible and mental. This is what the sage enjoys. He may be weighted with business responsibilities and surrounded by a family, but in his heart nothing holds him.

271

The sage affirms nothing, denies nothing.

272

He does not wish to be regarded as other than he is; not for him the canonization of a saint or the adoration of a god. Insight, and its application to human living, is the final fulfilment for all of us, shall be our natural condition.

273

Does he feel revulsions and attractions like other persons? He may, but the feeling is always within the larger circle of feeling the presence of Overself, with himself and with others. This compensating principle acts as a control and a balance. He is not ruled by the reaction, as others are, nor blinded by it to an egoistic judgement.

274

Something of Nature's vast impersonality, her indifference to the individual human, is in him.

275

The Sage looks out dispassionately upon the course of human life— which includes his own life—as if he were not personally involved in it, yet he does whatever ought to be done as if he were.

276

The man of high spiritual status is aware of this difference, but the awareness does not create any vanity within him, any self-conceit.

277

If there is an air of remoteness about him, perhaps because of his inner detachment showing through, perhaps because he is habitually centered in the Presence, it does not stop a quietly voiced greeting and amiable half-smile suddenly revealing the intention of keeping linked with this grosser world.

278

He is wide enough in his outlook to look at contradictory ideas and things with equal calm. For they all melt in the Pure Mind.

279

He will not have to think out the needed reaction, for it will flow naturally and spontaneously out of his inner being.

280

The sage's consciousness remains permanently serene and equable, at the same level whatever conditions prevail.

281

Compassion—a quality so real and vibrant in the Italians but sensibly practical in the English and Americans, so infrequent in the French but present in the Indians—is natural, quiet, and devoid of sentimentality in the sage.

282

He may still have his hygienic reactions, his aesthetic preferences, his individual tastes. He may still retain human aversions to dirty bodies, attractions to refined habits. Enlightenment has not turned him into an indifferent robot or a frozen creature or a zombie deprived of feeling. But his personal discrimination is calmly practised: behind it there is an impersonal detachment.

283

There is something which is always kept in reserve, a part of himself which is enclosed and which keeps other men at a distance, however cordial is his outer self. This enables him to keep always calm, whatever the outer provocations may be, to hold to an intense inner stillness.

284

He does not hope for anything nor wish for any special piece of good fortune—not because he is too pessimistic about life, but because he is so serene that he has stopped looking for something to come to him from outside that would bring happiness, stopped holding on to others, and stopped dreaming. THIS is reality; what the world can give is a dream.

285

When the hour comes to desert the body, he will be ready for the fated event, without that desperate struggle to hold on to a form which has served its purpose seen too often in the ignorant.

286

Such is his freedom from common ego-obsession and such the stretch of his compassion, that he makes whomever he talks with feel that he is genuinely and deeply interested in his or her particular affairs.

287

There is a friendliness in his look, goodwill in his face, that make acquaintance easy.

288

The sage can condemn nobody, can regard none as outside his range of compassion, and can find a place in his heart for the worst sinner. He knows that duality is but a dream and discovers himself anew in all sentient creatures. He knows that the world's woe arises out of its false and fictitious sense of separateness.

289

He receives too many confidences ever to be surprised by any of them, too many confessions ever to be shocked. But even if he had never heard or read a single one, he would receive them just as calmly. For his compassion and insight, his tolerance and realism embrace the whole range of human feeling or human behaviour.

290

He is always himself, without pose, without pretense, and without self-consciousness.

291

It is not the studied poise of good breeding but a natural poise upwelling from within.

292

His uniqueness extends through body, feelings, thoughts, character, outlook—it is total.

293

The ordinary man sees only his personal objective, but the illumined man sees simultaneously both the objective and the person pursuing it.

294

His silence bravely takes its stand on the fact that truth is a reality, is a power, is invincible.

295

He knows the proper value to stamp on fame, position, and wealth, and the proper place to assign them. He neither rejects them with harsh ascetic scorn nor seeks them with hard self-centered ambition.

296

The strength with which he has conquered both himself and life will be evident to those who are sensitive to more than merely commonplace things.

297

In every affair he knows where he stands, but more in the sense that he listens and obeys the higher guidance than in any other.

298

He learns from within, intuitively, much more than from without, the full teaching to which other men or their books have led him.

299

He is ever at peace within himself but does not necessarily care to advertise this fact to the world by wearing a perpetual smile.

300

For such a man all actions become ritual ones, all places sacred.

301

Even if a negative reaction to some untoward event were to enter his mind he would efface it instantly.

302

The adept is capable of immense power on the occasions when he unleashes it.

303

The illuminate is more likely to shun fame than to seek it. His humbleness is shown by the way he seeks anonymity.

304

The exquisite peace and serene passionlessness of his days have been fully earned, the power to withdraw his senses from objects whose pursuit wastes the lives of most men has been gained in long meditations, the insight which reveals the presence of God in all things has been born out of his many self-denials and self-surrenders.

305

Where other men see nothing, sense nothing, revere nothing, he does all these things. For him the Empty is the Full.

306

The life of such a man compares with the dead movement of a fixed spindle. While he sits calm within himself, his hands and feet and brain work actively amidst the world.

307

The sage is not tainted by calculations of gain or loss for he is egoless in his reckonings.

308

The quality of this man is utterly different from that of most men. Such is the impression a sensitive observer must feel.

309

If he talks out of his personal experience of the Spirit, it will not be an arrogant boast but a quiet statement of simple fact.

310

Peace trails in the wake of such a man as foam behind a ship.

311

He is no more capable of reviling other men, let alone hating them. Such evil thinking cannot even begin to enter his mind but must die stillborn.

312

No ugly qualities are left in him, no vicious remnants of the beast that became man.

313

What he feels within himself irradiates what he sees outside himself. The inner strength that he has received enables him to endure adverse circumstances in a manner that truly makes the best of them in the best sense.

314

The genuine illuminate will discourage all attempts at deification of himself whereas the pseudo-illuminate glorifies in it.

315

His eyes seem passionless to our own agitated ones. His mind seems impenetrable to our own easily read ones.

316

Even if the ego still lives in him, it lives thoroughly purified and utterly checked. His principle trends of thought and conduct proceed from a level beyond it.

317

His manner always imperturbable to the point of emotional aloofness, his views always impartial to the point of stepping aside from his own self-interests, his love of truth never deserts him.

318

The simple knowledge of his own status has no personal pride in it; therefore, no need exists to hide it behind a false modesty.

319

He may carry no outward credentials of his status yet there will be an inward presence of silent authority all about him, which not even his humility, his utter self-abasement can hide.

320

He is not outwardly too different from the rest of mankind. He is not a cold, unfeeling marble statue nor entirely remote from human interests.

321

It is easy to mistake his habitual reserve for cold disdain. But it springs from a wish to refrain from interfering with others.

322

He will not complain if other men irritate him, nor will he worry if problems beset him. This peace which he has found is unfaltering.

323
In this mystical detachment from people, the sage asks nothing from them and cringes before nothing in them. He is free and independent.

324
From this complete independence arises part of that authority with which his speech is filled.

325
He practises tolerance without condescension, conformity without hypocrisy, and freedom without license.

326
He knows and tolerates the weaknesses of humanity, and the vacillations of his disciples, without condoning them.

327
He neither approves nor disapproves of anyone.

328
He conforms to the higher laws, his life is based on the cosmic life, his thought and attitude are in harmony with the cosmic order.

329
Under the genuine friendly cordiality there is, although subtly felt, a measured distance of manner, a holding back in reserve and detachment.

330
It is true that there have been historic figures among the sages who conducted themselves with the tradition-bound aloofness of a Mandarin. But there were others, and they were probably the majority, who were approachable in a more human way.

331
These great elemental forces in him are purifying ones.

332
Be he a dictator holding the fortunes of a nation in the hollow of his hand, or a despised outcast, degraded, destitute, and sin-steeped, none is too high to find a place in the illuminate's orbit of contact, just as none is too low. For the first virtue of self-knowledge is the inner understanding of others, the intellectual sympathy with them.

333
Through this sympathy he is able to place himself at the point of view of each man with whom he has to deal, or of each school of thought which he has to lead to one beyond its own.

334
If it can be said that he has any negative attitude at all, it may be noted that whether Oriental or Occidental he has a strong disinclination to talk about the Quest to those who are uninterested in it, or antagonistic to it.

335
He holds his convictions calmly where others preach them violently.

336
He is as indifferent to laudatory articles about himself in the public prints as to condemnatory gossip in the private circles.

337
He can understand why they hold these views even though he does not share them.

338
The current of peace carries him along. He does not have to struggle for it.

339
Lao Tzu: The characteristic inner state of his ideal sage is, in his own word, "emptiness."

340
He will carry his attainment quite unassumingly and naturally: he will not ordinarily speak of it, but if he does it will be without any pretentiousness.

341
He is, in Homer's phrase, "within irradiate with prophetic light."

342
Gently he will disown any status which would elevate him too high in the world's eyes.

343
If he is given the work of writing down this teaching or the mission of proclaiming it quietly in speech, the way in which it is received by others will not personally and emotionally affect him much. Whether it be long neglected or immediately accepted is more their affair than his. He will be happy if people can take the offer and benefit by it, but if they do not, he is not rendered unhappy.

344
He will be neither over-emotionally sentimental nor utterly selfish in his relations with others. He will mind his own business which is a celestial one. He will tend to seem absorbed and will not be understood, but rather misunderstood.

345
He is, he must be, the least sectarian of men, the broadest minded, the most tolerant of observers.

346
He holds no self-image of a flattering kind to buttress his ego when dealing with the world, in which he prefers to remain inconspicuously—

unless a particular work of service withdraws him outwardly from this humility.

347

Those who are deceived too quickly by appearances to take the trouble to try and penetrate them may find him a cold man. But the truth is that he has feeling, not passion. There is dynamic power within him, but it is always impersonal and always calm. It is never used to gratify personal vanity or egoistic aggression.

348

The sage knows more secrets than he ever tells, and knows, too, how to keep them well.

349

The sage hears the answers of Life to the questions of man where the latter hears nothing.

350

It is impossible to forget the unfaltering dignity of such a man, in whom all those littlenesses which betray mediocrity have been submerged and dissolved forever.

351

Here at last is a man who stands out from the herd because of his essential goodness and complete integrity, his fine insight and lonely dignity.

God alone is perfect

352

The tendency to assume that the spiritual man was perfect in his youth and never made a mistake in his maturity, is common among his followers and passed on by them to the public—with the result that the latter stares at him with great awe as a rare phenomenon but does not dream that it is possible to follow in his footsteps to the same achievement. The truth is that he had his share of struggles and failures, that he was born with his own particular imperfections, and that he had to make the character and expand the consciousness which adorned his later years.

353

Nobody is perfectly fulfilled, completely virtuous, totally enlightened, on this physical plane. The best of sages and saints are so because of their inspiration's source, which is beyond other men's. But the channel is still human, still limited, and still liable to colour what flows through, as Ramakrishna himself admitted.

354

The body of every sage is still human and shares the same limitations as other human bodies. This is why he may suffer from the illnesses and diseases to which all flesh is heir.

355

We may admire, respect, and pay homage to these men without falling into the extravagance of regarding them as gods.

356

It is a common error to believe that such a man is freed from all limitations whatsoever and that the deliberate performance of miracles is not beyond him. But the truth is that not only is he not allowed by the nature of circumstances to help but he is also surrounded by barriers in what he is able to do for those whom he does try to help.

357

The belief that the adept can explain everything is a false one.

358

It would be in better harmony with the facts, and mysticism would lose nothing not worth losing by it, if the representation of great mystics as demi-gods and infallible entities ceased. They are human beings and sometimes they make mistakes.

359

No teacher can be all-knowing or all-powerful. Such attributes belong to God, not to man. Most teachers commit errors and possess frailties.

360

There is too often a tendency to regard him as more than human. It is true that in one sense and in one part of his inner being, he is. But this is no reason to lose all balance and lavish adulation indiscriminately upon him. For in a number of ways he is still an ordinary man.

361

Even the greatest of prophets may have his lesser moments, his lighter moods.

362

Why not look at discoverable realities rather than unrealizable expectations? These men, however high in development and however worthy of reverence, are still only mortals. They die like us, they get ill and suffer. They do not know everything. They are even fallible. Some hold views which are arguable at least, which have been dictated or influenced by local tradition, custom, or belief rather than by God.

363

The presence of insight does not exempt the sage from his human needs. He continues his daily functions as before.

364

Some people picture to themselves an ideal human being whose body exemplifies his mind—a perfect human type—and associate the historical saints, sages, mystics, and masters with their picture. But the biographical fact itself is never the same, could we get the true fact.

365

No one but Allah knows all. The sage is not a human encyclopaedia. Those who expect an answer to every question do not show up the sage's ignorance but their own.

366

The inspired man who is a genius in these matters need not be deprived of his humanity in order to hail him as a god. Even if he is used as a channel by the higher power, he is used *because he is a man living with, and working among, other men.*

367

Swami Virajananda, President, Ramakrishna Mission circa 1950:"The conduct and dealings even of a spiritual teacher, or of a fully qualified Guru may not be entirely without defects or imperfections, errors of judgement, or lack of proper understanding of some sort."

368

Though overshadowed continuously by this divine being that is really his own other self, he remains nevertheless quite human.

369

This rare wisdom does not prevent him from being a normal human otherwise.

370

To turn them into demigods, to believe that their intelligence is perfect, their character faultless, is to pervert the truth.

371

The adept has his limitations, like other human beings. He is subject to the same vicissitudes of fortune that they are. He is liable to the natural changes of life, to sickness and death. He is certainly not as powerful as so many credulous and superstitious believers imagine him to be.

372

To remind the worshippers that he is still a human being is not to criticize or denigrate him.

373

Cicero wrote nearly two thousand years ago that the ideally perfect men were "nowhere to be found at all." Who, except wishful thinkers and pious sentimentalists, can gainsay him?

374

Those who seek absolute perfection, whether in someone else or for themselves, seek what is unattainable in this world.

375

It is not possible to find human perfection, not even among the mahatmas. Travel, contact, and experience with them reveal that not one was always infallible, not one failed to commit errors of judgement.

376

Do such men of realization live among us today? Once I thought so, but now I must honestly confess that I have no proof of the existence of even a single one. Perfect men must have existed in antique times, if the accounts which have descended to us are correct; they may even exist today, but in the course of my world wanderings I could not find them. I found remarkable men, who were perfect enough in their own line, but the broad mantle of realization did not seem to fit their shoulders. I have resigned myself, however, to the acceptance of the probability that the race of realized sages is extinct today.

377

Is there any man—no matter how spiritual or how well-meaning he may be—who could safely be trusted with *absolute* power over other men? It is this, along with other and more important observations, that has given me the courage to reject all spiritual authoritarianism. Some defect or some evil is mixed into each one of us. Imperfection is our natural lot here on earth. In a well-varied experience of my own species and in fairly wide wanderings through this world, I have never met a perfectly good, perfectly wise, and perfectly balanced man. That is to say, I must now lament with Confucius: "A sage I have no hope of ever seeing."

Sage not easily recognized

378

It is to live realization while behaving in the perfectly natural human way, and it is in this last sense that an old Oriental text describes the sage as bearing no distinguishing marks upon his person.

379

From the moment when the divine soul succeeds in taking full possession of a man's thought and feeling, will and flesh, his motives, words, acts, and desires become obscure and mysterious to other men.

380

It is quite customary to associate the term "sage" with some ancient gentleman whose long grey beard is supposed to make him as wise as his years. But an old man is not necessarily much wiser than a young one. Wisdom cannot be measured by the calendar. We should not respect the years but their fruit. If a man has found wisdom at the cost of his years, we should respect him. But we should not fall into the concealed if persuasive fallacy of respecting his beard. The term "sage" also gives rise in many minds to the picture of a creature belonging to an extinct species, a boring creature with pompous speech and portentous manner. Yet the lack of ability to laugh at themselves—and certainly the lack of any sense of humour at all—characterizes fools and not sages.

381

You may meet such a man daily over several weeks and yet know nothing of his mind, have no insight into his true character. This is because you do not have the high-grade quality of perceptiveness needed to sense him. There is no level of contact, no real communication between you and him.

382

Not every illuminated man has his status admitted and his knowledge recorded. Some have not been found out by the world until years after they have been dead.

383

If a man has found his divine soul and it has found him, he is thereby set free of the rules, restrictions, and disciplines which ascetically fence the life of a man who has not. The cigarette in his mouth cannot burn away the divine presence in his heart.

384

The illuminate does not have to engage in a lengthy conversation to find out whether another man is also illumined. As Chuang Tzu tells, two sages met without speaking a single word for "when their eyes met, the Tao was there."

385

One may achieve personal influence without gaining personal publicity. There are masters who prefer this kind of anonymity.

386

We project our own undeveloped minds into these sages, and then expect them to behave according to our own undeveloped ideal patterns. If we are disappointed, the blame rests with us.

387

All speculation upon the motives and the methods of the illuminate will avail little. The light by which he works is denied to ordinary men. We should not try to bind him down to qualities which fit only those who grope in the dark or move in twilight. We should trust where we cannot see and wait patiently for the day of revealment, when we will find all made clear and all riddles solved to our satisfaction. It is an old truism in the East that it takes an adept to understand an adept, but the West will have to learn this truth by bitter experience with pseudo-adepts.

388

There may be signs of his spiritual status in the dignity and composure of his bearing, the deliberateness and truthfulness of his speech, and the impressiveness of his tension-free face.

389

No adept presents himself to the public as such; it is for others to read the secret of his attainment. And since only those who have developed the same capacities as himself can read it, he usually remains obscure and unknown. He does not even seek to recruit disciples. He knows that the few who could absorb his help will come by destiny.

390

Spirituality in his aura is not always immediately recognizable although it is always indefinable. The effect he has upon those around him cannot be measured by its immediate result but only by its ultimate one.

391

The world can judge only by appearances and always judges the worst; the world can never hope to understand the independence of a man like him who will not hesitate to take on even the *appearance* of wrong whilst seeking to render service. Actually he has to subscribe to an infinitely higher ethic than conventional society can understand.

392

He will certainly be unpretentious and may even be unimpressive, but that will be only to the external eye. To those who can see with the mind, the heart, and the intuition, he will be a rare messenger of divinity.

393

We cannot dictate the external form in which he will express his attitude. The illuminate will do just that which is demanded of him by the particular circumstances of the case at that particular time and in that particular place. There is nothing arbitrary about his action.

394

Some behave as if they know nothing, these hidden illuminati.

395

Most of us are not in a position to judge either the inner being or outer behaviour of such a divinely illumined man.

396

People have these men of the spirit among them and do not know it, often do not care to know it.

397

His is indeed a life full of paradoxes. Outwardly he may be a millionaire. Inwardly he owns nothing, begs at the door of God.

398

It is written in some ancient Oriental text that among the signs whereby we may detect a person to be an Illumined One, the condition of the eyes is most important and that in such a person they will resemble a baby's.

399

The extent of any other man's enlightenment is not easily measurable, much less so in those cases where the other is no longer alive or has never been met.

400

It is easy to create an idealistic figure in imagination and declare that he would always act in such-and-such a way, but in actuality his actions are unpredictable and what they are can really be known only when they happen.

401

He knows truth, has penetrated to Reality, feels the Unseen Presence but, because he is in the world and not in meditation, plays a scene. He acts as if he were a worldling.

402

A true sage is more often than not unhurried in manner and slow in speech and eye-movement.

403

How superficial the mind, how futile the expectation which believes that when it meets an adept's body it meets the adept himself. The body may be insignificant in size, unattractive in appearance, frail in health, all that is visible being indeed in complete and deceptive contrast to the man ensouling it.

404

The sage lives a stranger life than we deem. His surroundings change miraculously. Poverty is no longer drab poverty, while where we can see only pain he also feels peace.

405

However large his accomplishment, it will still be mostly personal and private, unseen by the world.

406

Such a man has little respect for traditions and less obedience to rules.

407

Such a man can be put into no neat classifications, filed under no categories. The content of his mind is unknown, the course of his conduct unpredictable.

408

"Musk is known by its perfume and not by the apothecary's label."— Sheikh Saadi

409

"By their fruits ye shall know them." This test is still safe and sound. By it the true sage may be separated from false prophets.

410

Cryptic and enigmatic his conduct may be at times to the ordinary observer's eye, but good and wise it will always be to the spiritually discerning eye.

411

What is unpardonable in an ordinary person may be excusable in a sage.

412

Proximity to him will not necessarily give lucidity about him. His inner life will remain absolutely inscrutable to those who lack the power to penetrate it.

413

Those who try to read his degree by the atmospheric gauge of accumulated knowledge will be disappointed.

414

Too many naïvely expect him to be what he cannot be; too many look for a materialization of a highly imaginary fairy-tale figure of their own creation; too many wrongfully demand a miracle-working, supernaturally saint-like and sentimentally loving creature from another world. They unreasonably and unrealistically want him to look like a spectacular angel and behave like a god untroubled by human needs. Is it a surprise that they are disappointed when they find him to be just a human being, a real person, someone who, as Ramana Maharshi once said to us when this very point was being discussed, "does not wear two horns on his head!"

415

He really lives and moves on a plane where the eyes of the multitude cannot follow him.

416

Is it not in keeping with the elusive character of God that the Masters who have attained communion with God should themselves become elusive?

Isolation, privacy, reticence

417

It is my experience of world-wandering that those who most know truth are themselves the least known among men. This is partly because so few seek that kind of truth which is theirs—the highest—partly because it is their own wish to remain inaccessible to all except these few seekers, and partly because their completely ego-free character is utterly without any ambition to put themselves forward in public under any pretext whatsoever, whether to gain the benefits and advantages of such a position or to practise so-called service.

418

However eager a Master may be to reveal truth, he is forced, by the indifference and miscomprehension of the world, to conceal it.

419

It is not an isolation due to arrogance, to too high a notion of his own status. It is the others who are really apart, by their animalism or egotism.

420

He is not alien to humanity but only alien to what is low and bestial in humanity.

421

If the adepts live in such splendid isolation, it is because they have to balance their greatly increased sensitivity in this way. It is not through any conceited sense of personal superiority that they keep apart from others. They are entitled to an environment which least opposes them, least emits discords at every thought, and most harmonizes with their nature and habits. They must themselves create such an environment: the world can not offer it. Thus the paradox arises that because they have entered into secret unity with all men, the adepts must stand aloof from all men!

422

The custodians of this knowledge may have the appearance of living aloof from the human race, but it is appearance only.

423

When he is among those who do not understand, nothing will shake his reserve on these truths. What else can such a man do but give only the surface of himself, only a part of his knowledge to them? If they are too insensitive to feel the subtle presence that he feels, and too self-enclosed to be interested in it, he can at least keep it from being profaned by sceptical remarks or sneering criticisms. The humble, who are not developed enough to understand but are willing to give their faith, may share his treasure to a limited extent; but the arrogant, who are too educated or too earthy to understand, may not. He is not hiding behind a mask—for he can still be sincere in all his talk or traffic with them—rather, he is keeping back his deepest self from full free expression.

424

The men who can save society are those whom it knows least and disdains most. They are men who have found out its shallowness and meanness and turned their faces toward Truth. They live aside and are not to be found in the ranks of clergymen, as a rule, for the latter help to pillar and prop society's crumbling edifice in order to save their jobs. But the men who have uncovered life, who can provide society with insight and foresight, make no attempt to press upon the public attention. When the world wants them, it will search for them. They can afford to bide their time for they know food is only for the hungry.

425

Even in the outer life, he and his kind must be reserved and withdrawn; it cannot be helped. He cannot descend any more to the residence of the inwardly shabby, the intuitionally destitute.

426

Although he identifies himself with their true welfare, he manages to keep himself detached from their personal affairs.

427

We humans are a race of walking and working somnambulists. Only the illuminate is really awake.

428

He finds the mass of humanity goes on as complacently unaware of its spiritual need as ever. It does not want the truth he has, but only the truth that suits, comforts, and preserves its ego. It wants a label, and he is as unlabelled as the wind which "bloweth where it listeth." The more original his presentation of the truth, the deeper the source from which he draws it, the less do most people, with their mass-conditioned minds, want it.

429

It is not the prophet himself who is conscious of his place in history but those in the circle around him, those who follow long after he is dead, and those who write about him. For the sense of mission, the relationship with past and future generations, the work to be done in the present epoch—all these things belong to the ego's thoughts about itself, to the concern with self. He is satisfied to let himself be used by the Overself, to abandon all care about them into its hands, to go where he is bidden and to do what he is urged to do. The thirst for fame and the striving of ambition are totally absent from such a man.

430

How can he crimp and cramp his private sense of truth within the narrow limits of some man's opinion? The strange infinitude of mind overpowers him, the mystic reaches of the Unknown haunt him continually; how then is he to walk into some mental prison and keep company with the spiritual captives of his time?

431

He stands outside all this drama and watches it as a spectator, sometimes with a slight smile of pleasure, sometimes with a mild frown of distress, never with a hard cold attitude but always with a settled resignation to the decree of karma or the will of Allah. If, now and then, he suggests a movement, a change, or a view-expanding idea to one of the actors, it is not to be regarded as an act of interference but as itself part of the person's own karma, or the higher will's grace.

432

He is neither unduly uncommunicative nor the reverse. He understands the need of respecting evolutionary need, rejects the theory of universal equality, and practises the discipline of speech. But his compassion is always active, his willingness to share truth and give blessing never absent. If in the presence of the Overself he realizes the futility of human speech about it, in the presence of groping, seeking, suffering men he holds back no word which will comfort, guide, or inspire.

433

If the sage gives the inner help which men need, he does so with no desire and no expectation of reward, as a physician might reasonably expect. He gives out of the fullness of his heart, out of his extraordinary capacity for sympathy through self-identification with others. But this may not often be understood, first, because he will not desert his habitual calm to put on an emotional display at the bidding of convention, and second, because he consults with wisdom as to what he shall do, which is not always what people want him to do.

434

The sage who works for the good of humanity must respect his own definition of good and his own knowledge of the best way to work. Otherwise, he would be no better than the social reformer, the statesman, the clergyman, and the moralist—he would have only an intellectual or emotional understanding of life, and not a mystical and integral one.

435

Do not reproach him for his reserve. He is ready to share and share generously. But it must be done in his way, at his time, and according to *his* circumstances. For his perception is unclouded by the ego, and yours is not. For when you make your demand on him, remember that there are many others making a similar demand.

436

He tries so to live as to acquit himself honourably before God rather than before men. He has lived long enough to hear many who once praised him, now abuse him. Hence he has lived long enough to know that unless he remains uniformly serene and inwardly detached from the world's opinion, there can be no true happiness for him. He has been taught by the Overself to stand unmoved by the disloyalties of so-called friends and the defections of short-sighted followers. He is too wise and experienced to expect either real justice or correct understanding from them. It will not be possible for them to understand him or his point of view or his logic by a mere exchange of words, so he refrains from attempting what is so useless.

437

Suffice that he replies with silence. If people cannot read that silence, cannot understand who and what he is from inner being alone, then they must go to the gossips, the critics, the enemies, and misunderstanders of him for an interpretation of his character, motives, and record. They will then take appearances for reality, and delude themselves and others. Therefore it is that with most of humanity he has and can have nothing to do. Occasionally he meets one who reads him with the inner sight, who speaks his wordless language, and then they recognize each other. For the rest, each descent from his solitude into society nails him to the cross.

438

It is not only that they feel so much at odds with the world that they stand aside from it and refrain from mixing in its society. It is as much or more that they have found a way of life which seems to them the best, the truest and the most spiritually profitable. They feel it essential to follow this way wheresoever it leads them, and whether in or out of society.

439

The sage will not need to advertise himself as such. People who are sensitive or discerning will come in time to recognize his rare inspiring quality. Others who are in vital need of the peace that emanates from him or of the truth that fills his words will learn, sooner or later, by some way or another, of his existence and beat a path or send a letter to his door.

440

The same lofty realization which brings him down to serve his fellow men, isolates him from them at the same time.

441

There is a wall between the adept and his detractors. They built it. They themselves must remove it. Nobody can do this for them, not even he. They must undo their self-perpetrated wrongs.

442

He is among the great solitary spirits of mankind, yet he can never be called lonely for in himself he is always sufficient.

443

He is forced to live among people who are mostly several hundred earth-lives younger than he, and consequently quite "unsympathetic" (in the European-Continental meaning of the term).

444

Whether he keeps in touch with human affairs or keeps away from them is a matter which is entirely personal in his view and dependent on time, place, circumstance, and need. He is not dogmatic about it, whether for himself or others, and would certainly not quarrel with them over it.

445

He has no need to acquaint others with the exalted nature of his insight, much less publicize it to the world at large. Just quietly being what he is will be enough. This will screen him from those who sneer, criticize, or attack: but the sensitive will appreciate him.

446

A Chinese proverb of antiquity says, "A dragon in shallow waters becomes the butt of shrimps." Hence, the illuminate does not advertise his sagehood, make a noise about his wisdom, or shout his power in public, but lets most men believe he is just like them. "The Tathagata (teacher) is the same to all, and yet knowing the requirements of every single being, he does not reveal himself to all alike. He pays attention to the disposition of various beings," said Buddha.

447

If the adepts prefer not to live with or near people, there are good and sufficient reasons for it. If their homes are exclusive, their contacts restricted, if they avoid familiarity, it is because their attainment has been paid for by their sensitivity. Truly has it been said that the gulf between the bad man and the good man is not so wide as the gulf between the good man and the adept.

448

Is there a moral obligation on him to share his knowledge with others?

In a sense there is. But he sees that their moral limitations and spiritual apathy restricts and cramps any activity in this direction. Also he learns that being himself is his best activity.

449

His power of keeping his knowledge a secret from those who are unready for or uninterested in it is perfect. Nothing in his words or manner may lead them to think that he knows immensely more than he tells them.

450

He knows how to protect his status well. In the presence of sceptics and scoffers, or the unevolved and unready, neither his outward manner nor his uttered talk will give any hint of it.

451

With all his reclusive habits, the sage is compassionate in temperament, benevolent in personality. Even when he avoids men, he does not hate them.

452

They feel tense, uneasy, and unsure in the presence of a superior class of beings. This he knows by experience and this is one reason why he keeps apart and alone; yet paradoxically it is also why he is kinder to them than a situation calls for, why he then behaves as if he were an equal and not on a different level.

453

In one sense his consciousness is insulated by its own superior quality from that of others, but in another sense it fleetingly registers or lengthily holds their states through his compassion, sympathy, or understanding.

454

He has no intention of meddling in other people's personal lives, no conceit that his duty is to change them, no willingness to take on responsibility for them. He commits them to the Overself and commends them to it. But this done, if intuitively or rationally he is led to suggest a purpose or remind them of a truth or point to a beneficial course or utter a warning, he will obey the leading—but always in response to their approach.

455

He is happier to move through this world incognito, if fate will let him, than celebrated.

456

Most people are always more impressed by outward show than by inner worth. But when the show is philanthropic service and benevolent activity dramatically performed, they are even more impressed. The recognition and appreciation are immediate. The man whose inner stillness admits spiritual forces into his surroundings remains unnoticed.

457

The readiness with which he once plunged into other people's affairs to help them, as he believed, will dissolve and disappear. He knows now that their real troubles remain unaffected by this surface aid, that meddling in their problems is not the right way.

458

He is surrounded by an aura which makes him seem more remote than he really is, which isolates him and overwhelms others.

459

It would be easy to surround himself with a crowd of fawning disciples and flattering admirers. But he could not accept such a role because he knows that they will refuse to let him be himself and will expect him to be different from what he really is.

460

He does not care to face an attitude which is hostile or indifferent; he does not even need to talk to men who begin by disbelieving him.

461

No sage looks proudly down on others from his pedestal, but that does not alter the distance that extends from their ignorance to his knowledge.

462

He does not require idolatrous homage from them, and indeed shrinks from it. His unaffected nature renders him desirous of being treated no better than others.

463

Without wearing the monk's robe, or the eccentric's long hair, he passes among men a hidden existence, a secret inner life.

464

The conventional world is so tied to, and therefore so deceived by, appearances, that it is only a tiny handful of people who meet such a man with the understanding and sympathy he deserves.

465

It is not personal desire which makes him refrain from communicating himself to others, but public circumstances. In this he obeys the Greek verse, "When to be wise is all in vain, be not wise at all." Why should he communicate the oracles of heaven to those whose minds run only to trivialities?

466

The illuminate prefers to pull strings from behind the curtain of obscurity.

467

He does not want to impose himself where he may not be wanted. He does not want to intrude on the mental privacy of others.

468

It is this quality of remoteness in him which baffles some people, provokes others, antagonizes many, but attracts a few. It makes him profoundly different from the average man, foreign to him and hard to understand.

469

The adept is built too high for ordinary men to appreciate him and too remote for them to understand him. It is inevitable that he should dwell isolated and aloof from all except those whose great aims justify the contact.

470

He will descend into the arena of this world only by the direct order of his Overself.

471

He dwells apart in solitude. Why? The world could not grant the existence of his tremendous modesty, his perfect poise, his freedom from chatter, his vast self-restraint, and so, failing to understand, it would misunderstand.

472

He prefers to remain anonymous, but if the mission requires it, he submits to publicity's glare.

473

Restrained in speech, withdrawn in self, he comes out of his inner world to meet his fellows only so far, and therefrom will not further descend. For it is a lofty world.

474

If, in their discretion, they suppress their true beliefs and hide their inmost mind from the masses as behind a veil, it must be granted that both history and psychology justify this caution.

475

They are reluctant to tell others about their inmost experiences; some even refuse absolutely to admit they have had such experiences if the questioner is unsympathetic or uncomprehending.

476

His rare experience, his precious wisdom, his special knowledge of life's higher laws are not put on parade to impress others. Rather does he behave among them as if he were, had, knew nothing exceptional.

Sage is usually misunderstood

477

The sage's enlightenment, like the man himself, eludes the unenlightened observer, who can not comprehend this kind of man, and so usually ends by misunderstanding him.

478

Such a man cannot help having his detractors, for people can see only what he permits them to see. And if that small part is misread by them, he has to remain silent. He will not force an affinity where it does not exist. They may have visited him and talked with him, not once but several times; they may think they know him well, yet in reality they have not met him and do not know him at all! Only the real pilgrims, who come with the correct mental attitude, have done so, and only they have been blessed by his grace and prized their good fortune at its correct value.

479

He must be prepared to find that others, because of their limitations— not necessarily or at all because they are evil—may seriously misunderstand him, misread his actions, and misinterpret his words.

480

Whoever has attained this blessed state would not be true to himself if he were not ardently happy to share it with others, if he were not ever ready to help them attain it too. And this desire extends universally to all without exception. He excludes none—how could he if the compassion which he feels be the real thing that comes with the realized unity of the Overself, that is, of the Christ-self, and not merely a temporary emotional masquerader! He himself could have written those noble words which Saint Paul wrote more than once in his epistles: "In Him there cannot be Jew or Greek, Barbarian, Scythian, but all are one man in Christ Jesus." Despite this, he soon finds that iron fetters have been placed on his feet. He finds, first, that only the few who are themselves seekers are at all interested; second, that even among this small number there are those who, because of personal dislikes, racial prejudice, social snobbery, or family antagonism, are unwilling to approach him; and third, that the mischievous agencies from occult spheres, through false reports and stimulated malice, delude a part of those who remain into creating an evil mental picture of him which is utterly unlike the actuality. For when such a man really begins to become an effective worker in this sacred cause, the evil forces begin their endeavours to pull him down and thus stop him. They may inspire human instruments with fierce jealousy or personal hatred of him, or they may try other ways. It is their task to destroy the little good that he has done or to prevent whatever good he may yet do. It is an unfortunate but historic fact that many an aspirant is carried away by the false suggestions emanating from such poisoned sources.

481
The true Prophet does not wear a single rag of the cloak of pretense. Therefore, he makes an easy mark for the poisoned arrows of his traducers. For the world does not willingly believe that a man can exist who tries to live his life literally on the principles of Christ's Sermon on the Mount. It prefers to believe that he has some hidden motive, that he lives a life of secret evil.

482
Those who do not know what the inward life means and consequently do not understand such a man—walking mantled in unique serenity as he does—often mistakenly regard him, if they themselves are of a markedly emotional temperament, as being cold, aloof, and reserved.

483
Another common mistake is to believe a sage to be less divine because he is more human than preconceived notions had imagined him to be.

484
The adepts are not creatures of sentimentalism. They do not love their neighbour in a gushy emotional way. How could they, when he expresses only his lower human nature or his beastly animal self? Not only do they not love humanity individually, they do not even love it in the mass.

485
Those who have malignantly attacked the person or injured the work of such a man through whom the divine forces are working for the enlightenment of mankind, create for themselves a terrible karma which accumulates and strikes them down in time. He himself will endeavour to protect his work by appropriate means, one being temporarily to withdraw his love from them for the rest of his incarnation until their dying moments. Then he will extend it again with full force and appear to them as in a vision, full of forgiveness, blessing, and comfort.(P)

486
Can those born blind be made to understand the difference between colours? The difficulty is insuperable. Realizing this, Emerson said: "Every

man's words, who speak from that life, must sound vain to those who do not dwell in the same thought on their own part."

487

There is a warmth, an intimacy in the Personal God, the Personal Master, which does not seem to exist in the impersonal ones. Nevertheless it would be highly erroneous to believe that they are cold and unresponsive, lifeless and stonelike. There *is* feeling but it is pure, refined, delicate, and flowerlike.

488

The illumined man gives himself, the ignorant one gives his possessions. If they are judged by appearances only, the truth of the situation will become reversed, and falsity will appear as truth. That is, the illumined man will seem the most uncharitable.

489

The master's motive may easily remain unknown to others, especially when he has a mission to fulfil for them, and by this ignorance they may just as easily misunderstand his actions. If this happens and they turn away from him, an opportunity for their higher growth will be missed. The distorted reading of his actions will also cause them to judge him unfairly and incorrectly. He will accept this injustice as part of the price of descending into an evil world where he does not really belong.

490

To expect from such a man at all times and in all places, as both sceptics and followers often expect, a pharisaical propriety of conduct simply shows how little they have comprehended the perfect selflessness and utter purity of his character. For they expect him to behave rigidly according to the patterns of conventional morality, although these are not always sincere or generous or wise. Because his guidance must come from within, from his diviner consciousness and not from outside, from a society led by its ego consciousness, there will be occasions when his actions will not conform to these patterns. And this is so in spite of the fact that he knows well, and obeys where possible, the requirement that he shall set an example to others. His nonconformity will then be denounced or misunderstood, reviled or viewed with bewilderment.

491

There are those who lightly appraise such a man's spiritual worth by the superficial signs which accident throws their way or by the stories gossip brings to their ears. They are wasting their time.

492

To offer no contradiction to false or slanderous statements made by others in their presence about a Spiritual teacher, is silently to consent to such criticism.

493

It is such a man who most serves his fellows yet who least receives the recognition of his service. This is because humanity fails to understand where its true interests lie, what its true goal is, and why it is here at all.

494

He will be the victim on one side of friendly enthusiasts who credit him with powers and adorn him with virtues which he does not possess, and on the other side of prejudiced enemies who malign him with motives and besmirch him with weaknesses which are wholly foreign to his temperament.

495

His illusionless life may not seem attractive to the mass of people who cannot afford the high cost of truth.

496

Too long has the word "Master" been bandied on the lips of people; they talk of the "Master" as of a politician—setting up to judge him or making wild statements about him or letting their imaginations run loose about him. It is not right that the Illuminati should be discussed so lightly and it is far better to let them remain as Illuminati to be thought of in silent hours of meditation and not to be analysed at our tea-tables as we analyse the events of the day.

497

Fools make complaint that the Prophet brings to them this old message of the eternal Deity that waits to light all human hearts and brings nothing new or fit for this age and hour. We may make a preamble to our answer with the statement that he indubitably gives such scientific and practical turn to his teachings as the time demands, but we must admit that his first and last words remain ever the same as the first and last words of all the illustrious divine teachers. For what other message can he give? When the soul hungers for a happiness it has hitherto been unable to find in its mud-pits of sensuality or in its marketplaces of barter, is he to offer it a stone of some economic doctrine and not the bread of spiritual nourishment? Is he come to confirm our self-deceptions and our self-grovellings and to give the lie to the divine bliss he enjoys every moment?

498

His continual serenity, his unemotional manner may draw the admiration of the discerning few, but it will also provoke the exasperation of the undiscerning many.

499

By what measure can they judge in reality which is unseen and not in illusion, the moral rectitude of a man who has been sent among them with a mission, who has not only secretly dissolved his human "I" but has secretly taken and faithfully kept the monk's renunciatory vows?

500

The vast reticence of such a man will be respected by those who are sensitive but may infuriate those who are not.

501

Because of the many *seeming* contradictions in his nature he may be much misunderstood by others.

502

Humanity venerates the memory of these prophets, but in decreasing degree. For they incarnate values, attainments, and qualities which most people feel are far above any likelihood of their own coming even remotely near.

503

Contrary to common belief, the illuminate is not a joyless griefless man who has crushed all human affection, sterilized all human feelings, sunk himself in physical inertia, and habituated himself to insensitivity toward the sufferings of others.

504

Such a man cannot be really known by those who have not themselves touched his height; part of him—the most important and precious part— must always remain an inscrutable stranger to them.

505

To one observer such a man seems to live inside himself, to another outside himself. To the first, he is held fast to some internal power; to the second, he is constantly practising self-identification with others.

506

His followers expect too much from him, perhaps because they credit him with powers far beyond what he does possess. This leads to a measure of disappointment.

507

If others think him aloof, cold, even unsympathetic, they may go further and misunderstand him. He is not shut stonily in his ego, as they think, but on the contrary, is much freer from it than they are.

508

It is possible that his actions sometimes puzzle those who put their trust in him. Those who judge only by appearances may be surprised and aggrieved at his seeming indifference. But with the efflux of time they may get to know more or all of the facts, and then their puzzlement will vanish.

509

They come to inspect the great soul, the Mahatma, as if they could really see him. They bring out their measuring equipment and pronounce verdict on his littleness or greatness. Their opinion is based on an appearance that is a possible illusion.

510

Just as Pythagoras and Socrates were maligned and even put to death by those who either misunderstood or misrepresented their teachings, so Epicurus, another Greek, has been maligned ever since his own time, although he fortunately died a natural death. Incidentally, he died of the stone. It could be that there was an excess of calcium in his body and that it had got concentrated in the wrong place, producing the stone in the bladder or the kidney—for he tried to live a simple life and ate only barley, bread, and cheese and drank only water. There was probably an excess of cheese in his diet, producing the excess of calcium. However the point I wish to make is that he is supposed to have preached heathenism, the pursuit of pleasure and enjoyment as being the highest good, but the truth is, as demonstrated by his simple life, that he was an ascetic. He did not believe in cluttering himself up with a lot of possessions and he sought the freedom from anxiety which this gave him. The freedom from those desires for luxuries and comforts which fill most people left him with a serene mind. This serenity was enjoyable and pleasant; so what he meant by pleasure was a pleasure of living the good life, not the pleasure of living the animal life. But if he is to be judged by his diet, his philosophy was incomplete and imbalanced.

511

Because he ever practises calmness, other persons may think him to be indifferent to them, to what is happening, and to his own actions, as if he were performing them somewhat casually; but in this they would be mistaken. For the detachment within him lies deep down and consists in a general attitude towards worldly life based upon knowledge, understanding, philosophy. He is not heedless but attentive, not unresponsive but touched by situations calling for sympathy, not neutral where right or wrong are concerned, not neglectful of duties and responsibilities, not care*less* in work but care*free*.

512

Suffering is real and painful when it comes. The sage is not heartless to its appearance in other people, but he understands it somewhat better than they do.

513

Such a man has enigma and paradox between him and the world's understanding.

514

It is easy for the populace to be deceived by his unassuming manners and unpretentious speech into thinking him to be anything but what he really is.

515

One and the same Master will appear to his followers as an incarnation of God, but to the worldly wise as a lunatic, if not a fraud. None of these views may be correct.

516

Although the sage can understand the points of view of the fool, the ignoramus, the worldling, and the bigot, they cannot understand his own.

517

It is the wise guidance of the Overself which persuades such a man to walk indifferently by when his name is vilified and to hold his tongue when his character is slandered.

518

Those who do not understand and appreciate this great control of feeling, and especially those who are highly emotional themselves, will see him merely from the outside and consequently misunderstand his character. They will consider him to be a cold, shut-in type.

519

The world will assess his motives at the lowest level, interpret his actions in the basest way. If he were to let it rot in its own ignorance, he would be well justified.

520

To evaluate the work and word of these men is to judge by appearances alone. For there is in both an incalculable element, a hidden worth.

521

The initiate does not waste his time in arguing with others, either to attack their beliefs or defend his Own.

522

If he seems outwardly distant and indifferent, we should understand that his distance and his indifference are not egoistic, and consequently are worthy of close examination and deep study. They contain a mystery as well as a paradox. For in his heart there flows, side by side, both a pure love for humanity and an utter detachment from humanity. It is in the very nature of his attainment of a true philosopher's status that he should be able to fulfil himself only by going beyond all selves—ours as well as his own.

Sages merit veneration

523

The world should be more grateful for the presence of such men. The good they do is mostly indirect, however, through intermediaries, or mostly hidden because psychological, so it escapes the world's notice.

524

Light the lamp and it will spread out its rays by itself. We are indeed blessed by the presence of these great souls on this earth and doubly so if we meet in person. They deserve not merely our respect but our veneration. But even if we are never fortunate enough to meet one of these masters, the mere knowledge that such men do exist and live demonstrates the possibility of spiritual achievement and proves that the quest is no chimera. It should comfort and encourage us to know this. Therefore we should regard such a man as one of humanity's precious treasures. We should cherish his name as a personal inspiration. We should venerate his sayings or writings as whispers out of the eternal silence.(P)

525

Such rare peace stands out in poignant contrast against the burdens and fretfulness of our ordinary lives. Such rare goodness is needed by a generation accustomed to violence, atrocity, bestiality and horror, lunacy and hatred.(P)

526

The World-Mind does not fully declare its intentions toward us humans but does give us enough inkling of them through the teachers and prophets of the race.

527

These great souls who have ascended to another plane of being altogether have sent us signals from that distant sphere. It is for us to heed those signals and to understand their meaning.

528

The knowledge of someone far better than oneself shows human possibilities. The longing to become like him provides one with an ideal for living.

529

The examples of good men help us when we compare ourselves with them, and especially our worst with their best.

530

History has honoured those individuals who have gone into the far places of this globe and explored them. It is now time to honour those who have gone deep, not far, within themselves and explored consciousness.

531

A real need of humanity eventually finds its expression in flesh and blood. Just as an oppressive tyranny ultimately produces the rebel who overthrows it, so a growing hunger for spiritual guidance ultimately brings forth those who are to provide it.

532

Those who have lavished their devotion on such an ideal, have lavished it wisely.

533

Just as Jesus was in reality greater than the rabbis whose unquestioned authority dominated the people of Israel, so any man today who reflects in all its purity the Overself's light, unshadowed by his personal opinions, is in reality greater than the impressively robed dignitaries of Church and State.

534

Philosophy views the various departments of world-activity from their standpoint as a *whole*. This rare synthetic outlook, this magnificent breadth of vision, this unique coordination of the entire panorama of life, enables the mystical philosopher to suggest the wisest courses of action to his fellow beings. Those who direct States put themselves and their people in moral peril if they ignore or despise his value.

535

We have paid, and are still paying, a heavy price for our comfortable conviction that the philosophic illuminate is a fool, to whom it is unnecessary to pay serious attention.

536

It is such men who ought to be made, not the leaders of mankind, but the counsellors to the leaders.

537

A single meeting with such a man brings forth our involuntary respect. A long association with him brings forth our loving devotion also.

538

If anyone brings him homage or reverence he takes it, not to himself but to the Unseen Higher Power, before whom he lays it.

539

Most men make their appeal to authority and are constantly at pains to quote letter and script for their words; others will gaze into their own glasses of vision and report upon the reflections of Truth that they descry within: but the illuminated ones live the life and so declare only that which they have experienced themselves; indeed what they say comes as from on high for us.

540

Those who inspire us to better ourselves, certainly deserve our gratitude and even deserve our love.

541

Every minute taken from the time of an illumined worker is selfishly taken from many other persons who may be in much greater need of it. It is a mistake to equate the time-measure of such a man with the average one by requesting "just a few minutes" for that is really equal to an entire day robbed from his time work, for which he was born and to which he ought to remain loyal and fully committed. Of course I do not refer here to those illuminati whose work is expressly done through personal contact with individuals or groups face-to-face, but to those who labour in studios, study-rooms, or benevolent meditation. If anyone really and truly admires them, or is grateful to them, and wishes to give form to his feeling, to the fact known, he will do better by writing a letter needing no physical plane answer and not by obstructing their work.

542

The great masters who taught men truth or gave them supreme works of art or lifted their feelings deserve a large gratitude for such benedictions.

543

It is those who create ways and means for others to follow in the search for spiritual fulfilment, the teachers and awakeners, who deserve our best honours.

544

Such a man is a focal-point for all that is noble.

545

A nature sensitive to the serenity, benevolence, and wisdom radiating from such a man will gladly give its homage to him.

546

It is a grave mistake made by ignorant persons or by proud ones to fail in holding such a man in deep veneration.

547

The gods keep a vacant seat for him in the high places, while simple men and women throw unseen roses of appreciation when he enters their orbit.

548

We should listen to the plain statements of such a man as the old Greeks listened to the enigmatic utterances of their Oracles.

549

Socrates tried to awaken the Greeks, Jesus tried to awaken the Israelites. Their failure was followed by consequences to their people which can be traced in history. If the higher power takes the trouble to send a messenger, it is better to tremble, listen, and obey than to sneer, reject, and suffer.

550

The comments made by sages upon the varied situations in human life are worth far far more than the commentaries written by pundits on the sacred or philosophic texts. The former are very much in a minority.

551

What he is testifies to THAT WHICH IS. Where lesser men have to shout their opinions, his silence is eloquent and, to the receptive, an initiation in itself.

552

There is no such act as a one-sided self-giving. Karma brings us back our due. He who spends his life in the dedicated service of philosophic enlightenment may reject the merely material rewards that this service could bring him, but he cannot reject the beneficent thoughts, the loving remembrances, the sincere veneration which those who have benefited sometimes send him. Such invisible rewards help him to atone more peacefully and less painfully for the strategic errors he has made, the tactical shortcomings he has manifested. Life is an arduous struggle for most people, but much more so for such a one who is always a hated target for the unseen powers of darkness. Do not hesitate to send him your silent humble blessing, therefore, and remember that Nature will not waste it. The enemies you are now struggling against within yourself he has already conquered, but the enemies he is now struggling against are beyond your present experience. He has won the right to sit by a hearth of peace. If he has made the greatest renunciation and does not do so, it is for your sake and for the sake of those others like you.(P)

4

THE SAGE'S SERVICE

A full identity of interest

The *Bodhisattva* is one who pledges himself to the spiritual service of ignorant unawakened mankind. For this ideal he sacrifices himself to the point of stopping his own liberation just when it is about to be realized.

2

The man who is delivered from sin and freed from illusion, who is emancipated from suffering for all time because the flesh can catch him no more, has earned the right to infinite rest in the eternal Void. But he has also the power to choose otherwise. He may stop at its very threshold and renounce the reward it offers. Since the phenomenal world has nothing to offer him, the only reason for such a choice can be compassionate thought for the benighted creatures he is about to leave behind.

3

If he refrains from the final mergence into *Nirvana*, it is not only because he wants to be available for the enlightenment of his more hapless fellows, but also because he knows that he has really been in *Nirvana* from the beginning and has never left it.

4

Among those who have attained this higher life, who feel its power and sense its peace, there are some who wish that others shall attain it too. We say *some* for the very powerful reason that not all are able to find it in their hearts to return to this bleak earth of ours, with its sickness and darkness, its sins and sufferings, its evil and ignorance, when there stretches invitingly before them the portals of a diviner world, with its sublime harmony and beauty, its burden-free peace and goodness. This is why Krishna is reported in the *Bhagavad Gita* as declaring that the greatest sacrifice man can offer is that of wisdom, which means simply that the enlightened man should give *himself* and use his wisdom for the benefit of others. This is also why Buddha asserted that the greatest charity is to give the truth to mankind. Therefore, the noblest sages give themselves secretly and concentratively to a few or openly and widely to the many to enlighten, guide, and inspire them. They know that this twofold way is the one in which to help mankind, that public work is not enough, that those who wish to do not only the most widespread good in the time open to them but also the most enduring good, must work deeply and secretly amongst a few who have dedicated themselves to immediate or eventual service in their own turn. Thus, compassion is rendered more effective through being guided by intelligence. To the few in the inner circle, the sage transmits his best thought, his hidden knowledge, his special grace, his most mystical power. How grand is the service such a sage can render all those who accept the light of his knowledge! Then indeed is he, in Shakespeare's phrase, "The star to every wandering barque."

5

Do not fall into the error of believing that, if he speaks openly these doctrines to others, or writes of them publicly, he is seeking to make proselytes. The religious missionary eagerly seeks to do so, but the philosophic expounder cannot. This is because he is not governed by the emotional desire to witness a large number of conversions but by the clear understanding of evolutionary operations—an understanding which enables him to see what is and is not possible, what is and is not suitable, at each stage of those operations. He is not, like the missionary, seeking any personal satisfaction by making an emotional or intellectual conquest.

6

The illuminate has a cosmic outlook. He thinks and feels for all creatures no less than for himself.

7

Do you think that these ancient illuminati, full of high intimations and carrying great lights in their hands, appeared before the world out of their silence and solitude to suffer its ridicule and contempt because they wished to brag about themselves or to amaze them? They came because they dared not disobey compassion's call save at the pain of being false to all that they knew to be true.

8

The sage makes the highest conceivable sacrifice in willing to return to earthly life for times without end solely for the benefit of all creatures.

9

People sometimes ask why anyone should give up even a part of his time to unpaid service. But the truth is that the sage is always paid by the friendship and gratitude, the trust and affection, which those he has helped return him. And if it be further said that these are mere intangibles which do not pay for the time and energy he gives, the answer is that they often are convertible into the most tangible of things. For if he is in real need of a home, a machine, a piece of domestic furniture, or a form of personal service, he has only to express that need and those whom he has helped will provide it. Nay, there are times when he need not even express it, when the silent magic of thought will prompt someone to offer the provision quite spontaneously and voluntarily. Anyway, the sage does not give his service with any thought about the getting or non-getting of rewards. He gives it because he thinks it right to do so and because he enjoys the satisfaction of giving a helping hand to the spiritually needy. In short, he is doing what he likes.

10

When a man has attained this stage of perfection he may truly rest, for Nature has achieved her task in him. Yet, if he chooses the path of sage-hood he must henceforth work harder than ever before! For he must now work incessantly through repeated rebirths for the enlightenment of others.

11

Whether or not a man will serve humanity after he attains self-realization is not an attitude he can completely decide upon or predetermine before he attains it. For the matter is then surely taken out of his hands altogether.

12

The question whether he shall share his knowledge with others or withhold it from them, will not be a real one to him. Its answer was settled long before, by destiny, by his character, by his past, by the World-Idea.

13

Helping others to attain what he has attained, guiding seekers to reach safely the glorious summit where he now stands, is not decided for him by personal temperament or choice but by the overpowering sense of a primary and paramount duty.

14

We are asked: What is the interpretation of a sentence in that excellent little book *Light on the Path* by Mabel Collins, which runs "For within you is the light of the world—the only light that can be shed upon the Path. If you are unable to perceive it within you, it is useless to look for it elsewhere. It is beyond you; because when you reach it you have lost yourself. It is unattainable because it forever recedes. You will enter the light but you will never touch the flame."

The meaning of this mysterious sentence is that the sage refuses to claim the ultimate mergence which is his right because he refuses to desert "the great orphan Humanity." He stops short at the very threshold of Nirvana simply to remain here and help others reach that threshold. Thus by his altruistic activity, meditative power, and intellectual penetration he continuously earns a title to that utter absorption of his ego in the unutterable Absolute which is Nirvana, but by his continuous self-giving for suffering mankind he never actually attains this goal. This extraordinary situation may be represented mathematically by the asymptote—a line which is drawn on a graph to approach nearer and nearer to a given curve but which never actually touches it within a finite distance. Only a man who feels with and for his fellow creatures will dare to make such a tremendous sacrifice of the supreme peace which he has won. How much more generous, how nobly grander is this example of ever-active altruistic service than that of ever-idle meditative reclusiveness!(P)

15

The sage will not be primarily concerned with his own personal welfare, but then he will also not be primarily concerned with mankind's welfare. Both these duties find a place in his outlook, but they do not find a primary place. This is always filled by a single motive: to do the will, to express the inspiration of that greater self of which he is sublimely aware and to which he has utterly surrendered himself. This is a point whereon many students get confused or go astray. The sage does not stress altruism as the supreme value of life, nor does he reject egoism as the lowest value of life. He will act as the Overself bids him in each case, egotistically if it so wishes or altruistically if it so declares, but he will always act for its sake as the principal aim and by its light as the principal means.(P)

16

It is not enough for the illuminate when the veil falls and the inner meaning of universal life is read. His efforts do not come to such an abrupt end. For he does not consider his own salvation complete while others remain unsaved. Consequently, he dedicates himself to the task of trying to save them. But in order to do this he has to reincarnate on earth innumerable times. For men can attain the goal here alone and nowhere else. This changes the whole concept of salvation. It is no longer a merely personal matter but a collective one. It also alters the concept of survival. This is no longer a prolonged enjoyment of post-death heavenly spheres but a prolonged labour through countless earthly lives for the service of one's fellow-creatures. And yet, even this sombre path bears its own peculiar rewards. For he shall receive the fraternal love of those who have been healed, the encouraging thoughts of those who are beginning to find a foothold in life, the pledged loyalty of those who want to share, with their lesser strength, the heavy burden through untold incarnations.

17

Bergson was right. His acute French intelligence penetrated like an eagle's sight beneath the world-illusion and saw it for what it is—a cosmic process of continual change which never comes to an end, a universal movement whose first impetus and final exhaustion will never be known, a flux of absolute duration and therefore unimaginable. And for the sage who attains to the knowledge of THAT which forever seems to be changing but forever paradoxically retains its own pure reality, for him as for the ignorant, the flux must go on. But it will go on here on this earth, not in the same mythical heaven or mirage-like hell. He will repeatedly have to take flesh, as all others will have to, so long as duration lasts, that is, forever. For he cannot sit apart like the yogi while his compassion is too profound to waste itself in mere sentiment. It demands the profound expression of sacrificial service in motion. His attitude is that so clearly described by a nineteenth-century agnostic whom religionists once held in horror, Thomas Huxley: "We live in a world which is full of misery and ignorance, and the plain duty of each and all of us is to try to make the little corner he can influence somewhat less miserable and somewhat less ignorant than it was before he entered it." The escape into Nirvana for him is only the escape into the inner realization of the truth whilst alive: it is not to escape from the external cycle of rebirths and deaths. It is a change of attitude. But that bait had to be held out to him at an earlier stage until his will and nerve were strong enough to endure this revelation. There is no escape except inwards. For the sage is too compassionate to withdraw into proud indifferentism and too understanding to rest completely satisfied with his own wonderful attainment. The sounds of sufferings of men, the ignorance that is the root of these sufferings, beat ceaselessly on the tympana of his ears. What can he do but answer, *and answer with his very life*—which he gives in perpetual reincarnation upon the cross of flesh as a vicarious sacrifice for others. It is thus alone that he achieves immortality, not by fleeing forever—as he could if he willed—into the Great Unconsciousness, but by suffering forever the pains and pangs of perpetual rebirth that he may help or guide his own.(P)

18

The mystic arrives at treating all people alike through the *emotion* of love; the illuminate arrives at it through the knowledge of *reason*. The first is likely to be changeable, the last permanent because emotion is variable, reason firm.

19

The mystic who talks of giving love to all mankind has still not realized Truth. What he really means is that he, the ego, is giving the love. The Gnani, on the contrary, knows all men as himself and therefore the idea of giving them love does not arise; he accepts his identity of interest with them completely.(P)

20

His goodwill to, and sympathy for all men, rather empathy, enables him to experience their very being in his own being. Yet his loyalty toward his higher self enables him to keep his individuality as the inerasable background for this happening.(P)

21

He seeks neither applause nor profit from others. On the contrary, he is ever willing to give them out of the spiritual store he possesses. But his giving is free from sentimentality and futility, because he restricts it by wise discrimination.

22

In one sense, it belongs to him alone. Did he not struggle with his ego so long, climb the ascending path of purification so arduously, wait in meditation so patiently? Yet in another sense it does not belong to him— his own work prepared the conditions, but the work of Grace, the influx from the Overself gave him the strength, truth, love, and peace. He must share what he has received, or at least proclaim its existence.

23

It is a compassionate obligation to share the fruits of such a rare attainment with less fortunate seekers. But only individuals of large generous natures can recognize this obligation.

24

The sage does not ask for service from others, but only to be allowed to serve them. He does not seek to attach them to himself, but only to God.

25

The illuminate never achieves perfect happiness because he is well aware that others are unhappy and that they are not alien to him.

26

When this wonderful compassion wells up within man, he can no longer remain enthralled by the satisfactions of his own personal peace. The cries which come to his ears out of the great black night which envelops mankind tell him that all is not well with such a self-centered life. He may not turn away from them by uttering the alibi that God is in his heaven and all is well with the world. No! He realizes that he must go down into the very midst of that darkness and somehow give out something of what he has gained, offer true hope to a hopeless epoch.

27

"Is it not because he himself is disinterested that the sage's own self-interest is established?" asks Lao Tzu. It is impossible for the materialist to perceive that we live and move and have our being in a universal Mind. But the sage, knowing this, knows also that this universal life will take care of his individual life to the degree that he opens himself out to it, to the extent that he takes a large and generous view of his relation to all other individual lives.

28

Amidst peaceful landscape in calm forest retreats or beside lonely sea-shores, where the attractions of Nature are all-powerful to him and where he could gladly spend the remainder of his life in solitude, a striking phenomenon will mark itself repeatedly on memory. Again and again, faces of different people will float up and confront him. Some will be the faces of friends or people known to him but others will be the faces of strangers. All call to him to leave his solitude and give up his silence. It is not difficult to understand this occurrence. The mountain eyrie, the jungle retreat, or the forest cottage may continue to attract him powerfully, but the awakening of his fellow men into truth must eventually seem a worthier objective than his own external peace.

29

So long as there are others acutely conscious of their spiritual need, so long must he go out among them. He does not do this by an external command but only by an internal one—the command of compassion. He no longer feels for himself alone but also for others. Indeed he cannot help doing so, for the same reason that Jesus could not help proclaiming the gospel to the Israelites, even though he foreknew the end would be impalement upon the Cross.

30

His service is done out of the pure joy of giving it.

31

The sage does not *have* to be told to help mankind in its struggles towards the light. He is a helper by nature. His compassion overflows and it is out of this, not out of condescension, that he works for them. But his help will not necessarily take the particular forms that humanity in its ignorance expects from him.

32

Fo Sho hing tsan: "I do not seek for any reward, not even being reborn in a paradise. I seek the welfare of man. I seek to enlighten those who harbour wrong thoughts."

33

He cannot help teaching confidence in the laws of life or expressing joy in the inspiration of life. He cannot help making strong affirmations of the Soul's dominion and power. He is exultant because he is in harmony with the universe.

34

The idea took possession of the Buddha that his doctrine was too deep for man's intellect and so he thought he would not teach it. However Brahma, the Lord of the World, came and begged him to have mercy on the erring world, for "the advent of Buddha is as uncommon as the flower on a fig tree." Then Buddha reflected as to who would be a proper person for him to teach.

35

The answer to the Buddha's soliloquy came, belatedly it is true but at the right ripened hour. It is: "Is the opinion of the ignorant many more important to you than the helping of the earnest few? If the first will disdain your words, the second will heed them. Who else can help them?" The final five words affected him deeply and forced him into action at last.

36

Such a man's actions, however much they outwardly appear to be like those of other men, are done under the impulsion of a higher will than the personal.

37

He has no wish to put his ego forward, makes no pretensions to spiritual superiority, yet he wishes to awaken others to the idea that enlightenment is possible, is worth seeking, and is accompanied by unparalleled felicity.

38

It is possible for man to realize his high aspiration. But will he then find that all is bliss as the Hindus say? How could that be when first he would become much more sensitive to the world's miseries and sorrows and, second, much more aware that everything that is, including himself, is merely a passing show—just like a dream of the night which vanishes in the morning? Will there not be a touch of melancholy in these two aspects of his awareness? The acceptance will be there, for he will be just as much aware of the Real which does not pass, but this acceptance will itself be touched with a kind of resignation. Is this what the religio-mystics mean when they so often admonish others to resign themselves to God's will?

39

The sage has no desire to gain followers, only to give service. His happiness comes from within. He looks to nothing and nobody for it. Nevertheless, if faith and friendship are given to him he is always grateful. And for such people he has the ardent wish that they too shall fully attain this great inward happiness and in their turn keep the presence of God alive in a materialistic world.

40

When he has found the truth, he has nothing to decide. He will realize that the ALL, this whole teeming universe, *is* himself, that all creatures and all men are one. Therefore their interests and their welfare become his automatically. Therefore he will come back to earth again and again to help all beings attain truth and happiness. The notion of choosing selfish bliss or unselfish service does not occur to those who have realized truth; it comes only to yogis and mystics who have experienced bliss in trance. But this is not the highest goal or plane; it is the highest *illusion*.

41

The thought of the burden that the sage has taken on himself may seem dreadful, but he has his consolations even though they are intangible. He has found unbroken peace and ultimate truth. He does not ask for more, not even the ecstatic bliss which delights the mystic, but which is necessarily intermittent. He knows that the whole creation is moving onwards to self-discovery which means it is moving onwards to find the same things he has found. The process is slow and painful, but it will surely be successful.

42

The sage has conquered separativeness in his mind and realized the ALL as himself. The logical consequence is tremendous. It follows that there is no liberation from the round of births and rebirths for the sage; he has to go through it like the others. Of course, he does this with full understanding whereas they are plunged in darkness. But if he identifies himself with the All, then he can't desert but must go on to the end, working for the liberation of others in turn. This is his crucifixion, that being able to save others he is unable to save himself. "And the scripture was fulfilled, which saith, 'And he was numbered with the transgressors.'" Why? Because compassion rules him, not the ego. Nobody is likely to want such a goal (until, indeed he is almost ready for it) so it is usually kept secret or symbolized. Again: "For this is my blood of the new testament, which is shed for many for the remission of sins."

43

What is the sage's reaction to the cosmos? It is very different from that of the ignorant who have never asked the question."What am I?" and who may regard the calm visage of a Yogi as a "frozen face." The sage has no sense of conflict, no inner division. He has expanded his notion of self until it has embraced the universe and therefore rightly he may say "the universe is my idea." He may make this strange utterance because he has so expanded his understanding of mind. Lesser men may only say "the universe is an idea."(P)

44

All these sufferers come to him in their need and expect so much from him, but he must expect and ask nothing from them; he is to be content with this one-way transaction. If he wishes anything in return—even an acknowledgment of service rendered, much less a payment in any mental, emotional, or physical form—the ego has reared its head and the service is impure. If he helps them, it is out of natural goodwill to all men.

45

The sage approaches them with compassion balanced by comprehension.

46

No mother asks why she should help her child or concern herself with the well-being of her husband. She identifies herself with them and takes it for granted that their interests are her own. Similarly, the illuminate takes it for granted that the interests of all mankind are his own and others are his family.

47

If the sage has to reincarnate perpetually because of his sympathy for the suffering world, if he cannot get freedom from this suffering cycle of rebirth, what is the use of the Quest and its labours? Reply: True, he can't get outer freedom, but he does get *inner* freedom, of mind and heart.

48

No worldly advantage can tempt the sage into desertion of his sacred task of serving humanity, nor can any egoism lead him into betrayal of those who trust him.

49

The goodwill which he shows to all men is devoid of any self-seeking motive, is a natural expression of the love which he finds in the innermost chambers of his soul.

50

The world play is but an illusion of the mind, but the integral vision of the sage enables him to act his part perfectly in the very heart of the world's tumult. The knowledge that all action is ultimately illusory does not prevent him being dynamically active. Supreme calm and silence reigns in his centre, but his harmony with Nature is such that he joins the world-movement spontaneously.

51

He does not fall into the error of a certain kind of ascetic who assumes a callous indifference to the sufferings of others as part of his plan to render himself invulnerable.

52

Such a man is truly a Christ-like one, inasmuch as he seeks to open the door of the kingdom of heaven for others as well as himself.

53

He may or may not know in advance that his efforts will avail little, but if the Power bids him say what must be said, he will accept the result calmly.

54

When there is no feeling of separateness from others, there can be no resultant feeling of doing good when helping them.

Help the sage gives

55

If he only holds before the aspirant a prophetic picture of man's higher possibilities, an ideal that transcends the commonplace trivialities of every-day, his service is sufficient. But in actuality he does very much more than that.

56

There are two ways in which an enlightened person may help humanity. The first is individual, therefore he becomes a teacher and accepts disciples. The second is general and may be entirely inward as in meditation, or quite outward, affecting the welfare of groups—whether small in number or as large as an entire nation. In rare cases this generalized help may even extend internationally.

57

He seeks no power over others, no claim to rulership over their lives, no disciples of his own, no train of followers clinging to his coat-tails. Yet he will not refrain from helping where such help is imperative, nor from giving counsel where the young, the inexperienced, the bewildered seekers have desperate need of it. But the moment after he will appear to have forgotten what he has done, so gracious is his delicacy, so strong his desire to leave others quite free and unobligated.

58

His inner state will not be easily discernible to others, unless they happen to be the few who are themselves sufficiently advanced and sufficiently sensitive to appreciate it. Yet it is his duty to announce the glorious news of its discovery, to publish the titanic fact of its existence. But he will do so in his own way, according to his own characteristics and circumstances. He will not need to announce it in a speech, or print it in a book; he will not publish the fact in daily newspapers or shout it from the housetops. His whole life will be the best announcement, the grandest publication.(P)

59

Without himself being a priest, he performs the true priestly office.

60

That strange and sweet spell flung forever over sensitive, ripe, and ready minds by a sage, when he uses his wisdom and goodness, is like a caduceus to enchant them into becoming seekers after truth.

61

He is a prophet without a church, a teacher without a school, a reformer without an institution.

62

The adept can do much more through the prestige of true ideas set down in writing than through the mechanical efforts of any formal organization, more by helping individuals than by creating a collective body which would one day exploit them.

63

He is the abstract, far-off ideal, but embodied visibly for our benefit and put near us for our inspiration.

64

Can one man transfer spiritual grace to another? If by grace is meant here can he give a glimpse of the Overself to another, the answer is Yes!—if the other is worthy, sensitive, and above all karmically ready. He can if the other man is capable of absorbing the stimulus radiated to him.

65

In the case of those who are ready for it or who have affinity with him, a master may be able to bring about a temporary illuminating glimpse through his inner contact with the other person by the power of his spiritual force. This force can be expressed through the Master's spoken words or in silent meditation.

66

Those who are always hoping to receive full enlightenment from a master, exaggerate the service he can render.

67

The most that a master can give is a glimpse, and that not to everyone. If the Zen assertion were true, if anything more than that, if full and final and durable illumination could be passed on to another, what Zen master could be so lacking in compassion as not to confer it upon everyone, everywhere? But it is not done simply because it cannot be done.

68

If a master could permanently add his spiritual vitality to that of all those who come as seekers to him, surely he would do so? History in the past times and observation in our own times shows no such desirable consequence of approaching him. But if a master cannot give illumination to a would-be disciple, he can show in his own person what illumination is. This is not less true of such men as Christ as of the minor prophets of the minor sects of contemporary history.

69

Those who penetrate into the holy of holies bless the world when they bring forth the treasures they find therein. What they achieve and accomplish mentally in the period of meditation, they will later express automatically in action during the days that follow. Theirs is the balanced life which is true sanity, so lacking in modern existence.

70

Unless he is bidden from the higher power (and he is sure of the source) to become an apostle, he will not take on the task of making available to others in such a public fashion, truths which most are not ready enough to recognize, which would create bewilderment or scorn in their minds. Nor, again, will he communicate privately without the inner command and thus become a guru to others.

71

The awareness that he existed on this planet made its grievous and troubled life more bearable, gave a little meaning to what seemed otherwise quite chaotic. For his own higher development reminded, nay assured, us that there *was* some sort of an evolution going on, that there *was* a goal and a purpose behind it all. Thus, merely to know that this man was alive, even though we might never again meet him and could never hope to become intimate with him, sustained our faith in Life itself and helped us to live.

72

The prayers of such a man are not lightly uttered nor egotistically born. Therefore they are always heard and generally answered.

73

He can communicate to others something of his mystical enlightenment through words and something of his mystical serenity through silence.

74

He carries with him a perpetual blessing, although it is seldom possible for those who identify themselves with their fleshly bodies to receive this unheralded gift with their conscious minds.

75

The sage may tell of truth, as he knows it, by refraining from speech and entering the Stillness. But if his interlocutors have not been previously prepared to understand what lies behind his silence, they may not benefit by it.

76

Serving humanity in his secret way, drawing benediction for all from this divine source, it would seem to be an unrequited activity; but he himself is included as recipient and beneficiary.

77

Like Jesus, Buddha preached to the masses. But other illumined men, like Atmananda and Mahavira, did not have this special mission and confined themselves to the educated and ruling classes.

78

Some come to illuminate, not to instruct.

79

Some who have attained true wisdom make no special attempt to communicate it through speech or writing, or to express it in action. Does this mean the world never benefits from them, as it benefits by the existence and work of even the humblest primary school teacher? It does not. For their contribution, though quite noiseless, is not at all valueless. It is to let the silent influence of their presence among us touch those who can receive it, even though they do so unwittingly.

80

This kind of illuminate is like a spectacle to be gazed at; he is not a teacher to be studied with. That does not mean he is useless to humanity. On the contrary, *the mere fact of his attainment is more valuable than any physical or intellectual service that could be performed.* But its value is mysterious and magical, for the moment perhaps better left undescribed.

81

He may leave his record in the silence, without producing a single piece of writing, without delivering a single lecture.

82

The greater his power, the less will he seek publicity. It is only if he knows that a mission has to be performed calling for public notice that he is likely to abrogate this rule. But of course there will then be no egoism and no vanity behind the abrogation.

83

Such a prophet is like a bell, calling its hearers to attend the true church within themselves.

84

His work is being done within the inner life of hundreds of human beings. His altruism is active more often behind the scenes of the world-stage than before its footlights.

85

The masters rarely emerge from their obscurity to positions of influence and prominence but their disciples may and occasionally do.

86

He will be content to plant seed-thoughts, and wait and work patiently, knowing and believing in the inherent power of true ideas to grow in their proper time into mature, fruitful existence.

87

The perfect concentration that reigns within his being can have the same effect when deliberately directed upon sensitive and sympathetic minds as the concentration of the burning lens upon dry paper. The devotee can be inspired, exalted, and illumined.

88

Once he has uttered the sacred Word, once he has revealed to men what they have not been able to know for themselves, he has done his work. If it fails to be accepted, if he gains no converts to belief in man's higher purpose, the blame is not his.

89

He cannot give spiritual peace to the spiritually peaceless as a lasting gift, but he can show them that it does exist as a reality and is no mere figment of the imagination. And he makes this demonstration by being just what he is and acting just as he does.

90

The sage starts no cult himself and founds no church. This is usually done by the disciples who gather together because he would not gather them around him.

91

Merely to remember with devotion that such a man is living on earth is to know, in some mysterious telepathic way, that there is inward sustenance.

92

The last thing he wants to do is to leave a sect behind him. Like the Buddha, he wants men to depend on the truth rather than on a person.

93

The words of a man so inspired, so wise, directly act on our minds and evoke our intuition.

94

The sage will help people on his own terms, not theirs, and guide them in his own way, again not necessarily the expected way.

95

Could we but trace some of these higher movements of history, we would have to trace their course back to the secret inspiration of some illuminates who live quietly and serve mankind without advertising the fact.

96

That which the illuminate will give out as doctrine will depend upon the conditions and needs of his epoch and place. He will be neither too active nor ultramodernistic.

97

He announces his revelation to his contemporaries in the mode that is his and theirs. In a scientific age he will present facts and reason logically.

98

Great Adepts are content to make history rather than figure in it, although their figures have glowed brightly in history like shooting stars and then disappeared.

99

His success in communicating truth will depend, on his audience's side, both on the degree of understanding it possesses and the feelings it evinces toward him.

100

It is not for him to work for humanity by helping particular persons and by alleviating isolated distresses. His form of service must stretch over wider areas, must affect a multitude of persons. But this is possible only if he works in deeper ground and through secret unobtrusive ways.

101

The world being what it is, human nature what it has long been, and human affairs all-too-repetitious, he will not waste time and energy attempting to re-arrange them by surface efforts.

102

He may do nothing more than put his mite of cheering truth and softening goodness into the grim world around him, but this will be enough. He cannot contribute more than he has. The ultimate result of this contribution may be little, but he has tried to do God's will on earth.

103

Just the fact that he is here, on this planet and at this time, makes its own contribution to humanity's welfare. This is still true even though he may not try to manage other people's lives on the plea of serving them. His service may not be immediately, or locally, apparent; it may need time to come up from the subconscious levels that are the deeper layers of mind and spirit, but it will be nevertheless real.

104

Although it is not his direct purpose, his existence will lessen humanity's suffering, increase its hope and goodwill.

105

He puts the teaching forward as far as it is proper for him to do so, but then leaves the matter. Those who receive it must take it up from there, or ignore it. He is not a missionary seeking to make converts.

106

Those who cross his path only once in a lifetime, as well as those who are often near him, receive instruction even though he is not outwardly teaching them. Such is the subtle impact his mind makes upon theirs, such the half-recognized influence of his greatness.

107

They tried to influence kings and rulers and leaders of men and culture. They even emerged into public view on rare occasions in order to quicken the pace of evolution by active external work; but when this happened, they did not usually reveal their true spiritual identity. Their efforts were not always successful because they had to deal with frail stubborn human nature and, moreover, they had to work within the karma of their own land.

108

Knowing such men convinces us better than printed arguments of the eternal Spiritual truths.

109

The truth flows from such a man all the time and not only when he speaks or writes. It flows silently. But whereas anyone can hear his spoken words or read his printed ones, not many can receive this voiceless and inkless message.

110

If he *must* lead men, he prefers to do so indirectly; if he is to serve them, he prefers to serve them unobtrusively; and if he needs to work among them, he seeks to do it self-effacingly.

111

It is only in the deepest possible sense that it may be said he is all things to all people, a spiritual opportunist who meets each man on his own level. But this is not to be taken to imply any desertion of principle.

112

Tradition tells us, and history confirms, that before passing away the illuminated man may preach the truth or write a record or communicate his knowledge to at least one other man.

113

In this state of direct relation with the soul's power, he feels and knows that his thoughts and prayers directed towards the good of others can help them.

114

The sage gladly opens to all qualified and eager seekers the mysteries and treasures of his own inner experience, that they may profit by his past struggles and present success.

115

He brings revelations to meet our gropings, inspirations to meet our doubts.

116

He becomes, for those docile enough to receive them, a bearer of grace and a vessel of truth, a bestower of comfort and a dispenser of confidence.

117

Chuang Tzu, the ancient Chinese mentalist sage, wrote: "All that was worth handing on died with them (the sages). The rest they put into their books."

118

Prophets and sages, teachers and saints receive the urge to share their knowledge and experience with others. Whence does this urge derive? Both lower and higher, personal and nonpersonal sources are possible. But if from the highest, then we may say that God sends his messages to mankind through these channels.

119

The sage who starts a movement or puts his thoughts out, acts as a lighthouse which guides many a fumbling but aspiring soul.

120

If he does not accept disciples individually it is because he serves men otherwise. Those who try to get such acceptance and find themselves rebuffed may consider him selfish, cold, remote. But they will be greatly mistaken. He can serve mankind—not each person separately but in groups or masses—and he may do this by lecturing, by writing, or simply by directing his meditation in the appropriate way. For a writer's books spread not only his ideas but also something of himself.

121

He can put thought on a high level but the way in which he does this depends upon him and his circumstances. He can do it personally as a private teacher, impersonally as a public lecturer or writer, or anonymously as a proficient contemplative.

122

All these men who have attained Reality inevitably leave a record for others or for posterity, but not necessarily with their name attached.

123

Has any one of the sages ever vanished without leaving behind a trace of Power, knowledge, goodness, and inspiration? Even if not in words or deeds, something is left in the unseen atmosphere.

124

They are not usually members of any sect, but circumstances or necessity may sometimes render it desirable that they be such.

125

The sage may or may not descend into the arena of action but if not he will still find ways and means to inspire, guide, or ennoble the actions of other men. He does this by teaching them and travelling among them, or by sitting still and meditating alone, or by disseminating writings among them. Even when he is unheard publicly he can help by the concentrated mind's great power.

126

He does what he can to introduce here and there into the consciousness of others, through whatever means he possesses, the seeds of higher ideas. These seeds may not grow and certainly may not fructify for many years, but that is not his affair. He knows that the vitality in these seeds and depth of mental ground in which they have been sown will inevitably lead to some result.

127

It is enough. He has sown the seed. He does not have to wait for roots to form, stems to grow, fruits to appear. His work is done.

128

In this momentous period the true sage has special work to do in trying to protect the human race from its own folly. One way is intercessory meditation which may help to mitigate the effects of the world crisis. This requires solitude. It is an impersonal contemplation and must not be disturbed by those who break into it, either to unload their personal problems or to offer personal service which in the end has the same result.

129

Yes, some of us are genuinely aware of the soul's existence and intimately know its freedom and blessedness. Modesty has hitherto imposed silence upon us about the fact, although compassion induced us to break it on occasions. But we mystics must now stand on our own dignity. It is time that the world, brought to its inevitable and by us expected materialistic dead-end, should realize at last that we are not talking out of our hats but out of a real and impeccable experience. It would be an unpardonable treachery to our duty in the final and terrible world-crisis of this materialistic age if, out of false modesty or fear of intimidation by a cynical society, we who daily feel and commune with the divine presence, who realize its tremendous importance for humanity's present condition and future life, fail to testify to its existence and reality. If today we venture to speak more freely and frequently, our ideas may drop into a few hospitable minds and sublimely penetrate their consciousness.

130

It is not the sage's function to tackle the worldly problems which governments usually deal with: the social, political, economic, and technical ones. His particular work is concerned with, first, his ordinary duty of professional service through whatever skill he possesses to earn his livelihood, and second, making truth available.

131

The mere existence of one who succeeds in identifying himself with the Overself benefits every sensitive person who meets him, even for a minute or two. Further, it inspires spiritual seekers who never get the chance to meet him but who hear favourably about him and respectfully receive what they hear. Finally, posterity benefits from the records left about him.

132

Each teacher—if he is divinely commissioned—leaves a deposit of truth after he dies.

133

The Master who leaves a record of his own climb, or a testimony to the goal's existence, or a path pioneered for those who would follow, or an instructed disciple here and there, leaves something of himself.

134

Even where help may not directly and outwardly be given when difficult circumstances press on a man, it may yet be indirectly and inwardly given to his mind, which has to deal with, or endure, them.

135

He can awaken some persons to this divine presence within themselves, but not all. He may do this mysteriously by some unknown process, or he may do it deliberately and with the display of his technique.

136

The abstract does not appeal to the masses, because it gives them nothing. But an embodied man can be seen, heard, and touched, to that extent can be understood, to that extent he gives them something; he can be followed, admired, feared, reverenced, or worshipped.

137

Secure as he is in his own peace of mind, it is inevitable that the more sensitive among those who meet him feel it too. But those who come with hostility, personal or intellectual, will be avoided if possible or find their time cut to the shortest if not.

138

Such a man has a catalytic action on the minds and even on the lives of those who come into sympathetic contact with him.

139

Just by being himself he makes the philosophic virtues real to others.

140

He does not need to be conscious of a clearly defined mission before he sets about doing something for the enlightenment of others. There is always some means open to him, some little thing he can do to make this knowledge available or to set an example of right living.

141

It is his duty to communicate what he feels there, what he finds there, to those who are excluded from it. If at times, and with sympathetic auditors, his duty becomes his joy, at other times and with insensitive auditors it becomes his cross. Jesus exemplified this in his own history.

142

The illuminate practises a wiser philanthropy than those who are presented as models of this virtue.

143
He has no wish to take charge of anyone's life or undertake the management of anyone's affairs.

144
He is not allowed by the code of ethics corresponding to his knowledge to make other people's decisions for them. Hence he can say neither yes nor no to such highly personal questions. But he *can* point out the consequences which are likely to follow in each case.

145
When we shall apprehend the meaning of life, we may discover that it provides its presage in such prodigies.

146
When the band of sixty young men met Buddha while they were looking for a woman of their pleasure, he said to them: "Abide with me a little while and I will teach you truth." Such is the power of the spoken word of the illuminate, when falling on a sensitive or sympathetic ear, that again and again we find in the history of the Buddha that he quickly converted and quickly brought to spiritual enlightenment those to whom he chose to address his speech.

147
The highest service they render is in silent contemplation, which inspires so many aspiring souls to a higher life. This is the truth.

148
The mere fact that these prophets, these light-bringers and way-showers have existed at all is enough to change a man's life if he is sensitive, reflective, and penetrative.

149
Even if he does no more than open the human mind to its higher possibilities, he does enough.

150
The fact that there have been higher men who have gone beyond the mass in goodness and insight, in serenity and radiant self-mastery, can be taken as a hint of re-embodiment's purpose.

151
He speaks or writes as one who is perfectly at home in these higher levels of consciousness.

152
If an illuminated teacher or an illuminating book cannot lead anyone into the Kingdom of Heaven and keep him there, they can at least give everyone a clue which, if followed up, may lead there.

153

Whatever help he can give through teaching is limited on the other person's side by both ability to understand and willingness to receive it.

154

He can give a man no other Grace than this, to point out the way to the Innermost Self. But there is none better.

155

He seeks to bring man back to the memory of his true native land.

156

There is no room for such a man in rigid official worlds. He could not even influence, let alone save, such a society. At best he can make some people more fully conscious of what they already dimly feel: that civilization is in danger and its leaders half-bankrupt; that society is sick unto death; that the individual needs spiritual help to endure and grapple with the depressing situation in which he finds himself.

157

What chance has the individual spiritual educator to continue his work when public and government alike accept the false suggestion that only through large organized groups and recognized traditional institutions can people be correctly led? The end of such a trend can only be as it has been in the past—monopoly, dictatorial religion, centralized tyrannical power, heresy-hunting persecution, and the death of individualism, which means the death of truth. Jesus, Buddha, Spinoza were all individualists.

158

He prefers to remain unrecognized for what he genuinely is so that others will not even suspect his true status—unless he deliberately wishes them to be made aware in order to help them in a special way.

159

Unless he has been invested with a special mission to speak or write to the world, the authentically illumined man will not publicly announce the fact of his illumination. Anyone who does is an impostor.

160

We may turn over the multitudes of tomes in which the opinions of man lie locked up, but one sage will tell us more Truth in a day than we are likely to learn from all that huge mass of speculation.

161

If world history shows little if any ethical progress on the part of humanity, are the sages to be blamed as futile? No. That merely shows the intractability of the human material they are working on, for their lives are given to doing whatever they can. They are not miracle men.

162

The best help he can give is to put a man upright on his own feet by helping him get his own experience of the glimpse. The man will then know that God really exists, that his own inner being is connected with God, and that he can draw upon this connection for moral strength and personal guidance, mental peace and spiritual knowledge.

Effects of the sage's presence

163

The response of others to the adept's presence is curiously opposite in kind: with a few, the finer evolved, it is beautifully comforting, exalting, pacifying, and draws their interest to him. But with many others it acts in reverse. His quiet ease puts them at ill-ease; his self-possession disturbs them. Either an unpleasant sense of guilt insidiously enters their feelings or one of resentment arises against someone who seems quite unlike other men, and whom they cannot therefore meet on even ground, who arouses their suspicions as being probably a fanatical religious heretic.

164

Those who are sufficiently sensitive feel, when they spend a short time with one who has learned to live in the Overself, a large relief from all their ancient burden of anxieties and difficulties and darknesses for a while. This effect is so extraordinary, its exalted peace so glowing, that although it passes away its memory will never pass away.

165

He who arrives at this stage becomes so wise and understanding, so strong and dependable, so kind and calm, that those who seek to foster these qualities within their own selves will receive from his word—sometimes from his mere presence—a powerful impetus to their progress. They will catch fire from his torch, as it were, and find a little easier of accomplishment the fulfilment of these aspirations. And those who are able to share in his effort to serve, to collaborate with his selfless work for the world, will receive daily demonstration of and silent tuition in those still loftier and more mysterious qualities which pertain to the quest of the Overself: in the paradox of dynamic stillness, inspired action, and sublime meditation. Yet he accepts worship from nobody as he himself worships none. For he will not degrade himself into such materiality nor permit others so to degrade themselves through their own superstition or someone else's exploitation.

166

His thoughts are permeated with unusual energy, and strange intensity, so that sensitive persons feel its atmosphere when in his presence or react quickly to its spoken and written expression when not.

167

Time-harried men and women, if they have not given themselves up to utter materialism and lost all their sensitivity, will draw serenity and touch repose when they enter his timeless atmosphere.

168

We do not have to become the privileged, personal disciple of such a man to benefit by him. If we have met him only once, for however short a time, merely to think of him helps us and merely to know of his presence in this world cheers us.

169

Those who are sensitive enough to be able to do so, become by faith and sympathy sharers in his own divine perception of the world. But whereas theirs is a glimpse, his is abiding.

170

The man who dwells in this light may transmit it to others if he is intuitively directed to do so or is charged with a mission involving others. But if others are hostile to it, there will be no felt result or perhaps even an uneasiness in its presence. This is a service of transmission or Grace, although not to be regarded as arbitrarily or capriciously given.

171

When he penetrates to the still centre of his being, the thoughts of this and that subside, either to a low ebb or into a temporary non-existence. Since thoughts express themselves in language, when they are inactive speech becomes inactive too. What he feels is quite literally too deep for thoughts. He falls into perfect silence. Yet it is not an empty silence. Something is present in it, some power which he can direct toward another man and which that man can feel and absorb temporarily—to whatever extent he is capable—if or when he is in a relaxed and receptive mood. The communication will best take place, if both are physically present, in total silence and bodily stillness, that is, in meditation.(P)

172

People react differently to his presence but only a few react rightly. Those are the ones with whom he has a spiritual affinity, and a prenatal link.

173

Association with or proximity to such a man not only brings out what is best in them but also, when it ends, invokes the reaction of what is worst.(P)

174

Constant association with him can only benefit the sensitive after all. It exalts and tutors them. But it leaves the insensitive exactly as they were before. Long ago Jesus pointed out the futility of casting seed on stony ground. Not that this lack of sensitivity is to be deprecated. Nature has set us all on different rungs of her evolutionary ladder. No one is to blame for being what he or she is.

175

If, through his complete calmness of manner, his presence was restful and agreeable to some people, it was disturbing to others. It seemed inhuman and mysterious. If some felt uplifted by his tranquillity and strength, others were frightened at its possible connotation of secret evil.

176

If the contact stimulates him before he is ready for it, then it will help his spiritual growth in some ways but hinder it in other ways. It may give him greater enthusiasm conviction and determination, but it may also inflate rather than abnegate the ego. This is another reason why adepts are hard to approach.

177

It is only for the sensitive that his bland serenity and benevolent smile will hold a distinct attraction, for it is only they who will feel the subtle unusual emanation from his person.

178

In the presence of an illuminate one feels, as Hawthorne felt and said of Emerson, so "happy, as if there were no questions to be put."

179

Mencius: "He who has wandered to the gate of the sage finds it difficult to think anything about the words of others."

180

The blessing of his compassion streams into one's soul.

181

In his presence, the disciple with true affinity feels an infinite rest.

182

Others avoid him after the first meeting because they cannot endure the uneasy feeling of guilt which arises in his presence. For their most secret sins and most hidden weaknesses are suddenly displayed to their mind's eye by the mere fact of his propinquity. It is an involuntary and mysterious experience.

183

Sometimes the interrogation in the eyes of an illuminate will prove fatal to the worldly foolishness we bring into his presence.

184

There is a silence which soothes and a silence which disturbs. With a genuine adept the first is felt, but with the other kind, the second.

185

Like a looking-glass, he shines back the image of what their conscious self turns away from but what their diviner self is silently pointing toward.

186

Those who feel this deep peace in the atmosphere around and between them, do not feel any need of words. The soothing stillness is their best communication and indeed gives the latter a quality of sacred communion.

187

Sitting in the aura of greatness that exudes from this man, a sensitive person absorbs some vitalizing element which gives him the impetus to nurture the quality of greatness in himself. The pretensions of the ego must collapse.

188

In this man's presence others often feel inadequate, often become acutely aware of their own deficiencies. Why is this? It is because they abruptly find themselves measured against his breadth of soul and height of wisdom. They become ashamed of their own littleness when it is shown up by his greatness.

189

They come to him with a head full of questions, but they find themselves struck with vocal dumbness in his presence. They come to him expectant of wonderful revelations, but they find that he takes care to seem and speak like other men and to keep his feet solidly planted on the ground of common sense.

190

They may draw near to him and cross his orbit for only a few minutes in a whole lifetime but it proves enough to inspire and irradiate the rest of their days. They now have not only the feeling that this man knows whereof he speaks but also the assurance that the Overself is utterly real and that the quest of it is the most worthwhile of all enterprises.

191

In his presence all that is best in a man receives stimulation and he comes closer to his true self. The significance of the meeting will emerge still more in after years.

192

He will be so quiet in his daily bearing, so calm in his dealings with others, that they will begin to sense despite his unfailing modesty that here, in his presence, there is a living echo from a higher world of being.

193
In his presence the shadows of depression or fear vanish. For then the disciple can look out on life with clearer eyes, seeing the Perfect which already exists beyond its imperfections.

194
Certain kinds of sensations, feelings, and thoughts are automatically repelled from the field of blessed consciousness in which the illumined man lives. All negative and destructive, egoistic and unruly ideas—certainly all those that the best conscience of the human race has stamped as "wicked" and generative of "evil-doing"—are not compatible with his purified state of mind and accordingly cannot enter it.

195
If he lets them, many will come to him in search of guidance help comfort or healing. Some will place their problem before him humbly and candidly, but others will be too afraid, or too proud, to do so openly.

196
Whether there is an actual transference of his power and light, or whether his actual presence and desire to help set up vibrations in the subconscious mind of the seeker, or whether he is merely a medium for higher forces, it is not easy to determine. The truth may well be a combination of all these three factors.

197
Constant contact with such an exalted personage is likely to influence others, but it is not possible to say when this influence will rise up into the conscious mind. The time will always be different with different individuals.

198
His silences may be exasperating to those who are insensitive and uncomprehending, but they will be exhilarating to those who have begun to learn how the Spirit operates.

199
In the presence of such a man, one instinctively feels that there are tremendous reserves of knowledge, virtue, and power within him, that he has so much more to give than is apparent.

200
His presence calls out the good, the true, and the beautiful in others.

201
The sensitive will quickly become aware of the hidden strength that is in him, the strength which kindles assurance in his own heart and confidence in others' hearts.

202

A benign influence diffuses itself from him and is felt by the sensitive, as if borne on telepathic waves.

203

This peace which he seems to diffuse is really there, is a central characteristic that never leaves him even when surrounded by dangers or beset by troubles.

204

A meeting with such a man, by those who are sensitive enough to register more finely than the gross senses can register, is always a benediction; the remembrance of him is always an exaltation.

205

By a principle of symbiosis, what he is, being now at the source of human power, spreads out and ripples its influence on the human group, which at the least keeps it from becoming worse than it is, and at the most lights up inspiration in certain individual minds and makes them benefactors of the race.

206

His goodness acts as a silent reproach to those who are unwilling to give up their badness: hence their discomfort.

207

His very presence is a silent rebuke to them; he stands there in all his integrity and spirituality—an embarrassment, for it makes such a contrast with their own worldliness.

208

In the serene presence of an illuminate, all criticism is charmed to antlike littleness. What can our broken thoughts do to injure or belittle one who is safely above all thought? And how dull seem these dogmas which we have brought into the neighbourhood of one who has liberated himself from all dogmas!

209

If "dead" illuminati can help the world as readily as those who are among us in the flesh, I would like to ask those who believe this why Ramakrishna uttered the following pathetic plaint as he lay dying in Cossipore: "Had this body been allowed to last a little longer, many more people would have become spiritually awakened." No, it is more rational to believe that a living illuminate is needed, that one who has flung off the physical body has no further concerns with the physical world, and that he whose consciousness is in the Real, uses the world (in the form of a body) to save those whose consciousness is *in* the world.

210

In the personal aura of such an adept, the sensitive person gets a feeling first, of peace, second, of security and safety.

211

Why do sensitive people feel protected and secure in his presence? It is because he knows and obeys the universal laws, invokes and attracts super-human power.

212

The impact of such a person on others may be the most memorable event of their lives or it may be the most trivial. That will depend on their own readiness to appreciate and estimate, their own capacity to absorb and receive. Take only the quality of his serenity, for instance, and imagine what it could mean to anyone thrown into contact with him during a frightening crisis.

213

In the presence of such greatness, a feeling of humility comes into a sensitive heart.

214

The uneasiness which many feel in his presence is partly caused by the fact that there are negative qualities in themselves which are not present in him. But partly it is also caused by their miscomprehension of his charac-ter. He does not attempt to criticize, judge, or condemn them, nor to approve or disapprove of them. He accepts that this is not his business for he accepts that evolution has made them what they are, both the good and bad in them. To this extent their uneasiness is unnecessary.

215

Some sages do not wish to enter into any precise relationship with others. They do not give personal initiation or accept disciples formally. But the sensitive will feel that some sort of inner benefit was got by the contact, non-visible and impersonal though it was.

216

The meeting with a higher personage, whether on the physical plane or on an inner one, is to be considered fortunate, and a blessing upon one's own higher endeavours.

217

Why is it that in India the crowds come from far distances merely to have the sight—perhaps for a few minutes—of a great soul? And why is this regarded as beneficial and worth the toil and trouble of the journey? Even if the opportunity to have a few words of conversation with him is quite impossible, it is still thought worthwhile merely to see him or be seen by him. There is, of course, the personal satisfaction of having seen him. Is that merely a sentimental and emotional satisfaction, or is there a scientific basis of fact making the visit worthwhile? The answer to this question can be found in the knowledge that the body is a battery and that there are electrical radiations from certain parts of the body, certain centres—the most important centre being the eye—and that through those radiations, a part of the aura is actually projected outwards. This would also explain why the Indians of the higher caste do not like to have their food looked at by those of the very lowest caste, which they would consider a polluting act.

218

The meeting with a great soul, a mahatma, is called *darsan* in India and is considered to convey some kind of a blessing. We now see the scientific grounds for this belief, even though the masses themselves are quite unaware of this fact but feel or have the faith that the blessing is there.

219

Once a man has found his way to truth he can speak of it simply, directly, and naturally, without personal pretentiousness or ostentation. Yet those who underestimate the worth of what he has to say would be in error. The insensitive and coarse may not feel it but the others will not need much dealing with him to find an air of distinction, not easily explicable.

220

There is power and strangeness in his presence, for it brings those who are sensitive enough to feel its quality to confess what they can hardly confess to their intimate friends.

221

He has no desires to satisfy through them, no claims to make upon them. Because they instinctively feel that nothing of the personal self enters into his dealings with them, they just as instinctively trust him. He becomes their confessional priest. They bring their secrets, their sins, and their confidences to his ears.

222

He who has conquered his own sorrows and abolished his own ignorance will find in time that others will come of their own accord to him. He will sit there imperturbable yet sympathetic, inscrutably poised yet gently understanding, while the sorrowful and the aspiring, the world-worn and the seeking, pour out their sorrows and aspirations, their sins and ideals as at a priestly confessional—yet without any assumption of priestly superiority, without any pretense of moral height, and without any quackery of pontifical infallibility. When he speaks, his detached, impersonal standpoint will help to reorient their own, will show the truth of a situation and the lesson of an experience as their desire-tossed ego could never show it. And all the while, the impact of his aura will gradually strengthen, calm, and uplift them if they are at all sensitive.

223

Sometimes the mere act of confession to an adept brings release to a troubled mind almost instantaneously and seemingly miraculously. Thus a highly placed government official who was troubled for many years with nightmares in which odious reptiles played a prominent role, was entirely and permanently freed from them by nothing more than mentioning his case to such an adept in whose attainment he believed. Again, an exceedingly busy businessman, who could find no time for meditation or spiritual study and saw no prospect of doing so for many years, became distressed and worried about this situation. He did not want to be submerged by material activities. He asked an adept for advice. He was told to begin each morning with a three-minute prayer and not worry. Since then his anxiety has vanished and he has enjoyed spiritual peace in the very midst of his work. At other times a question or two by the same adept will ferret out secreted episodes that are stifling progress or will bring up subconscious memories that are poisoning character. The third group of effects are perhaps the most wonderful of all because they deal with causes that are the most deep-rooted of all. The innate tendencies born of former incarnations may themselves be influenced beneficially by the healing association of an adept.

He may sit quietly and listen very sympathetically to the troubled outpouring of a sufferer. At the end of a single session, the healing vibrations of the adept's interest may spontaneously effect an apparent miracle. The burden of long-felt grievance may fall away, the pressure of agony be taken away. The sufferer's inner being will give up its secret sins, expose its hidden uglinesses, and surrender its private fears only to have them thrown instantly out of his mind and life.

224

Only the sensitive are likely to leave his presence uplifted, quieted, and reassured in mind. The others—and they are the majority—come with nothing and leave with nothing.

225

He who sits in meditation with a master may find an inner impetus developing out of the contact.

226

He may never utter aloud any prayer on behalf of others or pronounce any benedictory formula over them. Yet the silent descent of his grace may be acutely felt and gratefully received.

227

We may borrow inner peace and inner strength by the proximity of such a man. But with its cessation, the peace and strength depart.

228

Without opening his lips he communicates a message to every sensitive seeker who enters his orbit.

229

The effect of this meeting, provided the proper conditions exist, is to give the seeker a powerful psychic and spiritual stimulus.

230

The presence of one man demeans us and makes us seem less than we are, whereas that of another like this adept will dignify us and seem to bring the goal for a while within easy reach.

231

Those who are sensitive to true spirituality will always leave his presence with a feeling of having been greatly benefited.

232

From his own unshakeable calm, the sensitive draw respite from their troubles. From his own unusual experiences, the humble draw priceless counsel.

233

There is danger in the frown of one guided and overshadowed by the Overself, as there is blessing in his favour.

234

To come near to such a man is to come more closely to the possibility—which all possess—of finding God.

235

He remains calm amid adversity to a degree so extraordinary that others sharing the same trouble feel less borne down by it and more able to tackle it.

236

In his presence we are willing to sit without words merely to enjoy the peace which emanates from him.

237

To have sat within the aura of a great soul is a memorable thing, but to have communed silently with him while doing so is to have received a lifelong blessing.

238

In one adept's presence, some men felt as if they underwent a religious conversion—yet there was no particular brand of religion to which it could be referred.

Sage as catalyst for higher powers

239

His beneficent spiritual influence may profoundly affect others to the point of revolutionizing their attitude to life, yet he may be unaware of both the influence and its effect! The part of his mind which knows what is happening is not the true source of the grace; this flows through him and is not created by him.

240

Let us not ascribe to the ordinary self of man what belongs to the Overself. The mystical phenomena, the "inner" experiences engendered by an adept, are done *through* him, not *by* him.

241

Help comes, inspiration is derived, peace is felt, and the support of moral fortitude is obtained without personal intervention by the sage or without even his personal knowledge of the matter. It is automatic, a response from grace to faith.

242

The catalyst which by its presence enables chemical elements to change their forms does not itself change. In the same way the illuminate may be used by higher forces to affect, influence, or even change others without any active personal move on his part to bring about this result. He may not even feel, see, or know what is happening, yet he has started it!

243

He is an agent for the work of Providence, a carrier of its messages and forces. At times he is used with his conscious knowledge and acceptance but at other times without them.

244

Much occult phenomena of the adept is performed without his conscious participation and "above" his personal knowledge, as when various people claim to be aware of receiving help from him which he has no recollection of having given. It is the Overself which is really giving the help, their contact with him being merely like the switch which turns on a light. But a switch is not the same as the electric current which, in this simile, represents the Overself. Yet a switch is not less necessary in its own place. If he does not use it, a man may grope in vain around a dark room and not find what he is seeking there. The contact with an adept turns some of the power that the adept is himself in touch with into the disciple's direction. The flick of a switch is done in a moment, whereas the current of light may flow into the light bulb for many hours. The contact with an adept takes a moment, but the spiritual current may emanate from him for many years, even for a lifetime. Just as in the ordinary man's deep sleep no ego is working, so this is the perfect and highest state because no ego is working here either. It reproduces deep sleep by eliminating egotism but transcends deep sleep by retaining consciousness. Thus it brings the benefit without the spiritual blankness of deep sleep into the waking state. If it be said, in criticism of his unawareness of so much occult phenomena manifesting in his name, that this lessens his mental stature, he must answer that it also preserves his mental sanity. How, with a thousand devotees, could he be attending to all of them at one and the same time? By what magic could this be done and his peace remain, his sanity be kept? God alone knows all things in a mysterious everywhereness and everywhenness. How could he be as God and yet remain as man, much more deal with other men? For all occult phenomena belong to the world of finite form, time and space, not to the world of infinite spirit, to illusion and not to reality. And, if, in further criticism, it be said that his unawareness makes him seem weaker than an adept should be, he can only answer humbly that because he has surrendered his personal rights he is weaker and more helpless than the most ordinary man, that his situation was tersely described in Jesus' confession, "I have no power in myself, but only from the Father."

245

The strain of these hundreds of questioning, eager, demanding, struggling, and perhaps suffering minds constantly directed towards his own would be so tremendous if he had to bear it in the ordinary way that his own mind would break under it. He is given no rest from his task. But his extraordinary attainment provides his protection. They reach him mostly through the subconscious self, which automatically takes care of them and leaves him free of the burden.

246

The message or the manifestation may, on the surface, appear to come directly from the master. This may be quite true in some cases but it could not possibly be true in all cases. If it were, then he would have to look in a dozen different directions every minute of every day. But the fact is that he helps most people without being consciously and directly aware of them.

247

There is magical power in the thoughts of such a man. The mind, the animal, and the ego in him being mastered, many other things become mastered as a consequence. Rabbi Gamaliel, who once taught Saul and prepared him to become Paul, has put this secret into these words: "Do His will as if it were thy will, that He may do thy will as if it were His will. Annul thy will before His will, that he may annul the will of others before thy will." Jesus put it somewhat differently: "Seek ye first the kingdom of heaven and all these things shall be added to you. . . . Ask whatsoever ye will and it shall be done unto you." Those religionists who take the latter words as applicable to any and all prayers are woefully ignorant. They cannot properly be said of persons who have not attained sufficient mastery of self, who give nothing from within themselves except wishes and the words which clothe them.

248

He may well be unaware how subtly the force is working within him until he begins to notice its effects on others, as they themselves draw attention to it.

249

Such is the wonderful infinitude of the soul that the man who succeeds in identifying his everyday consciousness with it, succeeds also in making his influence and inspiration felt in any part of the world where there is someone who puts faith in him and gives devotion to him. His bodily presence or visitation is not essential. The soul is his real self and operates on subconscious levels. Whoever recognizes this truth and humbly, harmoniously, places himself in a passive receptive attitude towards the spiritual adept, finds a source of blessed help outside his own limited powers.(P)

250

He takes no credit to himself for these things. He feels he is only an instrument. All that he can do is to invoke the higher power, and it is this which makes these things possible. It is not really any power of his own that does it. But quite often he does not even have to invoke the power— and yet these things will happen all the same. Nevertheless, his followers are not attributing powers to him which he does not possess. For these happenings, after all, occur only as the result of the contact with him. He knows that in some mysterious way he is the link between the power and the event.

251

Although the master may not directly transmit the message or prompt the manifestation, he does exercise an influence which indirectly causes this to happen and indicates the direction in which it is to happen.

252

The power to inspire or comfort others can operate without his personal awareness and even without his own consent. Sometimes it will manifest itself merely as if he were present and close, to be felt but not seen mentally. Sometimes, a like form of his body or face will appear to the mind's eye along with this same feeling.

253

Those whom he never even meets but who direct their thought and faith towards him, receive inspiration automatically. The impact of his personality helps those whom he does meet, if they are sympathetic, but often without his even being aware of it.

254

It is not necessary for him to preach and sermonize others. Sometimes in a purely secret and unnoticed way, sometimes in a half-conscious way, those who cross his path temporarily and those who associate with him permanently will feel that the good is being strengthened in them. This is his silent service.

255

Just by being himself, without preaching, without trying, the sage may awaken in others whose lives touch his a longing for the higher life.

256

He has a peculiar power which acts upon the subconscious minds of those who have any contact or association with him.

257

The illuminate exerts his influence upon others spontaneously and effortlessly rather than deliberately and purposely. He need make no effort but the benign power and light will radiate naturally from him just the same and reach those who come within his immediate orbit. It is sufficient for them to know with faith and devotion that *he is* and they receive help and healing. The Overself works directly through him and works unhindered upon all who surrender themselves to it.

258

Because he has no feeling of egoism, he has no feeling of a mission to accomplish. Yet a work will be done all the same.

259

"The Sage works when apparently doing nothing; instructs without uttering a word."—Lao Tzu

260

The sage does not need to pray for anyone nor does the other person even need to know that the sage has thought about or remembered him. For we are all held within the World-Mind. But if the sage does not think of the person, the latter must believe, or remember, or ask, or think of the sage if help is sought.

261

Only such a man has the right to echo back the statement of Lao Tzu: "To do nothing is to do everything." For others to do so is to claim what is not theirs, and to breed laziness and parasitism.

262

By his being what he is, there is nothing to impede the flow of pure consciousness from him to those he contacts. The ego does not intervene, the lower nature does not interrupt, and without his making any deliberate effort something passes through and from him to benefit them.

263

Without his trying to influence others to reform their characters or to improve their thoughts, his influence will still appear whether they know its true source or not, and whether it is after the lapse of many years or not. Nor does he ask any credit for this result for he gives that to the World-Mind whose World-Idea is being realized in this and many other ways.

264

Quite often he does not need to do anything; it is enough if he beneficently remembers the person before emerging from his own periods of contemplation. Sometimes, even merely being present may act as a catalyst for remedial forces. If however he goes farther than this, and performs a specific act, the result must come.

265

Such a power is like a catalyst in chemistry. Itself invisible, it inspires others to visible deeds.

266

As the light of truth passes into him, he in turn refracts it to others, although only some will let it touch them.

267

Grace flows from such a man as light flows from the sun; he does not have to give it.

268

It will suffice for him to be what he is and thirsty seekers will draw from him in a mysterious, silent way what they need of his power and wisdom, his love and serenity. The beautiful statement of Bishop Phillips Brooks is worth quoting here: "It is the lives like the stars, which simply pour down on us the calm light of their bright and faithful being, up to which we look, and out of which we gather the deepest calm and courage."

269

He can take no credit of his own for the service rendered, and calls no attention to himself. How could he honestly do so when he is fully aware that it is only by ceasing from his own activities, by being inwardly still, and by abandoning his own ego that the power which really renders the service manifests itself?

270

Where do these phenomena originate? Not always from himself, but more often from outside himself, from the mysterious and unknown mind which is the soul of the universe and the ground in which all individual minds are rooted.

Sage works with few directly

271

The sun does not ask any plant, animal, or human if it is worthy before shedding benign life-giving rays upon it. The light is given without stint to all. Why should the man who has united with the spiritual sun of pure love within himself hold its warmth back from any living creature? Why should he make distinctions and bestow it only on a chosen few? The fact is that he does not. But the mass of men fail to recognize what he is, seeing only his body, and miss the opportunity that his presence among them affords.

272

It is certainly not all mankind, not even all those who cross his orbit, whom the sage is called upon to help but only those with whom there is either an inner affinity or a karmic link. "I pray not for the world, but for them which Thou hast given me," said Jesus in his last prayer with his disciples before the great betrayal. He could not undertake to save all men and women, for that were an infinite labour without end, but only some among them. At any given time there are several spiritual shepherds in the world, each with his own distinct and separate flock. It is inevitable and right that he should sieve humanity for those alone who need him or who were born to follow him or who seek the kind of guidance which he especially can give.

273

His compassion is broad-based; it is for all. But his personal work is extremely narrow for it is only for the few who will receive it most readily. This implies that he works among the sympathetic and mature, not among the hostile and immature. The reason for this is the need to practise economy of time and energy that he may not waste his arrows of effort on the vacant air. For a similar reason he prefers to enlighten the *leaders*, and let the flocks alone.

274

He will seek to give depth of instruction rather than width of influence. Hence his own activity will be directed towards a severely limited number. Whatever movement he inaugurates and personally leads will be small, indeed, for he will understand that were it to become popular and widespread its quality of thought would immediately degenerate, its purity of motive would instantly be degraded. He will count the years gloriously spent if, when the moment comes to drop the body-idea and pass through the portcullis of death, he can look back and reflect that a hundred men have firmly grounded their minds in truth and planted their feet on the road to eternal liberation through the work done by this transitory body. For those who welcome the Truth-bringer must needs be few, those who want the truth must be fewer still, and of these again those who can endure it when brought face to face with it are rare.

275

The sages of old deliberately restricted the public from their full knowledge so that their immediate following was always numerically insignificant. Yet the paradox was that they exercised an indirect influence disproportionate to their small numbers. This was achieved by (a) concentrating their tuition on men in positions of high authority or leadership, and (b) establishing popular religions and cults suited to the capacity of the multitude.

276

Few are fit and worthy to be taught by such a sage for few would accept him if he were clothed in an unattractive body, if his skin were the wrong colour or his stature dwarfed or his face ugly or his shoulders hunchbacked.

277

He is better occupied in quietly revealing his knowledge to the elect than in publicly defending it against those who are incapable of receiving it mentally, and therefore incapable of appreciating it morally.

278

Should a master composer spend his time teaching musical scales to children? Should an adept come out of his seclusion and spend his time teaching the mass of people? The answer to the first question is, obviously, no! The answer to the second question is, less obviously, but equally, no!

279

Many will admire such a teacher but few will emulate him.

280

The illuminate bestows his grace in vain on the man who will not yield up for a moment his intellectual pride and his incessant egotism.

281

For him to try to convince others of the truth would require that they are seeking truth. But how many are consciously and deliberately doing so?

282

The persuasive influence of his mind and the pellucid truth of his sentences do not register with many men. Fitness, readiness, and ripeness must be present first if receptivity is to be achieved.

283

No sage who has entered the great enlightenment is going to tell everyone he meets what has happened to him. Nor is he going to reveal everything he knows at the first few meetings even with those who want to find truth.

284

The sage does not try to collect a personal following, nor does he try to stop anyone who wishes to wander elsewhere. He does not wish to form a cult or even a school of thought. He seeks to attach only those who seek for the truth alone, both in his thinking and in his life. Sometimes he trains a few in meditation and instructs them in philosophy.

285

Unlike insane self-titled "Messiahs," he has no program of saving the whole world from its sinfulness, for the chances of such an enterprise are microscopic; but he has a program of finding his own kindred—those whose aspiration thought and prenatal relationship with him make them his natural followers.

286

Such a man may have many acquaintances, may make a modest number of friends, but he is unlikely to find more than a few intimates.

287

He sees that there is nothing he can do for people whose point of view is so undeveloped, so materialistic, so concerned with surfaces and appearances. He does not engage in the futile task of meddling with their lives. He does not attempt the impossible task of changing them suddenly. He leaves them to the natural processes of growth and to the cosmical forces responsible for their past and future course.

288

He is the silent background counsellor for a few men who have the opportunity and capacity to serve mankind.

289

These adepts help the few who are in a position and attitude to help a multitude.

290

He seeks no personal devotees but is glad over each person who becomes a follower of impersonal Truth.

291

The illumined man becomes a channel of the Holy Ghost, a chalice of the Prophet's Wine. Yet even he cannot turn the absolute mystical Silence into finite comprehensible speech for more than a sensitive few. With most people he finds himself utterly dumb because they themselves are utterly deaf. This is the tragic pity of it, that just because his words have a value far beyond that of other men's, there is no audience for them, so few ears to receive them.

5

TEACHING MASTERS, DISCIPLESHIP

Teaching and non-teaching illuminates

There is a widespread belief among questers that a man who becomes enlightened automatically becomes a teacher and attaches followers to himself for instruction. This is not inexorably so. He may, or may not.

2

Few have penetrated the secrets of being, fewer still have revealed them to others.

3

Not everyone who is illumined becomes a spiritual teacher of humanity. Only one whose previous tendency, general character, constant aspiration, allotted destiny, or personal capacity fits him for that function becomes a teacher.

4

It is not every spiritually enlightened man who is called to hold his lamp in mankind's darkness, or is required to be a teacher of others. This is a special art and requires special gifts. Those who attain enlightenment fall into two grades: the first, *mystics* who are possessed by the Overself but who can neither show others the way to this state nor expound in detail the truth they have realized; the second, *sages* who can do both these things.

5

To be a teacher, to be able to educate others in philosophic doctrines, to prepare pupils for the wise life, requires qualities which knowledge alone does not necessarily confer.

6

Every sage must be a teacher because every sage must wish to promote the enlightenment of mankind.

7

Not all those who attain sagehood necessarily become teachers in the *personal* sense. Such a one is entitled to choose anonymity. Unknown to the world at large, he still by virtue of that very attainment is a benignant presence mentally.

8

There are two kinds of masters: Inspiring masters like Ramana Maharshi, and Teaching masters, like Gurunathan. The first have greater power to inquire; they can show the goal but not the path to it; the second have a greater capacity to lead aspirants step by step along the path.

9

All qualified teachers are illumined but not all illumined men are teachers.

10

He could not tell others how to struggle out of the depths if he had not himself done so, how to realize the soul if he himself had not realized it. But this is only his first qualification. His second is that he has cultivated the special virtue of compassion for others throughout the whole course of his mystical life. Consequently he becomes its fullest embodiment when that life flowers into bloom. That is why he is a teaching sage rather than a cold self-centered mystic.

11

The men who have seen deeply into the hidden meaning of life are the men best qualified to guide us in matters of conduct and motive.

12

Only when truth already exists in the mind and heart of the teacher can he convey it in his teaching to the student. If it does not, then he is merely indulging in a piece of pantomime.

13

Whoever has attained this stage can pass on to the proper persons both a foretaste of mystical experiences which lie beyond them and an impetus to their quicker self-development. If he is only a mystic he may do so quite unconsciously, but if he is a philosopher he will give this wordless instruction quite consciously.

14

The enlightened man who has to deal with those who are not sensitive enough to receive clearly in the silence that which is his best communication, meaning most people, must then give it in a more familiar and easier form—words! But here the illuminate may himself be at a disadvantage. He may lack fluency and have a limited vocabulary—be inarticulate. Here others will be better served if the illuminate has wide command of good language; if he can teach in sentences that are clear, beautiful, powerful; if he is eloquent.

15

He whose course embraces a mission of spiritual service to others is invested with a greater power and enlightenment than he has actually earned. This does not make him greater than he is. But as the excess of inspiration gradually uses him as its channel, it becomes gradually integrated into his own character little by little over a period of several years.

16

We may sit before the saintly phenomenon and enjoy the peace issuing from him. But when we leave him, the peace leaves us too. We may have no such dramatic experience when working with the teaching Master. But he will guide our feet each step of the way; he will listen to our difficulties, problems, or questions and give us his wise counsel. That is the wide difference between these two types of illumined men.

17

It is true that many of those who attained enlightenment gave some of their wisdom or counsel to others but did so only incidentally or occasionally and to a limited extent. Others made it their chief and whole-time mission in life to teach others and preach truth. Those who did so had better capacities for teaching and preaching than those who did not. Moreover, they had to leave an example of conduct in their own lives worthy of being imitated—a duty which was not incumbent upon the non-teachers and was sometimes disregarded by them.

18

There has occasionally been a man who entered into awareness of the Overself without the help of a teacher and without the laboured struggles of most other men. He is like a horse which has crossed the river by swimming and without touching the ground. Such a man does not usually go out of his way to teach the path to others or try to help them individually, or even to announce the truth to the world. He is satisfied with his own place and with the knowledge that "God is in his heaven, all is well with the world." He is an inward-looking mystic who has a perfect right to enjoy his attainment.

19

There are two types of illumined men, of those who have attained spiritual perfection. The first have sought the goal for their own sake alone and are satisfied to rest on their labours with the attainments. The second type does not accept this rest, for their very search was made with the intention to share with others. The first type have been called, in the

Orient, Silent Masters, also Isolated Masters. The second type have been called Preaching Masters, also Teaching Masters and Compassionate Masters. In the case of the first type, the renunciation of the world is usually abrupt and sudden, though the period spent between renunciation and the attainment of Enlightenment may be long and weary. It is possible for one to become a Silent Master while yet a layman, but, in this case, the marks of a layman, such as the clothes he wears, immediately disappear. The spiritual attainments of a Preaching Master and those of a Silent Master are alike; but in the case of the latter, though he attains to supreme and perfect insight, yet his enlightenment is individual. His enlightenment is of benefit to himself alone; he does not proclaim to the world the great Truths discovered by him. He cannot instruct others "effectively"; his realization of the Truth is "like a dream seen by a deaf-mute." "Silent" is unsatisfactory because they do preach to those who come to them, though their preaching is restricted to admonitions regarding good, righteous, and proper conduct. They even have personal attendants whom the world may regard as disciples, but they give no instruction other than ethical instruction.

20

There are men of enlightenment who cannot throw down a bridge from where they are to where they once were, so that others too can cross over. They do not know or cannot describe in detail the way which others must follow to reach the goal. Such men are not the teaching-masters, and should not be mistaken for them.

21

The man of enlightenment who has never been a learner, who suddenly gained his state by the overwhelming good karma of previous lives, is less able to teach others than the one who slowly and laboriously worked his way into the state—who remembers the trials, pitfalls, and difficulties he had to overcome.

22

The Master *has* found his way to the Overself; he daily enjoys the blessing of its presence; he has passed from mere existence into significant living, and he knows there is peace and love at the heart of the universe. He wants now to help others share in the fruits of his discoveries.

23

The Master, who is a dedicated teacher also, wishes ardently for others on the Path to attain the goal and share its bliss.

24

If qualified disciples are few, competent masters are so rare as to be almost unfindable.

25

He who is to direct the steps of others along this path needs not only to be high in character and consciousness and teaching ability but also to be learned in the comparative history and comparative doctrine of mysticism.

26

Without inexhaustible patience and pedagogical talent, the mystic can hardly engage with satisfactory consequences in the task of instructing others. He may be highly inspired but, lacking these two things, he will do better for those who approach him by silence than by speech.

27

It is true that nobody can get sufficient data to determine the solution of the riddle of a single man's status, nobody can penetrate fully into any man's motives. I do not judge anyone and I ought not to judge. Nevertheless, his teaching alone is insufficient to testify to the true worth of a man; he himself is a testimony of equal value.

28

It is said in the old texts that the perfect Master feels not only for his disciples but for all those who are devotedly following the Quest, an affection similar to that of a cow for her calf.

29

If he has both inspiration and technique his message will carry authority, power, enlightenment, and hope to those who can receive it.

Advice, warnings to would-be teachers

30

He is a true messenger who seeks to keep his ego out of his work, who tries to bring God and man together without himself getting in between them.

31

A master whose experience and training enable him to detect the signs of what psychoanalysts call "transference" should be immune to any displays of undue affection from a disciple of the opposite sex. If he is not, if he feels he is only human and cannot remain satisfied with spending his life being a big brother to everyone, then he should descend from his pedestal and join his disciples in search of another—and stronger—teacher.

32

Beware of assuming the Master's role too prematurely. If you are not ready for it you may not only misguide your pupils but, as a Tibetan text says, fall into the ditch with them.

33

Do not pretend to be other than you are. If you are one of the multitude, do not put upon yourself the proud robes of the Teacher and pretend to be able to imitate him; unless you stick to the Truth, you can never find it. To put yourself upon the pedestal of spiritual prestige before the Master or God has first put you there, is to make the first move towards a humiliating and painful fall.(P)

34

The true adept does not sell either the secrets of his knowledge or the use of his powers. There are several reasons for this. The most important is that he would harm himself for he would lose the link with the very source of his knowledge and power. He does not possess them in himself but by virtue of being possessed by the Higher Self. From the moment that he attempted to make them a means of worldly profit, It would gradually begin to desert him. Another reason is that he would lose his privileged position to speak the pure truth. To the extent that he had to rely upon purchasers of it, to that extent he would have to shape it or conform it to their tastes and prejudices; otherwise they would refuse to have it. He would have to use his powers to please them. He would have to accommodate his knowledge to their weaknesses. He could succeed in the profession of teaching truth only by failing in his own duty of realizing truth. For the truth, being the one thing he got without price, is the one thing which he must give without price. This is the law governing its distribution. Anyone who violates it proves by this very violation that he does not possess truth in all its shining purity.(P)

35

A writer, teacher, preacher, or spiritual guide who gives out high ideals ought to be the first man to follow them himself.

36

It is inadvisable for the spiritual director to bring in his own personal experiences of the past and relate them to a student with the hope of making the student feel that the director has passed through similar situations and sympathizes with him. This brings in the personal element and annuls the detached impersonality which gives the director his authority and influence. Any stories of experience which have to be told can be given anonymously or in the third person.

37

The teacher's work will have to endure the malice of satanic human instruments and the misunderstanding of the superficial and ignorant.

38

When he becomes humble enough to recognize that it is not he that touches, guides, inspires, heals, teaches, warns, or leads others but the infinite power of the Overself, that he is only a medium for this power, then all his motives change. He no longer seeks to serve his ego but rather the Overself. And the better to do this, he tries to cleanse and refine his ego.

39

By what right can he guide others who himself prays daily to the Infinite Being for guidance? The answer is that it is not he who guides them, but the Infinite itself, which uses him merely as a medium, whose only virtue lies in being pliant and submissive.

40

If he is to tell them what is the matter with themselves and to tell them successfully, he will need tact, intelligence, patience, calmness, and courage. Nor will it be enough merely to possess these qualities, they must also be possessed to an infinite degree. Without that, he had better relapse into silence—for he would then only arouse their egos and introduce discord.

41

The man who is to be a true mouthpiece of the Overself, whose teaching or writing or preaching is to be intrinsically valuable for its revelation or inspiration, must forsake both the animal and the ego in him.

42

The man who goes around pointing out people's mistakes to them becomes unwelcome and unpopular. Even the spiritual guide is not an exception, for his criticism is received with treble force by those who worship him. A prudent guide will soon learn, by experience, that it is better to shut his mouth than to tell his disciples what they do not want, and do not like, to hear.

43

The self-centered neurotic especially, but also various other types, will pressingly invite you to become involved in his personal affairs. If you accept, you merely postpone the day when he must learn to handle them for himself. This does not mean that the wise counsel, the kindly word, may not be dropped here and there, now and then. But there is always the danger that pressure will be put on you to repeat yourself constantly, to live in his ego and in his past, present, or future with your disciple.

44

"Whoever gives advice to a heedless man is himself in need of advice," admonished Saadi of Shiraz (thirteenth-century Sufi master).

45

The danger of the ego accepting an homage which belongs only to the Overself, provides the successful teacher with his next test. To let disciples make his personality all-important and overlook the Overself which uses it, is to fall into error. Humility is here his only safeguard.

46

It is easy to be humble when obscurity, poverty, personal ugliness, or menial position forces it upon a man or woman. But to show this quality when every visitor bows low before him—that is the test!

47

One danger to a guru is that he may become surrounded by sycophantic followers, who will nourish and strengthen whatever undesirable egoism may still remain behind in him because his training was never completed. Another is that he may attract dilettante followers, who will waste his time and create needless useless disputes of interpretation among his more serious disciples.

48

The true master is he who points the way to the recognition of one's inmost self, not to the adulation of his own personal self.

49

If you wish to help a man, you can do so only by exposing him to the truth which refers to his level. To venture onto a higher one is perilous. He may even be hostile to it.

50

Teaching must begin with oneself if it is to become effective. The teacher must spiritualize himself and integrate his own personality before his words and silences can really be significant.

51

Lao Tzu says there will be no end to the work of reforming the world. Now since a man is part of the world, the same conclusion applies to the guru who would reform a disciple.

52

Do not be over-critical with students. They need help, which is best given through positive affirmations, Short Path joy, and radiant fulfilment.

53

He has to be more than careful of the way in which he speaks to his disciples. A single sentence could fill one of them with utter exhilaration for a whole day: another sentence could fill a second disciple with frowning melancholy for just as long.

54

The following points have to be learned if one hopes to fill the office of a spiritual teacher:

(a) Weaknesses of moral character must be mercilessly sought out and uprooted. No task should be undertaken which might induce their return.

(b) Whatever form of service is given must be accompanied by spotlessly pure motives—never out of desire for reward or expectancy of return.

(c) When the work of teaching involves one in no personal expenses he cannot meet out of his ordinary professional earnings, he should not accept emolument. This is considered bad karma.

(d) When the work of teaching brings one in contact with the opposite sex, he must not take advantage of his influence to have any but the purest, spiritual relationships. To break this rule is again to invite bad karma.

(e) One should not meditate haphazardly with anyone and everyone who comes to him.

These are serious dangers to which the would-be teacher must be extremely attentive. It is partly to help counteract these dangers that I have explained the philosophic discipline and emphasized the need of cultivating reason in my last seven books.

55

When it is useless to tell him the truth in words then don't: tell him in the Silence. But if he is to hear you, then you must already live from within.

56

When a spiritual teacher does not take precautionary care to keep from colliding with those establishments called churches, governments, and colleges, he runs the risk of being crucified. If he is to utter truth, he will find it hard to ignore the plain fact that they stand for dogmatic closing of the mind, for timid clinging to outworn threadbare and useless doctrines.

57

To become an open channel for that high power, its servitor in this darkened world, its messenger in this bewildered epoch, is honour but also burden and privilege and responsibility combined.

58

That Javanese custom whereby a guru does not humiliate a seeker by scolding him for an error in outlook but tells him an anecdote from which the seeker can himself infer that he is wrong, is worth noting. A positive approach gets better result than a negative one.

59

He who takes on the role of a spiritual counselor must be prepared not to lose patience too soon.

60

He may like to see those near and dear to him share the same faith and undergo the same disciplines. There are ways and means whereby he can utilize prayer, meditation, and personal example to promote this end. But all the same he will find himself up against the hard fact that, by its very nature, spiritual growth in another is not to be forced.

61

It is well to remember that the revealing god is also the concealing god.

62

No attempt to enlighten an individual should go more than a single step in advance of that individual's mental power and moral stamina.

63

A spiritual teacher who wants to work publicly must concede ground to orthodox religion and should conciliate the feelings of orthodox ministers.

64

Give the man what he really requires at the moment, not what he may require if and when he reaches a higher stage of development.

65

A teacher, to be most effective, should present his teaching in a dress and colouring appropriate to the age in which he lives. He must "tune in" to the needs and hopes, the thoughts and sentiments, the lives and surroundings, of the people of his age.

66

Only one who has reached the degree of competency and the state of purity requisite for such work, may rightfully teach others or enter into the spiritual counselling relation with them.

67

To play the role of spiritual adviser to any person is to accept a grave responsibility.

68

I would revise an oft-quoted sentence so that it reads: "When the master is ready, the pupil appears!"

69

Let not the guru get in the way of the student when the latter is ready to try his wings, make the first flight of a grown-up, and begin to be an individual.

Value of a qualified teacher

70

If he can find a Master-Inspirer, he will find his greatest help in the Quest.

71

It is essential to find a reliable guide who can indicate the higher studies which should be pursued; knowing this, the sage will gladly give his services to those aspirants who seek him out.

72

The benefit of approaching a master *as a disciple* is that he provides inspirational stimulus and aspirational uplift. He pours a current of power into the disciple who then finds renewed strength to continue the Quest in a general sense. In the special matter of practising meditation, he is able to go into it deeper and to sustain it longer.

73

The contact with a true teacher is always significant, always fruitful. Old perplexities will be illumined for him and new avenues will be opened for him.

74

There are plenty of teachers to cater to the surface-seekers of this world. The true master does not choose to be one of them. He can be of service only to those who comprehend that the object of life is not to stand their bodies on their heads but to put the truth into their heads. But such seekers are few. For the one feat is spectacular and dramatic whereas the other is silent and secret. The real teaching work will be noiseless, without show, and in the background—behind the scene and not before the curtain.

75

The great teacher leaves his impress and exerts his influence upon his disciples without robbing them of their capacity to grow into their own individual freedom.

76

A true teacher will teach and guide but only to the extent that the pupil can absorb the teaching and is ready for it. In that way he will leave the pupil his independence and not order and command him. He will make him realize that his own endeavours must be looked to for advancement and his own strength must liberate him.

77

It ought to be the guru's task to get his disciples to act nobly or discipline self not because he orders them to do so but because they feel it is what they want to do of their own accord. Such subtle inner work is uncommon for such gurus are uncommon.

78

The old Oriental way was to tell the student to perform certain exercises blindly, to follow certain rules unquestioningly. The modern Western way is to give him the reasons for what he is told to do—so that he can work consciously and understandingly.

79

The sage tries both to do his disciples' thinking for them and also to provoke them into thinking for themselves. Nevertheless the statements he makes are suggestive and not controversial.

80

One of the great errors propagated by these swamis is to suggest that because Ramakrishna could transmit his spirituality by a touch of the hand to a few persons, he could therefore transmit it to everybody in the same way. He would assuredly have done so had it been possible, for he wanted to serve humanity. But as a Tamil proverb says: "Though one teaches an ass by speaking in his ears, we obtain nothing but braying." That, after all, only a tiny handful of persons were so "saved" by Ramakrishna is enough evidence to refute this senseless suggestion.

81

The teacher ought not to be looked upon as someone with whom to consult in every personal difficulty as it arises. His function is to teach the general principles of philosophy and it is the disciple's function to learn how to apply them to his own individual life. So long as he carries every personal trouble to the teacher, so long will the term of probation fail to come to an end.

82

The guide is successful partly to the extent that he makes the disciple aware of his own subconscious resources.

83

The master expounds truth to the disciple, telling him again and again, "You are THAT reality which you seek: give up the ego and know it." This holy message echoes itself repeatedly within the disciple's mind and eventually he too realizes its truth in his turn.

84

It is the Master's business to lead his disciples to make their own discovery of the hidden track to the Overself.

85

A primary duty of the teacher during the phase of self-purification is to tell the disciple about his weaknesses, show him his failings. This is a disagreeable duty, but any teacher who evaded it would fail in his responsibility.

86

It is kinder in the end to tell an aspirant quite candidly the truth about his shortcomings than to keep his illusions alive. For they are the true cause of his misery, the root of his sorrow; why not let him look them in the face? If he is to grow at all, the shock of discovering them is inescapable anyhow. A teacher's duty is not to keep him emotionally comfortable, not to keep silent because it is easier to do so than to reveal what the seeker needs to know. The easy way renders a disservice. The hard way is the right way in the end. The sooner he attributes his troubles to some fault in his own character, the sooner are they likely to come to an end.

87

To counsel those in trouble to adopt escapist forms of relief does not really help them, even though it may seem to do so. This is often an easier way out for the counsellor than compelling them to face unpleasant truth about the inexorable necessity of working on themselves to remove the cause, when the trouble is only an effect, likely to be repeated in the future.

88

The expert teacher encourages aspiration, instructs truth-seeking, and guides meditation.

89

The guru gives his service both in monition and admonition, both in strengthening conviction and fostering aspiration.

90

He is a messenger come from a far place to tell people that there is a reality, and that truth awaits them; he points out the direction where they are to be found, and how.

91

If he is to serve them well, rather than merely serve them, he must be aware of the conditions under which they actually have to live, the capacities they actually have, and the needs which are most immediate. Then, when he attempts to show them the way to an inner life which is potentially theirs, when he points out the higher needs which those conditions seemed to blot out—perhaps because they were ultimate—he will be better able to relate the teaching to them.

92

The response depends upon the level at which a man's mind is functioning, upon how much he is held down by his own past, upon what kind of outlook his experience and reflection have brought him to, upon the company he keeps and the surroundings in which he dwells, upon the condition of his body, upon the balance within himself and in his relationship with the world, upon what intuitions, counsel, visions, revelations, and instructions in the higher laws he has received from other men—if dead, through their writings or, if alive, through hearing their talks or lectures.

93

Such a concept of life is too precious to die out even if it is precious only to a scattered few. Be assured that they will take the greatest care to preserve its existence within the mind and memory of their race. And they can do this in two ways: first, by recording it in writing; second, by training disciples.

94

A true guide will surely serve his disciples, sometimes without the title of teacher, certainly without the pay of one who works for self. He will teach a small number so that, after attaining a certain degree of mystical understanding and practical advancement, they in turn may become helpful guides of others.

95

He has to give out what those whom he is addressing can understand and not outstrip their development. He may, for this purpose, either simplify the teaching or keep back the more advanced portions, those dealing with the transcendental mysteries.

96

What is the use of giving instruction which is unsuited to those who are instructed? Will it avail them to give instruction which is suited only to those who are far more advanced, far more ready, far more receptive? Whoever does this either lacks discrimination or shows vanity, that is, he needs to learn either wise prudence or true humility.

97

Such is the World-Mind's grace that it inspires men of the most different types to arise and help their fellows, men as widely apart as General Booth, who founded the Salvation Army, and the late Lord Haldane, who sought to translate his philosophical vision into unselfish public service. Thus, even in the darkest epochs someone eventually appears to help the most ignorant, the most sinful, and the most illiterate, even as someone eventually appears to guide the virtuous, educated, and intellectual. Inability to comprehend the highest truth or inability to live up to the loftiest ethics is not made by true sages a bar to bestowing help. They assist the undeveloped from where they now stand. And such is the wisdom of these sages that they know just how much to give and in what form it can best be assimilated, even as they know when it is better to convey material assistance only and when ethical, religious, mystical, or philosophical instruction should also be given.

98

The capacity to receive truth is limited by the moral, intellectual, and intuitional limitations of the receiver. Hence the sages put their teachings in a form proportionate to the receptivity of their audience. They keep silent on what it is unprofitable to mention because impossible to grasp.

99

The first work of the sage is to plow up the field of his pupil's mind, to make it fit to receive the fresh seed.

100

He has no desire to get men interested in his own personality, to have them turn to, and rely on, himself but would rather turn them toward their own higher nature.

101

The master who gives truth is a greater creator of values and contributor to humanity than the greatest music composers.

102

When eloquence is united with enlightenment, we may expect sentences which pierce us with their rightness, which are rich in truth and stimulating to goodness.

103

His statements make truth clearer, his declarations are like a sparkling drink.

104

The Master can help the aspirant with the benefit of a lifetime's experience on the Quest and with the Grace he has attained from having to endure the vicissitudes, ordeals, temptations, and tests which mark the way. From such a one, the aspirant can learn painlessly in a short time what another has to learn through years of suffering and blundering alone.

105

For the earnest seeker, a master will not only provide all these helps, he will also give assistance in the art of meditation so that it will be more easily and quickly learned than could otherwise have been possible.

106

The help provided by a master during a joint meditation period is provided by his simply being there! His presence may help to deepen the student's own meditation.

107

He who has awakened his own super-physical energy, intuited his own higher knowledge, can develop a skill beneficial to others whenever they come within his orbit. For he can inform them of what they can do to themselves *for themselves* and how they can do it.

108

To receive instruction from an inspired teacher or from inspired books has been the most common way in most cases resulting in enlightenment. This, of course, has been accompanied by following the practices, doing the exercises, making the studies, and undergoing the purifications required by the teaching. But there have also been a few cases where enlightenment has come by itself, spontaneously, without either the help of a teacher or the labour of a training. Such men can thereafter radiate their grace as much as the others but, not having travelled the path to enlightenment, cannot properly or adequately or satisfactorily engage in teaching and act the master.

109

It is not for a master to make his disciples' decisions for them.

110

His statements may or may not be justified by argument and certified by documentary quotations, for he leaves it to others to take them up or not as clues, hints, suggestions, to be tried experimentally on the way.

111

He cannot tell with certainty whether he is on the right path. It is then that he needs a guide.

112

The master will benefit his students not only by his verbal or written instruction but also by his example and counsel.

113

He does not insist, like lesser men, on making his disciples into facsimiles of himself, subject solely to the influence of his personality.

114

Those who expect him to work some spiritual sleight-of-hand to turn their lower nature into the higher one instantly will not find fulfilment of their expectation.

115

The help which the master gives is intended to bring the disciples to the point where they can help themselves—or he is no true master.

116

His work is to tell men what they have deep inside themselves.

117

It is not only on the stage reached in growth that the kind of teaching given a man must depend, but also on his temperament.

118

The adept's external moods are infinitely variable, simply because humanity is infinitely variable, and he changes his conversation to suit the mood of his hearers. It is never his aim to appear wise by giving out ideas beyond the understanding of his audience. Always he adjusts his teaching to meet the needs of his students. He is quite unmoved if others think from his variability of behaviour that he knows not Brahman.

119

By refusing to divide his mental life, by stubbornly holding to this higher level of statement however much it bewilders, repels, puzzles, or dismays undeveloped audiences, by rejecting all compromise of principles, convictions, or doctrines, the teacher of nonduality stirs and shakes the seeker into the beginnings of new experience and forces him to stop and discover his own inadequacy and think out afresh his position, outlook, or beliefs.

120

Anyone who expounds this, the highest of all metaphysical positions, puts himself and his audience in a paradoxical position. Those who say they are his disciples obviously do not understand his teachings, for if they had mastered them they would know that there is only the One, that the disciple-teacher idea insinuates plurality. Indeed, there would then be many egos surrounding another ego, many little illusions surrendering to yet another illusion.

Seeking the sage

121

"Association with the sages happens partly by merits and partly by devotion to God, but always as if by accident like a fruit suddenly fallen from empty void."—*Tripura Rahasya*

122

It is a fact which wide experience confirms that a spiritual guide, one who has himself realized the goal, one who has both the willingness and competence to lead others individually step by step along the path, is hard to find.

123

If you want to meet such a man, it will not be by seeing his body with your eyes nor by hearing his speech with your ears. It will be by sitting with him in the deep silence, whether of your own mind if you can achieve it, or of his if you cannot.

124

The would-be disciple must feel strong affinity for a master and the master must feel strong sympathy for him before any lasting relationship can be set up between them.

125

There is one master to whom the seeker is predestined to come and before whom he is predestined to bow above all others.

126

When the first meeting with the destined master takes place, the seeker will experience an emotion such as he has had with no other person before. The inner attraction will be immense, the feeling of fated gravity intense.

127

He may have a strange feeling of having always had this affinity with him and being destined to have it always in the future. This arises partly from association in a previous reincarnation and partly from the destiny of this present one.

128

The sympathetic accord between a piano and a tuning fork is like the affinity between a silently blessing sage and a devoted person.

129

With him one feels that one can talk and be heard and be understood, whereas with so many others one can only talk and be heard.

130

He may not be a perfect master, he may commit grievous errors of judgement and display regrettable deficiencies of personality, yet still he will be *your* master. No one can take his place, no one else can arouse the feelings of affinity and generate the harmony which he does. If because of his defects or lacks you reject him for another man, you will be sorry for it again and again until you return.

131

It sometimes happens—although uncommonly—that the feeling of inner affinity with a certain illuminate exists deeply and strongly in striking opposition to the attitude taken up intellectually towards him. The desire for personal independence of thought, movement, and self-expression may prevent external submission. The attitude of self-reliance may be so ingrained that one is reluctant to become dependent on another. There may be a marked difference of doctrinal view. The physical actions or arrangements of the illuminate may be disapproved. Yet the subtle inexplicable mystical attraction may be overwhelming. His wisest course is to recognize that this is his divinely ordained spiritual godfather, to confess his sonship, and to accept the relationship rather than resist or reject it. No label need be affixed to it, mysterious though it be, and certainly not the conventional master-pupil one. He will humbly be outwardly free but inwardly tied.

132

The process of differentiation must inexorably take place and nobody can stop it even if one wanted to. For a teacher has to find his "own." Those who belong elsewhere will sooner or later leave him, but those who belong with him will stick on through storm and sunshine. How foolish then to try and hold followers against their wish; what a waste of time and emotion to seek permanent discipleship where in the very nature of the case it is impossible.

133

Those who are fit to follow him, who are bound by ancient and unseen ties, will continue to do so; but the others—whom he accepts through soft heart and soft brain rather than right judgement and ripe understanding—will sooner or later avail themselves of the opportunity to walk another path and follow another light.

134

Many are too modest to venture to seek his acquaintance personally, although charmed by his teaching, and so miss the possible chance while he is still alive.

135

If he wants desperately to talk to the adept, let him throw his thought on paper and send it in, today or twenty years later—it matters not. Nothing can change between them if God has appointed the adept to a spiritual relation with him. It is above earth, time, and space. It will be fulfilled only in the kingdom of heaven.

136

He ought to make the most and the best of such a chance.

Approaching the sage

137

Unless an adept is approached in the right receptive spirit, he will reveal nothing of what he is or what he has to give.

138

We must enter their presence as humble heart-open seekers; we must be teachable if we would not return empty-handed.

139

The prospect of having to meet such a man frightens some persons, although when it is actualized the fear melts away in the benign aura of his kindliness. It is the reminder of their own weaknesses, their own dishonesties, which the meeting seems likely to create, the possibility that his clairvoyance may penetrate the ugly side of their character, which instigates their hesitation.

140

They are somewhat over-awed by his reputation, or his status, and so often leave his presence with unvoiced questions.

141

His reticence is not invincible. He will break it, and gladly, if your interest or hunger encourage him to do so.

142

If he has to meet someone who is regarded as a sage, he may quickly feel the stillness surrounding the man. If they sit down together and he feels disinclined to break the silence, it would be better not to do it but to take it as a signal to flout convention and let the initiative be taken by the sage himself.

143

The aspirant need hide nothing from such a man, for the depths of human sin and misery as well as good and joy are alike open to his understanding.

144

One enters his presence with humility—for here is a man immeasurably greater than oneself—and with relief, for it soothes and calms as nothing else does or can.

145

Enquirers can get from meeting a Master a benefit proportionate to the attitude they bring to it: if faith, devotion, humility, they open his door to the same extent; if scepticism, doubt, coldness, or suspicion, this door remains shut.

146

The student may have reached a crisis in his inner life when he met one so much more advanced than he. The other may foresee that there will be repercussions on the physical plane as a result of the inner changes taking place. The student should not fear to follow the intuitive urge which he will feel and he should be told that he must not remain enslaved by his past.

147

After a meeting with a master, it is more prudent to go straight home and meditate upon it than to go hither and thither on any other business. For that day is a serious one, that event a momentous one, and forces can then be released to the receptive, stilled, and waiting mind that are shut out by the busy indifferent one.

Qualifications for discipleship

148

The sage is not eager to welcome those whose chief qualification is only an ephemeral enthusiasm. To admit the wrong class is to bring eventual disappointment to the student and eventual loss of time and energy to the teacher. Hence he must avoid contacts likely to prove unprofitable to the candidate and unsatisfactory to himself. The only way to make a success of his tuition is to choose his students, not merely to be chosen by them. Every candidate must be adequately qualified before admission to his intimate circle, and must pass through a probationary novitiate before acceptance as a regular full-fledged student. He cannot afford exaggerated optimism about human beings. Hence those who are silently enrolled as pupils must first serve a term of probation, to be weeded out if proved unfit and to be rejected if proved unreliable. The proof of their fitness will therefore come from themselves.

149

Discipleship under such an adept is a privilege which can never be bought. It is a truism that almost everything in this world has its price in gold. Here, however, is one thing which can be bought only by the price of personal qualification.

150

There are certain qualifications which a candidate must possess before he can be accepted as a personal disciple. This is the old tradition in the Orient. It is considered a waste of time for anyone lacking such fitness to seek initiation, which would bring confusion to himself and danger to others. Consequently, although an Oriental master may give advice, grant interviews, or correspond with hundreds of persons, he will personally instruct or train very few of them.

151

The candidate for admission into a Japanese Zen training community was at first strongly but courteously refused admission. If he was half-hearted about the matter he departed and was not heard of again. If however he was wholeheartedly keen, he returned again and again but still met with refusals, ending even in being forcibly thrown out! But if he applied once more after this happened, he was cordially welcomed and put on probation.

152
He too has the power to be a master. But he himself must evoke it.

153
Too many are wholly unprepared to become the pupil of a master and tread the way of discipleship. Instead of asking for what they have neither the strength to endure willingly nor the balance to pursue safely, it would be wiser and more prudent to prepare themselves first.

154
Discipleship imposes certain responsibilities upon the disciple also. It is not a one-way street. Not only is correct instruction on the teacher's side needed, but conscious effort on the disciple's also.

155
The teacher is compelled to restrict his help to those seekers who have already made the necessary elementary efforts in their own behalf.

156
It is impossible to avoid the happening that a number of persons will persistently attach themselves to a teacher of philosophy and, out of compassion, he will let them remain, although they are only capable of absorbing and following religio-mystical doctrine. In most of these cases, the persons will—after having gained a certain amount of benefit—feel that the philosophic path and goal is somewhat beyond them, and so retire from it of their own accord. In other cases, after this period of benefit has elapsed, the teacher may shake them off by some act or remark which hurts their ego or shocks their preconception. Those who still remain despite these tests will be treated with especial care thereafter and given the blessing of his grace.

157
The custodians of this teaching judge their responsibilities well when, in view of the power which is released by its secret exercises, they are extremely careful in accepting a candidate and even then admit the accepted neophyte only after a period of probational training and discipline.

158
No one, not even an adept, can help another when that other lacks the capacity to recognize help when it is brought to him. This is why the wisest men have been so guarded in their contacts with the masses, so reserved in their publication of the truth, so seemingly detached from their fellows.

159
If they cannot comprehend his quality intuitively by his silent presence alone, words will be useless.

160

When a spiritual teacher is asked to accept a student, he tries to discourage the seeker, because he knows by personal experience what a long and painful road it is. One has to learn to crush his own personal feelings. This is doubly difficult for a woman because nearly all women are more emotional than men. The essence of this path is the giving up of the "I," the ego, which means that in a crisis the heart must weep tears of blood. Deep wounds are made, which only time can heal. They will be healed some day and when the storm of hurt feelings goes completely, a great peace arises.

161

Whoever wants to seek for Truth will learn more if he sets up as a standard: Nothing but the best—why settle for less?

162

No man can function as a spiritual counsellor for long without sadly noting how few finish the grade, how many slip into a smug complacency.

163

Buddha said: "Seeking the way, you must exert yourselves and strive with diligence. It is not enough to have seen me! A sick man may be cured by the healing power of medicine and will be rid of all his ailments without beholding the physician. He who does not do what I command sees me in vain. This brings no profit. Whilst he who lives far off from where I am and yet walks righteously is ever near me."

164

The teacher is expected to put the candidate on a probation of testing period for a whole year if possible, for six months if not, for three months at the very least, before accepting him as fit for instruction.

165

He can leave his wisdom to his disciples only in the form of words, which are merely its shadow. They must work on themselves, gain it afresh if they want it.

166

Any more than a parent can pass on all his experience to his children, the sage cannot pass on what he has learned to those who are unready for it.

167

If they are initiated into the secrets of this hidden teaching, it is because they were well equipped to study it. It is not a privilege arbitrarily given to a select few.

168

The great helpers and prophets have made little more than a dent in the total volume of human misery and human evil. God offers time and guidance but man must supply his own effort and his own aspiration.

Master-disciple relationship, general

169

In the annals of wisdom it is said that hard it is to find a true master, but harder still to become accepted by him. For the relationship between pupil and teacher develops into a grave one, with certain self-sinking duties on the former's part and certain self-giving responsibilities on the latter's.

170

We know that Plato regarded his birth during his master's lifetime as better than all the good fortune that aristocratic birth had bestowed upon him. And yet Socrates himself declared that he had no regular disciples and that anyone or everyone was free to hear him.

171

It is better for both master and disciple if their times together are short and well-spaced apart. For then the master will be better regarded, more respected, and found mentally, while the disciple will be less manacled, more independent, less imitative, and more correctly related inwardly. In brief, the actuality will be more commensurate with the expectation.

172

Their relationship must have a solid foundation on which it can be built. It must have love, affinity, and trust.

173

The disciple who was most constantly in attendance on Buddha was Ananda. The disciple who followed him about for more years and for longer journeys than any other was Ananda. Yet the disciple who was among the last of all to attain Nirvana was also Ananda. The lesson is that if a disciple gets attached to a competent master his progress will be facilitated, but if he gets over-attached to the personality of his teacher, then his further progress will be hindered. For his ultimate task is to free himself from all attachments and to learn to stand resolutely on his own feet.

174

His personal career and domestic decisions have to be made independently of the teacher's advice as long as he is still on probation. Only after formal acceptance and the final sealing of the inner relation could any spiritual teacher accept the responsibilities involved in helping a student form decisions. Until then, all experiences, whether pleasant or unpleasant, will be helpful because either the student will learn from the results of his own decisions if he analyses them impersonally, or he will show what is in him by the manner in which he faces the tests and ordeals of this probationary path. Of course, in perplexing circumstances it is quite difficult to make his own judgements. But every difficulty causes an inner struggle which has its evolutionary value from a long-range point of view.

175

Some men are cast in too independent a mold to become any other man's disciple. Whether this is for their benefit or loss, depends on the individual case.

176

With the passage of time the disciple should be led toward more and more self-sufficiency, if he is to realize the goal one day. Yet we find too many of the Oriental disciples showing less and less of this quality the longer they stay with a master. This is evidence of his failure to lead them aright, and of the fact that a man may be an illumined soul and yet not be a competent teacher.

177

All this heavy leaning on a master is a kind of secondhand experience, a living and copying of someone else's life, an imitation and not a realization.

178

Those who depend too much on a master violate one of the principal conditions of yoga, which is solitude. The yogi is to isolate himself not only physically but even inwardly from all other persons. This is because he is to turn to God alone.

179

It is not merely an association but an active collaboration.

180

The disciples are enslaved to their Master, the Master is enslaved by his disciples. A real relationship between them, with true spiritual profit, can begin when both sides can give and receive in utter freedom.

181

The advanced mystic appreciates the genuine and sincere statement that he has been taken by someone as a guide. However, if he does not set himself up as a teacher and consequently does not give personal instruction, the student must be reminded that his guide is a fellow student only. Nevertheless, if the student feels that it helps him to do what he has done, and if he understands fully what his position is, he should continue; and the advanced mystic to whom he has turned will remember it, let him not doubt that.

Master is symbol of Overself

182
Those disciples who can see their master only in his physical body and find him only in his monastic ashram see and find only his illusory appearance, not the real master. *He* can be seen and found only in themselves. The other and outward manifestation is a substitute who exists for those who are unable to understand mentalism or are unwilling to take the trouble to do so.

183
It is the mystic's ego which constructs the image of his teacher or saviour, and his Overself which animates that image with divine power. This explains why earnest pupils of false teachers have made good progress and why saviours dead for thousands of years still seem to help their followers.

184
The man who creates a new movement, pioneers a great reform, brings a better faith to a nation, or marches a victorious army across a continent is the burning lens of the new *idea* that is to appear. There must be a definite centre on the physical plane; there must be a human focus through which a new concept can shine out upon humanity. In the same way, there is needed a human teacher through which the Infinite can move the unawakened out of their apathy, give forth its light to instruct men's minds and its heat to inspire their hearts. Such can be no ordinary teacher, of course, for he must carry credentials brought down from heaven.

185
Every circumstance and environment, every fresh experience and personal contact is an instruction sent by the one unseen Infinite Mind, who should be regarded as the real Master.

186
The shortest way from ego-consciousness to the higher self's is represented by the master, by devotion to his person and following of his precepts. For he alone is, at one and the same time, both visibly outside us as a physical being and invisibly inside us as a mental presence.

187

The Orientals believe that the Teacher is sent by God to seeking humanity. We believe that the Overself within them draws him to them. He is then used as a medium to help them until they can become conscious of their own Overself. If the fullness and depth of the Godhead are inaccessible to all, its intermediary within is not. This—the purest, deepest, quietest part of them—is the Overself, and this is where the Teacher really lives when he withdraws from outer activity. At other times his presence acts as a link for those who would otherwise have to construct their own.

188

In the end, it is no external person who can save us but only the internal soul itself. The master may point out the way to discover that soul, he may even be useful in other capacities, but he cannot do what it is ultimately the business of the divine in us to do.

189

Only when well-advanced does he learn that the help he thinks he got from a guru came often from the Universal Being. It was his own personal thoughts which supplied the guru image, but the power which worked was from that Being.

190

Speaking loosely, almost figuratively, it may be said that in a kind of way the master localizes the Infinite Being for those who cannot reach it directly. This is actually true during the long period of discipleship and quest, for that is still the period of illusion. The final attainment puts an end to illusion, and then the sense of infinitude which was felt with the master is found to have its source within the disciple himself.

191

It is their own action which brings them into the relation of disciple; it is not anything of his doing. What is his role? Certainly not the one which fits the common idea of a guru, the religio-mystic one. He only makes them aware by his mere being, silent presence, or by speech or writing, of a higher level to which their response is aspiration, to which they add discipleship.

192

He calls them his students; they call themselves his disciples. The difference is wide and significant of their respective standpoints.

193

A relationship which has not been started, cannot be terminated. A sage who, in his own view, attaches no one to himself is free of responsibility for anyone, however much others insist on calling themselves his disciples. But such sages are the rarest among the three kinds.

194

When he knows that it is useless to seek real being anywhere else than within himself, he knows aright. No distant place, no other person, is needed. "A fool seeks for the Buddha," wrote the Ch'an Master Hui Hai centuries ago, "not for the mind. A sage seeks for Mind, not for the Buddha."

195

When you come to see that his presence is not required to keep you close to the truth, that it is with you, in you, and a part of you and so his coming or going is really irrelevant, you will begin to feel an indestructible peace.

196

He knows well enough that he has no power to exalt a man spiritually or to change him morally. When that seems to happen, it is really the man's Overself which is the effective agent and which has been using his destiny to prepare the man for the event long ahead of its actual and visible occurrence.

197

The Master's purpose is to bring the disciple into the same condition as that which he himself enjoys; and because it is an internal condition, the disciple can make his efforts to find it effective only by approaching even the Master himself internally also, and not externally.

198

The worship which is directed on a physical level toward the figure of a fallible human being, must be deflected on the philosophic level toward the impersonal Overself of the worshipper. He will continue to honour the man but only for what he really is, not as a god.

199

The true disciples seek to attach themselves to no embodied master; how can they when freedom is the goal? They will honour and consult such a man but they will not desert the disembodied Principle within themselves for him. The inward freedom which opens the way to It must be matched by an outward one.

200

Your idea that the Teacher is the Overself is rarely found among Westerners but often among Orientals. But how can this be possible? What is the Overself? Answer this correctly and you will comprehend how impossible such an idea must be.

Go back to the hidden Ground of everything, the passive Mind or pure Being, the First, the unconditioned Origin of all. This is utterly inconceivable and unknowable. The very concept of it, this infinite mystery of mysteries, is so awesome that the little mind of man hesitates and trembles when it even approaches it in the deepest meditation. It is beyond the capacity of that mind to penetrate the reality behind the concept. A mediating principle is necessary here. This exists in the Overself, which is nothing more than a germ of that same infinite M I N D, although to the adventurous mystic it seems the unlimited End of all.

If this were not present in man, not only would mystical experience be impossible for him but all religious intuition would be mythical to him. This is the divinity within him, but it is only a spark. The fullness of the flame is with the Godhead alone.

This is why philosophy repudiates the Oriental notion which merges the human individual in God or the Occidental notion which identifies Jesus with God. In the first case, the merger is actually with the Overself. In the second case, his inner life took on a divine flavour; his mind entered a deep intimacy with the Overself. He was always conscious of the sacred presence in his heart. But even though Jesus came so much nearer to God than has the rest of mankind—with the exception of the other Masters—he still remained within the limits of human organization. Where Christian religion goes beyond such a claim it is the result of a mixture of unseeking ignorance and deliberate imposture. But in the earliest Christian circles, which had some pretense to culture, the truth was known. The name "Christos" or "Christ" meant man's higher self and was used in the same way that the term "Overself" is used today. "Jesus Christ" meant that the man Jesus had been "Christed" by becoming consciously fused and unified with his Overself.

Hence you may correctly say that the Teacher, Prophet, or Guide is a medium for the Overself. While he is still embodied, still using an intellect and body (an ego), he can only be a medium, not more. He *is* the Overself but working through, and therefore necessarily limited by, a human individuality. It is true that in the deepest rapt meditation he can divest himself of this individuality and become the pure Overself in awareness, but that is an unusual state and you must consider him as he is in ordinary life.

201

It is the practice of a holier mediumship than that which, among spiritists, commonly passes by this name. The spirit which takes possession of him is no human one but Divine Power in him itself, the Overself.

202

He is a human agent of the superhuman grace.

203

He is a transmitter, or a carrier, of divine forces, radiations, and states of being.

204

Forget the teacher's person, remember the teacher's doctrine.

205

He is the gate through which his disciples pass to reach the higher power.

206

He is symbolic of the Overself's reality as well as an expression of its power.

207

A complete surrender of will and reason to any teacher is risky—for both persons. Only a truly great soul can afford the risk. In any case the final submission should be made to God alone, or rather to the god within, the Overself.

208

Since the connection between him and the Universal Spirit is a direct one, any submission of his inner being to another man—even if for the ostensible purpose of realizing his connection and attaining fuller awareness of it—would not be a help but an interference, not a continuance of the path travelled towards this objective but a deviation from it.

209

When he has fully learned this lesson he will look to no other human being for that which his heavenly Father alone ought to be looked to.

True relationship is internal

210

The Sufis consider the relation between teacher and disciple as a sacred eternal tie that can never be broken, as the mystical union by which two souls become so close by the telepathic link as to live and feel almost as one.

211

Between the two there is an impalpable bond which keeps them spiritually in contact. There is an intangible cable along which messages are conveyed and through which communion is made.

212

It is a privilege to come into the company of a great soul, but even more so to come into intuitive affinity with him. This is far more necessary than coming into geographical propinquity with him, for when that happens the link will not be severed by death, but his unseen presence will continue to be a vital thing.

213
Either at acceptance or later, the disciple experiences an ecstatic reverie of communion with the teacher's soul. There is a sensation of space filled with light, of self liberated from bondage, of peace being the law of life. The disciple will understand that this is the real initiation from the hands of the teacher rather than the formal one. The disciple will probably be so carried away by the experience as to wish it to happen every day. But this cannot be. It can happen only at long intervals. It is rather to be taken as a sign of the wonderful relation which has sprung up between them and as a token of eventual attainment.(P)

214
This silent wordless unavowed bond holds him far tighter and ties him far longer than any emotional vocally expressed one could do.

215
The true initiation proceeds in perfect silence. No words are needed.

216
It was a lifting-up into his mind when you had reached the very edge of your own mind.

217
From that moment the master's presence will be felt constantly as close to him, not leaving him but remaining with him. They will be together in a tender indescribable relationship.

218
The attitude of the student towards his teacher is of great importance to the student, because it lays an unseen cable from him to the teacher, and along that cable pass to and fro the messages and help which the teacher has to give. The teacher can never lose contact with the student by going to another part of the world. That unseen cable is elastic and it will stretch for thousands of miles, because the World-Mind consciousness will travel almost instantly and anywhere. Contact is not broken by increasing physical distance. It is broken by the change of heart, the alteration of mental attitude by the student towards the teacher. If the attitude is wrong, then the cable is first weakened and finally snapped. Nothing can then pass through and the student is really alone.

219
In the case of initiated disciples, suspicion cuts off the force inside the

inner cable at once, while doubt renders it only intermittently effective. In the case of persons who approach him from the public outside, these attitudes yield consequences which depend partly on the master's own attitude toward them and partly on their karma.

220

Because the master knows and regards his own self to be impersonal and immaterial, mental and not physical, the aspirant does not *have* to meet him personally in order to get inspiration from him. It is enough to meet him mentally by faith, remembrance, and devotion to get the desired result. Indeed, unless the aspirant makes *inner* contact with the master he does not become a disciple at all. No outer contact and no verbal communication will suffice to give more than a pretense of discipleship; the reality can be given from within alone. The truth is that no one becomes the disciple of an adept merely by verbal intercourse; he becomes so only when he has attained enough purity and developed enough power to meet the adept telepathically in meditation. Until that time he is still in the outer court of the temple.

221

The mere physical proximity of teacher and disciple does not constitute their association. Unless the lesser man catches by empathy and cultivates by effort something of the greater one's thoughts and feelings, he does not associate with him at all, whatever his body may be doing. It is not the person of a master but his Idea that is important.

222

There is no distance in Real Being. Therefore the disciple living in one place on this planet is as near to the master as the disciple living in another country. The belief that his personal proximity in a physical body is better than his mental proximity in spiritual development is a human and understandable illusion.

223

Where the disciple is attuned and devoted, the master genuine and compassionate, there is, there can be, no failure in communication between them. The master's presence will remain with the disciple, will not desert him, and will remain fresh even when a thousand miles in space and two hundred weeks in time separate them.

224

The mysterious feeling of the presence of his spiritual guide will come unsought at some times but it must also be deliberately cultivated at most, if not all, times. This is done by holding his mental picture before the mind's eye.

225

The inner contact with the master may variously express itself in vision or in feeling, either separately or both together. With the advanced disciple it will not matter how it is expressed, for the result in contact and communion will be the same.

226

The disciple must feel that he is living inside the teacher at times and that the teacher is living inside him at other times.

227

He will find, by actual personal experience, that the master's words are true, that the master's inward presence is often near him in ordinary hours and sometimes startlingly vivid in meditative hours.

228

He has to catch the mental radiations from his master and transform them into intuitions and inspirations as a radio set catches electrical waves from a broadcasting station and transforms them into sounds.

229

The disciple who believes himself to be in continual contact with a master unconsciously projects his own influence, limitation, and suggestion into the figure he sees, the message he receives, or the intuition he feels.

230

To achieve this frequent inner contact with the spiritual counsellor telepathically, the disciple must relax his mind from everyday affairs and concentrate upon the quest anew, must separate it from its burden of cares and desires and doubts, must let everything else go except the thought of the counsellor with whom he seeks to re-establish the consciousness of inward contact. He must abate the everlasting dominance of the personal ego and come as a humble child into the presence which he seeks to invoke.

231

When this personal purification has been undergone and inner contact has been established, the disciple will find his master ever present and recognizable when called upon, ever responsive to the obeisance of his thought and feeling.

232

The response from the master flows back to the disciple quite automatically every time he fulfils the required conditions for establishing inner contact.

233

The response from his guide will be automatic and telepathic. The latter does not need to be aware of what is happening, and in most cases will not be.

234

It is not often the master himself who thus personally communicates with, helps, inspires, or uplifts the student; but it is more often his unconscious influence, his unconscious power.

235

Just as magnetism is actually transmitted to a piece of inert steel by its mere contact with a magnet, so spiritual inspiration is transmitted to a disciple by his physical or mental contact with a master.

236

The impact of such telepathic blessings upon the disciple's mind may be instantaneously felt. Or it may first start a subconscious process working which will produce the same result more slowly and less certainly.

237

Although there is always this general response to each of the disciple's turnings towards his master, there is also the special response deliberately made on the master's own initiative at special times and impressed on the disciple.

238

There will come moments when a serene peace and an impersonal joy well up without external cause and quite suddenly within his being. They may or may not be accompanied by a mental picture of the Master, but he will intuitively feel that they derive from him and instantly connect their arisal with him. He will not be wrong. For whether at that moment exactly, or at an earlier one, the Master has indeed remembered the disciple.

239

An important part of the process used by a master is to hold the mental picture of his disciple continually inside his own heart. Inevitably, this draws forth the pupil's affection and creates desire for union with his master. The effect will be like the sun holding a tiny seedling continually within its rays. The seedling cannot escape natural growth through the action of the sunlight nor the inevitable seeking for and love of the sun itself. In the same way the pupil, who is thus given an adept's grace, may depart from or desert him but in the end will have to recognize the presence of the adept, the efficiency of the adept, and spontaneously love the adept again. To complete this process, the pupil should keep the mental picture of his master continually in *his* heart, too. This directly helps himself and enables the master to help him inwardly more effectively. If the latter did nothing more than this, its power would be enough to advance the disciple a long way. But of course he does so much more by way of pointing out the path, clearing intellectual doubts and difficulties, encouraging, inspiring, and so on.

240

The help is given telepathically and the student will begin to sense during quiet periods and at odd times the current of peace flowing toward him.

241

It is not the human thoughts which the teacher sends out, so much as the spiritual power within the disciple which is aroused by those thoughts, that matters.(P)

242

We are asked why, if thought-transference be a fact, the hibernating hermit should not still represent the loftiest achievement, should not in fact be as antisocial as he superficially seems. He may be hidden away in a mountain cave, but is not his mind free to roam where it likes and has not its power been raised to a supreme degree by his mystical practices? We reply that if he is merely concerned with resting in his inner tranquillity undisturbed by the thought of others, then his achievement is only a self-centered one.

There is much confusion amongst students about these yogis who are supposed to sit in solitude and help humanity telepathically. It is not only yogis who sit in solitude who are doing so. Nor is it needful to be a solitary to be able to do so. The truth is that most yogis who live in solitude are still in the student stage, still trying to develop themselves. And even in the rarer cases where a yogi has perfected himself in meditation, he may be using the latter simply to bask egotistically in inner peace for his own benefit and without a thought for others. It is only when a man is a philosophic yogi that he will be deliberately using his meditational self-absorptions to uplift individuals and help humanity for their good. If the mystic *is* using his mental powers for altruistic ends, if he *is* engaged in telepathically helping others at a distance, then he has gone beyond the ordinary mystical level and we salute him for it.

The Adept will not try to influence any other man, much less try to control him. Therefore, his notion of serving another by enlightening him does not include the activity of proselytizing, but rather the office of teaching. Such service means helping a man to understand for himself and to see for himself what he could not see and understand before. The Adept does this not only by using the ordinary methods of speech, writing, and example, but much more by an extraordinary method which only an

Adept can employ. In this he puts himself in a passive attitude towards the other person's ego and thus registers the character, thought, and feeling in one swift general impression, which manifests itself within his own consciousness like a photograph upon a sensitized film. He recognizes this as a picture of the evolutionary degree to which the other person has attained, but he recognizes it also as a picture of the false self with which the other person identifies himself. No matter how much sympathy he feels for the other man, no matter how negative are the emotions or the thoughts he finds reproducing themselves within his own being, it is without effect upon himself. This is because he has outgrown both the desires and the illusions which still reign over the other man's mind. With the next step in his technique he challenges that self as being fearful for its own unworthy and ultimately doomed existence, and finally dismisses the picture of it in favour of the person's true self, the divine Overself. Then he throws out of his mind every thought of the other person's imperfect egoistic condition and replaces it by the affirmation of his true spiritual selfhood.

Thus, if the Adept begins his service to another who attracted by his wisdom seeks counselling or by his godliness seeks his inspiration, by noting the defects in the character of the person, he ends it by ignoring them. He then images the seeker as standing serenely in the light, free from the ego and its desires, strong and wise and pure because living in the truth. The Adept closes his eyes to the present state of the seeker, to all the evidences of distress and weakness and darkness which he earlier noted, and opens them to the real, innermost state of the seeker, where he sees him united with the Overself. He persists in silently holding this thought and this picture, and he holds it with the dynamic intensity of which he only is capable. The effect of this inner working sometimes appears immediately in the seeker's consciousness, but more likely it will take some time to rise up from the subconscious mind. Even if it takes years to manifest itself, it will certainly do so in the end.

We know that one mind can influence another through the medium of speech or writing: we know also that it may even influence another directly and without any medium through the silent power of telepathy. All this work takes place on the level of thought and emotion. But the Adept may not only work on this level: it is possible for him to work on a still deeper level. He can go into the innermost core of his own being and there touch the innermost core of the other man's being. In this way, Spirit speaks to Spirit, but without words or even thoughts. Within his innermost being there is a mysterious emptiness to which the Adept alone gains access during meditation or trance. All thoughts die at its threshold as he enters it. But when eventually he returns to the ordinary state and the thinking activity starts again, then those first series of thoughts are endowed with a peculiar power, are impregnated with a magical potency. Their echoes reverberate telepathically across space in the minds of others to whom they may be directed deliberately by the Adept. Their influence upon sympathetic and responsive persons is at first too subtle and too deep to be recognized, but eventually they reach the surface of consciousness.

This indeed is the scientific fact behind the popular medieval European and contemporary Oriental belief in the virtue of an Adept's blessing and the value of an Adept's initiation. The Adept's true perception of him is somewhere registered like a seed in the subconscious mind of the receptive person, and will in the course of time work its way up through the earth of the unconscious like a plant until it appears above ground in the conscious mind. If it is much slower in showing its effects, it is also much more effectual, much more lasting than the ordinary way of communicating thought or transmitting influence. In this way, by his own inner growth he will begin to perceive, little by little, for himself the truth about his own inner being and outer life in the same way that the Adept perceives it. This is nothing less than a passage from the ego's point of view to the higher one.(P)

243

The picture of bringing a disciple to God for inspiration, improvement, purification, or blessing belongs to an inferior mode of working. The superior one is to shut him out of consciousness, along with his defects, and let in only the presence of God—nothing else. This is nonduality.

244

The master's presence has a paradoxical effect upon disciples. While with him they feel that they amount to nothing, that the contrast between his inner greatness and their inner littleness is tremendous and they are humbled to the dust in consequence. But soon after they leave his presence an opposite reaction develops. They feel that they do amount to something, that they are approaching the verge of spiritual attainment, and they are stimulated and excited as a result.

245

The fact that a teacher does not permit a physical meeting, even after some years of waiting, does not mean that he no longer regards you as his disciple.

246

Discipleship is a mental relationship that needs only a single meeting on the physical plane to become established. The student should remember that in such a relationship it is the mental rather than the physical contact that counts.

247

Deprived of the physical presence of his master, he is forced to seek and find the mental presence. At first he does this as a substitute for what he cannot get, but later he learns to accept it as the reality.

248

It is not really necessary to have more than one physical-plane meeting with anyone whom he chooses as a spiritual guide, because after that the inner current of help can be found on the mental plane. Such an inner link is much more real than an outer one and will in the course of time provide him with all the help he needs.

249

The image of the master will afterwards come back to the disciple again and again after this first meeting. They may never have a second one on the physical plane, yet its inner relation, the mental contact, will never die.

250

Several years may pass without a single meeting between them, and yet it will make no essential difference in their tie, or in the love which the one feels and the compassion which the other gives.

251

It must be pointed out again that a single meeting on the physical plane is usually quite enough to start the current working which provides a contact and draws spiritual help. The real help is inward and mental, and it is drawn partly to the degree of his faith in the source of that help and partly to the degree of his obedience to the practical teachings.

252

Through the use of memory and imagination in recapturing the picture of a first meeting, he may maintain the inner contact.

253

The spiritual help which he may be in a position to receive, will come just as effectively on the mental plane if he has enough faith in the principles of mentalism to believe that it can come this way.

254

The master not only becomes the inspirer of his interior life but also the symbol of it. When time and distance separate them, the remembrance of his name is enough to find his presence, and sometimes even his power, within the disciple.

255

The best remembrance, and the one which will please the advanced mystic most, is a renewed effort at self-improvement, and the renewed determination to eliminate evil qualities from the character.

256

He will come to the belief that, at certain times, the master is actually beside him, inspiring or warning him.

257

So vivid and intense are these experiences that the disciple believes he is holding genuine converse with his master.

258

The disciple who wants to "tune in" to his distant master's meditation should note the hour at which the latter usually sits for this purpose each day or night, and then find out what local time in his own district corresponds to it. If he himself will then meditate at this hour, he will have a better chance to "tune in" than at any other one; but of course a fixed inner contact will always help him to do so anyway.

259

The human embryo gets its earliest nutrition in the mother's matrix by absorbing it from the fluids which surround it; this process of nourishment by osmosis leads to its growth and development until the first of its organs, the heart, is born. Then, with the later appearance of blood-tubes, the little creature begins to pump blood and feed itself. Osmosis is a process which may help us to understand its parallel—*Sat-sang*—in the disciple-master relationship.

260

The guru and disciple sit in meditation, the one drawing the other to this divinity within.

261

It is a mingling of minds, a contact of hearts, where waves of peace pass from master to pupil, stilling restless thoughts and healing the world's hurts.

262

He will draw strength and imbibe calm from these meditations. These qualities, drawn from the master, will infuse themselves in a mysterious manner into his own being, remaining vivid for hours, sometimes for days.

263

Such experiences of a seemingly divine inflow are not imaginary ones but are the genuine reception of grace. Help is being given even when there is external silence. Do not measure its volume against the volume of physical communications.

264

Why does he sometimes see the guide's photograph emanating light and charging him with spiritual power? A photo, after all, is a light-phenomenon charged with the electromagnetic ray connection of the person photographed. When the guide tries to help, his auric mental energy immediately expresses itself through the picture and affects the seeker's mind as its percipient. However, at a certain stage of development, when that energy of the Overself which the Indians call *kundalini* is being awakened so as to enable him to do what is then put into his hands to do, the photo carries something more than mere thought; its mental radiations are actually transmuted into light-radiations and so it may at times appear to be suffused with light. And, needless to say, the most sensitive points in such a picture are the eyes; the help given will therefore affect these points most.

265

The person who is distracted by the Master's physical picture and by the attraction or repulsion it exercises on his personal feelings will not be able to attend intuitively to the Master's mental picture and spiritual aura.

266

The teacher feels that some advanced students are bits of his own self functioning, however imperfectly, at a distance, so loyal are they to him and so devoted to the same cause.

267

Because this ever-and-everywhere-present Mind has become the basis of his life, even when he has travelled to the other side of the world, he always has a curious feeling of never being absent from his pupils and of his pupils' never being absent from himself. And because of the intimate telepathic communion which is constantly going on between both, they also will have occasional flashes of the same timeless spaceless feeling concerning him.

268

The power of the higher Self is such that he who becomes its channel can affect others—if Grace be granted them by their own higher Self—by the mere thought alone. He will need neither to be near, to touch, nor to speak to them.

269

The illuminate can transmit his grace directly from mind to mind or indirectly by means of the visual glance, the physical touch, the spoken word, or the written letter.

270

He finds that, by the strange magic of telepathy, he can pass on to certain other minds something of the lustrous beatitude which pervades his own heart.

271

To those who reject the idea of a Master's grace and declare their disbelief in its possibility in a world governed by strict cause and effect, the answer is: The meaning of the word suggests something or anything of an immaterial, moral, or material nature that is given to man. Why should not the Master, who has attained a higher strength, wisdom, and moral character than that which is common to the human race, give aid freely out of his beneficent compassion for others struggling to climb the peak he has surmounted? And to those who deny that he can transmit his own inner life to another person, the answer is: In its fullness he certainly cannot do so; but he certainly can impart something of its quality and flavour to one who is receptive, sensitive, and in inward affinity with him. If this too is denied, then let the deniers explain why both the power of the Master and the sense of his presence pervade the disciple's existence for many years after his initiation if not for the rest of his life. Finally, it is a fact, but only personal experience can prove it, that inspiration may be felt coming strongly from a Master who is not physically present but far away. What is this inspiration but something added to the disciple which he would not otherwise have had—that is, grace!

272

Those who turn to an illumined man for inspiration have the possibility of getting it, no matter how large a number they may be. They can attune themselves to his mind by sympathy, faith, and devotion—conjoined with sensitivity. Even if they all turn to him at one and the same moment, the inspirer can come into direct inner touch with them through the medium of a telepathic mental bridge. This is done automatically, spontaneously, and subconsciously.

273

With a Teacher, it is the inward relationship that matters. What, then, is going to happen when there is only one Teacher and many thousands of students? How can all the wishes, dreams, and thoughts reach him, yet leave him time for his work? Obviously, it cannot be done. So Nature steps in and helps out. She has arranged a system very much like a telephone switchboard. The incoming "calls" are plugged into the subconscious mind of the Teacher. The "line" itself is composed out of the student's own faith and devotion; he alone can make this connection. Then, his wishes, dreams, and thoughts travel along it to the subconscious of the Teacher, where they are registered and dealt with according to their needs. In this way, they do reach the Teacher, who can, at the same time, attend to his own work. Sometimes, Nature deems it advisable to transfer a particular message to the conscious level. In such a case, it may be answered on either the conscious or subconscious level. Occasionally, too, the Teacher deliberately sends one out when he is guided to do so.

274

DISCIPLESHIP [Essay]

Discipleship is for those who make the quest of the Overself the deep underlying aim of their existence, who take alive and keen interest in the particular form of it outlined by P.B. in his own books, who are critical enough to understand the unique value of his teaching and grateful enough to proffer its disseminator their abiding personal loyalty. Disciples naturally look for discipline, but P.B. neither seeks the first nor stipulates the second. Discipleship is for the few because while there are many who read the books, there are but few who follow the quest; there are many who will take the first few steps but few who will take the last ones; many who can swallow fables but few who can swallow facts.

It is for those to whom the quest has become their life, their goal, their refuge, and their strength.

The true relation of discipleship cannot be established by any merely vocal asking for it and being vocally accepted. Nor can it be established by any formal outward rite or ceremony. Nor by mail order, that is, by a written request and a certificate granting it. It can be established only when it becomes first a mental fact, an inward relation, a telepathic link, and when second these things are based on the disciple's side on complete faith, devotion, loyalty, and willingness to subordinate his own little ego, his own limited intellect, should they ever find themselves opposed to the master's guidance.

This last must not be confused with blind slavish obedience. It is a realization of the need for superior guidance until that glorious moment arises when the guidance can be dispensed with, when the master himself is transcended by union with the disciple's higher self.

In other words, there must be internal evidence of the relationship's having been established, for then alone does it become a reality and a certainty.

This relationship is very rare in the modern world because most people are too materialistically minded to contribute proper efforts towards its making. They think that by associating with a master and by seeing his physical presence they have found him. This is not so. They must find his mental presence within themselves before they can begin to say they have really found him. The relationship is also rare because few such teachers are to be found in the world. For a man may attain the heights of self-realization and yet neither his characteristics nor his karma may permit him to perform the work of teaching along with his realization.

All this is the true explanation of the word "Sat-sang" (that is, association with the illumined, or with a Master) which is so often mentioned in Indian mystical circles as being the first condition to be sought for to make discipleship effective. But in present day India Sat-sang has been materialized into a physical association only, so that aspirants think they have only to go and live in some guru's ashram in order to become that guru's disciple. But this is only an imitation of Sat-sang, and the false belief partly accounts for the disappointing results noticeable in so many ashrams in that country. It also partly explains the melancholy warning given by the master K.H. in the book entitled *The Mahatma Letters*, wherein he laments the fact that so few of the pilgrims who set forth on the ocean of discipleship ever reach the longed-for land of attainment.

No man is so secure that he can afford to walk the path entirely alone, or so sure-footed that he does not feel it necessary at times to call to his aid those who are qualified to help him negotiate the difficulties.

Why is it that so many—if not most—seekers feel the need of a personal spiritual teacher? Beyond the obvious need of intellectual instruction, practical guidance, and emotional inspiration, there is a further, a profounder, and sometimes an unconscious need. The formless Infinite is a conception the human mind can hardly comprehend, much less hold for any sustained period. But the name and form of another human being who has himself succeeded in comprehending and holding the conception constitute an idea and a picture easily within mental reach. Reverent devotion given to him and imagination directed towards him set up a telepathic process which eventually elicits an intuitive response from the devotee. For in this process there is an interchange of vibration between the two whereby something, some mysterious quality of the sage's mind, is drawn into the devotee's mind and gives the devotee a feeling, however imperfect, of what the Infinite Spirit is really like. The mental image of his master can be carried by the devotee anywhere and everywhere and provides his own mentality with a definite resting place, without which it would be yearning vaguely and struggling aimlessly. But because such a relationship depends on two factors whose reality has not yet been fully granted by the educated world, it may be laughed at as an imaginary one. These two factors are telepathy and intuition. Therefore only those who have themselves experienced it can say how utterly true and intensely real it is. This is why the *Bhagavad Gita* says that out of love for his devotees, God the impersonal assumes the form of a personal guide. This is why Jesus proclaimed himself to be the door. If so many students are running hither and thither in search of a master, it is not only for the commonly given reasons that they do so, but also because of their need of a personal symbol of the impersonal God, their need of a human gate to the gateless Void. But let us not forget that this need is really a manifestation of human weakness. There are some seekers who can draw from within themselves the guidance they need, the light upon their path, and the intuition to comprehend the Absolute. They can get along quite well without a master. Indeed it is better for them to work in lonely independence for they have the best of all masters, the Higher Self. But such souls are fortunate and blessed, and those others who do not come into their category need and must find a spiritual leader. First they must find him in the world without. Later, with more understanding and increasing development, they must find him within themselves.

The service of such a guide in helping seekers to understand spiritual truth and in sustaining their interest in it is necessarily great. He will equip them with sound metaphysical knowledge and impart to them the primary elements of the hidden teaching. It is essential to pass through a course of systematic instruction involving the highest discipline before this knowledge can be got. His own informed mind will enlighten theirs and his inspiring words will stimulate aspiration. He will be to them the voice of research and meditation far beyond their present capacity. Also he enables them to conserve their interest after the first flush of enthusiasm for the teaching has inevitably lost some of its emotional intensity amid the pressures and oppositions of a sceptical world.

Even when whatever is good and true from amongst current notions in different schools of thought is selected and sifted, and a compact doctrine is formed from the results, the tremendous vitalizing power of a master is often needed to make such truths tangible.

The teacher examines the aptitudes and trends of aspirants and prescribes accordingly. The disciple is not told directly what to accept, but is so guided that he is given the chance to perceive the facts, follow the reasoning as if it were his own, and reach for the conclusions apparently by himself. In reality throughout this process he is aided by the teacher, yet so subtly that in perfect freedom he develops his own capacities, for it is the aim of the true teacher to put the red corpuscles of self-reliance into his pupils.

The adept opens up a line of communication between his disciple's conscious mind and the secret conscious spiritual self. Thus in due time, the disciple receives from his master the full truth of the world.

The wonderful influence which a true sage exerts upon a receptive student is well-exemplified by the statement of Alcibiades about his former master Socrates: "At the words of Socrates," he says, "my heart leaps within me and my eyes rain tears when I hear them. And I observe that many others are affected in the same manner. I have heard Pericles and other great orators, and I thought that they spoke well, but I never had any similar feeling; my soul was not stirred by them, nor was I angry at the thought of my own slavish state. But this Marsyas [Socrates] has often brought me to such a pass that I have felt as if I could hardly endure the life that I am leading; and I am conscious that if I did not shut my ears against him and fly as from the voice of the siren, my fate would be like that of others—he would transfix me and I would grow old sitting at his feet. For he makes me confess that I ought not to live as I do, neglecting the wants of my own soul, and busying myself with the concerns of the Athenians; therefore I hold my ears, and tear myself away from him. And he is the only person who ever made me feel ashamed, and there is no one else who does the same. For I know that I cannot answer him or say that I ought not do as he bids, but when I leave his presence the love of popularity gets the better of me. And therefore I run away and fly from him, and when I see him I am ashamed." (from Plato's *Symposium*)

The relationship between the spiritual counsellor and his disciple must first find an inward harmony as its basis. After that harmony there will emerge a telepathic reception on the part of the disciple. There is often much misunderstanding about this type of communication. Let it be stated categorically that whatever the counsellor communicates it would necessarily deal with the general rather than with the particular, with the higher emotions to be cultivated rather than with the things and happenings of this world, with the spiritual qualities to be unfolded rather than with the material affairs and special situations of the external life. It is common enough, however, for the seeker's ego to mistranslate the character of the help given to him, to turn the impersonal into the personal, the lofty into the lower, and even the pure into the impure.

It is rarely understood here in the Occident that where spiritual help is given telepathically, it is given as a general inspiration to remember the divine laws, to have faith in them, and to follow the higher ideals. It is not given as a particular guidance in the detailed application of those laws, nor in the day to day outworking of those ideals. The teacher gives by radiation from his inner life and being, and the disciple draws it into his own mind by a correct approach and mental attitude towards the teacher. What he receives, however, is impersonal. His own ego will have to convert it into a personal form and will have to apply the ideals instilled into him. Another misconception is also very common: "Is it not the master himself who helps me at such moments?" is a question asked in astonished surprise by those disciples who feel his presence keenly, see his image vividly, and converse with him personally in experiences which are genuinely telepathic in character. The answer is that it both is and is not the master himself. The minute particulars of the pictorial experience, or the actual words of a message are supplied by the disciple's own ego. The mental inspiration and moral exaltation derived from it and the emotional peace which surround it are drawn telepathically out of the master's being. Both these elements are so commingled and diffused with one another in the disciple's mind, and so instantaneously too, that inevitably he gets only an unclear and partial understanding of his experience. The truth is that the master does not necessarily have to be conscious of the pupil's telepathic call for help in order to make that help available. Nor does he personally have to do anything about it in order to ensure that his help is transmitted. Just as it is said that the cow's idea of heaven is of a place eternally filled with grass, and that a man's idea of God is a magnified human being, so it may be said that the uninformed aspirant's idea of a spiritual guide is often only an improved and enlarged version of himself. The master is pictured as being filled with oozing sentimentality, however pious, vibrating with personal emotion, and fluttered by his disciple's changes of fortune—as being almost always on the verge of tears with sympathy for others, as fretting over every little fault and change of mood in his disciples every hour of the twenty-four, every day of the week, every week of the year. It is imagined that the master seeks only to influence pleasurable experiences towards his disciples and to divert painful ones—as though pleasurableness were the only good and pain the only evil. It is easy for people to open the doors of a weak sentiment or to gild the bars of the cage of selfishness and forget the living prisoner within. To them the Illuminate is a paradox of conduct. For the same law which stays his hand from giving promiscuous relief also bids him render unto each man his due.

If he places himself in the proper attitude the disciple may be ten thousand miles away from the master and yet receive not less fully and not less adequately the bestowal of Grace, the telepathic awareness of a higher presence, the divine renewal of his inner life.

The mental image of his absent master may come before him bearing any one of several different suggestions, reminders, inspirations, or consolations.

But it is for the pupil himself to cultivate perfect poise between the two extremes of utter dependence upon a teacher and complete reliance upon himself. Both extremes will obstruct his advance upon this path. Nor will it be enough to find the mid-way point between them and adhere always to that point. The definition of poise will vary at different stages of his career. At one time it will be absolutely necessary for him to cultivate self-reliance, whereas a couple of years later it may be equally necessary to cultivate a mood of dependence. What is proper at one time or period may not be proper at another. Which phase is to be uppermost or when both are to perfectly balanced is something which can be decided only by a mingling of inner prompting, logical reflection, and other circumstances.

"To the real enquirers after knowledge, the master's words will enable one to know his own self. A teacher's Grace, if it becomes *en rapport* with his disciple, will of itself in a mysterious manner enable the disciple to perceive directly the Brahmic principle within. It is impossible for the disciple to understand how Brahman is prior to his direct perception. It is indeed very rare to attain that state without the help of a Guru."—*Yoga Vasistha*

The master flings his divine grace direct from his own great heart into the heart of the disciple—this is the true initiation.

"The master who has completed his quest commences it anew with every disciple."—the Persian Sheikh Gazur-i-Elahi the Sufi

There are always the few who respond to the master's voice more quickly than others, and hence receive more fully. When he finds querents who are completely unready to grasp the subtle truth which he expounds to those more familiar with his philosophic ideas, he takes up the viewpoint of the questioner and gives him a lift upward from his present state.

If some complain that he is inaccessible, this is because real intercourse with them is impossible, because they can meet him only on surface levels where all that is said or done vanishes futilely in the air. But if anyone comes to the master as a *seeker* to discuss the higher purposes of life, he is quite ready to do so. The fact that he seldom gives himself to others shows only that so few come to him in such a spirit. And for those who do he cannot eliminate the long search for truth, but he can shorten it. The intuition of the seeker which brought him into touch with the teacher has, however, to be put to the test during the probationary period. If during this contract time the seeker allows nothing, no outward appearance or inward doubt, to break his loyalty to the Guide, then the day will surely come when he can enter into full discipleship; but if, judging by intellect alone and deceived by superficial circumstances, he falls away from faith in his guide, then the rare opportunity will pass and be wasted. In that event he will spend the years groping amid semi-darkness for the entrance to the path which he has missed, but to which his teacher would gladly have led him in due course.

The master's Grace and guidance abides with his disciples so long as they abide inwardly with him.

At the moment of death of a disciple, the teacher will always be present spiritually to help him pass out of the body in a peaceful state of mind. If, as should be, the disciple places his last thoughts and faith in the teacher, that will call to the teacher wherever he may be, and he will appear to the mind's eye of the dying disciple.

And a master who has led even one *chela* some distance on this path will never be content to let him reappear on this earth without the hope of finding further guidance, further support, and further teaching. The master will never be content with the passionless peace of Nirvana the while his former students struggle in the maze of passions and suffer thereby. He is no master of the true doctrine that all beings are oneself in reality who could desert his students to gain his own ease. The awareness of his identity with ALL will surely and compulsorily arouse his profoundest compassion with those earnest seekers who know not whither to turn for genuine help during their groping amid the darkness. And this will lead to a single and certain result: that at the moment of dying he will WILL his own rebirth again and again until his flock are brought safely through the narrow gate which leads to the kingdom of heaven. Therefore it is said, for such is the mysterious reality of his telepathic power, that the birth of the guru sends forth an echoing vibration within the universe, which acts as a call to his unborn *chelas* to incarnate with him, and as a command to the principle of rebirth to make effectual the event. Thus he sacrifices himself for the salvation of his chelas.

Discipleship. Seeking the master:
The word "guru" is sacred throughout India. Although a Sanskrit term, it has been incorporated into most of the varying tongues and dialects in the different provinces and is even used in several books written by Tibetan mystics.

Guru means teacher; and a teacher who has realized his responsibility and tested his views, who has proved his competence and established his trustworthiness, is very hard to find.

If a seeker cannot find himself, let him find a teacher. If he cannot find such a one, let him find a disciple. If he fails in that, too, let him find a book written by a teacher.

We are affected by our associates; he who keeps company with criminals is apt to descend into crime himself; he who seeks the spiritually minded as friends is apt to ascend to spirituality.

There are various teachers in the world, but each can only teach according to the experience he has had. Because we believe that meditation has a place and a purpose in life, this is no reason why we should raise every idiot who practises it to the stature of a sage, nor why we should esteem every charlatan who plays with it, as a saint.

There are several self-styled spiritual guides who can guide their flocks into all kinds of queer experiences, but they cannot guide them into the Kingdom of Heaven. That territory is barred to them. Consequently it is barred to those who meekly walk behind them. The reason for this is quite simple. Jesus explained it long ago. The lower ego with its baggage of desires is too big, while the door leading into the Kingdom is too small. In all their activities, these teachers fail to achieve a truly spiritual result because they are thinking primarily of themselves rather than of what they are supposed to be thinking. In some cases the process is an unconscious one, but in many it is not.

The difference between a false teacher and a genuine one is often the difference between a dominating dictator and a quiet guide. The false teacher will seek to emasculate your will or even to enslave your mind, whereas the true teacher will endeavour to exalt you into a sense of your own self-responsibility. The teacher who demands or accepts such servility is dangerous to true growth. In the end, he will require a loyalty which should be given only to the Overself. The true teacher will carry your soul into greater freedom and not less, into stabilizing truth and not emotional moods. The true teacher has no desire to hold anyone in pupilage, but on the contrary gladly welcomes the time when the disciple is able to stand without help from outside.

But because talk is easy and redemption is not demanded except in the distant future, these false teachers thrive for a while. Many of them are but students, yet find it hard to take the low places where humility dwells. Hence their gravity; hence the laughter of the gods at them. Could they but laugh at themselves awhile, and perhaps at their doctrines occasionally, they might regain balance, a sense of proportion—but greatest of all true Humility. They are not necessarily deliberate misleaders of others, these self-appointed saviours, but their mystical experiences have given them false impressions about themselves. Their authority is fallible and their doctrines are false. They find it easy to deliver themselves of lofty teachings, but hard to put the same teaching into practice. These gurus promise much, but in the sequel do not redeem their word. These self-styled adepts appear to be adepts in circumlocution more than in anything else.

Those who openly court worship or secretly exult in it cannot possibly have entered into the true Kingdom of Heaven. For the humility it demands is aptly described by Jesus when he describes its entrance as smaller than a needle's eye.

Would-be disciples who are so eager to fill this role that they are swept straightaway into enthusiasm by the extravagant promises of would-be masters, usually lack both the desire and the competence to investigate the qualifications of such masters. Consequently they pay the penalty of their lack of discrimination.

If a nation accepts and follows a wicked man as its leader, then there must be some fault in it which made this possible. And if a seeker accepts a false guide on his spiritual path, then there must be some false intuition, false thinking, or false standards which made this possible too.

There are various ways of appraising a teacher at his true worth. We may watch his external life and notice how he conducts his affairs, how he talks and works, and how he behaves towards other men. Or we may dive deep into his interior nature and plumb the depths of his mental life. The latter course presupposes some degree of psychic sensitiveness. The best way is to combine both, to penetrate the unseen and to observe the visible.

Nanak, founder of the Sikh faith, uttered this warning: "Do not reverence those who call themselves guru and who beg for alms. Only those who live by the fruits of their labour and do honest and useful work are in the way of truth."

Spiritual knowledge is not to be bought and sold. Indeed it could not be. That which could be got and given in this way is only the pretense of it. It is utterly impossible for a man who has entered into communion with the World-Mind to sell his powers for money. The very act would of itself break his connection with it, leaving for his possession only those undesirable lesser powers which come from contact with the fringes of the nether world of dark spirits.

I dislike, and shall always dislike, any attempt to cash in on the spiritual assets of a teacher or his teaching. Those who begin to hawk the things of God, however indirectly and remotely, become nothing but common hucksters.

The aspirant who expects a guru to be like himself, only somewhat better, a guru made in his own image, rejects the teacher who does not fit in with his preconception and goes on looking for the impossible.

The ideal sage is not the wandering *sadhu* but the working one, he who works incessantly to relieve the sufferings of his fellows and to enlighten them.

There are too many aspirants who are hoping, like Micawber in Dickens' story, for something to turn up. In their case it is a spiritual master who will not only take their burdens and responsibilities off their shoulders but, much more, translate them overnight into a realm of spiritual consciousness for evermore. They go on waiting and they go on hoping, but nothing turns up and no one appears. What is the reason for this frustration of their hopes? It is that they fail to work while they wait, fail to prepare themselves to be fit for such a meeting, fail to recognize that whether they have a master or not they must still work upon themselves diligently, and that the harder they work in this task of self-improvement, the more likely it is that they will find a master. They are like children who want to be carried all the way and coddled while they are being carried. They are waiting for someone to do what they ought to be doing for themselves. They are waiting to receive from outside what they could start getting straightaway by delving inside themselves.

Because of bad karma and inherent insensitivity most people fail to recognize the master as such, and therefore fail to take advantage of the opportunity offered by his presence among them.

Only the master's body can be perceived by the physical senses. His spirit must be received by intuition. If acceptance or rejection of him is based on the physical senses alone, then only a false master will be found, never a true one. If the idea of him is predetermined by conceptions about his appearance, and if he is accepted only because he looks handsome or speaks well, and rejected because he is lame, blind, or diseased, then the true master will never be found, only charlatans and imposters.

He who says, "I want no mediator between myself and Truth," has the right instinct but the wrong attitude. None save self can make the divine discovery for him, but this is not to say that an adept who has attained the inward light cannot come to the one stumbling in darkness and give a guiding hand. As a matter of fact the true teacher does much more than this. He even gives that stimulus which carries us over the quest so steep and difficult, so beset with snares, and so often clouded over that a guide who has travelled the path already is more necessary than we dream. It is he who points out the direction when all are uncertain, who encourages when our pace slackens, who strengthens when our will weakens, and who becomes a bridge as it were between our present standpoint and a diviner one.

The oracle of wisdom must find a seat, the stream of divinity must find an outlet. Hence the need for a teacher.

If it be asked, are the great Adepts accessible by the masses and willing to bestow help upon them, the answer is that they are not. They leave the masses to the infallible workings of gross Nature, which influences and develops them by its general internal evolutionary impetus; they leave even ordinary aspirants to the guidance of more advanced ones. In one way they stand like helpless spectators of the Great Show, for they may not interfere with but must ever respect the freewill of others, whose experience of embodied life is regarded by them as sacred. For this experience incarnation is taken, and its lessons are a fruit of which not even the Adepts may rob any man or woman. They reveal themselves to, and shed their aid upon, the few who can win their own way to their presence by preparatory self-purification, mystical methods, and philosophic understanding. Their duty is to guide such as have earned the right to their guidance and who can inwardly respond to them. From the foregoing statements it should now be obvious that the teachers who accept any and every applicant, themselves belong to the lowest rung and possess an imperfect character.

There is a craze for Messianic revelations. The weak and credulous will always worship the bold. Hence any man who has seen a corner of the veil lifted can come forward as a god who has seen all the veil lifted, and he is sure to collect an obedient flock. Such men are very apt at creating personal fantasies. They appear in their own eyes as God-sent guides and liberators.

It is a strange but saddening thought that all these would-be Christs are conscious of a world-wide mission which they have to perform, whereas the real adept is unconscious of having any mission whatever. The Infinite is embodied in him and carries out its work perfectly without calling up his own separate ego-hood. Since the latter has been blown out like a candle he cannot be conscious of having a mission. Only those who are still under the delusion of separateness can harbour such an idea.

The conclusion is that instead of wandering about looking for Christs to come, we should be better employed wandering inward looking for the Christ there, the Christ within. Such a truth is our best Saviour and the surest Avatar of our time.

Discipleship. Meditation:

To practise meditation on the way of discipleship is always simple, and often easier than all other exercises. It is to repose physically, let the personal life subside mentally and emotionally, think reverently and devotedly of the master, and thus surrender the ego to him.

The same technique applies to the connection with the guru. After he is "seen," you should take the plunge and try to "feel" his presence as the next stage. Later you should transfer to yourself *as your own* that which was formerly the characteristic of his presence, and this you can do only by dismissing him. When the teacher disappears for you in personal emotion, it is because you see him from the *Atmic* standpoint, impersonally; later the love will return as intensely as before, but you will find yourself free. You will not be *attached*.

Initiation cannot be conferred as lightly as many seekers imagine. It must be gained by one's own unremitting effort to understand; it must be attained by fitting oneself through constant reflection. It is the fruit of growth, not only the gift of a teacher. Not that the teacher is not needed: his guidance, instruction, and counsel are prerequisites of its attainment. And it should be observed that what he leaves unsaid is at times as important as what he says.

It should also be remembered that if visions arise of a deceased saint or a living guide it is because there is the conscious or unconscious wish to have them. This does not mean they are without reality or without truth. It means that the form in which spiritual help is expected contributes to the actual shaping of that help. It means that each individual receives his spiritual experience in terms which have the most meaning for him and which therefore make that experience most useful to him.

It is very hard to concentrate attention upon something which has no visible points, and that is the nature of the pure Spirit—formless and shapeless. The easier way is to form a mental picture of someone who represents the incarnation of your highest ideal, and to whom you are deeply attracted because he makes this ideal real for you, and then to strive in imagination for inward unity with him. When the living presence is felt, it is like meeting a friend; when the vision only is perceived, it is like seeing his painted portrait. Then meditate on the attributes of a divinely inspired character, on the qualities of a divinely guided life. Later, the time will certainly come when the mental picture will disappear of its own accord and will be replaced by the consciousness of pure Spirit which the master has represented for you.

In the Tibetan systems of meditation, at a certain state the worshipper of a god has to think of himself as being the god.

Discipleship. The disciple's work. Difficulties, Errors:

It would be wrong to believe that the attainment of a high degree of initiation into mystical truth makes any man or woman absolutely infallible in personal judgement or absolutely infallible in personal character.

He who is only a disciple himself has no right to become responsible for the inner life of another. But within the degree of both his understanding and his misunderstanding of truth he may cautiously, judiciously, offer a helping hand to others who may be even more precariously placed than himself. Both he and they should do this with a clear understanding of their situation, without exaggeration on his part and without fanaticism on theirs.

It is easier for women to follow the path of devotion, for men to follow the path of discipline. And the easiest form of the first path is to choose, as an object of this devotion, some individual who reflects the divine qualities. More women than men are usually to be found circling around a prophet, a saint, or a guide. They are drawn instinctively to personalities, where they cannot so easily as men, absorb principles. This is all right so long as they do not lose balance. But unfortunately this is what they often do. The relation between them and their leader then tends to become unhealthy for both and enfeebling for them. The noble devotion to him which they may properly show becomes frenzied attachment or foolish deification. This enlarges personal egoism instead of dissolving it, and real spiritual development is hindered by the very thing which ought to help it.

Eventual graduation of disciple

275

In an adept's presence, as in the sun's presence, things begin to happen of their own accord. People feel a spiritual quickening and begin to call him master and themselves disciples. The whole institution of discipleship is nothing but a convenient illusion created by people themselves and tolerantly permitted by the adept for their sakes. He himself, however, is aware of no such thing, has no favouritism, but sends out his light and power to the whole of mankind indiscriminately. Yet this is not to say that the disciples' illusion is a useless or baseless one. It is indeed very real from their standpoint and experience and affords the greatest help to their advancement. Ultimately, however, towards the final stages of the path, they discover him entirely within themselves as the infinite reality, not disparate from themselves, and the sense of duality begins to disappear. Later they merge in him and "I and my Father are one" may then be truly uttered.

276

The realized man leaves no lineal descendants to take over his spiritual estate. Spiritual succession is a fiction. The heir to a master's mantle must win it afresh: he cannot inherit it.(P)

277

Emerson could not be deceived by common theories in the matter when he wrote: "When a great man dies, the world looks for his successor. He has no successor."

278

When the concept of the ego is put aside, all those other individuals who are associated with it will be put aside with it. This will apply not only to family and friends, as Jesus taught, but even to the spiritual master.

279

Ernest Wood, *Practical Yoga*: "There was a tradition in some occult circles that when the pupil reached the highest initiation, he had to kill his teacher. The meaning is simple—the master is not the form that appears and speaks words. In nine cases out of ten that form is created by the pupil even when the words speak truth. The master in the pupil thus speaks to himself. And inasmuch as the pupil has come to life, he must perform that meditation in which the form vanishes and the life alone shines forth. Akin to this is the tradition that the personality of a Master is an illusion."

280

Only when he has reached a point where he no longer thinks of the Master as another person but as the core of his inner self, can it be said that the Master's work for him is done. When Jesus said that he who eats His flesh and drinks His blood abides in Him and He in him, he meant no theatrical rite of purely ceremonial order such as is performed outwardly through the Eucharist today. He meant this inwardly achieved union here described.

281

The guru is useful at a certain time and for a limited time, to help us rise from level to level in our spiritual life. But since the aim of evolution is to bring us to ourselves, to *Atma*, unless we drop the very guru-idea itself at a certain stage, we shall stop our further growth.

282

If the disciple is held too long in dependence by his guru, it may prevent him finding out his powers.

283

It is a good master who is ego-free enough to recognize that his work is done, and it is a faithful disciple who will accept the fact and let him go. The master knows that however helpful he himself was in the past, his presence will henceforth be a hindrance. The disciple knows that it will now be better to depend upon his own intuitive self and work out his own salvation.

284

There is a right time for all things. The symbol which has been such a grand help must now go. It has served him well, but to cling to it always will be to stop on the way to his great goal. The reason for this is quite simple. The Real is beyond all individualization, all ideation, and all picturization, because it is beyond all form, all the senses, and all thought. While anything—any particular human image or idea—occupies his mind, no matter how exalted it may be, he is giving himself up to that thing, not to the ineffable Real itself. Unless he frees his mind from it, he will miss aim. Hence he must withdraw attention from the concrete symbol and bestow it henceforth on the lonely formless void which is then left. Nothing and nobody must then be permitted entrance therein. Most aspirants naturally shrink from this step, shrink from deserting what has been such a faithful helpful friend in the past, but it is one that cannot be avoided.

285

This last stage, where the presence and picture of the Master are displaced by the pictureless presence of the disciple's own spirit, is accurately described in the words of Jesus to his disciples: "It is expedient for you that I go away: for if I go not away, the Comforter will not come unto you . . . when he, the Spirit of truth, is come, he will guide you into all truth." Any other interpretation of them leaves them without reasonable meaning.

286

When a man has at last found himself, when he has no longer any need of an outside human Symbol but passes directly to his own inner reality, he may stand shoulder to shoulder with the teacher in the oldest, the longest, and the greatest of struggles.(P)

287

The adept is happy indeed when a student comes into the full realization of the Kingdom of Heaven, for whoever finds it, naturally wants to share it with others.

288

There are untouched forces back of self which we seldom include when we reckon up our mortal accounts. One of these is that aspect of God in man which we denominate Power. Once found it makes us feel greater than we seem. When the divine will works through our hands, we may go forth into the world and master it. Strong in this consciousness of Power, we can advance without fear, asking favour of none, yet conferring it upon all we meet.

Part 2:
WORLD-IDEA

Spiritual feelings are good and necessary but they are not enough; they need to be completed and complemented by spiritual knowledge. We have much to gain by learning the laws and knowing the processes which the World-Mind has imprinted upon the cosmos. Otherwise we are likely to violate those laws or interfere with those processes through ignorance. The result will then be suffering and unhappiness.

It is Man's true business in this world to discover his real self and to ascertain his relationship to the surrounding world. His mind will then shine with the Secret glory of human nature and his life will come into harmony with the cosmic order and beauty.

1

DIVINE ORDER OF THE UNIVERSE

Meaning, purpose, intelligent order

Is life only a stream of random events following one another haphazardly? Or is there an order, a meaning, a purpose behind it all?

2

Philosophy offers as a first truth the affirmation that we live in a universe of purpose and not one of caprice.

3

We live in an orderly universe, not an accidental one. Its movements are measured, its events are plotted, and its creatures develop towards a well-defined objective. All this could not be possible unless the universe were ruled by immutable laws.

4

There is an invisible mechanism within the universe and an intelligent mind directing this mechanism.

5

The cosmic order behind things is a divine one or it would be supplanted by nothing less than chaos. It is creative, intelligent, conscious—it is MIND.

6

The universe could not exist as such if there were not some sort of equilibrium holding it together, some sort of balancing arrangement as in the spinning of the earth on its axis and the planets around the sun. A little thought will show the same principle in the just relation of human beings to the World-Mind and among themselves. Here it appears as karma.

7

If moon, earth, and planets came into existence, and were thenceforward directed, by mere chance or whim, there would be no pattern in their positions and no rhythm in their movements; that is, there would be no world-order. Were the sun and stars involved in the same caprice, we would not know when to expect daylight and darkness, nor where the North Pole would be found. But because there *is* a World-Idea, there is law, orderliness, and some certainty: there is a universe, not a chaos.

8

If there were no World-Idea, then would all things be governed by mere chance, then would all be in dense obscurity; all our lives would flit through past, present, and future in a haphazard way.

9

The universe would be without meaning and without purpose if it were itself without the World-Idea behind it.

10

If there were no World-Idea there would be no world as we now know it, for its elements would have interacted and associated quite irresponsibly by mere accident and chance. In the result the sun might or might not have appeared today, the seasonal changes would have no orderly arrangement nor food-crops any predictable or measurable probability; instead of man there might have evolved a frightful monstrosity, half-animal and half-demon, utterly devoid of any aspiration, any conscience, any pity at all.

11

Those sceptics who assert that the universe is meaningless are themselves making a meaningful statement about it. That is, they are unconsciously setting themselves up as being more knowledgeable about whatever intelligence lies behind the designs and patterns we see everywhere in nature.

12

The great worlds which move so marvellously and rhythmically through our sky, however, must leave the more reflective minds with a wondering sense of the sublime intelligence which has patterned the universe.

13

The materialist who sees in the course of Life only a blind, irrational, chaotic, and arbitrary movement, has been deceived by appearances, misled by the one-sidedness of his own psyche.

14

There is enough evidence in Nature and in humanity for the existence of a Higher Power. Those who say they cannot find it have looked through the coloured spectacles of preconceived notions or else in too limited an area. There is plenty of it for those who look aright, and who widen their horizon; it will then be conclusive.

15

There are orderly patterns in Nature which we can call "laws" in its timings, properties, measurements, and lives.

16

The cosmos exists in a great harmony for it obeys laws which are divinely perfect.

17

It requires deep thought to discover that the improvements in Nature's laws which can so easily be suggested would, in the long term, probably lead to worse results than those now existent.

18

There is an established order in the universe, scientific laws which govern all things, and no magician who seems to produce miracles has been permitted under special dispensation to violate that order or to flout those principles.

19

Consider how orderly is the periodicity of giant-dimensioned planetary travels as well as of microscopic atomic weights.

20

Can we rightly say it is mere chance that our earth rotates around the sun, and does so in a certain precise measured rhythm? Is there not evidence of intelligence here?

21

Wherever we search in the universe, whether among the stars or the molecules, its structure reveals both orderliness and intelligence.

22

In his essay upon history, Emerson wrote, "The facts of history pre-exist in the mind as laws."

23

The presence of these laws should not make us picture the universe to ourselves as if it were a kind of manufactory filled with the whirr of wheels turning mechanically and automatically—ugly, lifeless, and loveless—utterly indifferent toward the hapless individuals who happen to find themselves in it.

24

The elements which chemically make up the physical universe interact mechanically. But because it *is* a universe and not a chaos there is a directing Intelligence behind the orderliness of this interaction.

25

When the existence of the Power is granted and its reality accepted, it will be easy to grant and accept that causation is everywhere present. Life in the universe then becomes meaningful.

26

Because the universe is mental in origin and character, it cannot be devoid of intelligibility and purpose.

27

This far-stretching universe is the expression of a Mind and therefore it is under the rule of law, not chance, for all laws are the consequences of mental activity.

28

If the universe were obviously based on mere chance, if it were in a state of complete disorder, if the moon, the sun, and the earth wandered about at their individual will, and if no sign of organization appeared anywhere in it, then we might justly assert that there was no Mind behind it. But because we see the very contrary of these things all around us, because the energy out of which the universe is made is everywhere inseparable from thought, we can definitely assert that a World-Mind *must* exist.

29

Events may seem to happen at random, but it is not really so. They are connected with our own thinking and doing, with the pattern of the World-Idea and with the activity of the World-Mind.

30

Everything around us and every event that happens to us is an expression of God's will.

31

The forces in the universe and the figures on the universal scene are all connected with each other and are all related with the World-Mind. Nothing stands alone except in its illusory belief.

Ultimate "rightness" of events

32

If God expresses His will through, and in, the universe then why are the horrors we find there unbeatable by any of the tortures perpetrated by man? The wanton malignancy of certain parasites, ants, worms; the poisonous bites and stings of certain insects and reptiles; the dreadful fish like piranhas which strip unfortunate wretches to a skeleton in a few minutes; the infectious germs in jungle and city alike; the intimidating hordes of vermin which threaten to multiply and destroy other forms—are they all God's goodness?

33
Even believers may sometimes ask themselves the question: "Is God blind and unseeing to human suffering—so small an item in the vastness of His universe—or callous and indifferent to it?"

34
Those who see no sign of God in the universe, and leave it at that, are at least in a better position than those who think they can detect an underlying hostility in the universe.

35
The absurdity of life and the insanity of man cast doubt upon the sanity of their Source. But this is a surface point of view.

36
The order which has been established throughout the cosmos is a perfect one. If the human mind fails to see this fact, it is partly because human feelings, prejudices, aversions, and attractions sway it and partly because the World-Idea unveils itself only to those who are ready.

37
The universe is perfect because God is perfect. But it is for each man to find and see this perfection for himself, otherwise the trouble and tragedy in life may obstruct his vision and obscure his path.

38
If the Mind behind this universe is perfect, then the pattern of the universe itself must be perfect too. And so it will show itself to be, if we muster up the heroism needed to cast out our feeble, sentimental, and emotional way of looking at things, if we put aside for a few minutes our personal and human demands that the universe shall conform to our wishes.

39
The more intellectual they are, the more they feel that God has somehow blundered, that they could have made a better or kindlier job of the universe than he has, and that too much unnecessary suffering falls upon his creatures. The sage, however, with his deeper insight and his serener mentality, finds the contrary to be the case and is set free from such bitter thoughts.

40
It is preposterous presumption to look in the divine Intelligence for what can only be found in the limited and little human one. Men judge the world without knowing the World-Idea, certainly without conscious contact with the World-Mind.

41
The moment we establish a right relation with the Mind behind the

Universe, in that moment we begin to see as ultimately good certain experiences which we formerly thought to be evil, and we begin to see as dreamlike many sufferings which we formerly saw as real.

42

The answer to those who admit they can understand and accept the existence of suffering when it is the result of karma caused by man's conduct toward man, but cannot understand and accept it when caused by Nature's havoc, by earthquakes and floods, by wild beasts and tornados, may not be a palatable one. It is that calamity and suffering, destruction and death, are ordained parts of the divine World-Idea, which needs them to ensure the evolution of entities. It is also that, after all, these things happen only on the surface of their consciousness, for deep down in the Spirit there is perfect harmony and unbroken bliss.

43

Just as we find strife, violence, and evil on the surface of human existence but divinity, harmony, and peace at its core, so we find cruelty, suffering, and malevolence on the surface of the world's existence but intelligent beneficent purpose at its core. It is ultimately an expression of God's wisdom, power, and love.

44

When I go into the innermost depths of my being I find that all is good. When the scientist can go into the innermost depths of the atom he will find that all is good there—and consequently in the entire universe constructed from atoms.

45

He looks at the universe with reverent eyes. What he sees is an infinitely variable manifestation of divine intent, divine Idea, hidden behind the conflict of opposites, the clash of yin and yang. The point of equilibrium brings the struggle to an end, revealing harmony instead.

46

The World-Idea is perfect at every point and every stage of its eternal unfoldment.

47

In glimpses of the World-Idea, human observational and intellectual beings discover an arrangement of things and creatures, of activities and circumstances, whose beauty and wisdom in one place evokes their constant wonder, but whose ugliness and horror in another place draws forth their strong protest. There is no answer to this enigma but simple religious trust for the shallow multitude and movement to another level by mystical experience for the serious seekers. In the first case there is the *hope* that in a

God-governed world all is arranged for the best, while in the second there is the overwhelming *feeling* that it is so. The philosopher is also possessed of hope and feeling but, venturing into a wider area, adds knowledge.

48

We see the underside of the pattern only—and merely a part of it at that—and inevitably judge Nature to be cruel, "red in tooth and claw." If we could see the upper side and the whole of it, the pattern would show itself perfect.

49

From this ultimate point of view there are no sins, only ignorance; there are no clumsy falls, only steps forward to the heart's wiser levels; there are no misfortunes, only lessons in the art of disentanglement.

50

Pain and suffering belong only to this physical world and its shadow-spheres. There is a higher world, where joy and happiness alone are man's experience.

51

The structure and working of the universe may not be stamped with "goodness" as we understand it, nor with "perfection" as we envisage it. Consider them from all aspects, however, in a philosophical manner and you will find them essentially "right."

52

Because there is a Divine Mind back of the universe, there are Divine Wisdom and Goodness in the universe.

53

The universe of our experience is governed by justice and wisdom, by ultimate goodness and infinite power.

54

The universe has infinitely more intelligence behind it than the men who live in it. This remains true even though there is much that seems unnecessarily brutal and unacceptable to compassionate believers in a divine order.

55

Let evil appearances be what they are, the revelation of insight contradicts them and shows the divine presence throughout the whole universe and behind all happenings.

56

Even the violent, sudden, and unwanted decease of such a multitude of persons in war, pestilence, famine, or eruption has a positive meaning in the divine World-Idea and is not at all vain or useless.

57

The truth about cosmic laws is sometimes terrifying to our human fears, sometimes repulsive to our human feeling. It may fitly be called ugly at such times. But the infinite power behind those laws is always beautiful.

58

In spite of contrary appearances this is still God's world.

59

We live in an orderly world but not in a humane one.

60

We must find the faith and some of us even the certitude that if it had been possible to think a better cosmos into being, the World-Mind's infinite wisdom would have done so. We cannot believe in God without accepting God's universe also.

61

We must accept and submit to the World-Idea with its ascending hierarchy of creatures and pre-established order of things.

62

If we do not know why we are here, the Universal Mind does. We may and must trust it.

63

When Lao Tzu saw the wonders of the World-Idea he could not help writing: "The Supreme Essence nurtures all things with care and love."

Nature of the World-Idea

64

Whatever we call it, most people feel—whether vaguely or strongly— that there must be a God and that there must be something which God has in view in letting the universe come into existence. This purpose I call the World-Idea, because to me God is the World's Mind. This is a thrilling conception. It was an ancient revelation which came to the first cultures, the first civilizations, of any importance, as it has come to all others which have appeared, and it is still coming today to our own. With this knowledge, deeply absorbed and properly applied, man comes into harmonious alignment with his Source.(P)

65

Thought is the product of mind. The unique, perfect, and all-harmonious thought evolving the cosmos is the World-Idea.

66

The World-Idea is self-existent. It is unfolded in time and by time; it is the basis of the universe and reflected in the human being. It is the fundamental pattern of both and provides the fundamental meaning of human life.(P)

67

The World-Idea holds within itself the laws which rule the world, the supreme intention which dominates it, and the invisible pattern which forms it.

68

There is an infinite number of possibilities in the evolution of man and the universe. If only certain ones out of them are actually realized, this is because both follow a pattern—the World-Idea.

69

All the activity of this entire universe is God's activity. Everything is being carried on according to the pattern and the rhythm set by the divine World-Idea.

70

All the forms and developments, the creatures and objects which make the never-ending picture of the cosmos derived from the World-Idea; everything conforms to it.

71

Just as the World-Idea is both the expression of the World-Mind and one with it, so the *Word* (*Logos*) mentioned in the New Testament as being with God is another way of saying the same thing. The world with its form and history is the embodiment of the *Word* and the *Word* is the World-Idea.

72

The pattern of the whole universe is repeated in the pattern of the solar system, and that again in the atom's structure. There is no place and no being where the World-Idea does not reincarnate itself.

73

The World-Idea provides secret invisible patterns for all things that have come into existence. These are not necessarily the forms that our limited perceptions present to us but the forms that are ultimate in God's Will.(P)

74

The deeper thinkers among our astronomers see no beginning and no end to the universe; it is to them a process and not a static thing. To this view a philosopher would echo assent, but in accordance with the World-Idea. Just as the wave of life prepares, enters, and leaves our human bodies, so does it prepare, enter, and leave each of the numerous universes.

75

The World-Idea permeates all existence, patterns all forms, and expresses itself in all evolution.

76

When the revelation of the World-Idea came to religious mystics they could only call it "God's Will." When it came to the Greeks they called it "Necessity." The Indians called it "Karma." When its echoes were heard by scientific thinkers they called it "the laws of Nature."

77

What we call here the World-Mind's master image is not quite different from, although not quite the same as, what Plato called the eternal idea and what Malebranche called the archetype of the universe.

78

Mahat, the divine ideation of the Hindu teachings, may possibly be correlated with the World-Idea, but I have not examined the doctrine. Nor do I know whether Plato's divine archetypes meet exactly the same definition. But I do know that all three constitute the world as seen by the Universal Mind.

79

Plato's doctrine of a timeless world of archetypal ideas which are copied imperfectly in the physical one may be compared with the doctrine of the World-Idea stated elsewhere in this teaching.

80

Jung's archetypes, as far as I know his thought (and I am not a student of much of it), apply to the unconscious of the human being. The archetypes of the World-Idea, if you wish to call them that, apply universally and are not concerned with the human species alone.(P)

81

The Stoics pointed to Reason (*Logos*) as the divine spirit which orders the cosmos. Plato pointed to Mind (*Nous*) in the same reference.

82

There is a universal order, a way which Nature (God) has of arranging things. This is why what we see around us as the world expresses all-pervading meaning, intelligence, and purpose. But we catch only a mere hint of these veiled qualities—the mystery which recedes from them is immeasurably greater.

83

The intelligence displayed by Nature is an infinite one. This fact, once recognized, forces us to concede that there is a deeper meaning and a wiser purpose in life than our puny intellects can adequately fathom.

84

The World-Idea is secret, its activity is silent, but its effects are everywhere visible and audible to us.

85

Immanuel Kant referred to "the hidden plan of Nature." Thus, without benefit of any mystical revelation but with that of acutely concentrated deep thinking to guide him, he sensed the presence of the World-Idea.

86

It is safe to assert that *nearly all* the activities of the cosmos are beyond ordinary human sense observations. Without the aid of special apparatus or thinking power we are unaware of them.

87

The World-Idea contains the pattern, intention, direction, and purpose of the cosmos in a single unified thought of the World-Mind. Human understanding is too cramped and too finite to comprehend how this miraculous simultaneity is possible.

88

The World-Idea is the *whole* idea that no human mind can grasp in its time-long entirety and its spiralled cycles.

89

In some way that the limited mind of man cannot understand by its ordinary processes, the universe exists in the World-Idea out of passing time and in an unbroken Now.

90

The World-Idea manifests itself by degrees but the Idea itself is a perfect whole.

91

The World-Idea not only includes everything existent but also everything which is yet to exist.

92

We may think of the World-Idea as a kind of computer which has been fed with all possible information and therefore contains all possible potentialities. Just as its progenitor the World-Mind is all-powerful, all-present, and all-knowing, it is also possible to think of the World-Idea as being this all-knowing, omniscient aspect of the World-Mind.

93

What is most extraordinary about the cosmos is that although it is a coherent Whole, yet it is one that is greater than, and different from, the sum of its parts.

94
The World-Idea is forever realizing itself in the actual, a process which is ceaseless and infinite, without known beginning or known end.

95
The World-Idea works itself out in time, which is the form wherein the thoughts appear, and in history, which is the record of time.

96
In the larger workings of the World-Idea we may see the rise and fall of entire cultures, civilizations, religions, and even whole continental areas with their inhabitants and races.

97
The World-Mind's World-Idea unfolds with absolute regularity and perfect sequence.

98
The World-Idea is slowly expanding itself on earth, incarnating itself.

99
The World-Idea is embodied in the world itself.

100
All that we perceive of the universe in which we live incarnates some part of the World-Idea.

101
The universe is a system of geometric forms.

102
The connection between number and form is easy to see: the multiplicity of forms makes the universe. The harmony of all three is their divine ordering—a part of the World-Idea.

103
The two elements become the five, the five become the seven, the seven become the twelve. And so the universe grows up.

104
There is a mathematical order in the cosmos, a divine intelligence behind life, an Idea for human, animal, plant, and mineral existences.

105
We see the entire cosmos is ruled by rhythm; its operations are cyclic: consequently this must be expressed through number and order.

106
Both mathematics and metaphysics deal with abstract concepts. Neither a point nor a line is more than an idea; the points and lines we see are different from the mathematical definitions of them. Pythagoras gave a prominent place to mathematics in his philosophy and claimed that the universe was built on Number.

107

The geometrical orderliness of the World-Idea gives us assurance, re-stores meaning to the external universe, and extracts the hope that the anguish of these decades will be amply compensated.

108

Pythagoras pointed out that the universe is based on number. This would mean there is a mathematical foundation to the cosmic order. The most important of the happenings was the 26,000 year cycle whereby the celestial pole moves in a complete circle around the ecliptic pole.

109

The World-Idea must not be regarded as something inert, nor only as a pattern, but also as a force through which the World-Mind acts, and through which it moves the universe.

110

The World-Idea would be more correctly understood for what it is if regarded as something dynamic and not static. It is a mental wave, forever flowing, rather than a rigid pattern.

111

The World-Idea is all one projection containing countless different forms and stages of itself undergoing countless changes. It is not a single static rigid thing.

112

It is a paradox of the World-Idea that it is at once a rigid pattern and, within that pattern, a latent source of indeterminate possibilities. This seems impossible to human minds, but it would not be the soul of a divine order if it were merely mechanical.(P)

113

The archetypes of the World-Idea are ever-new yet basically ever-an-cient. The states of development, function, consciousness, appearing as mineral, plant, and man repeat themselves without end but the detail within them is less rigid.

114

The World-Idea contains within itself, like a seed, all the elements and all the properties of a universe which subsequently appear. In this sense they are predestined to recur eternally even when they dissolve and vanish. The ancient Egyptian text puts it: "I become what I will." The World-Idea is thus the pre-existing Type of all things and all beings.

115

There is an Order in the universe to which it has to conform. Yet it is not so rigid as the carrying out of an architectural plan. Nor like an architect-built world does it allow only for creation and maintenance; for it allows for destruction too. I call it the World-Idea.

116

If this universe was built, like a house, on a plan, its own life and the life of all things in it would be fated within iron walls. If, on the contrary, its course was an extempore and spontaneous one, with each phase freshly decided by the situation of the moment, it would be too much a matter of chance and fortuitous happenings. That would be as dreadful as the other.

117

It would be a mistake to believe that the World-Idea is a kind of solid rigid model from which the universe is copied and made. On the contrary, the theory in atomic physics first formulated by Heisenberg—the theory of Indeterminacy—is nearer the fact. It does not seem that Plato meant the same thing when he described his theory of Ideas as referring to eternally existent Forms, but mentalism does not at all liken them to goods laid up on shelves in warehouses. Here they are simply the infinitude of possibilities, varieties, permutations, and combinations of elements through which the Infinite Mind can express itself in an infinite universe without ever exhausting itself.

118

The notion that the universe is laid out on an architectural plan holds some truth but more error. Its truth appears in the geometrical pattern of the World-Idea, its error in the separate building materials theoretically involved. For of Matter there is none.

World-Idea is ultimate determinant

119

Nothing can come to pass that is contrary to the will of the World-Mind, or that is not already mysteriously present in the World-Idea.

120

All is formed according to the World-Idea, shaped and permeated by its expression of the Divine Will. All things which exist and all events which happen fulfil the World-Idea and are necessary to it.

121

In the ultimate sense, all history—whether planetary or racial or personal—is preordained. No chance event, no human planning can defeat the divine World-Idea.

122

The universe takes the pattern it does out of realization of its own inherent and latent possibilities. The Divine Will prevails everywhere within it, from atom to planet.

123

The World-Idea must subsist through all the spectacles of history, must remain the beginning, the middle, and the end of it all, must operate and dominate inside and outside men's will.

124

The World-Idea is what is ordained for the universe, its divine prescription.

125

In the end the World-Idea must triumph. Nature, whose guests we all are, issues her dictates and executes them by her own power.

126

All things must in the end as in the beginning conform to the World-Idea or there would be no order in the universe.

127

Universal laws will not suffer defeat.

128

All is known to the World-Mind—not only as it was in the past but also as it will be in the future. If it were otherwise then the World-Mind would not be able to maintain the universe in complete function and all its parts in complete relation, nor would it be able to move all the planets in rhythmic revolution. God could not be God if everything were not exactly knowable and every consequence predictable in advance. But that in its turn could not be unless everything were predeterminable too. This is contrary to common modern and Western belief that it is what we, as human beings, freely choose and do, and what we try to get in satisfaction of our desires, which determines what course the future takes.

129

If we all lived in a chaos and not in a cosmos, then it could be said that man's will was completely free. But in that case the sun's will, the stars' wills and the moon's will, would also have to be completely free. All things and all lives would then be subject to caprice, chance, and disorder.

130

The World-Idea is perfect. How could it be otherwise since it is God's Idea? If we fail to become a co-worker with it, nothing of this perfection will be lost. If we do, we add nothing to it.(P)

131
No man can do anything to alter the World-Idea. It is God's Will in every possible meaning of the word.

132
The World-Idea will be realized anyhow, whatever human beings do or fail to do.

Uniqueness, non-duplication

133
The World-Idea contains so many combinations of pattern and characteristic that the possibility of living human creatures duplicating one another during the same historic epoch is non-existent.

134
There is no thing or person, no creature or object, which has not its individual place in the cosmic pattern. Such is one item of this revelation.

135
Each item in the World-Idea is unique: nowhere is there another precisely like it.

136
The characteristics of a natural thing which it shares in common with similar things in its category are not alone: there are others which belong solely to it alone, for Nature produces no two things wholly alike.

137
Differences in function exist throughout Nature—variety is everywhere—but this need not imply difference in status.

138
Every imaginable kind of human comes sometime somewhere to birth.

139
No one else has a self like yours. It is unique.

140
Be it creature or plant, it seeks expression for those attributes of which its form is both symbol and meaning.

141
The amazing uniqueness of each human being's body extends not only to its measurements and its movements but also to its psychic aura; there is not one which is not special, different in some way or to some degree.

142
No two persons have the same appearance. Nor, if we could examine them, the same minds.

143

Not only are no two creatures alike, but no creature ever has two experiences which are alike.

144

Plant several seeds from the same plant. They will not grow up into identical plants but into individually different ones, no two roots, stems, or branches being alike.

145

What is the reason why each man and woman is unique? This solitariness is true not only of the body but also of the mind. No other man in this world today is like me. The true answer to the question is also the only possible one. The Infinite World-Mind manifests itself in an infinite variety of forms in the attempt to express its own infinitude. But since every form is necessarily limited, full success is necessarily impossible. The process of creation will be an eternal one.

146

No two men are ever alike, no two hands are ever the same. The Infinite Being tries to express itself in infinite individuality, just as it tries to reproduce itself in infinitely varied degrees of consciousness.

147

Each man is unique because the Infinite Mind has an infinite number of diverse ways in which to express itself.

On the "why" of "creation"

148

By an act of faith we may accept the religious belief in creation, that God brought the universe to be, and it was. By an act of logic, we may think that the universe formed itself according to the mechanical laws of nature.

149

The Medieval concept of the universe as a drama being played out according to a plot, a first beginning and a final end fully revealed to man, is unacceptable. For the universe is beginningless and endless, its ever-changing activity moving too mysteriously for the finite brain of humanity to comprehend much more than just a significant hint.

150

Is the World-Mind having a game with its hapless creatures, or playing tricks on itself, or expressing its own irrationality and idiocy? My first Buddhist teacher jocularly suggested that the Creator must have been in a state of complete inebriation when He made this universe. But, of course, we have no right to demand that our small finite minds should have the secret revealed to them. They are incapable. Yet intellectual curiosity and spiritual aspiration for truth keep pushing us to seek answers for apparently unanswerable questions.

151

Radhakrishnan rightly says that the human mind, whether in his own country or in the West, has been unable to solve the problem of creation. But this failure was inevitable. The human intellect created the problem for itself; it is an illusory one: it simply does not exist in fact, in Nature. The problem vanishes when the intellect itself vanishes—as both do in the deepest contemplation.

152

Since no one could have been present before that Beginning which the West calls Creation, no one could *directly* know why the universe was manifested at all. But the intuitive intelligence of the sages penetrated to this idea, that the infinite potentiality and indefinite expansion or contraction of the universe expresses in space-time form and motion the infinity of the incomparable Void, the unique Reality.

153

This Universal Pulsation and Rest has repeated itself, in its own varied way, endlessly. So the great Revealers tell us. Why is not known, not even to them. All starts and ends in Mystery. For our own Revealers not only were in communion with levels of consciousness beyond the earthly one but had received visitation from others coming from higher planets.

154

If it be asked why the world was brought into existence, what can insight say, what can anyone say? That God made the human beings in order to be sought, known, loved, and found? That God made the universe as a mirror in which His image is reflected, and man as a mirror in whom His attributes appear? That man is a fragment forced by his innermost nature ceaselessly to desire reunion with his divine source?

155

Why creation of the universe? Alone, the eye cannot see itself; but with a second thing present, a mirror, it can do so. This universe is as a mirror to the World-Mind.

156

Through an unlimited variety of creatures, conditions, and objects, God is forever seeking to see his own attributes. Because God is infinite, this process of creation must likewise be unlimited in every way; it is "a becoming" and never achieves a final result. How could it?

157

The universe is beginningless and endless; it is its appearance which is intermittent and temporary. It cannot be said to have been created or to have needed a creator. That which has always been in existence, though intermittently in manifestation as man sees it, which has had no beginning or end, requires no Creator. There is nothing for him to create.

158

We reject all theories of the Divine Principle having a self-benefiting purpose—such as to know Itself or to get rid of its loneliness—in manifesting the cosmos. It is the Perfect and needs nothing. The cosmos arises of itself under an inherent law of necessity, and the evolution of all entities therein is to enable them to reflect something of the Divine; it is for their sake, not for the Divine's, that they exist.(P)

159

But if the universe has no internal purpose for the World-Mind, it has one for every living entity within it and especially for every self-conscious entity such as man. If there can never be a goal for World-Mind itself, there is a very definite one for its creature man.(P)

160

There is a rhythmic in-breathing and out-breathing that is God's relation to the universe. Only when we understand the foreverness of this relationship do we understand that there can be no ultimate purpose from God's point of view, only from man's.

161

It is not possible to answer the question "What is the purpose of creation?" But this will not deter the practical person and genuine seeker from continuing his attempt to fulfil the immediate purpose which confronts all human beings—that of awakening to the consciousness of the divine soul.

162

If there were really a purpose in the bringing of the cosmos into existence, there would have to be an ultimate end to the cosmos itself when that purpose was realized. But this is irreconcilable with the eternal nature of the universe.

163

The management of human affairs, the values of human society, and the operations of human faculties are basic influences which necessarily shape

human ideas or beliefs about divine existence which, being on a totally
different and transcendental level of experience, does not correspond to
those concepts. The biggest of these mistakes is about the world's creation.
A picture or plan is supposed to arise in the Divine Mind and then the
Divine Will operates on something called Matter (or, with more up-to-
date human knowledge, called Energy) to fashion the world and its inhabitants. In short, first the thought, then, by stages, the thing is brought into
existence. A potter works like this on clay, but his mind and power are not
transcendental. The Divine Mind is its own substance and its own energy;
its thoughts are creative of these things. Not only so but the number of
universes possible is infinite. Not only this, but they are infinitely different,
as though infinite self-expression were being sought. The human understanding may reel at the idea, but creation has never had a beginning nor
an end: it is eternal. Nor can it ever come to an end (despite rhythmic
intervals of pause), for the Infinite Being can never express itself fully in a
finite number of these forms of expression.(P)

164

There is no once-for-all creation at a certain moment in time by a First
Cause, but only the appearance of it. There is a series of appearances, as
beginningless and endless as the unseen Mind Itself, which is the other
aspect of World-Mind, and which is the Real behind all appearances. The
creationist doctrine of Semitic and other later religions is not an ultimate
one but an understandable one, given to the multitude as something
comprehensible by limited mentalities. And we must remember that each
"creation" is incomplete, partial, for humans know only their present level
of experience and not what else is behind it.

165

The origin in time and early history of the world, the varied phases and
permutations of its evolution, are concerns only for those who believe in
causality as an ultimate truth and fact. There is certainly the appearance of
causality in the world, but when enquired into it is found illusory. The
notion seems impossible but Planck has scientifically shown that strict
causal sequence does not operate in the realm of ultimate atomic particles
of the physical world.

166

Philosophy does not accept the Semitic belief in a world created for the
first time by a personal creator, and this is as true of the highest Greek
philosophy as expressed, for instance, in Aristotle's work on metaphysics
as in the highest Asiatic philosophy associated with Buddhism and Hindu-
ism.

167

The word "creation" is inadmissible here for it signifies producing something out of nothing. No one, not even God himself, can produce something out of nothing. Therefore, the orthodox Christian idea of a mysterious creation is completely untenable.

168

That the existence of manufactured things indicates a manufacturer is sound logic, but to apply the same analogy to the world is not. For the world is something quite other than them; it is in a category not only altogether apart from them but altogether by itself.

169

There was never a time when the universe was created or fabricated by a Creator or Maker. This is a case of man making God in his own image.

170

Through successive cycles the universe comes and goes, is born and dies, as the World-Mind rethinks the World-Idea or lets it lapse.

171

The universe was never created for the first time for it has always and incessantly appeared and disappeared, activated and rested, come forth, evolved, and retreated into latency.

172

There has never been a time when there was not a universe, by which I do not mean our own.

173

There is nothing arbitrary in this "creation." It is really self-determined. Everything brings itself into existence under the necessity of its own being and the laws of its own possibilities.

174

Where a circle begins it also ends; the universe is like that: it has no real beginning or ending. It is not a creation in the Biblical sense but an intermittent continuation.

175

Aristotle: "The universe unfolds out of its own essence, not being made." We could add that its pattern unfolds too out of the World-Idea.

176

The universe has never had a beginning, and cannot have an end, but its forms and states may change and therefore must have a beginning and end.

177

It is more correct to speak of the universe's birth, not of its creation.

Universe as emanation of Reality

178

The universe was not made, in a workshop sense; it was emanated. It flowed out of the Original Source and it will flow back there at the appointed time.

179

The cosmos is neither a phantom to be disdained nor an illusion to be dismissed. It is a remote expression in time and space and individuality of that which is timeless spaceless and infinite. If it is not the Reality in its ultimate sense, it is an emanation of the Reality. Hence it shares in some way the life of its source. To find that point of sharing is the true object of incarnation for all creatures within the cosmos.

180

Two points should be clearly understood. First, the world of external Nature, being eternal, is not brought into existence by an act of sudden creation out of nothing. Second, this world is rooted in the divine substance and is consequently not an empty illusion but an indirect manifestation of divine reality.(P)

181

A thought exists in intimate relation with the mind that produces it. The world-thought exists in intimate relation with the World-Mind, God. The world is not bereft of reality although it does not possess ultimate reality.

182

The world is neither a trap nor an illusion, neither a degradation of the divine essence nor an indication of the divine absence.

183

What is the meaning of the world? If it is nothing more than an illusion, it can have no real meaning at all. But if it is an expression of infinite intelligence it must be everywhere pervaded by immense meaning.

184

The truth is ever here, whether unwritten and bodiless or scripted and described. The image of it can be looked at by other generations long afterwards, but the reality of it remains always in the World-Idea and is never lost.

185

If the world is sheer illusion, how could man—himself a part of this illusion—ever know the Real? Were he merely an illusion he could see only further illusion. Were he part of the Real he could see only further reality.

186
Since our experience of illusion is itself in accordance with the World-Idea, why should we be afraid of admitting its existence? What we should be afraid of is letting it blot out Reality.

187
The whole universe is a symbol, whose meaning can be read only when we have learned the alphabet of philosophic laws and experiences.

188
Our world is but a fleeting symbol, yet we may not disdain it. For it is the arched entrance under which we must pass through to the infinite life.

189
The world is a spectacle presented for our meditation in depth. It is a clue, a pointing sign, and even a mystery play.

190
What is the universe but a gigantic symbol of God? Its infinite variety hints at the infinite endlessness of the Absolute itself.(P)

191
The world stands for something else: it is, first, a token that God exists and, second, an image of God's being.

192
The universe is a cipher which needs to be decoded. The scientist does this on one level of investigation, the metaphysician on a different level; the religionist does not attempt the effort but reveres the cipher's Author.

193
Was it not Goethe who wrote: "Everything which happens is only a symbol"? Is not the whole gigantic cosmic effort in the end only a symbolic expression indicating that paradoxically it is and is not?

194
The more we learn about the universe, the more mysterious it becomes.

195
The World-Idea has been represented by diagrams (*mandala* and *yantra*). The World-Mind has been embodied in images and idols. These things can be and are used in religious worship and mystic meditation. The idol acts as a reminder to its devotee; he is not a fool to confuse the piece of stone with the power of God.

196
We live in what appears as a multiverse, a timed and spaced existence—in short, a finite one. But those who can pierce through to its secret—and some have done so—find that it is actually the Unconditioned revealing itself *as if* it were the Conditioned.

197

This universe appearing in time and space under innumerable forms, its particles and planets ever in motion, hides as its supreme secret THAT which is timeless and placeless, without shape, intangible and immobile. Is this not the greatest paradox, this solid something whose essence is Nothing?

198

Few men know God even when they see him, as they unrealizingly do when they look around at the world or even when they merely look at it.

199

The phenomena of the world-form tyrannously and completely masks its reality, so completely that only a dwindling number of people even suspect there *is* any reality behind it. Spiritual intuition has never been so dormant among the race as during the past hundred years. Form, which should have been a wicket-gate giving entry to its diviner significance, has become a prison in which they are held captive by their own obtuseness.

200

Chuang Tzu wrote: "There is great beauty in the silent universe. There is an intrinsic principle in created things which is not expressed. The Sage looks back to the beauty of the universe and penetrates into this principle."

201

These seeming shadows of the spiritual domain are more real than the tangible things which are everywhere taken for reality.

202

The question "Are inanimate things included in the infinite life?" must answer itself, if you take one of the meanings of this term as being the Great, the All. As a matter of fact, however, science now knows that there are no inanimate things. Its high-power microscopes reveal the presence of minute living cells in materials and substances and liquids which are seemingly dead, and its sensitive electrical instruments reveal the presence of energies in others, such as steel. In the end we have to come back to the basic idea that the universal existence is like (but is not actually) a dream inasmuch as it is all a series of mental experiences projected from one's own mind. And because even the inanimate things such as tables and houses which a dreamer sees are really his ideas—that is, reflections of his own mind and therefore of his own life-energy—consequently they are not really dead things. So too for the mountains and rivers in God's dream. From this standpoint there is no such thing as death, only life. But of course the life of a limited world is poetically like death when compared to the life of the divine world.

203

There is a marked intelligence within every atom of the cosmos and within every living creature within the cosmos. So far as the human mind shows forth its own native intelligence it reveals, however faintly, the presence of that master-intelligence out of which it spends itself.

204

The circling earth makes its way through space just as a man makes his way through city streets. It is an intelligent living entity.

205

If there is life in the plant kingdom, there must be consciousness also. What, then, is this consciousness? It is like that of a deep sleep. Nay, we may even go back further and assert of the mineral kingdom that there is life in it, too. For the cells of plants are built up out of the molecules. It is impossible for the human mind to conceive of what the mineral consciousness is like, but the closest description would be that of the deepest trance.

206

Whether in the fragile chrysanthemum or the sturdy redwood tree there is life, intelligence, and being. They are fellow dwellers on this curious planet just like all of us.

207

When we gaze observantly and reflectively around an object—whether it be a microscope-revealed cell or a telescope-revealed star—it inescapably imposes upon us the comprehension that an infinite intelligence rules this wonderful cosmos. The purposive way in which the universe is organized betrays, if it be anything at all, the working of a Mind which understands.(P)

208

God's immanence is reflected throughout the whole universe. God's reality is indicated by the very existence of the universe. God's intelligence is revealed by the intelligence of the creatures in the universe.

209

To recognize that the order of the cosmos is superbly intelligent beyond human invention, mysterious beyond human understanding, and even divinely holy is not to lapse into being sentimental. It is to accept the transcendence and self-sufficiency of THAT WHICH IS.(P)

210

Thought is the spirit of the universe, thoughts are the forms of the universe.

211

Everything in the universe testifies to a super-intelligent power being behind it.

212

We live in a universe that is spun out of the divine intelligence and sustained by the divine energy.

213

At the centre of each man, each animal, each plant, each cell, and each atom, there is a complete stillness. A seemingly empty stillness, yet it holds the divine energies and the divine Idea for that thing.(P)

214

The Void which man finds at the centre—whether of his own being or of the universe's—is divine. It holds both godlike Mind and godlike Energy. It is still and silent, yet it is the source of all the dynamic energies, human and universal.

215

God, the infinite power, is everywhere present and always active. All beings draw their little power for the purposes of their transient self-centered lives from it. In the same way the infinite Mind provides the mainspring for the activity of each little egoistic mind.

216

The smallest one-celled creature is alive with an energy which comes from the universal energy that is the expression of the World-Mind.

217

The same energy which runs in waves or flows in streams of particles through the universe's atoms courses through man. In both cases it issues forth from a centre which is divine.

218

There is no moment when the unseen divine activity is not present in the universe. Everything is being carried on by the divine Power and divine Wisdom.

219

The secret stream of a diviner life flows ceaselessly beneath our mundane existence.

220

The cosmic order is divine intelligence expressed, equilibrium sought through contrasts and complementaries, the One Base multiplying itself in countless forms, the Supreme will established according to higher laws. The World-Mind is hidden deep within our individual minds. The World-Idea begets all our knowledge. Whoever seeks aright finds the sacred stillness inside and the sacred activity in the universe.(P)

221

It is not only man that is made in the image of God: the whole universe likewise is also an image of God. It is not only by coming to know himself that man discovers the divine life hidden deep in his heart: it is also by listening in the stillness of Nature to what she is forever declaring, that he discovers the presence of an infinite World-Mind.(P)

222

He comes to see the whole cosmos as a manifestation of the Supreme Being. It follows that involuntarily, spontaneously, he brings himself—mind and body, heart and will—into harmony with this view.(P)

223

Each individual centre of life and intelligence is a replica in minuscule of the World-Mind itself.

224

Man and nature are metaphysically an appearance, physically an expression, and religiously a creative projection of God.

225

The World-Idea is slowly but rhythmically being unfolded from the Infinite Mind. Yet if we could speak in spatial terms of what transcends space, we could say that the Idea and its process of unfoldment occupy no more than a single point in that vast Mind.

226

Although the universe expresses Mind, it does not exhaust it. The universe is not the entire God-Consciousness.

227

If the Infinite Being is represented by an infinite number of atoms, ways, creatures, and relationships, both harmonies and oppositions, this is only to be expected. If it is itself inexhaustible, its manifestations must be the same.

228

The universe only partially expresses the characteristics of World-Mind. Its own tremendous spaciousness strives—but of course always strives in vain—to unfold the infinitude of World-Mind.

229

Not only man was made in the image of God, but also the universe. It is as geometrically infinite as God is absolutely infinite. There is no limit to the number of things in it, no limit to the differences among those things, and no limit to the space it occupies.

230

The number of objects and creatures, stars and suns is by a natural necessity infinite. Infinite being can only express itself infinitely. The worlds cannot be counted; the space which contains them cannot be measured.

231

We live in a universe which is only one amid an infinity of other universes whose patterns, as we find with individual living things, show infinite differences of detail while sharing certain basic general forms.

232

If there is infinite variety in the teeming life of the universe, this arises partly because of the need to satisfy the infinite number of possibilities through which the infinite life can alone express itself.

233

Descartes argued that the universe could not be infinite since infinity was an attribute which the Deity alone possessed. He considered the universe to be undetermined, indefinite.

234

The notion of infinity implies that it cannot be extended, and whoever understands this will not look in this world for anything which contradicts the implication.

235

It is quite logical that this vast range of the most varied forms should have come into existence. How else could Infinite Being express itself under the limitations of the physical world except so continuously, so endlessly and differently?

236

The infinite permutations of Nature are so vast and so varied only because they are an attempt to express the infinite being in terms of time, space, form, and motion. But such an attempt can never come to any finality; it is endless: a forever-turning spiral.

237

In the world's life there is every kind of joy and every kind of suffering, because there is every kind of creature. The world could not have been manifested at all if it had not manifested infinite variety as an expression of the infinitude of the divine power behind it. Surely this is what Plato saw when he described time as the moving image of eternity.

238

The tremendous monumentality of the World-Idea, the staggering breadth of its scope and variety are a mere hint of the divine wisdom behind both.

239

Somewhere in her writings Blavatsky says that the universe, however vast, is finite. But Epicurus, in a sharply termed piece of logic, tries to demonstrate that the universe is infinite. He says, "That which is finite has an end; who would deny that? Again that which has an end is seen from some point outside itself; that too must be granted; but the universe is not seen from without itself; we cannot question that proposition either; therefore since it has no end the universe must be infinite."

240

Each universe, however vast, is finite. But the possible number of universes is not. The Infinite Being, by some strange necessity (from the human standpoint, contemplating a fathomless mystery), forever sponsors fresh universes as old ones decay and disappear. In this way It seems (again from the human standpoint), by giving expression to an infinite number of universes, to be expressing Its own infinite nature.

2

CHANGE AS UNIVERSAL ACTIVITY

Everything changes

Like Nature, the world, I myself, all existence is subject to change. It is inevitable. What can we do except accommodate ourselves to this inexorable law?

2

If there is any law which governs human existence it is the law of change. We forget it at our peril. Most ancient societies forgot it and suffered.

3

For they cannot escape change, nor the sorrow that change brings, nor the loss of individual existence which it also brings. Such is the universal law which dominates all things and all creatures. When we try to press a permanent happiness out of this world of impermanent things, we are deceiving ourselves.

4

Whether he comes to this truth near the end of a lifetime after long and varied experience or early in it by intuition, the effect is salutary, if saddening: perfect and continual happiness would include perfect and continual functioning of the body, good health, good teeth, good eyesight, good digestion, and all the rest. How few of the saints and the wise in history's records had excellent bodily condition to the end? No!—Buddha's law of decay after growth is still valid.

5

Nothing remains; everything is subject to change. Whether you rebel against this stark fact or resignedly accept it, it stares you in the face unaffected by your personal attitude. Call it Buddhistic if you like, or call it Christian if you prefer, for Jesus said: "This world will pass away."

6

It is hard to bear the remembrance that whatever else may happen change is certain, in one way or another, at some time or another. This is the "eternal flow" of ancient Greek thinkers and Buddhist sages.

7

Not only is everything subject to change but everything also exists in relation to something else. Thus change and relativity dominate the world scene.

8

Even Nature, used to existences extending through millions of years, is itself subject to this ever-changing process. What chance then is there for the creations of man? How could they hope to endure? We may think of the Sphinx and the Pyramid as likely to outlast the hours—but stay! look at their neighbour, Sahara: today a vast sea of sand, but formerly a vast sea of water. So we must conclude that all is perishable—yet, to complete the picture, we must admit also that all is renewable.

9

The one feature of life and the universe which does not change is change itself! It is an inexorable law, as Buddha himself persistently reminded his hearers.

10

Wherever we look or search, probe or analyse in this universe, we find nothing that is permanent. Everything is moving slowly or swiftly to a change of condition, whether this be growth or deterioration, and moves in the end to complete disintegration.

11

There is no stability anywhere but only the show of it. Whether it be a man's fortunes or a mountain's surface, everything is evanescent. Only the *rate* of this evanescence differs but the fact of it does not.(P)

12

Throughout all things in the universe and not only in the plant and animal kingdoms, Buddha found the presence of what he called "growth and decay," and later what Shakespeare called "ripe and rot."

13

There are no golden ages, no utopias, no heavens on earth. This world is a scene of continuous process, or diversification—which means it is an ever-changing scene. Sometimes it is better, sometimes it is worse—if looked at from a human standpoint—but none of these two conditions remains forever fixed. Only romantic dreamers or pious, wishful thinkers look or wait for one that is. What we may reasonably look for and, if fortunate, hope to find, is an inner equilibrium within ourselves which will yield a peace or a presence. Let us not lessen what we are by refusing to accept the responsibility, by practising self-pity, or by blaming environments. They have their place and may make their contribution, but in the end it is our own ignorance of our own possibilities which is the basic cause.

14

Whatever is done to improve human affairs and arrangements will not last. The time will come when it will need to be improved again. In just the same way even the planet itself changes its features, turns tropical zones to temperate ones and great seas to sandy deserts. Only in the Void is there no activity, no change.

15

If anything is perfect it cannot be improved. Whoever therefore demands perfection must understand that he is demanding finality. Could there be such a thing in this ever-changing world?

16

There are no permanent solutions because there are no permanent problems.

17

Millions of animal and human bodies have entered the earth's composition through drowning in vast floods or dying in droughts, famines, and epidemics, through earthquakes and eruptions. It has been an immense graveyard and crematorium. Yet equally it has brought into living existence millions of new beings.

18

Men and women terrify themselves with mental pictures of age, of its diseases and infirmities, its growing cancers and shrinking arteries. Yet they seldom relate their personal experience to the wider scheme of things, to the universe as a whole. If they did, they would soon see that not only are decay and disintegration everywhere in nature, but brutality and murder are there also on an appalling scale. Millions of animals, insects, birds, fish, and sometimes humans, attack, deform, mutilate or kill other creatures.

19

Civilizations do not progress; they grow, but they crumble by their own weight, or, rather, overweight.

20

If anything ever impressed me with the truth of civilization's transformatory nature it was my reading of the Frenchman Volney's book *The*

Ruins of Empires, together with my visit to the remains of two cities. One, Anuradhapura in Ceylon, sixteen miles long and sixteen miles wide stretching in the sunshine with thousands of golden and silver pillars, was eaten up by jungle growth or dissolved into dust! The other, Angkor in Cambodia, displayed huge temples rising out of the thick clogging undergrowth and broken, weather-beaten statues of the Buddhas tangled with, or root-bound in, gnarled wrinkled trees.

Metaphysical view of universal change

21

Despite the ever-confronting evidence that change is ceaseless throughout the universe and through all human experience, we persistently get the feeling of solidity in the universe and permanency in experience. Is this only an illusion and the world merely a phantasm? The answer is that there IS something unending behind both.

22

There is no stability anywhere in the universe, given enough time, and there is none in human life. Yet the craving for it exists. There is a metaphysical meaning behind this phenomenon. It exists because *THAT which is behind the craving person* is the only stable thing there is, or rather no-thing, because IT has no shape, no colour, is soundless and invisible and beyond the grasp of ordinary thoughts. It is this hidden contact, or connection, which keeps man seeking for what he never finds, hoping for what he never attains, refusing to accept the message of ceaseless change which Nature and Life continue to utter in his ears, and opposing the adjustments that experience and events demand periodically from him.

23

There is no permanency anywhere except in ourselves. And even there it is so deep down, and so hard to find, that most people accept the mistaken idea that their ego's ever-changing existence is the only real existence.

24

The earlier non-existence of the cosmos is only physically and not metaphysically true. Even when its form was not developed, its essence was and shall ever be. Whether as hidden seed or grown plant, the appearance and dissolution of the cosmos is a movement without beginning and without end. Science establishes that the cosmos is in perpetual movement. Philosophy establishes what is the primal substance which is moving. Although the cosmos is a manifestation of World-Mind, it is not and never could be anything more than a fragmentary and phenomenal one. The World-Mind's own character as undifferentiated undergoes no essential change and no genuine limitation through such a manifestation as thoughts.

25

This is a universe of unceasing change, both within its atoms and within itself—hence of unceasing movement in the same two categories. It is an *active* universe. Yet at the heart of each atom there is quiescence, that mysterious stillness of the unseen Power which must be, and is, the Power of God.

26

The new physics finds creation to be a continuous process, which has never had a dated beginning in the past. Its atoms and universes appear and disappear. What does this indicate? That the unspaced untimed No-Thing out of which all this comes is itself the Reality, and the Universe a showing-forth.

27

In *The Hidden Teaching Beyond Yoga*, I wrote that the one certain thing about the universe is change. This is because from the moment that Spirit began to go out into seeming time, place, form, relativity, and individual souls, it left behind the infinite stillness of Absolute Being, the motionless Void. The appearances taken could only be fleeting and changing and could only keep this same characteristic until they returned to the still Source. This restlessness was the inevitable consequence of consciousness' becoming immersed in the unconscious, of Reality's becoming the victim of illusion, of the Perfect's becoming shrunk into the imperfection. It can not be content to remain with such limitations. So desire for change begins but is *never* satisfied, is ever active but is ever changing its objects to new ones.

28

"Each [thing] is proceeding back to its origin," said Lao Tzu. This is why change is incessant in the universe, why only the Origin is without it, and why Lao Tzu further explained that "to understand the Changeless is to be enlightened."

29

Lao Tzu wrote: "I come back to the Beginning! I beat down to the very origin of things. It is astonishingly new. Yet it is also the End of all. It is both return and going-out. All begins in death."

30

There is a central calm behind the universe's agitation.

31

The fluidity of human life, ever moving onward and onward and carrying us all with it, is a hint that it is not the ever-real.

32

Energy radiates, whether in the form of continuous waves or disconnected particles—"moment to moment" Buddha called it. It is this cosmic radiation which becomes "matter."(P)

3

POLARITIES, COMPLEMENTARIES, DUALITIES OF THE UNIVERSE

Paradox, duality, nonduality

Paradox is both the primal and the final truth. Life, whether we approve of it or not, is like that. Things are dual and so is man's nature a pairing of negative and positive. But even more is the entire cosmos itself both real and unreal.

2

"The truest sayings are paradoxical," declared Lao Tzu, and to prove it wrote a little book which was full of them. The proverb applies as much to the entire universe which science is probing as to the mysterious divinity behind it. What is more, we humans meet at times with the most astonishing situations which exemplify paradox to the full.

3

Lao Tzu's *Tao Teh Ching* is a book of paradoxes. Yet it summarizes the highest wisdom, the Mystery behind the world, life, everything. It is the essence of yin and yang, the principle of polarization, the method of dialectics.

4

Every individual comes, in time, into possession of that very peace. The answer, so often summed up in one word, is paradox. For this is what sums up the world, life, and man.(P)

5

The nature of the world's substance is paradoxical. The nature of the world process is dialectical. Questions about them cannot truthfully get a straight clear-cut answer. It is of those who demand it that Buddha must have been thinking when he remarked, "Grasping after systems, imprisoned by dogmas in the world." He even went so far as to refuse to deal with these controversial metaphysical questions.

6

The fact is that the higher truths are embedded in pairs of things and forces and paradoxes of situations and happenings. This applies to the universe as much as to man.

7

The truth of paradox is possibly too deep for most persons to accept; apparently it is too self-contradictory. That is why the balanced mind is needed to understand that the contradiction is joined with complementary roles.(P)

8

In Chinese philosophy the Absolute is often represented by a simple symbol: a plain white circle surrounded by a plain black line. Out of the Absolute comes forth a point. This point is the World-Mind. With it there simultaneously manifests what the *Bhagavad Gita* calls the pairs of opposites and what the Chinese call yang and yin. Yang is symbolized by a kind of white crescent with a black dot in the broader end, yin by a black crescent with a white dot. It is not exactly a crescent because one end swells out like a balloon, while the other end remains sharp and pointed like a crescent. When the two symbols are put together in a single picture surrounded by the circle of the Absolute they form a single but complete symbol of the All. The Chinese call it the *T'ai Chi*. In Indian philosophy the Absolute is called Nonduality and the polarized universe is called Duality—or to be more precise *Advaita*, meaning the not two, and *Dvaita*, meaning the two. Yang is considered to be the positive element and yin the negative one; there is nothing in the universe which is not subject to the tension between these two elements. Therefore we human beings, who are part of the universe, are also subject to them. Their interaction brings about birth, life, and death.

9

In the Chinese figure which symbolizes the cosmic dualism of Yin and Yang, the two curving lines—one thickening and the other thinning, one emerging from a point and the other returning to it, one representing Mind Absolute, and the other representing Mind Active, that is, the World Mind—we see illustrated the equilibrium which keeps everything together. There is a balance of forces whereby those who know have to live as if they did not know—that is, live in the tumultuous world as if its physical reality were the only one it possesses.

10

Everything comes in pairs as death with life and darkness with light. Whatever seems to be necessary to existence is so only because its opposite is equally necessary. Duality is a governing factor of the world and everything within it including ourselves. That alone is outside the world, is nondual, which is the untouchable Reality. This is the Chinese idea of yin and yang, and the *Bhagavad Gita*'s expression "the pairs of opposites" conveys the same idea. Duality is a fact. It is here. But it is also an illusion and the opposite truth which completes it is the nondual. We may deplore the illusory nature of our existence, but we need not get lost in it for it is fulfilled, completed, and finalized in its complement the Real.(P)

11

All human thought and experience move through the contrasts between two things or through the difference between them. Otherwise, it would not be possible for us to think or to have experience. In all human consciousness there is two-ness: thought and the object of thought, self and the thing it is aware of. But in the deepest trancelike meditation, this duality vanishes and only pure consciousness, the nondual Reality, exists.

12

Neither Yin nor Yang can stand alone: each is necessary to the existence of the other. In this world of *Maya*, that duality is the fixed truth; but in the world of Real Being, duality is transcended and neither Yin nor Yang operates there.

13

The Infinite Power divides some of its own stillness into the pairs of opposites and sets them in constant vibration and movement.

14

The positive energy of the universe, called yang by the Chinese, was pictured by a straight unbroken line whereas the negative energy that is called yin was pictured by a broken line. Everything in the universe as well as everything in man is a combination of these two forces; neither is absent but their proportions may vary widely. It is interesting to see why this symbolism was used. A solid line stands for a strong line whereas the broken one stands for a weak one. However, although the broken line also stands for femininity and the single one for masculinity this is not to say that the "weakness" and the "strength" have any moral signification or judgement; it is neither a reproach nor an approval. It is simply a difference of function: one giving and the other receiving; one developing out of a point, a seed, the other returning to that condition; one expansion, the other contraction; one the sun, the other the moon.

15

Yang is the creative agent in the cosmos; Yin is the destructive one.

16

Heartbeats, pulsations of wrist, in and out breathings, waking and sleep, rest and activity—all rhythms, alternations, and opposites = Yin + Yang.

17

Everything is polarized, whether in the visible universe or in the invisible forces of life itself. This fact is what the Hindus call the pairs of opposites and the Chinese call the Yin and Yang. All things are complementary and compensatory, yet, at the same time, antagonistic. If Yang gives us energy, Yin gives us calm. Both are necessary.

18

All through Nature these two opposing principles Yin and Yang reveal themselves. All through human existence these contraries show themselves. Most of the ancient mythologies recognized it and certainly most of the Oriental religions, too, from the Far East in China and Persia to the Near East in Lebanon and Syria.

19

Mystic ecstasy of union with the universe is Ishvara's creativity or Yin and Yang. It is Krishna's and Shiva's Dance, hence mystic delight. One sees light, feels love, joy; but it's behind the world misery which Buddha saw. Both are together.

Opposites constitute universe

20

The World-Mind is able to think the World-Idea only under the form of opposite conditions existing at the same time. No world could possibly come into existence without these contrasts and differences. Their presence accounts for the existence of the universe; their movement toward equilibrium with one another accounts for its history.

21

If we humanly dislike the very idea of this duality, this constant tension between two forces, this perpetual opposition by evil, disease, destruction, we must remember that if it did not exist then neither the entire universe itself nor the human being within it could exist as such. The two contrary principles must exist together or not at all.

22

What I learned from the Hindu texts about Brahma breathing out the universe into physical existence and then back into Himself, not only referred symbolically to the periodic reincarnations of the universe but also and actually to its moment-to-moment rhythm of interchange of contrasts, differences, and even opposites. It is this interchange which not only makes universal existence possible but also sustains universal equilibrium. Without it there would be no world for man to behold, no experiences in it for him to develop, no conscious awareness in time and space.(P)

23

Everything in Nature is included within this law of contrasting conditions. Nothing is excepted from it. Even the universe of definite, spherical forms exists in its opposite—formless space. We humans may not like the law; we would prefer light without shadow, joy without pain; but such is the World-Idea, God's thought. It is the product of infinite wisdom and as such we may trust and accept that it could not be otherwise.(P)

24

The presence of pain, cruelty, even evil, seems clear enough on this planet at any rate. So men must be forgiven if they doubt and question God's goodness or break out in open rebellion against God's wisdom. We may tell them that nothing can be created without also creating its opposite. But that, like all the other explanations, will not satisfy the deeply probing intellect, even though that same intellect would be unable to find out how a one-sided planet could possibly exist.

25

Throughout the universe we see these opposites paired together, for indeed the universe itself is a manifestation of duality.

26

The opposites come into being because they are needed. Without them the Great Work of the universe could not be accomplished. Hence Lao Tzu: "Being and non-being create each other."

27

The World-Idea provides for a network of interwoven forces of contrasting colour and opposing direction.

28

It is this alternate tension and release of opposites, this Yang and Yin principle of the Chinese sages, which makes the universe what it is.

29

The course of life is so arranged that it gives clear evidence of Yin-Yang's activity. It appears in the contradictions, the opposing attributes of important situations, whether personal or national, and it appears in Nature in climatic oppositions during the changing year.

30

The tension of opposites which is depicted in a Tibetan mandala, with its grouping of heavenly and hellish forces upon a common centre, refers to this same idea.

31

We could see no form of anything at all if all were in the dark nor even if all were in the light. The contrast of shadow *and* light is needed to define the form. Opposites are always necessary to each other. This is why they are present throughout the universe and moreover present in all possible combinations and proportions in all possible rhythms and patterns. It is present in life, in all things, in planets and seasons. It is the eternal and invariable law of manifested existence.

32

For anything to exist for us at all, it needs an opposite to compare it with, or it will remain non-existent to our consciousness.

33

Thinking cannot come into existence at all unless it recognizes the pairs of opposites.

34

We could not appreciate Good if we had not experienced Evil. We could not appreciate Reality if we had not become lost in Appearance. It may be that for us humans, the ultimate meaning of the cosmos lies implicit in this truth.

35

The acting self needs an outer world and an inner one—both.

36

All things in man's experience can be classified into pairs of opposites—that which experiences and that which is experienced. In each pair the first member itself becomes, on analysis, the second member of another pair.

37

Whatever we look at, we see only in a relationship of contrast to something else. It is a mistake to consider this opposition to be antagonistic. On the contrary, each should be considered a part of the other if our perception is to be true and our judgement correct. This teaches us to synthesize, to look at both sides of a thing, to include both points of view in an argument, and to add the similarities also instead of noting the differences alone.

38

It may be unusual, inconsistent, startling, to propose that we think in terms of opposing ideas, of conflicting statements, and find identity in variety, but that is Nature's own way—her Yin and Yang.

39

It is a teaching which plays on contradictions and finds room for opposites. It sees them both in the structure of the universe and in the movement of evolution. It puts them in its approach to human problems.

40

Each view of a thing or idea implies the existence of the contrary view.

41

To understand that the universal evolution depends upon a two-way interconnected movement, and that its comprehension requires us to think about it in oppositional terms, is to be liberated from the narrow, one-sided, incomplete, and intolerant thinking which is responsible for so many absurdities and miseries in human history.

42

Optimism becomes as unreasonable as pessimism when both ignore the two-faced character of fortune and Nature, the Yin-Yang interplay.

43

A view of the World which fails or refuses to recognize that the opposites are essential to it, which accepts its beauty but not its ugliness, is not complete and only half true.

44

Nothing exists without its contrary: if there is suffering as well as sweetness in life, that is no accident, nor is it brought into the scheme of things by human evil alone.

45

In the end, a man must recognize that there are two forces at work in Nature—and therefore in his own life—the one benign, the other hostile.

46

The good and the evil are so mingled together that it is futile to expect to find one without the other.

47

If he hears the lark singing and notes its joy, he hears also the captured prey of hawk and owl and notes their screams. If he admires the beauty of Himalaya, he remembers the large number of living creatures buried at its upheaval.

48

The brutality of Nature is certainly present but so is its beauty. If the piranha fish devours any live creature mercilessly, the lark flies delightedly.

49

This play of opposites exists not only in Nature but also in human destiny. We observe repeatedly how fortune and misfortune are either intermingled or follow one another in phases. The modern Italian writer Cesare Pavese received in 1950 the highest literary praise of his country, yet, before the year came to its end, he took his own life.

50

There are two principles which are fundamental in the operations of our universe, even though they are opposed to one another. We humanly label one good and the other bad, not seeing how one is necessary to the existence of the other and both to the universe.

51

A world without pain, without suffering, is a utopian, impossible world.

52

The complete truth is that the universe is neither hostile, as many scientists conclude, nor friendly, as many religionists believe: it is both.

53

Geometrical patterns and designs not only symbolize the universe's structure and nature, process and operation; they also show its harmonies and symmetries, conflicts and oppositions, its lights and shadows.

54

Both forces—the static and the dynamic—are present in existence, in Nature and human life.

55

In the universe everything has its opposite; the one cannot exist unless at some point in time the other also exists.

56

The contradiction between yin and yang is a surface one only. They interact with each other and work together dynamically in association with the World-Idea.

57

It would be a mistake to believe that these two forces, although so very different from each other, are fighting each other. This is not so. They are to be regarded as complementary to one another. They are like positive and negative poles in electricity, and they must exist together or die together. They are inseparable, but the need between them is correct balance, or equilibrium.

58

This is the universe's final fact, life's last twin-secret. The pairs of opposites really secretly combine, co-operate and assist each other, despite their outward appearance of antagonism.

59

The structure of the universe is built on two principles which, although opposite in tendency, work together to produce Nature's harmonious order.

60

Heraclitus taught that the universe was a conflict of opposites controlled by what he called Eternal Justice and what we call Karma.

61

All things in Nature show this polarity of opposed characters. All forces and movements in Nature show it in their striving to adjust, balance, reconcile or unite their contradictory activities and conflicting rhythms.

62

There is hardly any situation which does not have its composition of Yin and Yang, good and bad, at the same time. A favoured life is faulted at some point, an ill-favoured one compensated for in some way. The inexperience of youth is balanced by its vitality, the accumulated experience of old age is countered by its infirmities.

63

Every yin is ranged by Nature along with a yang, everywhere there are the pairs of opposites. Here what was once a clear-watered lake is becoming rapidly polluted, dirty looking. On the lake the white swans which move so gracefully can behave very viciously to one another. At their feeding time I have seen them bite the younger members of their tribe to drive them away. I have also seen, many years ago, a swan literally bite the hand of a child which was trying to feed it and inflict a severe wound on the child. Moreover, this powerful bird has been known to break a man's arm with a single blow of its bill. Yet the swan looks so innocent and beautiful that it occupies a place in the spiritual symbolism of India.

64

When one understands this play of Yin and Yang in all existence, and therefore the double nature of human nature, one dislikes pinning a precise tag of classification on anyone, putting him under a rigid category of goodness alone or badness alone.

65

The presence of Yin and Yang shows itself everywhere: in the human being—so admirable in technological achievement, so ignoble in political strife.

66

Yin and Yang work side by side or fight face to face or compensate one another.

67

Yin is forever accompanied by its opposite Yang, which flows in an opposing current.

68

These opposite tendencies co-operate to produce an equilibrium in Nature.

69

The notion that anything outside of God can exist or have meaning by itself is a false one. The universe is what it is only because it depends on an equilibrium of opposing forces or of pairs of things united in opposition.

70

The objective of Balance is held not only before man but also before the universe itself. The movements and forces within it are set for attraction and repulsion, opposition and contrast, so that as they balance themselves its own equilibrium is maintained.

71

The cosmos has its own integral balance, or it could not remain a cosmos. And it must keep this balance all the time and in all places.

72

Abrupt changes in history and brusque changes in ideas came in our time partly because they were karmically due, or even overdue, and partly because of pressure from the World-Idea. All this means that the so-called good and the so-called bad interplay again to find a temporary equilibrium.

73

Nature keeps her equilibrium by bringing in counter forces, or complementary ones, to correct or balance any condition where too much has gone too far.

74

When the pairs of opposites, the contradictory forces, are brought into a reciprocal unity, equilibrium is established and harmony prevails.

75

The opposites and the different meet here, are held in equilibrium, balance and supplement one another.

76

It includes opposites, reconciles contradictories, unites differences.

77

In this world, everything exists with an opposite, as stated in the *Bhagavad Gita* and referred to in the Chinese doctrine of yin and yang. These opposites are contrasts, but also complements and in this sense dependent upon one another. The art of life, so far as these opposites affect us, is to establish a proper equilibrium between them.

78

It is the equilibrium in which the paired opposites and the tension between them come to rest.

79

Experience teaches human beings that life is governed by duality, that like Nature itself, it holds contrasts and oppositions within itself. Just as day and night are positive and negative poles, so are joy and sorrow. But just as there is a point where day meets night, a point which we call the twilight, so in our experience, human experience, the joys and sorrows have a neutral point—and in Nature, an equilibrium. So the mind must find its own equilibrium, and thus it will find its own sense of peace. To see that duality governs everything is to see why human life is one tremendous paradox.(P)

80

He accepts the tension that exists between the indivisible and interdependent opposites which compose life but puts it into his own inner harmony and tranquillity.

81

Yin and Yang are not the opposing principles of good and evil in life but are the heavenly and earthly energies. They complement each other; although independent, the effect is to work together. The one is positive and the other is passive. Finally, they test and complete each other. The philosophic ideal is to balance the two harmoniously.

82

The polarity of yin and yang goes through all existence and therefore all experience. Neither can be destroyed, but what can be done is to bring them together, to reconcile them on a higher plane.

Cyclic unfoldment, reversal

83

The World-Idea is not like a human architect's planning. It is a mighty creative idea, pressing forward into activity, or retreating inward to repose, according to cyclic need.

84

The World-Idea contains the twin forces of evolution and involution—the two go together—but although they are simultaneously present in the whole, they act separately and at different times on each individual cell,

0

entity, creature, or substance. Their presence and activity can be seen both in Nature and in human life.

85

The history of universal events, the ceaseless developments and evolutions as well as the retrogressions, cataclysms, and destructions, the energies and substances, express the World-Idea. It is inherent in all things, latent in all laws of Nature.

86

There are ideas which become obsolete and are allowed to die. But three ideas are so fundamental that they will always reappear. They are built into the universe and therefore into man himself.

87

These three cosmic forces—Attraction, Repulsion, and Rest—constitute the triune manifestation of the World-Idea. You will find them in every department of existence.(P)

88

There is a movement in the universe which during one phase seems constructive, but in a later phase seems destructive. But both are really part of its order, its divine order, for the two phases belong to each other, complement each other, and are necessary to each other.

89

There are two poles of this universal movement: the one, a going-out, affirming, and the other a coming-back and denying. All nature is bisected by this two-way process.

90

The life of the universe moves through a series of evolutionary oscillations between rest and activity.

91

It is the increase of one movement which runs parallel with the decrease of the other movement. One is constructive even while the other is destructive.

92

The rhythmic life alternates and reacts. It brings alternation of the alternations and reactions against the reactions.

93

Just as humans and animals pass through their cycles of infancy, youth, maturity, and senility, so does the planet itself which is their abode.

94

The cycle of existence is never-ending. Whoever understands this truth and his own relationship to it will become humble.

95

Existence is an endless affair but it has periods of rest and withdrawal, changes of form and body, of consciousness and selfhood. We are developments brought forth from it and taken back into it.

96

The universe plays its little part on the surface of unknowable and ineffable Mind and is gone—only to reappear at some immensely far-off time.

97

Worlds come into being, are maintained for a long or short while, change, and dissolve. As we can readily see by observation and experience, this is not less the situation for the creatures—including human creatures—who inhabit these worlds. Yet most people are too unprepared, too weak and too shallow, to be willing to take in these truths.

98

Infinite Mind releases from within itself an infinite variety of suns, stars, planets, substances, plants, and creatures. Even the process itself is an infinite one, countered only by necessary dissolutions and destructions, pauses and rests. Even universes get old and die off. All that is released into manifestation is subject to this perpetual law of movement and change, growth, decay, death, reappearance, and recurrence.

99

The universe comes into being, maintains its varied operations, or passes into dissolution by inherent necessity.

100

The entire universe will dissolve and vanish into the unseen Power whence it came. But there are many other universes and galaxies to replace our own.

101

Dawn follows night in the vast cosmos with rhythmical recurrence. Therefore the sages say that there is neither beginning nor end to the universe but the perennial flow of eternity. The Final is likewise the First. We must understand clearly that creation and dissolution, evolution and involution continue to recur perpetually. It is not a question of long periods of time coming to a final close. This rhythm of the universe is incessant. According to the Chinese wisdom, when either of the two aspects has developed to its utmost limit, then it begins to transform itself into the polar opposite of its own accord. Our own proverb "The night is darkest just before dawn" is also apt here. In the sky we see the same phenomenon. The moment when the waxing moon has reached its fullest is immediately followed by the moment when the process of waning begins. The highest position of the mounting sun is no sooner attained in the overhead sky at noon the great orb begins its downward descent. At new moon the waning process comes to an end and the reverse process occurs. The same turning point is reached at winter and summer solstices. The interrelation of these phenomena with the larger phenomenon of the universal creation and dissolution may be seen. At the extreme point of either process there is a turning.

102

Every movement in Nature ultimately reverses itself, but the point of reversal is not reached until it has gone to the extreme. With the reversal it begins to develop opposite qualities. This is an old and well-known idea in China, not only among the people but also among the philosophers. Lao Tzu, for instance, says, "To go farther and farther means to revert back again."

103

In this shuttle-and-loom, two-way alternating rhythm of the universe, when the forces attain the midpoint of their arc, they start working in reverse, going down instead of evolving up, decaying and destroying instead of nurturing and vitalizing, yielding pain instead of pleasure.

104

Every condition in man, every effect in Nature is forever seeking to attain its own fullness. Yet the moment that is attained and a pause ensues, it reverses its direction and begins to seek union with its opposite. Thus it balances itself in the end.

105

Evolution is never a straight line. It could not be, in a two-way universe. At the crisis-point on each way a shock becomes necessary to force a turnabout. This is the same point referred to by ancient Greek thinkers, where everything destroys itself in the end by its own excess. Heraclitus meant the same when he too taught that all things tend to turn into their opposites.

106

The movement in one direction sooner or later provokes a counter-movement in the opposite direction. This reaction leads to resistance at some point or points; it may also lead to friction and then to fighting.

107

Each phase of this to-and-fro movement covers long periods. When the impetus in one direction exhausts itself, the opposing impetus awakens from tranquillity and is active.

108

When the movement in one direction has exhausted itself, there is a pause, and then a reversal directs the movement into the opposite direction.

109

The flow of Nature follows the course indicated by the Principle of Reversion, which throws it back after a time in the opposite direction.

110

When the point of farthest travel is reached, the forces reverse themselves. In this way, excess disciplines and even defeats itself. In this way too the universe and all the different kinds of existences in it are kept in equilibrium.

111

In the to-and-fro movement of animal breathing, we have a key to human development. Study it well with this aid and you will discern a forward and backward movement, a pendulum-like swing, here too.

112

Everything in the universe is subject to a pendulum-like movement. It shuttles to and fro with a coming-to-be and a ceasing-to-be effect.

113

A time comes when he must weary of his paradise, when a desire appears for the conditions which he was formerly glad to leave behind but now would be glad to take up again. Thus it is that man shuttles through this universe of opposites.

114

Just as the ink-ribbon of an old-fashioned typewriter automatically reverses itself when the end is reached, and then winds in the opposite direction, so does the flow of a nation's historic development change its outward and inward course when karmic requital and balancing need call for such reversal.

115

Physics finds that nothing is ultimately permanent, that everything moves from its present condition to its opposite. Need we be surprised that history finds somewhat the same cyclic movement in the activities of mankind, that deterioration of even the best comes with time, that improvement of even the worst follows too?

116

It is as true in the domain of inner life as in the outer one that Nature must restore equilibrium when it is lacking, must compensate opposing forces by balancing them. There could not be any stable universe if it were not continuously being equilibrated in some of its parts. This is happening by obedience to a law, not by chance. It is happening wherever the movement or development of man and Nature reaches an extreme, when it forces a reversal of direction of the movement backward toward the other and totally dissimilar extreme. The pattern followed is therefore a rhythmic one, shuttling between one pole and its opposite.

117

In the history of man, when the point of fullness in any particular development is approached, a contradictory movement begins to come into play and, at first gradually but later suddenly, reverses the direction of his tendencies. In this way not only are neglected potentialities activated but also some sort of an equilibrium is maintained. These critical turning points are always marked by great and violent upheavals.

118

The universe is not only constructed by divine intelligence on a two-way oscillating rhythm, but also on a balancing force between both movements.

119

If man upsets Nature's equilibrium by excess, she sets up a reversal in compensation, a movement toward lack, restraint. This is the endless oscillation of things, history.

120

There is a threefold movement in nature and life—forward, backward, and neutralizing.

121

There is a Buddhist theory that everything that has been will be again, repeating itself by a precise mathematical law when the same particles of matter are brought together again. There is also a Hindu theory of perpetual alternation between change and changelessness, of endless rhythm and periodicity which provides no evolutionary goal but makes life an end in itself.

122

The view held by Ouspensky and Gurdjieff, and by certain Buddhist sects from whom the latter derived it, that Eternal Recurrence is the eternal law, that perpetual repetitive movement is the universal condition, is questionable at the very least, unjustifiable at the very most. If the human race, for example, were doomed to repeat all its mistakes and misdeeds again and again, its life would be senseless. Such an outlook is not far from the merely materialistic one.

123
The idea of recurring historic cycles is not alone Buddhist and Asiatic, but also Greek and European (held by Nietzsche in modern times and Pythagoras and Zeno in ancient times).

Spiral movement of universal flux

124
All things move forward, stop, and wheel back on themselves. They increase and strengthen but also bend and submit. This advance and retreat is both a cycle and a spiral. It is not blind, for thus it establishes equilibrium and obeys law, that is, it gives meaning.

125
Nowhere in Nature does a situation, a circumstance, a creature, or a person recur exactly as before. It is true that Nature repeats herself, but during the interval the spiral has wound its way onward.

126
In the spiral's form we see the coming together of that which is the hidden being and that which is the visible one, so the full truth is revealed. It is true of a creature or a globe.

127
Wherever you see a spiral form in nature, you will find it stands for a form which is developing, growing, changing, or moving.

128
The spiral expresses this Yin-Yang polarity as it twists from each side to the opposite one. Among the power-phenomena of Nature, the whirlwind takes the same form.

129
The cycles which show the path of universal movement are not horizontal ones, but ascending spirals. If there is a return to the same place, it is on a higher level each time.

130
The inward-going and outward-turning forces of the cosmos work with perfect reciprocity and carry everything with them by turns. The line they follow is a spiral curve. The neutral points where they meet are points of rest and inactivity. Thus, although they oppose each other, they also balance each other.

131
The movement of every energy and trend takes a curved direction. This is why there is no straight-line, lapse-free evolution in human nature or

history. And the curve develops itself with time into a circle, and this again with further time into a spiral.

132

The history of the universe is a history of cycles: of birth, development, disintegration, death, and rest endlessly repeated on higher and higher levels. The energy impulses which rise from the Void and accumulate as electrons, only to disperse later, reproduce the same cycles through which the entire universe itself passes.

133

The large clear cosmological vistas of philosophy reveal the unfaltering return of the evolutionary spiral upon itself and help us to appreciate the superb harmony of the World-Idea.

134

With every finished cycle the evolutionary line moves up higher and thus becomes a spiral.

135

The evolutionary movement moves through a series of advances and retrogressions, and through slow steps broken periodically by violent spurts.

136

Evolution threads its way spiral-fashion, mostly by slow, unhurried inches but at critical periods by mounting leaps. Nor is it seen aright unless its complement and corollary, involution, is seen along with it.

137

All things and all beings, all events and all phenomena are interrelated in an endless chain. In this way evolution circles the universe again and again, spiral-like.

138

Evolution is not only accomplished by a series of rising and falling arcs but also across long flat plains.

139

Development is not continuous. It moves forward through alternations of lulls and renewals, peaks and valleys and plateaus, in rhythmic fluctuation.

140

The course taken by the universal movement may be upward in spiral evolution or downward in spiral retrogression.

141

The materialist who asserts man to be wholly the product of environment is half right. The immaterialist who asserts the opposite is likewise half right. This is because development moves alternately in two opposed directions, never stays in a single one.

142

The course taken by each life-entity in its slow development is neither straight nor direct, but a winding one, going forward and backward upward and downward, curved like a series of interwoven spirals.(P)

143

Why should the waves of life-entities take this spiral-like two-way course? Why do they not go along a direct single one? The answer is that they have to gather experience to grow; if this experience includes totally opposed conditions, *all* the parts of each entity can grow, all its latent qualities can be stirred into unfoldment. In the oppositions of birth and death, growth and decay, in-breathing and exhaling, youth and age, joy and suffering, introversion and extroversion, spirit-form and body-form, it fulfils itself.(P)

144

If these alternating sequences through which every entity has to pass were subject to endless repetition, we would be entitled to criticize the absurdity and uselessness of it all. But they are not. If the repetitions do occur, they do so on a higher level each time. The net result is genuine evolution of the entity.

145

The cosmic movement traces a circular path, which is why the evolving entity has to pass through opposite extremes and why it is guaranteed a fullness of experience. In no other way could its progress toward a higher level be made sure by the periodic arrest of its downward courses. Contrast and difference are innate in the divine World-Idea to control and adjust the conflicting and opposing forces.

146

Life subjects man to "the pairs of opposites," throws him into the conditions he needs to balance his experience. In undergoing this reversal of pattern, he is compelled to draw upon all his latent resources, not merely upon one of them.

147

The movement along a turning spiral road through one birth after another, will in time pass through seemingly unrelated extremes and unfriendly opposites.

148

We see a perpetual struggle going on in the cosmos between two contrary forces. It appears not only in Nature's operations but also in man's inner being. Thus there is no continuous upward movement but rather an alternation, which is of a cyclic and spiral kind. Repulsion follows attraction in the human mind, decay contradicts growth in the universal life.

4

TRUE IDEA OF MAN

Man more than animal

What is man? This is the most important question which has ever been put before the mind.

2

The idea of man which exists in and is eternally known by the World-Mind is a master-idea.(P)

3

When we can learn what the true worth of man is and wherein lies his real salvation, we shall learn the most practical of all things. For this, more than anything else, will show us how to live on earth peacefully, prosperously, healthily, and usefully.

4

If a man does not know what he is in the very essence of his human beingness, he does not really know what he is talking about.

5

Scientific concepts of the nature of man which leave out the intuitive and spiritual element in it as existing independently and in its own level, will always remain inadequate to explain man, however brilliant they themselves admittedly often are.

6

If man's life were nothing more than a physiochemical process, then man's highest aspirations and intuitions, unselfishness and aestheticism would still need an explanation.

7

For more than a century we have been listening to what men think about the universe. It might be more illuminating, now, to learn what the universe thinks about man.

8

The more he perceives the immensity of intelligence behind the World-Idea, the more he perceives the insignificance of his own entity in relation to it. This increasing humility is in striking contrast to the increasing pride which so many intellectuals develop.

9

It is not arrogantly to overrate the function of man in the universe to say that he has a co-operative and creative role to play in it. Those who point to his insignificance and helplessness do well, but they do not do enough.

10

If experience teaches anything at all, it teaches the littleness of men but the greatness of Man.

11

Science frightened man when, in the last century, it told him that he was not the constant attention of God, as he believed, but a most insignificant particle in an immense universe.

12

Against this immense cosmic background, we may see the paltriness of human pride, the ridiculousness of human conceit.

13

Although it is not possible to offer irrefutable scientific proof of the doctrine of spiritual evolution, it can be shown to be as reasonable a doctrine as any of its rivals. And for those who have had mystical experience of the divine presence behind the mind, of divine wisdom behind the cosmos, it is the only acceptable doctrine.

14

The Darwinian idea of evolution as a struggle for existence is blind; the philosophic idea sees it as rhythmic unfoldment, following a spiral pattern and accompanied by involution.

15

A different view of the descent of man may be obtained if we start with the theory that the human form was born out of a pair of apes, that it originated by a process of natural selection. But we still need the Missing Link. This is something which will never be found by the methods of scientific investigation. There is *evolution* only in outward appearance but *unfoldment* in inward reality. The human entity paradoxically contains within itself all lower forms of life from the very beginning, although they are quite different from the one it manifests when fully developed. The living, intelligent human entity preexists elsewhere, and takes up its physical residence on earth only when that is ready for it. From the moment this specific unit of life separated from the cosmic Life, through all the different experiences whereby it developed, and through all the different kingdoms of Nature, its spiritual identity as Man was predetermined.

16

The materialistic belief that man has evolved from the monkey is not accepted by philosophy. The race of apes came from a conjunction of primitive man and female beast. It was a degeneration, not an evolution.

17

It is true that we got our bodies, as Darwin says, from the best type of animals on earth through a utilization of them at the time of conception. The progeny was animal plus human.

18

The monkey did not precede man, as so many materialistic biologists assert, but appeared after him. Had it really preceded him it would not have been in existence today, for in every case of the evolution of species the predecessors die off and disappear.

19

There is a long evolutionary arc between a thinking animal in human form and a beauty-inspired man.

20

According to philosophic tradition, we are in the "monkey" stage of development where our relationship toward the full "human" stage is as far away as that of a monkey is to a present-day man.

21

The "half-ape," half-human being which passes today for a real "man" will one day give place to the real thing. Only then will it deserve the appellation.

22

The grossest humans, not far from animals in habits and ways, and the most unrefined primitive communities contain this possibility of eventual development. But its realization can come only with time, with birth after birth slowly and spirally unfolding the World-Idea.

23

Is man only a reasoning ape—a creative animal? The religious instinct, the ethical conscience, the metaphysical faculty, and the mystical intuition proclaim, with one voice, the answer: "No!"

24

Man is the keystone of the arch of material life, whereas an animal lives solely under the impulses of self-preservation and self-procreation. Only in man can this Divine Being arrive at Self-consciousness, because only man can develop intelligence in its fullness. The intelligence which animals possess, however excellently it suffices them, is after all one which is concerned purely with objective things. Animals cannot move in the realm of abstract ideas, but man can escape from the concrete through his developed reason, his religious feeling, his mystic intuition.

25

So far as man is an animal body, he shares with the other animals their interest in eating, drinking, and copulation. But their interest does not go beyond this point whereas his does. He wants to know about other things and to express what he knows or to receive communications from others concerning what they know.

26

No living creature in the kingdom of animals knows more than its immediate surroundings or cares for more than the sustenance of its immediate existence. It lives in an immense and varied universe but that fact is lost to its mentality and outside its interest. Only when the evolving entity attains the stage of developed human beings does this unconsciousness disappear. Then life takes on a larger meaning and the life-force becomes aware of itself, individualized, self-conscious. Only then does a higher purpose become possible and apparent.(P)

27

Is there any animal which tries to understand the meaning of its life, much more the meaning of life in the whole cosmos? Only when its consciousness has advanced to some extent into the human kingdom does the beginning of such an attempt become noticeable.

28

When Consciousness in any creature reaches by successive periods of growth the stage where it asks itself "What am I?" thus betraying developed intelligence of a kind which no animal possesses, it is ready to seek the Spirit.

29

The moral idealism and metaphysical thinking which is possible to man is impossible to animals.

30

What animal could hold any metaphysical theory, could generalize ideas about space, time, and mind, could analyse situations and relationships, could be seriously concerned about a higher ethical problem?

31

No animal has the capacity to get outside itself and to perceive itself quite impersonally. Some humans do have it and more will have it as they develop their potentialities.

32

A self-conscious creature is one that not only knows its own individual feelings and thoughts, its own mind, but can also reflect upon them. The animal has not reached this stage but the human has.

33

Tied to the physical body as he is, the outlook would seem bleak for man if there were no way of going beyond it. For then he would be but an animal. But he has mental and emotional possibilities and capacities, imaginations and sensitivities, which can carry him where animals cannot penetrate.

34

There are certain ideas which belong exclusively to the higher part of man's nature. We would look in vain into any animal's mind to match them.

35

Man is the only creature among earth's animals which aspires to reach beyond himself, which has the inner urge to grow. He also is the only creature which desires to know what life is here for. The human animal is unique.

36

Yes, let it be admitted that man moves and acts with an animal body but let it not be forgotten that he thinks with a human brain and feels with a heart capable of responding to calls for charity. More, there is something in him which aspires to spirituality.

37

Growth is the characteristic of the plant kingdom, movement of the animal, thought of the human.

38

The mineral, the plant, and the animal have the infinite Life-Power within them, too, but they do not know that they have it. Man alone can know his own divinity. Indeed he is not truly a man until he has known it.

39

What the fishes and flies cannot attain, the human can. And that is the Supreme Awareness, the Divine Being discovered under the cosmic masquerade.

40

The animal's active possibilities are limited to eating, drinking, sex, and obedience to, or service of, human masters. It has no cultural possibilities, no aesthetic faculty or artistic appreciation, no intellectual development. But the highest possibility which separates man from beast is attainment of insight into truth, experience of his divine source.

41

All animals must reincarnate but men may take to the Quest and with time stop the process.

42

A tension holds all things in equilibrium between coming together of their elements, temporary maintenance of their forms, and passing away into dissolution. This includes the mineral, the plant, the animal, and the human. But when we look at the last-named, a new possibility opens up which could not have happened to Nature's earlier kingdoms. All things dissolve in the end, I wrote, but man alone dissolves *consciously* into a higher Consciousness.(P)

43

We are not just higher animals and nothing more but are possessed of something that the other animals do not possess—a self-consciousness which can be developed until it matures into a thinking power as well as a totally superior kind of awareness—that of the Overself.

44

A human life presents the only opportunity for attaining the realization of Overself. It ought not to be taken away from any man, however evil he may be, and however remote from this goal, in punishment for his crime.

45

How can men be so blind to the truth of their very being? Their quality of consciousness provides the clue, but it must be followed up, which few—and no animals—do. This is no shame for the animals, for they cannot, whereas men can but do not.

46

It is questionable whether the advantages of being a human creature are outweighed by the disadvantages. The Buddhists think they are, the Epicureans think they are not, but the Vedantins think man is an immensely fortunate creature. Why? Simply because he may use his human faculties to transcend his present level and, as they call it, "realize himself."

47

The choice between submitting or not submitting to his animal genes and hormones belongs to man, but the tendency to follow them belongs to the earlier stage; it is very, very ancient and is coming under his control very, very slowly. He fulfils himself as truly human when this transcendence of his ancestry is complete.

48

If man walks upright, and most of the animals do not, it is because this upright posture is symbolic of his gradual progression into ruling his animal body and animal nature.

49

The ordinary ego-driven unenlightened man is acted on by lower cosmic Nature, just as plants and animals are. But in a human animal, individuality and intellect are additionally present—whether slightly in the savage or markedly in the highly civilized person. The enlightened man is also acted on, but in his case it is by higher cosmic Nature. Instead of being guided by passion and desire, he is guided by intuition. The changeover from lower to higher requires his contribution, his effort to control nature, to discipline individuality, and to achieve self-mastery.

50

It is not only in the possession of reason and the reception of intuition that the human form of life is superior to the animal, but also in the exercise of will.

51

Man, by contrast with the animal, is an individualized creature. He is aware of his own separate identity and special personality. The animal is not individually responsible for its actions, being *entirely* responsive to its surroundings and herd instinct. If man feels the same responsiveness, he modifies it by his own particular characteristics.

52

Whereas the animal and even the plant are moved solely by instinct—unless they have lived closely with man—the human being adds a new urge, that of *conscious* development through intelligence.

53

The impersonal and eternal part of us is the god in us, symbolized by the upper half of the Sphinx's head, as the lower half symbolized the human part, and as the body itself symbolized the animal part.

54

We cannot separate the importance of the body from the importance of the mind. We are animals in one part of our nature, human beings in the second part, and sometimes angelic in the third part. All make one creature. We learn what our bodies are through the physical senses. We learn a part of what the mind is through our thoughts. We learn still more about the mind's deeper phases through our non-thoughts—that is, intuitions.

55

Such is the triple nature of man—a lower self of animal instincts, a middle self of human thoughts, a higher self of divine nature.

56

We may well wonder how animal lust, human cunning, and angelic nobility can come to be mingled in a single entity. That indeed is the mystery of man.

57
When the whole cosmos shows its double-face of Yin and Yang, shadow and light, we must expect the individual creature to show the same. Hence man is half animal and half god, with reason as their link; he fulfils himself only when he establishes an equilibrium between them.

58
Nature is what it is—bipolar—so existence involves struggle and conflict for all of us until the genius in a million finds the point of equilibrium between the two opposing pulls, between the savage and the saint in him.

59
The animal nature is naturally selfish, the spiritual nature unselfish. Between these two poles, man is brought more and more into conflict with himself as he evolves.

60
Because they are human animals tied to a divine spirit, we see men and women as erratic in their behaviour and irrelevant in their purposes.

61
They bear the human form externally but are largely predatory animal internally. Mind—that is, character and consciousness—is the real essence of a man.

62
There is the brute and the angel in almost every man. But how much there is of the one and how little of the other, differs with every man.

Divine essence of Man

63
The ideas in a man's mind are hidden and secret until he expresses them through actions, or as speech, or as the visible creations and productions of his hands, or in behaviour generally. Those ideas are neither lost nor destroyed. They are a permanent part of the man's memory and character and consciousness and subconsciousness, where they have been recorded as automatically and as durably as a master phonograph disc records music. Just as a wax copy may be burnt but the music will still live on in the master disc, so the cosmos may be annihilated or disintegrate completely but the creative idea of it will still live on in the World-Mind. More, in the same way a man's body may die and disintegrate, but the creative idea of him will still remain in the World-Mind as his Soul. It will not die. It's his real Self, his perfect Self. It is the true Idea of him which is forever calling to be realized. It is the unmanifest image of God in which man is made and

which he has yet to bring into manifestation in his everyday consciousness.(P)

64

If the world is a thought in the mind of God, then men are thoughts in the World-Mind, who is their God in reality and in logic. If all thoughts must go in the end, this is true also of the World-Mind, except that here millions of years are involved.

65

The World-Mind works in and through everything. The World-Idea reveals a mere hint of its wisdom and intelligence to that projection from Itself which is man.

66

Every law of the universe and every principle of its operation can be found reflected in the nature and life of every man.

67

In the complicated structure of the human personality, we find different levels of being, with different forces operating at each level.

68

Man is what he is. Nothing can alter that. Out of the immortal, benign, eternal Mind he came, to It he shall return. Meanwhile It is his very essence, that is, It is life.

69

Man is Mind individualized.

70

We must see in each man the beginning of a fresh and unique attempt of the Infinite to express itself in the finite world of space-time.

71

The Unseen Power, *Al* (without beginning) *lah* (without end), is One. Every other kind of power derives from It. And this holds true even of the little power which a little ant shows. Hence the energies of a human being are linked with It. From this we may deduce that he is unaware of, and not using, all his potential resources.

72

Though it seems entirely our own faculty, this thought-making power is derived from a hidden one, the Universal Mind, in which all other men's minds lie embedded. What he does with this power is a man's own concern, for better or worse, yielding him more knowledge or more ignorance.(P)

73

The man who, according to the Bible, is made in the image of God is not the earthly man, visible to all and speaking in a voice that sounds in physical ears. He is to be found in the deep centre of consciousness, where there is only a Void, and he speaks in silence to the attentive mind, not to other persons.

74

The man that is made in the image of God is not physical man or desire-filled man or thought-breeding man but he who dwells behind all these—silent, serene, and unnoticed.(P)

75

Here, and here alone, is the real meaning and true portrait of a man.

Purpose of human life

76

What is the inner purpose of human life as apart from its outer object?

77

What is the highest end of the life of man?

78

We may not be able to comprehend the universe's meaning—why it should come into existence at all—simply because human capacity is too limited; but we should be able to comprehend some meaning—enough for practical purposes—in our own personal existences.

79

To enquire into such matters is very far from being a remote and unimportant affair, for on its final results depend the answers to such questions as: "Does this earthly life exhaust all possibilities of human life?" "Is there anything more than death for man to expect as the final experience life offers him?"

80

"What are we here for?" asked Empedocles, and several reflective thinkers have since supplied their answers. Each is different, but each is only a single part of the total answer.

81

If we begin at some time to wonder at the starred sky and go on to speculate at our human destiny, there will be moments when a feeling rises that there must be something behind it all. They pass and mystery engulfs us again.

82

If we do not know the "why" of universal existence, we do know the "why" of human existence. It provides the field of experience for discovering the divine soul. The integral quest which ends in this discovery is, consequently, the greatest and most important of human undertakings.

83

Where is the possibility for the puny intellect of human beings to hold in its consciousness simultaneously and all-embracingly the innumerable stars, planets, suns, systems, galaxies, and universes? Yet man's curiosity cannot be stilled; his eager mind insists on knowing more and more, his ever-upwelling stream of questions never stops flowing. What do these two conflicting situations mean when put together? The answer is simply that there *is* something which he can and must know in order to fulfil himself, but it is not a piling-up of numbered facts; it is nothing other than his relation to the source of the cosmos.

84

Man's experience is so limited and his mental equipment so small that his attempt to understand the universe would seem impertinent were it not for the assurance of great prophets and seers that where intellect and sense fail, intuition succeeds.

85

The structure of the human being—his bodily senses and mental faculties—does not permit him to get more than a limited awareness of his environment. The remainder—which may be very large—is not only unknown but likely to remain unknowable. This means that what he does know, being neither complete nor completely true, concerns a world that is only relatively real. The world as it really is in itself escapes his knowledge and remains the greatest mystery. Only those who are piqued by their ignorance of reality look beyond science, beyond the intellect even, for truth.

86

If human life has any higher purpose, it is that the human ego should find its way back to that harmony with the Overself which has become disturbed but never disrupted.

87

We must all give life what it demands from the human—that it shall seek to transcend its present state, that is, transcend itself in the end. For life as we know it is only one expression of the World-Idea, the inexorable will of the World-Mind.

88

Everywhere in the advanced countries specialists, experts, and scientists are seeking more knowledge of the human body and its world or are applying this knowledge to practical use. Yet the highest work in which intellectual power can engage is to seek the reason for human existence. This will lead it to discover, and bow before, the World-Mind.

89

If a creature is capable of conceiving the highest purpose for human life as something which transcends physical existence and even overpasses its ordinary thinking and image-making existence, there is here a phenomenon where this creature is either intuiting or predicting its own destiny. And it must be something glorious, something whose nature few cultures and civilizations have yet enjoyed.

90

The goal of life is to be consciously united with Life.(P)

91

Man's need is twofold: recollection of his divine nature and redemption from his earthly nature.

92

If it be asked whether there is any purpose in life, the answer must be "Yes!—to perfect ourselves and know ourselves; to find the happiness which comes as a fruit of such fulfilment."

93

Attaining to our manhood is good chiefly as it provides us with the chance, during subsequent years, of attaining to our higher selfhood.

94

The higher purpose of existence is to advance man until he can live in the awareness of his divine selfhood.

95

It is within the ultimate capacity of man and part of the higher purpose for him to achieve this awareness.

96

Revelation establishes that the sequence of events in our universe is an orderly one, while observation confirms it. They do not just happen by chance, and chaos is not their background. Many will admit this but yet they are unable to admit that this orderliness is not limited to stars and planets alone, nor to the chemical elements also, nor to the physical forces of Nature in addition. They are unable to extend it to human life, to its birth, course, fortunes, and death. But the philosophic revelation tells us that law and order are here not less than elsewhere. It is unreasonable to suggest that although they rule all the lower kingdoms, they do not touch us. Our experiences too are controlled by heaven's laws.

97

There is order in the starry systems, on the planets, and on this earth, because the World-Idea provides law and pattern. What is true of the universe is true also of man, of his body and his inner being.

98

There is an orderly structure in the universe and an orderly pattern in the lives of its creatures. If everything else is governed by laws, why not the growth of man's spirituality?

99

All personal fates are fulfilled within the larger predetermination of the World-Idea. And only within that larger meaning can men find any real meaning in their own lives.

100

The divine pattern is there not only in Nature but in Man, not only in inspired written revelations but in secret unwritten meditations.

101

You are part of the World-Mind's World-Idea. Therefore, you are a part of its purpose too. Seek to be shown what that is, and how you may realize it, rather than mope in misery, frustration, or fear. Look upon your situation—personal, domestic, career, mental, emotional, spiritual—as having significance within that purpose, as teaching you some specific lesson or telling you what to do or not to do.

102

It is nonsense to say that any man is alone in his trouble. He is in the great World-Idea, part of it, belonging to it, sustained by it.

103

Men imagine they are acting for their own personal objectives only and for their own personal choices. They believe that they are moving through their life-scenes by their own freedom. But the fact is that, all unwittingly, they are acting for the World-Idea and moving by the power which inheres in it.

104

What are we to say of the many whose lives evince no purpose, whose years show no progress? This judgement is a surface one. All people respond to the power of God, and perform their role in the idea of God, however slight be the measure of their response or however hidden be their role.

105

Every person is unconsciously trying to fulfil a higher purpose set for him by the Overself, and all the purposes fit together and combine to form a part of the World-Idea.

106

Humans are part of the World-Idea; most of what comes *to* them is within that part too: much of what comes *from* them likewise. They are free only within the World-Idea.

107

Whether we like it or not we must submit to the World-Idea. It is there and must be accepted—reluctantly, resentfully, or blindly and devotedly. None of us has total freedom; that is an illusion, for it could never exist in a world based upon orderliness and equilibrium.

108

The World-Idea contains from the beginning to the end each individual life in its picture. How much freedom that life really contains is a matter for seers to say, not for intellectuals to debate.

109

How old is the series of experiences through which we moved unknowingly towards our present evolutionary position! How lofty is the level toward which we have yet to climb! How ironic is the discovery that what we thought was being done by free personal choice was merely blind obedience to universal force; that where we believed free will was exercised, there we merely conformed to the World-Idea!

110

The World-Idea is the ordained will of the World-Mind. Within its large outlines, change is impossible. All its parts serve them. But it would not be correct to assert that we humans are slaves of that Idea. Somewhere within each part some sort of freedom is possible.

111

That in the end nothing that the human will can do can sway human life into divergence from the World-Idea, that All is fixed by it, is not quite correct. The main outlines of World-Idea can certainly not be affected, however, for they are inherent in the nature of things.

112

Every man is offered a chance to live again, not once but as many times as will bring him to his diviner being and establish him in that. Human existence is a kind of bewitchment; we experience what we are made to experience. All is simply the expression of the World-Idea—that is, of God's will—but we share in the making, participate in the divine ideation.

113

In the end the World-Idea triumphs as, in reality and actuality, it is doing at every moment. Even man's own personal will unwittingly prepares itself for such eventual conformity.

114

The pressure of the World-Idea shapes his tendencies and his circumstances, denies him any other freedom than the mental position which he finally takes up, than the alliance with or rejection of moral conscience.

115

The World-Idea's end is foreordained from the beginning. This leaves no ultimate personal choice. But there's a measure of free will in a single direction—how soon or how late that divine end is accomplished. The time element has not been ordered, the direction has.(P)

116

Both the ordinary man and the enlightened man are playing the role allotted to them in the divine World-Idea. Neither could change that part of the planetary fate. But whereas the first is doing it unwittingly, blindly, and at times rebelliously, the second is doing it knowingly, perceptively, and submissively.

117

There are no mistakes anywhere in the World-Idea, nor even accidents. But there is enough flexibility in its human part, enough freedom there, to make it seem *as if* there were some mistakes and some accidents.

118

The meteor which moves across the earth's orbit is as much beyond man's control as is his larger part in the World-Idea.

119

Is the human race nothing else than God acting out a multitude of different parts in a tremendous play?

120

If this were so, all men would be no different than the mere figments of imagination of authors creating characters in novels. But living men *are* different. If they were just as illusory as those creations there would be something wrong with philosophy, with mind, and, let it be said, with God. It is needful to penetrate reflectively more deeply to bring light upon this point.

Glimpsing the World-Idea

121

When one is allowed a glimpse of the World-Idea, he feels that he understands at last why he came here, what he has to do, and where his place is. It is like an immense enlargement of the mind, an escape from the littleness of the ego, and a finding-out of a long-hidden secret.

122

When the fact of the World-Idea flashes into his mind, he stands like Hillary on Mount Everest. At last this bewildering enigma which surrounds and entraps everyone everywhere assumes pattern, the countless events and things and processes leave their isolation, their useless chaos, and fit together.

123

He has come to the inner sight of the World-Idea's meaning for him: that he is to use the human self to lift his nature up from the animal one, and that he is to put himself at the service of his angelic, his best, self, to lift his nature up from the ordinary human. In this way he co-operates with the World-Idea. This is the use he is to make of his life on earth: his personal life, his family relations, his professional career—all must become subject to the higher purpose. The resolve made, the matter of success or failure is no longer urgent, for every subsequent embodiment will point in this direction. Philosophy has instructed him in the unreality of time and has revealed to him his indissoluble connection with the Overself. All this was seen by the sages long ago and symbolized by them in the Sphinx and the Pyramid.

124

He sees that life is encircled by a great Being, that the Mind behind the universe—although so still and uncommunicative and, apparently, unconcerned—is in reality sending its messages in varied ways all the time.

125

The world is no longer merely itself. Henceforth it is the expression of a divine Idea.

126

It is then that the awareness of the World-Idea comes to him, explaining his planetary surroundings and enlightening his situation therein. Every relationship and every event is then seen to be significant, falling into place in this amazing pattern.

127

He sees the world forever changing its forms, forever in process, and he himself as part of it under the same doom. All is appearance, not reality. But he sees also the Essence.

128

This is the world as my experience showed it to be, the world as it was revealed to me by the Overself.

129

In those divinely captured moments when ego is loosened and Overself is present in awareness, the amazing pattern of the World-Idea shines clearly.

130

He becomes awed, through such heavenly glimpses, by the tremendous intelligence behind and within the Cosmos.

131

He will begin to see an intelligence moving in and through the universe which he had not seen before. The universe will no longer be a strange symbol without any meaning.

132

There is a wisdom within the cosmos beyond our telling or knowing, but we may feel its presence in tranquil moments if we turn in reverence to it or in remembrance of it.

133

To feel the divine presence is much more common an experience than to perceive the divine purpose.

134

The World-Idea authentically exists but not in the way that physical things exist. No human mind can receive and hold it in the same definite way it can receive and hold all other ideas. Even in those exalted psychological states or mystical experiences when the world's meaning is perceived, its inner drama understood during a brief glimpse, the seer gets only the fragment which his mind can take in, limited and conditioned as he is.

135

The vast coverage of the World-Idea, coupled with the microscopic spaces in which it is equally manifest, transcends human grasp. A few have been lifted out of themselves, like Buddha and Arjuna, to receive the Cosmic Vision for historic purposes. The others receive glimpses, at best, of parts only, but even these are awe-inspiring.

136

What they may expect to find with intellect is at most the slow uncovering of little fragments of the World-Idea: but with intuition the subtler meanings and larger patterns are possible. These include but also transcend the physical plane. A few fated persons, whose mission is revelation, are granted once in a lifetime the Cosmic Vision.(P)

137

The six *darsanas* are ways of looking at the world, of seeing it metaphysically: a *darsana* is the vision a man has of revealed truth of the universe, God, and man.

138

No human mind is capable of ultimate knowledge of all the universe's secrets, nor of absolute comprehension of what is in the World-Mind, no matter what the Indians claim or what the Westerners assert so glibly about God.

Co-operating with the World-Idea

139

Wise men co-operate voluntarily with the World-Mind before they are forced into going along with it and its expression, the World-Idea.

140

Only to the extent that he unites his own little purpose with the universal purpose can he find harmony and happiness. Its strength will support him firmly in adversity and misfortune, as it will carry him triumphantly through misery and hostility.

141

He who begins to sense the World-Idea, as expressed through him and his environment, has still to put aside self—with all its short-sighted emotionality and sentimentality—if he is to accept the Idea as perfect.

142

The more one learns about the World-Idea, the more one wonders at it. To go farther and co-operate with it is to find peace.

143

To bring himself consciously and deliberately within the World-Idea is a holy act. He is within it anyway, but without the consciousness.

144

His personal share in the World-Idea is limited to reception of it in every corner of his conscious being.

145

If Nature keeps her lips inexorably shut to the questions of those who abuse her, she graciously opens them in perfect response to those who ask with a quieted, co-operative and harmonious ego.(P)

146

We can be co-workers with the World-Mind only to the extent that we withdraw from our ego. Then only are we able to receive correctly the wonderful revelation of the world's meaning and laws, so that we can participate intelligently and lovingly.

147

When he sees the meaning of life, he cannot help but give it his acceptance. Circumstances previously rebelled against now fit into a reasonable place in the pattern of things.

148

Nature gives her message to man, and gives it all the time all at once. But man hears it only in bits and pieces, even when and if he hears it at all.

149

How to live well while in this world does not only mean how to live comfortably, nor even morally, but also how to live in harmony with the World-Idea. To be unaware that there is any such meaning to existence is to be unable to live really well and truly wisely as a human being.

150

Bring in a single light and there follows recognition of several objects in a room; there is knowledge of their existence, their form, and often their function. In the same way, some knowledge of the World-Idea makes possible the clearer comprehension of human existence, its hidden purposes, goals, and enigmas.

151

I have only a very partial knowledge of the World-Idea but it is enough to throw a practical working light upon our business here on earth.

152

Only when man finds out his correct relation to the universe and to his fellow creatures will he find his own well-being.

153

We too are elements of the world like the mountains and flowers around us and need to understand it in co-operation with the need to understand ourselves. The two cannot be separated without loss to our own fullness of understanding and practicality.

154

"He who knows not the world-order, knows not his own place therein."—Marcus Aurelius

155

Since the human being is one among many other creatures existent in the cosmos, if he is to know himself properly he must know enough cosmology to enable him to do so.

156

Because the World-Mind is here the cosmos is there. Because the cosmos is there you are there.

157

Such knowledge will enable him to make the best use of himself and his environment, for its beneficial influence will pervade his general life and work.

158

To what ideal ought the young advance? This is where foreknowledge of the World-Idea is helpful to them.

159

The value of a knowledge of cosmology is that it makes a man feel, intellectually at least, that he is part of something immensely great and immensely significant.

160

The highest mystical teachings end, and can only end, in proclamation of the One Reality or, more properly, the Ineffable, the One-without-a-Second. Nothing much can really be affirmed about It other than that It IS. But revelation cannot end with this affirmation. For man finds himself subject to the necessities of a physical body living in a physical environment. The higher laws governing such earthly existence affect him vitally. He ought not to remain ignorant of them, if he is to live in harmony, not conflict, with these laws.

161

All spiritual study is incomplete if it ignores the facts, truths, laws, and principles of cosmogony. To attempt to justify this neglect with the accusation that they belong to the world of illusion is silly and useless. For the accuser must still continue to live in an illusory body and use an illusory self governed by those laws. After every such attempt and for each violation of those laws—upon which the order and harmony of the universe depend—which his neglect brings about, he must pay the penalty in suffering.(P)

162

As knowledge of the true facts about the world in which we live becomes available (and I mean by knowledge not only scientific knowledge, but also spiritual knowledge and psychical knowledge), more and more the human race will discover that it has obligations to the cosmos, and that they cannot be ignored without retribution.

163

It is not possible, and it is not necessary, for any human mind to learn all the higher laws governing life. But it is possible to learn some of them and also the archetypal ways in which the World-Idea manifests. With them, one has something of a key to the unknown laws.

164

It must be remembered that these higher laws are established throughout the cosmos, not merely in our part of it; that this higher truth can never undergo any alteration in itself, whatever way different men of insight may speak about it; that we human beings have the privilege, when purified, of partaking in the real holy communion which alone fulfils our highest prayers.

165

Those who seek to do God's will must first seek to discern it not only within themselves but also in their environment outside. For this a study of the pattern of the World-Idea is necessary.

166

Spinoza saw that the whole universe conformed to a world-order under what he named "laws of necessity." But the source of these laws was God. He saw too that Man, in the effort to understand all this, and drawn by an intellectual love of God, would unfold intuition and come closer to God.

167

Learning what these cosmic laws are and trying to live in obedience to them is the only way whereby humanity can do what is best for itself. It will have to come to such obedience through the lessons of experience and cannot escape it.

168

The more a man learns what laws move this universe in which he exists, the better will he find the universe to be and the happier will his existence be.

169

In the long slow course of development, as it stretches out with time, men will come to understand the true nature of the universe around them and the correct nature of their relationship to it. It will be a logical corollary that as they come thereafter to understand also the harm they do themselves by every violation of the higher laws they will begin to change their thoughts and amend their conduct.

170

It is not possible to know what lies at the heart of the great mystery, but it is possible to know what it is not. The intellect, bound by the forms of logic and conditioned by the linkage between cause and effect, here enters a realm where these hold no sway. The discoveries of Germany's leading nuclear physicist, Professor Heisenberg, were formulated in his law of indeterminacy. The ancient Egyptian sages symbolized this inscrutability under the figure of the Veil of Isis. The ancient Hindu sages called it Maya, that is, the inexplicable. Argument and debate, ferreting and probing among all available facts, searching and sifting of records are futile here. This is the real truth behind the doctrine of agnosticism. Every man, no matter who he be, from the most knowledgeable scientist to the profoundest philosopher, must bow his head in acknowledgment of this human limitation. He is still a human being, he is not a god. Yet there is something godlike within him and this he must find and cling to for his true salvation, his only redemption. If he does this he will fulfil his purpose on earth and then only he finds true peace of mind and an end to all this restless, agitated, uncertain mental condition. Study what this planet's best men have given us. It is no truer message than this: "Seek for the divine within yourself, return to it every day, learn how to continue in it and finally *be* it."(P)

World-Idea guides evolution

171

The forces which move men and bring about events are not always to be found by rational analysis. There is another factor present which eludes such analysis. It may be called the evolutionary intent of the World-Mind.

172

All things and beings flow forth from the illimitable Power, all derive their consciousness from It. Nor may we stop with this acknowledgment. For they derive whatsoever they have of intelligence from It, too. Is it not a grand thought, full of promise and hope, that in the gradual progression of this intelligence from minute cells to celestial beings, it passes upward through man, enabling him in time to attain and know his own Divinity?

173

The World-Idea is drawing us little by little after the pattern of its own infinite perfection.

174

To say that man is unconsciously seeking God, or rather his Higher Self, is the truth. To say that God is seeking man is an error based upon a truth. This truth is that in the divine idea of the universe, the evolutionary development of life-cells will bring them slowly up to an awareness of the diviner level; but the Higher Self, having no desire and no emotions, cannot be said to be seeking anything. Indeed, the evolutionary pattern being what it is, there is no need for it to seek, as the development of all beings from primitive amoeba to perfect spiritual consciousness is assured.(P)

175
We may call it evolution if we wish but the actuality is not quite the same. The universe is being *guided* to follow the World-Idea—this is the essence of what is happening.(P)

176
The pattern of evolution is an endless one. The meaning of the pattern could not but be a wise one.

177
Because mind is the basal reality, all this majestic progression is nothing else than an evolution from lower to higher forms of intelligence and consciousness.

178
Within the Overself, the infinite absolute principle of mind, there arises the idea of the cosmos, and from this original idea proceed all other mental constructions that constitute a universe. Because the Overself is formless and unindividuated, we have to picture it under the glyph of darkness. The cosmic idea will then appear as a primordial germ of light, called by the Hindus *Hiranyagarbha* (the golden embryo). The entire panoply of suns and stars and creatures is contained latently within this point of light. This first-born God is the primal Idea.

179
World-Mind, concerned only with Its own larger purposes, which are hidden from us, directs us in that light.

180
We must begin by recognizing that this planet exists for a specific purpose and that the evolution of all creatures upon it is part of that purpose.

181
This earth, with the varied experiences of good and evil, joy and suffering, peace and peril which it offers us, is a school of initiation leading primitive animal man into the development of awareness until he reaches the first discovery of his Overself.

182

The world exists for the training of ever-ascending living things—from their early start as protoplasmic cells to their later development as human beings.

183

Despite the pious assertions of our Western theologians, the world does not exist solely for the benefit of the human species. It is a means of development and expression for all kinds of creatures, a development in which the humans share so largely.

184

Who can calculate the number of years which shaped the primal atom into its latest form—the modern man?

185

The differences in consciousness between an amoeba, an insect, an animal, and a human represent a line of growth.

186

Because evolution is not merely a physical matter of size and shape, because it is primarily a mental matter of intelligence and consciousness, philosophy finds the ant nearer to man than is the panther.

187

Animal life climbs ever higher in the scale of evolution, reappears in forms of a more developed type. That is one compensation for the manner of its death, which is so often to be devoured by other forms.

188

Everything that has feeling or awareness, however dim, is capable of developing to higher and higher forms of existence. But only when it is individuated and attains the human form does it fulfil its possibilities.

189

The human foetus grows through various stages, each of which corresponds to a parallel stage of the whole human race's own previous evolution.

190

Examine any living organism you choose and you will find that its conception, birth, and growth show an innate evolutionary trend. The process of passing from an embryonic stage to a more evolved one involves considerable differences physically. It is equally true, although less apparent, mentally.

191

The nature and functions of man are reflected in miniature in the cells which compose his body, while he himself reflects those of the Universal Mind in which he is similar to the cell.

192

There is not one cell in the whole organism of man which does not reflect in miniature the pattern, the proportions, and the functions of the immense cosmos itself.(P)

193

The microorganism has within it all the varied possibilities of becoming a human entity.

194

The body's physical cells disintegrate into the earth and become part of the soil until they take new forms in plant and animal life. Just as a class in school one day breaks up and all the students go their separate ways, and in its place another class is formed, so the units are fully individualized only when they enter the human stage. Until then they very, very slowly approach this release, just as an embryo in the womb approaches the form of a newborn baby.

195

The human body is composed of millions of tiny different intelligences, each having its own specialized life, all having developed from a single generalized cell. Some cells die within hours, others within days or even longer after the body's own death.

The fertilized egg contains all the organs of the human being in miniature. They merely grow and become big to produce the adult.

196

It is an astonishing thought that the entire human body, from its head to its feet, is contained in miniature in the cell from which it starts existence. No microscope can see it, for it still is only an *idea*. But given time the idea finds expression in a form.

197

In our bodies, the phagocyte cells follow the very opposite path to all the other cells, scattering and moving restlessly where the others are settling down into groups.

198

There are millions of living cells which, in their totality, compose the human body. Each has its own separate birth, life, and death.

199

Nature extravagantly spends large fragments of time on outworking her high purpose; a million years to her are nothing remarkable. We poor mortals, however—being helpless prisoners in the captivity of time, whose tyrannous character we have yet to understand—are eager to see improvement and progress before the same day's sun has set. We need but to consider the enormous duration of the aeons which have straddled the globe since the first Lemurian lived and loved.

200

Those who get discouraged by seeing how slow is humanity's moral growth, and how few are the signs of its spiritual awakening, may gain fresh hope if they study the World-Idea.

201

There are different stages in the development of people: some stand on the lower, some on the higher ones—and others fill in the space between. There is no equality among human beings, in character or manners, in intelligence or intuitiveness. Those who resent this fact may deny it, thereby revealing their incapacity for understanding truth. Exploitation of the lower types by the higher ones has bred the resentment, and this in turn has blinded the eyes or the mind.

202

By his own reaction to the fragments of knowledge of the World-Idea which come to a man, he reveals himself, his kind of character and stage of development.

203

The wise and the foolish, the enlightened and the ignorant, the good and the bad, dwell on the same earth outwardly but on different planets inwardly.

204

The human being slowly unfolds its possibilities through the workings of manifold experiences. In this there are to be seen conscience, guiding it along ever-higher moral paths; capacity, expressing its active power and creative talent; and intelligence, teaching it to discriminate between foolishness and wisdom or to penetrate through appearance to reality.

205

It is significant that animals tend to live in herds. As man matures, he reaches more and more individuality.

206

Slowly, at times pleasurably and at times painfully, the human entity builds up its consciousness and capacities through the ages.

207

If human needs brought us thus far, human curiosity is bringing us into another kind of cycle.

208

Yet this perception of the ultimate goodness behind life, the ultimate triumph of light and love, need not keep us from recognizing that there are evil tendencies in many men. We may recognize them as motes in the beam, as dust in the sunray, for we must not lose our perspective about them; but we may still regard them as temporary phases of human vicissitude that will be over-passed and left behind as the slow course of evolution carries out its work upon the human race.

209

There is no immediate guarantee that the good man may not become a vicious one. The evolutionary arc does not rise with utter smoothness; there are strayings aside, fallings down, and erratic jags. But there is an ultimate guarantee that the experiences of life are so ordained as to open the eyes and direct the will of every man at some point, and to repeat this process at intervals until he does so of his own spontaneous accord.

210

Easy hopes about perpetual progress and shallow optimism about scientific improvement are alike going to be frustrated so long as the higher development of man himself is less valued.

211

Things and information are accumulated. This is naïvely called progress, although the man who uses them is as bad as before—as his inability to stop warring clearly shows.

212

The mere movement in time does not automatically bring progress.

213

If left to their own capacity, many would fall back and fail to grow. But life or Nature does not leave them unassisted like that. For there is the World-Idea, the vital spark, the germ born of World-Mind, the mental picture held by the higher power, which pushes each living cell to fulfil itself. But there is also ignorance opposition and deterioration. Man must make his contribution and *in the end* does so. He has to. As the World-Idea unfolds, he gets more self-control and gains self-knowledge until he discovers the Overself.

214

There is no choice in the matter, ultimately, although there is immediately. The entire human race will have to traverse the course chalked out for it, will have to develop the finer feelings, the concrete intellect, the abstract intellect, the balance between the different sides. If men do not seek to do so now, it is only a question of time before they will be forced to do so later.(P)

215

Man will be redeemed and saved. This is not mere pious wishful thinking but ineluctable destiny. The divine World-Idea could not be realized if this redemption and this salvation were not eventually possible and inescapably certain.

216

It is easier to transform a wilderness into a garden flourishing with plants and flowers than to transform humanity into a spiritual race. But time and life, evolution and experience will all combine to do it. The movement up to higher levels will be slow and painful, the maturation of human character retarded and halting, but they will be sure because they are written in the fate of man.

217

Set, in the Egyptian religion, was the Destroyer, the leader of the powers of darkness, the opposer of Life and the adversary of aspiring man; hence he was turned into Satan by the Christians, into Shai'tan by the Israelites. But just as Set was defeated in the end, his power broken and his submission as a penitent accepted, so man, the prodigal son, will return and will be saved, despite his sins. The covenant has been made: there is ultimate hope for all.

218

The World-Idea is operative on every level. It invites savage humans to outwit their fellow animals by beginning to use brain-power through arrows, slings, and primitive traps; at a higher level to compete with fellow humans and rise economically and socially by using the same power; at a still higher level to reduce sufferings and self-made miseries by practising control over self and avoidance of injury to others; then, at a still higher level, to discover and nurture their spiritual nature.

219

Men are what they are. We have only to look around and see how the great Avatars have not much saved the human species. It is still more or less what it was thousands of years ago. If those men of light and power could not change the masses, how can others do so? Is this a doctrine of hopelessness? No! Men will have to change despite themselves, but it will be under the inexorable pressure of the World-Idea, which will be their teacher, their guide, and their enlightener, because it is the expression of the World-Mind.

220

As the two interact—the human purpose and the World-Idea—each man slowly unfolds his intelligence, which is the fusion of intellect with intuition, and this culminates in Enlightenment, the ultimate and revelatory Insight.

221

The movement upward from the ego's "me" to the real "I" consciousness is as sure as the movement of the planets themselves.

222

Human life does not escape the working of divine law. Human thought, feeling, and action all fall within its circle. The law is unalterable and absolute, universal and sure. It always operates, even when its operation is quite unseen and unknown, because the development of human entities is a part of its own reason for existence.

223

In the end, and whatever his heredity or environment may predetermine and irrespective of his own free choices, the development as well as the history of man must move in obedience to the World-Idea. What that is is known in its completeness only to the World-Mind, but sudden or fleeting glimpses of some tiny part of it have come to a few seers. Yet they have been received, recorded, and handed down as tremendous revelations—and quite rightly.

224

The compulsion exercised by the World-Idea is a secret obscure one, but it may become clearer and plainer as events unfold and experience increases.

225

The achievement of these goals is not left to the effects of chance or the whims of men. It is the half-hidden, half-declared purpose of Nature, and as such is quite compulsive.

226

The mass of people are like blind worms wriggling through the earth. They toil but do not know that the real value of their labours is not in the passages they make for air and moisture or in the fertile mould they carry to the soil's surface. No!—it is in the evolutionary consequences *within themselves*.

227

They have tried and tried to find their own substitute for the higher-than-animal life, but it is ordained that satisfaction of the physical needs of the human species is not enough to give them fulfilment, and that not even the satisfaction of their cultural needs can do so. They are forced in the end to push onward and upward.

228

Life is governed by its own mysterious laws, driven in certain directions by its own mysterious momentum, conformed to a hidden scheme by its own mysterious quality. Nature is significant. The human entity is not just drifting. It will certainly arrive somewhere.

229

Human beings are not only what their past births have made them but also, in the most popular and least accurate language, what God has made them.

230

We have to pass from prattling about man's long-past Fall to declaring his newly possible Rise. It is time to take a better view of him, and certainly of his prospects.

231

Recognizing this, humanity will within a certain time—not in our time—humbly submit as it once did in prehistoric times to rulers guided by true sages and adopt the higher forms of government inspired by the true facts of life. Philosophers will then be not merely the witnesses of their age but also its activators. Then only will humanity at last prevent outer war, even though its own moral nature will still need much more growth. With that recognition, Nature herself will grow kindlier and the area of other forms of human suffering will diminish noticeably.

232

Even though we will reach a higher kind of civilization one day, human differences will continue to express themselves.

233

Nobler and wiser types of humanity, standing at loftier altitudes of consciousness, will begin to emerge from the mass. If they are all too few today, they will be more numerous tomorrow.

234

We are very far from the true man which we are destined to become, the evolved masterpiece of Nature. We possess only rare inklings of the day when the ego's "I" will be transformed into the Overself I-ness.

235

The waves of life have moved across other planets before arriving on this earth and, when this has outserved its usefulness, will move on again.

236

The inhabitants of each planet belong to different stages of evolution: some higher and some lower. This applies not only to the human inhabitants but also to the animal and even the plant inhabitants. They pass in great waves from one planet to another at certain stages of this evolution, going where they can find the most appropriate conditions either for expression of their present stage or for the stimulation of their next immediate stage. Consequently the stragglers and laggards who fall behind pass to a planet where the conditions are of a lower nature, for there they are more at home. On the other hand, the pioneers who have outstripped the mass and can find no conditions suitable for their further development pass to a planet in a higher stage.(P)

237

The notion that God created this world spectacle for the benefit of man alone is an absurd and unwarranted anthropolatry, but the notion that life first attains individual self-consciousness in man is justified in philosophy and by experience. What is it of which he alone is conscious? It is of being himself, his ego. In all earlier stages of evolution, consciousness is entirely veiled in its forms and never becomes self-aware. Only in the human state does individual consciousness of being first dawn. There may exist on other planets creatures infinitely more intelligent and more amiable than human beings. We may not be the only pebbles on the beach of life. Nevertheless the piece of arrogance which places man highest in the scale of existence contains the dim reverberation of a great truth, for man bears the divine within his breast.(P)

238

Human beings have made too much fuss about themselves, their own importance in the cosmic scale. Why should there not be other forms of life superior to them, conscious intelligent beings higher in mentality, character, and spiritual knowledge, better equipped with powers and techniques?(P)

239

Even a partial awareness of what it means to be a man—as above an animal—capable of thinking abstractly, conscious of the vastness of the universe and the littleness of the ego, asking the age-old questions about meaning and purpose in life, sometimes getting a glimpse of a few words of the answer through religion, art, Nature, mysticism, joy, suffering, or intelligence, even this is enough to make him wonder what follows in development after him, higher than himself, if not here then perhaps on other planets or in a fourth dimension. Such beings must already exist somewhere. Are they the gods of ancient fable and myth, disfigured or miscomprehended in human narratives by the passing of time? Were they visitors who helped infant humanity reach its teens and then left it, withdrew, except for rare appearances as avatars, angels, or lawgivers?

240

There are existences for beings on levels and in times and spaces different from ours. The level we know and the humans we see only partially manifest the World-Idea.

241

The multibirthed nature of human experience fits in with the shimmering galaxies of the multiverse itself. "We are not alone" could be echoed back by this planet Earth itself.

242

There are beings not subject to the same laws as those governing mankind's physical existence. They are normally not visible to men. They are gods.(P)

243

The Gods are both symbols of particular forces and beings dwelling on higher planes.(P)

Evolution's goal is not merger

244

Can it be true that all this vast travail, all this long long ingathering of experience, all this travel to the farthest limit, is only to end in negation, in unlearning all knowledge and returning to where we started? My heart does not believe it, my reason cannot accept it.

245

The human entity has travelled through joy and suffering, experienced birth and death, experimented with good and evil for the very purpose of becoming a fully conscious entity. How then could annihilation—Vedantic or any other kind—be its ultimate fate?

246

Is it for this, that man should end as a mere speck of dust, that he was born? Consciousness, aspiration, insight, and inspirations, artistic creations and scientific revelations, the noblest ethical feelings—all useless because the being they serve is destined to vanish utterly? If all man's seeming progress comes to an end with his death, his own end, how futile it is! It helps little to say that others will benefit by it, for this merely shifts the futility to them, for they too will die. The human situation is unsatisfactory, as the Buddha tirelessly asserted and as the Biblical Psalmist succinctly lamented.

247

We have not come from oblivion. All our past is present in our characters, capacities, and tendencies; therefore we shall not go into oblivion. There is no death—only a change of state.

248

We know that the cosmos manifests itself out of the divine Mind, and within it, too. But why there should be such a manifestation at all, we do not know. Many students raise this query and are dissatisfied at the failure to obtain a good answer. But the fact is that such questions cannot be adequately answered on the same plane as that on which they arise. If we could shift our consciousness to a higher one, we would find that they simply do not exist there. However, although complete adequacy may be unattainable, some sort of working answer can be formulated and used for and by those who are unable to effect such a shift. If the human entity has no other purpose to fulfil on this earth than to return to the sphere of its origin, then it had no business to leave that sphere. There must be something to be gained by its earthly journey, if the universe has any sense in it at all.

249

His destination is also his origin. But to say that he was born in the eternal Spirit starts the question, "How can time, which is placed outside eternity, bring him to eternity?" The answer is that it does not bring him there; it only educates him to look for, and prepares him to pass through, the opening through which he can escape. Need it be said that this lies at the point where ego surrenders wholly to Overself?

250

The Goal towards which man is slowly travelling by successive steps is a threefold one: the fully developed environment, the fully developed intelligence, and the realized soul. The last is the best and the other two are but servants of it, for here he comes first to a comprehension and then to a realization of himself. Yes, he is on his way to the grand awakening into full self-consciousness.

251

All this vast evolution of environments and their entities has but one ultimate aim from man's point of view and so far as he is concerned. It is to bring him into a miniature likeness to his divine Parent, to make him into an image of godlike beauty, power, wisdom, and being.

252

Yes, the earth has been, through this long travail of countless ages, bringing forth the mineral, the plant, the animal, and the human kingdoms. In man, she has given birth to a child who is destined to rule with her when his Intelligence becomes perfected and consequently when he is able to rule himself.

253

The process of human evolution serves a twofold purpose. The first is to develop the physical, emotional, and intellectual characteristics. The second is to lead the individual to enquire into, and become fully conscious of, his divine origin.

254

The journey of life is both an adventure and a pilgrimage. We pass from body to body to collect experience. The fruit of experience is Enlightenment: the knowledge of Overself, established awareness of its presence; and knowledge of the Unseen Power behind the universe, established connection with it.

255

We are here in this world for a higher purpose than the obvious physical one of self-preservation, for even that is contributory to it. We are here to evolve into the consciousness of Overself. Every physical experience is only a means toward such spiritual development.

256

Students who have come finally to philosophy from the Indian Advaita Vedanta, bring with them the belief that the divine soul having somehow lost its consciousness is now seeking to become self-conscious again. They suppose that the ego originates and ends on the same level—divinity—and therefore the question is often asked why it should go forth on such a long and unnecessary journey. This question is a misconceived one. It is not the ego itself which ever was consciously divine, but its source, the Overself. The ego's divine character lies in its essential but hidden being, but it has never known that. The purpose of gathering experience (the evolutionary process) is precisely to bring it to such awareness. The ego comes to slow birth in finite consciousness out of utter unconsciousness and, later, to recognition and union with its infinite source. That source, whence it has emanated, remains untouched, unaffected, ever knowing and serenely witnessing. The purpose in this evolution is the ego's own advancement. When the Quest is reached, the Overself reveals its presence fitfully and brokenly at first but later the hide-and-seek game ends in loving union.(P)

257

What is the use, ask many questioners, of first, an evolution of the human soul which merely brings it back to the same point where it started and second, of developing a selfhood through the long cycles of evolution only to have it merged or dissolved in the end into the unselfed Absolute? Is not the whole scheme absurdly useless? The answer is that if this were really the case, the criticism passed would be quite a fair one. But it is not the case. The unit of life emanated from the Overself begins with the merest glimmer of consciousness, appearing on our plane as a protozoic cell. It evolves eventually into the fullest human consciousness, including the intellectual and spiritual. It does not finish as it began; on the contrary, there is a grand purpose behind all its travail. There is thus a wide gulf between its original state and its final one. The second point is more difficult to clear up, but it may be plainly affirmed that man's individuality survives even in the divinest state accessible to him. There it becomes the same in quality but not identical in essence. The most intimate mental and physical experiences of human love cast a little light for our comprehension of this mystery. The misunderstanding which leads to these questions arises chiefly because of the error which believes that it is the divine soul which goes through all this pilgrimage by reincarnating in a series of earthly forms. The true teaching about reincarnation is not that the divine soul enters into the captivity and ignorance of the flesh again and again but that something emanated from the soul, that is, a unit of life that eventually develops into the personal ego, does so. The Overself contains this reincarnating ego within itself but does not itself reincarnate. It is the parent; the ego is only its offspring. The long and tremendous evolution through which the unit of life passes from its primitive cellular existence to its matured human one is a genuine evolution of its consciousness. Whoever believes that the process first plunges a soul down from the heights into a body or forces Spirit to lose itself in Matter, and then leaves it no alternative but to climb all the way back to the lost summit again, believes wrongly. The Overself never descends or climbs, never loses its own sublime consciousness. What really does this is something that emanates from it and that consequently holds its capacity and power in latency, something which is finited out of the Overself's infinitude and becomes first, the simple unit of life and later, the complex human ego. It is not the Overself that suffers and struggles during this long unfoldment but its child, the ego. It is not the Overself that slowly expands its intelligence and consciousness, but the ego. It is not the Overself that gets deluded by ignorance and passion, by selfishness and extroversion, but the ego.

The belief in the merger of the ego held by some Hindu sects or in its annihilation held by some Buddhist ones, is unphilosophical. The "I" differentiated itself out of the infinite ocean of Mind into a distinct individuality after a long development through the diverse kingdoms of Nature. Having thus arrived at consciousness of what it is, having travelled the spiral of growth from germ to man, the result of all this effort is certainly not gained only to be thrown away.

Were this to happen then the entire history of the human race would be a meaningless one, its entire travail a resultless one, its entire aspiration a valueless one. If evolution were merely the complementary return journey of an involutionary process, if the evolving entity arrived only at its starting point for all its pains, then the whole plan would be a senseless one. If the journey of man consisted of nothing more than treading a circle from the time of his emergence from the Divine Essence to the time of his mergence back into it, it would be a vain and useless activity. It would be a stupendous adventure but also a stupid one. There is something more than that in his movement. Except in the speculations of certain theorists, it simply does not happen.

The self-consciousness thus developed will not be dissolved, extinguished, or re-absorbed into the Whole again, leaving not a trace behind. Rather will it begin a new spiral of evolution towards higher altitudes of consciousness and diviner levels of being, in which it will co-operate as harmoniously with the universal existence as formerly it collided against it. It will not separate its own good from the general good. Here is part of the answer to this question: What are the ultimate reasons for human wanderings through the world-process? That life matters, that the universe possesses meaning, and that the evolutionary agonies are leading to something worthwhile—these are beliefs we are entitled to hold. If the cosmos is a wheel which turns and turns endlessly, it does not turn aimlessly. Evolution does not return us to the starting point as we were. The ascent is not a circle but a spiral.

Evolution presupposes that its own possibility has always been latent within the evolving entities. Hence the highest form is hidden away in the lowest one. There is development from the blindly instinctive life of animals to the consciously thinking life of man. The blind instinctive struggles of the plant to sustain itself are displaced in the evolutionary process by the intelligent self-conscious efforts of the man. Nor does this ascent end in the Vedantic merger or the Buddhistic annihilation. It could not, for it is a development of the individuality. Everywhere we find that evolution produces variety. There are myriads of individual entities, but each possesses some quality of uniqueness which distinguishes it from all others. Life may be one but its multitudinous expressions do differ, as though difference were inherent in such expression.

Evolution as mentalistically defined by philosophy is not quite the same as evolution as materialistically defined by Darwin. With us it is simply the mode of striving, through rhythmic rise and fall, for an ever fuller expansion of the individual unit's consciousness. However, the ego already possesses all such possibilities latently. Consequently the whole process, although apparently an ascending one, is really an unfolding one.(P)

258

Although the possibility of this discovery and awareness of Overself and establishment in it has always been with every man at every moment, the probability has not. For he has to develop the equipment for maturing from animal *through* man's gathered experience to this full establishment in full union with his highest being. The savage may get the glimpse, and does, but this is only a beginning, not an end. The teaching favoured by Indian metaphysicians that we came from God and shall return to God is an oversimplification which generally leads to misunderstanding. Then all this long pilgrimage with all its sufferings becomes a senseless waste of time and an idiotic expenditure of energy—if not on our part then on God's. It is like banging one's head against a wall in order to enjoy the relief which follows when the action ends. Through lack of a cosmogony the proponents of this teaching are compelled to explain away the purpose of all this vast universe as non-purpose, using the term *maya*, one of whose two meanings is "mystery." The Infinite Being, whose Consciousness and Power is behind the universe of history, can itself have no history, for it is beyond time, evolution, change, development, can have no purpose which is gainful to itself, cannot be made the object of human thought correctly because it utterly transcends the limitations of such thought. But all this is not to say that the World-Mind's activity is meaningless, Idea-less, and fruitless. The very contrary is the case.

259

But because causation is shown to be illusory, and the cosmos uncreated and unending, this does not mean that our cosmology denies the truth of evolution. It denies only the conventional attitude towards evolution. For it takes all change and hence all progress out of the realm of ultimate reality and relegates them to where they belong, to the realm of immediate appearance.

260

Just as there have been misconceptions about the role played by the personal ego and the physical ego in the life of mankind—misconceptions which have arisen by holding on to ideas which are out of their time and place—so the question must be asked, *did* these egos come, as the Orient mostly believed, by a process which launched them on a path where, as the poet Sir Edwin Arnold has beautifully put it, "The dew-drop slips into the shining sea" where the ego is utterly annihilated, where the personal self is completely dissolved in a sort of mass-consciousness, where all that it has gained from experience, all that it has learned from intelligence, is to be dissolved and thrown away as futile and useless although ages upon ages have been taken for the process? Or will there unfold a higher type of individuality, one that is free because it has *earned* its freedom; free to exist in harmony with the universal harmony, with the Universal Mind. If nonduality, the goal of Advaita, is to be the end of it all, the vast work of time and space seems to have been in vain, a ghastly repetition of what was not worthwhile. Or is there another explanation which philosophy offers? The answer is: there is.

261

If anyone finds anything in this universe about which to complain, if he criticizes its defects and deficiencies, its evils and imperfections, let him remember that a universe which is perfect in the sense that he means does not and could not exist. Only God is perfect. Anything else, even any universe, being distinct from God, cannot also be perfect. Consequently it will display tendencies and situations open to human criticism. Even though a universe is a manifestation of God, it cannot become as perfect as God without becoming God—when it would itself vanish. Nevertheless its divine origin and sustenance are revealed in the fact that all things and all beings in it strive for perfection even if they never attain it. This is what evolution means and this is the secret spring behind it. For in seeking to return to their source, they are compelled to seek its perfection too. That is, they are compelled to evolve from lower to higher states and forms, from evil conditions and characteristics to ideal ones.

262

It is not a game of hide-and-seek that God is playing with man, not a sport for God's own amusement as some Hindu sects believe, but a process of evolvement intended to give man insight into the Real and power for co-operative participation. It is a treasure-hunt through many earthly lives.

263

We murmur against the world's obstructiveness to our aspirations: the body is our stumbling-block. Yet if we had to live always as disembodied spirits, our spiritual development would need an immeasurably longer time to accomplish itself. The sharper focus of physical consciousness quickens our pace.

264

Man, in his earlier phases of being, was connected with the Overself and aware of it. But his connection lacked his own control. Eventually, to fulfil the purpose of evolution, he lost this connection and with it his awareness. Now he has to regain the connection and reawaken this awareness by his own efforts and out of his own inner activity, through his own desiring and in his own individual freedom. What has he gained by this change to compensate the loss? His consciousness has become more sharply focused and consequently more clearly aware.

265

Our source is in the Overself; our growth is but a return to it, made fully conscious as we were not before.

266

The immediate purpose of human incarnation and evolution is to develop a true and full self-consciousness at all levels from the lowest to the highest. The man who does not know himself beyond the physical intellectual ego is still only half-conscious.

267

As a man truly evolves, he is guided more and more by intelligence and consciousness. It is a false evolvement which guides him into cunning and selfishness.

268

The idea of human perfection would mean the attainment of a static condition, but nowhere in nature do we find such condition. Everything, as Buddha pointed out, is in a state of becoming, or as Krishnamurti number two calls it: Reality is motion. Buddha never denied that there was anything beyond becoming. He simply refused to discuss the possibility, whereas persons like Krishnamurti two stop there and affirm it as being the ultimate. There were very good reasons why Buddha refused. He was living in a country where the intelligentsia were lost in fruitless and impractical speculations, and where the emotional were lost in religion, endlessly ritualized and filled with superstition. The mystics were lost in the impossible task of making meditation their whole life. Nature forbade it and brought them back. Becoming and motion are processes, but Being, pure consciousness, is not. In the experience of a glimpse we discover this fact. Being transcends becoming, but it is only the Gods who live on the plane of Being; we humans may visit it, even for long periods, but we must return.(P)

Part 3:
WORLD-MIND

Is it so unimportant to form an idea of God which shall be as near the truth as possible through containing so little error as possible? The Spirit which inspired and instructed Moses did not think so. "Thou shalt have no other Gods before me," it said. That is, we must not label the wrong thing with the name of God, or hold the wrong idea about him as if it were the correct one. "Thou shalt not make unto thee any graven image" was the next commandment. But an idol does not necessarily have to be made of stone or metal. It can be made of an idea.

If anyone wishes to call World-Mind the Lord of the Universe, he will not be wrong; but then if someone else wishes to assert that World-Mind cannot be a Personal God, neither will he be wrong. Is there any possible reconciliation of these two views? Yes, for in both cases these are only mental formulations, and it is impossible to describe God positively, accurately in intellectual terms. All mental concepts of God have to be discarded in the end. No dogmatic statement can hold the truth *as it is*: we merely get from the statement something to satisfy the intellect. For the Real is ineffable, that is, undescribable and untouchable by the ordinary finite capacity of humans. But because there is something godlike, somewhere, in man, intuition may reveal it.

1

WHAT IS GOD?

Differing views of God

We must differentiate between the invented God of religion and the imagined God of mysticism, on the one hand, and the real God of philosophical truth, on the other. The creator-God of religion is a more erroneous conception than the immanent God of mysticism, but both are alien to truth. Both have failed to fathom the Unconditioned, Nondual, and Illimitable God.

2

There is a universal principle of Eternal Intelligence behind all existence. If the follies of superstition and the bigotries of religion caricature it, the verities of philosophy and the insights of wisdom restore a true picture.

3

We are not atheists. We do hold that a reality higher than the crudely material one exists. If the name of God is given to this reality, then we accept God; but we do not and will not accept the erroneous and degrading notion of God which most men have.

4

This higher concept of God is much more respectful and much more reverential than the old traditional one.

5

Most of the current ideas about God are hazy, uncertain, unsettled, and even absurd. *The Wisdom of the Overself* represented an attempt at clear exposition of that truth about God which philosophy has found out.

6

The conception of God held by traditional established religions is not the same as the philosophical conception of the World-Mind except in some points. There are noteworthy differences.

7

If by God you mean something higher than mere material existence, then we do not deny God. It is the false notions of God that we deny, the grotesque caricatures that appear in churches and temples and sermons and books. We look on this higher Reality as something not afar off from the *essence* of our own selves. We have discovered that the common every-day life does not exhaust the alphabet of existence, that there is something sublime beyond it and yet akin to us. We *do* honour and revere such a God, if you wish to call It such, because we believe It to be the true God.

8

God—a term which signifies a certain mathematical formula to some moderns and a certain mental figure to some primitives—exists all the same.

9

There is some truth in the claim of both Japanese Buddhists and Western materialists that human beings created the idea of God and later believed in their creation to the point that they found it necessary to worship God. But this is not the whole truth and, left by itself, it may become misleading. It must be properly inserted in its place within the whole truth, whose first and basic tenet is that there is something real behind the idea of God, although the idea itself may be a product of imagination.

10 ·

Mixed up with different theologies, dressed up with different rituals, God remains identic and does not change.

11

Men of inferior intelligence quite naturally want a God who will be attentive to their requirements, interested in their personal lives, and help-ful during times of distress. That is to say, they want a human God. Men of superior intelligence come in time to consider God as an impersonal essence that is everywhere present, and consequently embodied in them-selves and to be communed with interiorly too. That is to say, they recog-nize only a mystical God. Men of the highest intelligence perceive that the "I" is illusory, that it is only ignorance of this fact that causes man to regard himself as a separate embodiment of the divine essence, and that in reality there is only this nondual nameless being. How impossible it is to get men of inferior intelligence to worship or even to credit such an Existence which has no shape, no individuality, no thinking even! Hence such men are given a figure after their own image as God, a deity that is a personal, human, five-sensed being.(P)

12

World-Mind, Lord and Creator, Maker and Ruler of all things, is not a glorified aggrandized human being.

13

We are not to believe that the World-Mind *deliberately* directs the universe and *consciously* attends to every detail of its operation. That would be to turn it into a Big Man—and to minimize the powers of Mind.

14

According to the simpler unintellectual religious views, the universe requires a Being to create it, then to maintain it, and lastly to guide it along a certain orderly way.

15

This is the mistake all too often made by those who ask the age-old questions: they see that every creature's life has a beginning, so they assume God must have had one too. But the Life-Force which appears anew in every babe comes from God; it has always existed, taking on countless outward forms. God, its source, has always been and never began. Any other assumption makes Him like the creatures—finite—and is a false one that contradicts the very idea of God—the Infinite.

16

Man gets no such treatment from life that he could believe it takes heed of his personal feelings. It treats him quite impersonally, as if it were itself quite impersonal. Thus the test of experience contradicts the belief in a personal governor of the universe.

17

If you discuss the concept of God as a creator, you discuss a personality. But such must have a beginning and an end. If you discuss the concept of God as Impersonal, however, these limits are no longer a necessary part of it.

18

We arrogantly superimpose our merely human ideas upon the Universal Mind and impertinently expect it to display anthropomorphic attributes, under the delusion that they are divine ones merely because they are displayed on a gigantic scale.

19

It is inevitable that we believe that the Infinite Power works as we humans work but it is also fallacious.

20

To think of God as a person is to think of a finite and imperfect being. God is a principle of being.

21

The Deity cannot be limited like a finite human being, using a personal will to achieve a particular end, or thinking in a series of successive ideas that move through time. A less erroneous picture is that of the electronic computing machine, which performs millions of different operations in a single second.

22

It is impossible for a rational mind to believe that the Infinite and Eternal Deity is subject to momentary changes of mind or suffers occasional lapses from continuance of the cosmic laws.

23

The Greek conception of the world being directed by Intelligence is surely higher than the Hebrew belief in a capricious, jealous, and angry despot of a personal God.

24

God is Love and Justice, Wisdom and Truth and Law, attributes which have been worshipped by man from ancient times.

25

The God who magically creates and personally manages the world, as separate from him, is the first simple concept of simple men. The God out of whose being the world beginningly and endlessly comes into birth is the next developed concept of more cultured men.

26

The notions of Deity which popular religion provides for its followers are well suited to the early stages of mental development but not to the more advanced ones. A child needs the comfort of living with its father and mother, but an adult becomes self-reliant enough to live on his own. The popular notions of God as a Father or as a Mother belong to the early stage and objectify God as some kind of glorified human being. They are human ideas picturing a human Deity. To this stage, too, belong not only the notions of a jealous, wrathful, or capricious God, but even those of a sentimental, kindly, emotional, elderly gentleman who is constantly hovering around to listen to the prayers of his devotees—and then running off to fulfil their wishes or, according to his mood, refusing to do so. The maturer notion provided by philosophy will naturally seem cold, and cheerless to those who need the popular one.

Is God good, conscious?

27

If, when we say that God is good, we really mean it in the circumscribed sense of the word, we would thereby imply that God could be better also—in which case God would no longer be God, being a changeable being, an improvable being. It was Spinoza's defect that he failed to perceive that the ultimate principle baffles such positive description and transcends such nameable attributes as "good." He fell into it through allowing his overly mathematical intellect to unduly tip the balance against his mystical intuition. His God had different qualities, even though their number was infinite. This made it a limited God. There is no way of describing the mysterious principle behind all existence that will be a correct way. Words drawn from the language of finite human creatures are inapplicable to the infinite principle that transcends those creatures. If we do use them here, it is only for the sake of literary convenience and with a presupposed understanding of their relativity, not for their literalness.

28

Since we see so many forms in Nature which are gloriously beautiful, and yet at the same time so many which are repulsively ugly, we may rightly conclude that *both* beauty and ugliness, the opposites, are present in the World-Idea and hence in the World-Mind. The same may be said of loving-kindness and merciless cruelty. For these attributes are merely human conceptions. The Infinite Mind is infinitely larger and more impersonal in outlook than is the human mind.

29

It will be found by experience that preoccupation with such questions as "Why does God allow evil in the world?" will fall away under the influence of the Witness Self. The question is relative to and relevant only in the sphere of the personal self in interaction with other personal selves, and in that sphere it has no answer. In the sphere of the Overself the question does not exist. "Come unto Me, all ye who are weary and heavy laden and I will give you rest" is still as true as when spoken by the Christ nearly two thousand years ago.

30

It is the outward appearance of their environment and the inward reality of their egoism which make so many thinkers doubt whether God is perfectly good.

31

"I am indifferent to all generated beings; there is none whom I hate, none whom I love," declares Krishna in the *Bhagavad Gita.*

32

The statement in the book *Mahatma Letters* which denies the existence of conscious God is nonsense if it means that God has no mind. However, what it probably means is that God has not the kind of limited five-sense consciousness to which human beings are limited. One trouble is that it is ordinarily believed that a God who is not a Person is no God at all because

He will not be a thinking, intelligent being. It is so customary to associate consciousness with individual consciousness that it seems almost impossible to grasp the concept of omnipresent, everywhere-diffused, all-inclusive Mind which is not a mind.

33

When the book *Mahatma Letters* tries to turn God into blind law, it is again likely to fall into nonsense if it denies real Being to God. What it probably denies is the limited kind of being which is the only kind our human faculties can imagine.

34

The Real, as the ultimate source of all knowing and feeling beings, cannot itself be unknowing and unfeeling. We could not deny consciousness to It without denying consciousness to man. But being absolute and infinite it does not know and feel in the same limited way which confines the knowledge and feelings of finite humans.

35

It is more correct to speak of Mind as the All-Conscious than as the unconscious. What we may rightly say is that, viewed from the side which alone is known to us, a certain phase of it appears to be unconscious. The higher teachings state that all the phases of Mind are conscious ones.

36

There is a curious and mysterious statement in more than one ancient Hindu philosophical text to the effect that God cannot know himself. What does it mean? The sun's light is needed to end the world's darkness but not needed at any moment by the sun itself since it is all-light: therefore the sun could not shine upon itself, could not light up itself. In the same way, God can gain nothing more by making himself known to himself, since he is already all-knowledge. In this sense only—and not in the sense of inability to know—is the Hindu statement to be interpreted.

God beyond finite knowing

37

Any mental picture of God is just as much, in its own way, an idol as any carved stone or wood figure may be. Those who worship the one are violating the second Commandment as much as those who worship the other.

38

Everything, be it person or idea, that you set up in place of the true God is an idol. In every act of such worship you commit idolatry.

39

If divinity cannot be represented by any idol, any graven image, neither can it be described by any word. All verbal descriptions are non-descriptions.

40

What Jesus called "the only true God" is the ultimate formless reality, not the thoughts about it or the pictures of it created in human imaginations. It is an object of insight, not of sense or thought.

41

Try as much as you can, but in the end you will find God is not something imaginable.

42

Nobody can tell us what God looks like, for God has no form at all.

43

God must be found *as He is in reality*, not as He has been in human imagination.

44

We feel the presence of a divine power, but we are baffled by its motives.

45

Neither thinking nor any other kind of human activity can grasp the full truth about the World-Mind. Not even at the height reached by sage or adept is this possible.

46

If God were not a mystery He would not be God. Men who claim to know Him need semantic correction; this said, their experience may yet be exceptional, elevating, and immaterialistic. But let God remain God, incomprehensible and untouchable.(P)

47

God is a mystery which no man can truly understand, no language can really express, and no idea can fully embody.

48

The one infinite life-power which reveals itself in the cosmos and manifests itself through time and space, cannot be named. It is something that *is*. For a name would falsely separate it from other things when the truth is that it *is* those things, all things. Nor would we know what to call it, since we know nothing about its real nature.(P)

49

The consciousness and nature of the World-Mind is utterly beyond the capacity and power of any human being to understand, much less to explain.

50

The universe's first principle, be it called God with the religionists or energy with the scientists, is beyond the power of human understanding. At its very best it can know only its own reaction to that Principle.

51

The Biblical announcement "I Am That I Am" is easier understood as "I Am As I Am." It can have no other meaning than the uniqueness and incomprehensibility of God. For every attempt to bring God within the range of the intellect always fails, and every attempt to bring God within the range of the imagination merely symbolizes. If, then, the original sentence is to be understood still more easily, let us read it as: "I am THAT which knows all and sees all, but can be known and seen by none."

52

The atheist says, "God is nowhere!" The mystic says, "God is now here!" The philosopher says, "God is!"

53

Man's mental apparatus being so limited, the truths he conceives through it must be limited too. He cannot possibly know what God is like but only that God—some sort of higher power—is.

54

The Bible's phrase wherein God is self-described to Moses as "I am that I am" is more philosophically correct and more linguistically right, in the original Hebrew sense, if Englished as "I am what I shall be."

55

It was his consciousness of being united with this timeless pre-existent as well as ever-existent Life that enabled Jesus to announce: "Verily, verily, I say unto you, Before Abraham was I am." "I am that I am," was the revelation of God to the Hebrew Master, Moses. "That I am," was the revelation of God to the anonymous Hindu Master of the *Upanishads*.

56

All verbal definitions of the World-Mind are inevitably limited and inadequate. If the statements here made seem to be of the nature of dogmatic concepts it is because of the inadequacy of language to convey more subtle meaning. They who read these lines with intuitive insight allied to clear thinking will see that the concepts are flexible verbal frames for holding thought steady in that borderland of human consciousness where thinking verges on wordless knowing.(P)

The active God we worship

57

The first great truth is that a Supreme Mind minds the universe.

58

All scientific evidence indicates that there is a single power which presides over the entire universe, and all religious mystic experience and philosophic insight confirms it. Not only is this so, but this power also maintains the universe; its intelligence is unique, matchless, incredible. This power is what I call the World-Mind.(P)

59

What is in itself and at once assembled as the highest concept of human beings, the greatest power ruling existence, the supreme Mind before which all other minds must bow, the primal consciousness which outlives every form of existence because IT alone is, was, and shall be? There is no name attached to it, this ineffable silent mystery of mysteries. Yet it is there. Everything tells us so, from the vast universe itself to those seers and sages of ancient Greece, India, and China who have broken through and away from human limitations. Can we wonder that with one God there came one energy and one substance?

60

That being whom the ancient Japanese called "The Master of the Universe" was the same as what the ancient Hindus called Ishvara. Mind, Life, and Power are in that being. It holds the universe in its Mind: therefore we creatures of the universe are held too. We would not live for a moment if this incomparable being were not here too.

61

The World-Mind is unique, different from any other existing or conceivable mind in the whole cosmos. Indeed, all these others can only arise out of and within it, but can never equal or transcend it.

62

There is only a single absolute unconditioned entity. Yet from it there extend countless finite and conditioned entities. They are visible to the sense of sight, physical to the sense of touch; yet it is neither.

63

The meaning among cultured Muslims of the Islamic phrases "*La Llaha*" "*Il-la lahu*" is: first, the denial of plurality and the affirmation of Unity in the Supreme Being; second, this Being is also the only real activating Force in the cosmos.

64

Behind all the innumerable creatures in this universe and behind all the innumerable phenomena of the universe itself, there is a single, infinite, eternal, supreme Intelligence.

65

It is something that never had a beginning and can never have an end. It does not change, although the world born from it does nothing else more incessantly than change.

66

We talk of being, but it is not to be found in time, nor in the mind and feeling of the conditioned self. And yet all these have emerged somehow out of it. Is it, then, that God is being? In the end it must be so.

67

Only in such a language as Sanskrit does one find a word which covers this ample meaning, that truth and being are one. The word is *Sat*.

68

World-Mind emanates and activates the cosmos into a fresh cyclic being. This continues under its sustenance but, again cyclically, it absorbs the cosmos in the end. Thus it is the closest to the common idea of God, the Personal God to be worshipped.

69

The World-Mind may be worshipped by religious devotees or meditated upon by others as present in their own souls.

70

I know that the word "God" is a tainted one, that it has been used by hypocrites and scoundrels, by brainless idiots and selfish vested interests, and had perhaps better be bypassed. Yet it comes into my consciousness at this point in time, in this particular place, when my own preference is, as often, to use the words "The World-Mind."

71

No human idea can account for its own existence without testifying to the prior existence of a human mind. The world as idea can only account for its own existence by pointing to a World-Mind. And it is equally a fact that the highest kind of existence discoverable to us in the universe is mental existence. In using the name "Mind" for God, I but follow some of the highest examples from antiquity, such as Aristotle in Greece, Hermes Trismegistus in Egypt, Asvaghosha in India, and the Patriarch Hui Neng in China.

72

For us who are philosophically minded, the World-Mind truly exists. For us it is God, and for us there is a relationship with it—the relationship of devotion and aspiration, of communion and meditation. All the abstract talk about nonduality may go on, but in the end the talkers must humble themselves before the infinite Being until they are as nothing and until they are lost in the stillness—Its stillness.(P)

73

Behind it all is the Great Silence, broken only by the projection of new worlds and the re-absorption of old ones, the unutterable and unknowable Mystery, unreachable and untouchable by man. Tiny creature that he is, with the tiny mind he has, THAT is utterly beyond him. But from the Grand Mystery, the active God of which this planet Earth is a projection has in turn projected him. Here, communication in the most attenuated intuitive form is possible, even holy communion may be attained. This is the God, the higher power, to whom men instinctively turn in despair or in aspiration, in faith or in doubt. Sometimes a mere fragment of his work is revealed to a chosen prophet in the Cosmic Vision, an awe-filled experience.

74

Sometimes a person is granted a glimpse of the World-Mind. This, if it happens, does so during meditation usually, but not always. It is then both a physical and a mental grace, for the sight is, says the Indonesian text, "similar to the brightness of a million suns."

75

We are surrounded by a world which seems both real and outside us. Nothing that we can find in this world corresponds to this idea of God. Are we to assert that it is illusory or that God exists but is remote from this world? The mystic can reply: "I know from experience that the idea is true and the existence is everywhere."

76

Modern man looks in all sorts of impossible places for an invisible God and will not worship the visible God which confronts him. Yet little thinking is needed to show that we are all suckled at the everlasting breast of Nature. It is easy to see that the source of all life is the sun and that its creative, protective, and destructive powers are responsible for the entire physical process of the universe. However it is not merely to the physical sun alone that the aspirant addresses himself but to the World-Mind behind it. He must look upon the sun as a veritable self-expression and self-showing of the World-Mind to all its creatures.(P)

77

The sun is God's face appearing in the physical world.

78

Those who love to see the sun in its mystery-laden risings or witness its equally mystery-laden settings bear outward testimony to an inward relationship.

79

The sun seen by men is both their symbol of God's power, glory, beauty, life, and light, and also the actual indicator of God's central heart, the Presence Invisible.

80

We must honour the Universal Ruler of things and beings as the flower honours the sun, for it is also the Source of Life.

81

It is right to venerate the sun, for without it we could not keep the body alive, could not grow the food we need.

2

NATURE OF WORLD-MIND

Attributes, characteristics, powers

He who made the world still upholds it. He rules the entire universe, this great Being, and regulates the karmic destinies of men.

2

The World-Mind brings our universe into being and governs it, too. The enormous number of objects and creatures which appear through Its agency, through Its power and wisdom, cannot be limited to what is visible alone, and must fill a thinking person with wonder at all the possi- bilities—a wonder which Plato said must be the beginning of philosophy.

3

The Infinite Intelligence knows and controls all things, all situations.

4

"Are not two sparrows sold for a farthing? And one of them shalt not fall on the ground without your Father" (Matthew 10:29) puts simply that an infinite intelligence controls this entire universe, and that it is as present in the smallest event as in the greatest.

5

This is the Power that carries everything along, every entity, and which provides the universe with its continuity.

6

In the sense that the World-Mind is the active agent behind and within the universe, it is carrying the whole burden of creation; it is the real doer, carrying us and our actions too.(P)

7

There is a Mind which keeps the planets in their allotted orbit and the lives of men in their largely self-earned destinies.

8

The World-Mind is God as universal intelligence and creative power.

9

The World-Mind is called *Adi-buddhi* in the Nepalese-Tibetan esotericism: meaning Divine Ideation, the First Intelligence, the Universal Wisdom.(P)

10

We are frequently informed by religious and mystical sources that God is Love. It would be needful for those who accept this statement to balance and complete it by the affirmation that God is Pure Intelligence.(P)

11

Love is not the ultimate but only an attribute of the ultimate.

12

The intelligence which works so untiringly in the world around us knows what to do without having to prepare a plan. It does not need to think in the way human beings think. Being infinite, its wisdom is infinite.

13

The Intelligence which formulated the World-Idea is living and creative—in short, Divine. The so-called laws of nature merely show its workings.(P)

14

If the divine did not have real being, with all its attributes of consciousness, intelligence, power, and love, we ourselves would not exist.

15

Those who cannot comprehend the infinity of intelligence behind the world around them can hardly be expected to comprehend that it has an independent existence as an attribute of pure Spirit.

16

The World-Mind holds in one eternal thought the entire World-Idea.

17

The World-Mind knows and experiences everything and everyone. It also knows the Supreme non-thing, the Real, while knowing the illusoriness of the cosmos.

18

The World-Mind knows all because it is eternally in all.

19

The mental activity of the World-Mind is not, and cannot be, an unconscious process. In the elemental, the mineral, and even the plant kingdom this may seem to us to be so; but if the first act of mentation which began the evolutionary process was not done unawares, then the entire projection of the entire cosmos, at all the different stages of this process, also cannot be unknown, at any moment and in any point, to the World-Mind.

20

In its own mysterious way, the World-Mind is all-embracing, aware of everything, every entity and every activity.

21

The World-Mind is not only Lord and Governor of the world but also Lord and Governor of the illusion which makes the world so vivid to the ignorant; that is, It is itself the All-Knowing, the All-Seeing, Conscious of the Real.

22

That One Mind could possibly comprehend all could only be possible if that one Mind were *behind* all.

23

The World-Mind is common to all human minds and is the field of their interaction, and the notion that A and B are independent and isolated minds is superficially correct but fundamentally fallacious. There is a common ground of mind, a hidden linkage, and the ideas of one can be transmitted to the other, albeit often unconsciously.

24

No event could be outside the knowledge of God, no entity could be beyond the power of God.

25

Were the World-Mind beyond, because outside, the finite universe, then it would be limited by that universe and thus lose its own infinitude. But because *it includes* the universe completely within itself while remaining completely unlimited, it is genuinely infinite. World-Mind is neither limited nor dissipated by its self-projection in the universe. If World-Mind is immanent in the universe, it is not confined to the universe; if it is present in every particle of the All, its expression is not exhausted by the All.(P)

26

Inexplicable and incomprehensible though the fact must be to the human intellect, the One infinite Mind never loses its own character even though it is seemingly incarnated into the myriad forms of an evolving universe, never loses itself in them.

27

It is a wisdom expressed through the World-Idea, but not confined to it.

28

Amid all this apparent self-division into innumerable selves, the World-Mind remains as intact and inviolate as ever it was.

29

The World-Mind alone has come into the limitations of physical existence without being held down by them, without being other than itself.

30

The infinite power is without a history but the ideas in its consciousness
do have one. Nothing ever happens to That which is out of every kind of
time and space, which transcends every kind of shape and change. But its
ideas pass through experience after experience because they appear in
timed succession and pictured form.

31

World-Mind is omnipresent.

32

The divine Mind is implicit in every universe, the divine Power is impli-
cated in every cosmic activity.

33

This is the reality that is hidden in me and you, in the whole universe
itself. It acts everywhere and exists eternally.

34

It is the unseen divinity that is responsible for the seen productions of
Nature and Time, and hence the divine is present in every atom of so-
called matter and in every individual human being.

35

The farewell greeting "God be with you!" is really a reminder which
means "God will be with you wherever you go for He is everywhere."

36

Thus make it. Unseen itself, its presence is seen in every earthly form;
unthinkable though it be, its existence is self-manifested in every
thought.(P)

37

The universe comes forth from the World-Mind, from its own being
and its own substance. Therefore the universe is divine, therefore God is
present in every atom and likewise in every one of us. Whoever denies the
existence of God denies the very essence of his own self.

38

Whether the divine power is looked upon as being inside or outside
oneself—and both views will be true and complementary—in the end it
must be thought of without any reference to body and ego at all.

39

In no part of space does the World-Mind exist, and at no point in time is
it to be met.

40

Why is God so hidden, the Overself so elusive, the Spirit of the World as if it never were? Because the eternal and infinite Being is forever seeking to express itself in the universe in which these attributes can appear only under time and in space, that is, never in their full and real nature. This means that God is not in this world (as he really is) and that his elusiveness could not be otherwise if he is to be the true God.

41

Reality is everywhere and nowhere. The world is impregnated with it. Mind and flesh dwell within it.

42

The World-Mind is in us all, reflected as "I." This is why ever-deeper pondering and penetration are needed to remove the veil of individuality and perceive BEING.

43

Swami Narayananda said, "God is the Subject of all subjects. In one sense He can never be known. It being the very Subject of all subjects how can we know it? To know means to objectify a thing, and the Supreme Subject can never become an object. In another sense, God is more than known to us. For it is our very Self. What proof do we want for our very existence?"(P)

44

Television brings simultaneously to millions the same picture, the same personalities, and the same voices. Just so is God present simultaneously to every individual in the whole world.

45

The World-Mind enters into the consciousness of all beings at one and the same time.

46

We describe this mysterious life-power as infinite because so far as we know, so far as reason can guide us or intuition tell us, so far as the great seers and prophets teach us, it is boundless in time and space; we can trace no beginning to it and see no ending for it.

47

There is an ancient recension of the *Bhagavad Gita* in Kashmir which contains a number of verses missing from the one hitherto translated into English. In chapter XI, between stanzas 44 and 45, it has the following: "Thy divine deeds, the former miracles, the sages of yore remember. There is no other creator of the world; thou alone art, both founder and disposer and omnipresent Being. Could any miracle be impracticable for thee? Or could I mention one possible for thee through someone else only? Since thou art thyself the Creator of everything therefore all this is but thee. The most wonderful deed is not difficult for thee."

As source of all

48

The point which appears in space is a point of light. It spreads and spreads and spreads and becomes the World-Mind. God has emerged out of Godhead. And out of the World-Mind the world itself emerges—not all at once, but in various stages. From that great light come all other and lesser lights, come the suns and the planets, the galaxies, the universes, and all the mighty hosts of creatures small and great, of beings just beginning to sense and others fully conscious, aware, wise. And with the world appear the opposites, the dual principle which can be detected everywhere in Nature, the yin and yang of Chinese thought.(P)

49

The Godhead is a great Void and has no direct connection with the cosmos. When the hour ripens for the latter to appear, there first emanates from the Godhead a mediator which is the active creative agent. This is the World-Mind, the Logos, Brahma.

50

From the Void emerges the Central Point. The Point spreads the All. So the World-Mind and the Grand Universe appear in existence *together*. No thing is exactly like any other nor is any individual history the same as any other. No entity or circumstance is perpetuated: each passes away and the entity reappears later in another form.

51

If the divine activity ceases in one universe it continues at the same time in another. If our World-Mind returns to its source in the end, there are other World-Minds and other worlds which continue. Creation is a thing without beginning and without end, but there are interludes and periods of rest just as there are in the individual's own life in and outside the body.(P)

52

Logos in Greek means not only the word through which mind communicates or expresses itself but also the thought behind the word. So the Biblical phrase "In the beginning was the *Logos*" means that first of all there was the MIND, here divine mind.

53

Men need and speak numerous words to express themselves, but God needed and uttered only the one creative silent Word to bring this infinitely varied cosmos into being.

54

However far we trace back the line of cause and effects it must come to an end in the lone cause, the great mystery which is the unseen power.

55

The sign for infinity is a circle. The sign for unity is a vertical dash. Hence 9, the figure nine, combines both and the figure six also, but reversed. Unity is the creative beginning of all things and infinity is that wherein they dissolve.

56

The World-Mind is the conscious Power sustaining all life, the intelligent energy sustaining all atoms, the divine being behind and within the universe.

57

Just as the echo can have no reality, no existence even, without the sound which originally produced it, so this entire universe can have none without the Infinite Power from which it originated and on which it is still dependent.

58

Call it God or Allah, the Creator or Tao, it is the First, the Source, the Origin from which all energies and things come into being.

59

The World-Mind is the creative principle of the universe.

60

The World-Mind eternally thinks this universe into being in a pulsating rhythm of thought and rest. The process is as eternal as the World-Mind itself. The energies which accompany this thinking are electrical. The scientists note and tap the energies, and ignore the Idea and the Mind they are expressing.(P)

61

There is a double alternating movement within Mind: the first spreading out from itself towards multiplicity, the second withdrawing inwards to its own primal unity.

62

Hidden behind the so-called material universe is the Power which emanated it, which is present in all atoms. Hidden behind the Power is the eternal Mind.

63

There is no power in the material universe itself. All its forces and energies derive from a single source—the World-Mind—whose thinking is expressed by that universe.(P)

64

There is an aspect of the World-Mind which, manifesting as protons and electrons, expresses its energies, forces, and powers. The atom is made from divine stuff. The world, which is made from atoms, is divine.

65

The same energy which is behind the universe is converted into the "matter" of the universe. But it remains unexhausted and unconsumed. God is its source, and is inexhaustible.

66

MIND is the Real, Energy is its appearance. Matter is the form taken by radiation or energy. It is not that the truth lies between two extremes but that it lies above both.

67

Is it not a miracle that physical objects, minerals like coal and oil, can be turned into heat and light and power, that is, into energies, as men are doing today?—that matter can be transmuted into electrical energy, which can be turned into sounds, pictures, songs, and words as it is thrown across the world? But what is the essence of this energy, whence does it come ultimately? Where else but from the Great Mind which activates the universe?

68

Physics derives the world of continents and creatures from energies; these in turn derive from a mysterious No-thing. There is no room here for materialism. For if nothing material can be found at that deep level, mathematical evidence points to Mind.

69

The substance of matter has shifted from the visible world to an invisible one but precise, if difficult, mathematical formulas tell us that it is there, while exploding atomic bombs demonstrate its power. At this point matter disappears; its substance becomes its source. All things and all energies come from this source. It is the ONE, unique. It is life for us all and death for us all.

70

Mind has its own energy, which mysteriously constructs forms in space and time, forms of planets, suns, galaxies, the cosmos.

71

Energy is expression in movement of the unseen substance. Matter is its apparent form. All things are made from it. We are a part of it.

72

At the very end of all their explorations of the atom, what do the scientists find? Empty space, no thing-in-itself, a gap out of which pour flashes of energy.

73

The World-Mind acts by its own power, underived from any other source.

74

This entire universe is a tremendous manifestation—the One turned into the Many—of a single Energy, which in its turn is an aspect of a single Mind. Whatever its nature, every other force derives from this Energy, as every other form of consciousness derives from this Mind.

75

The statement "Light is God" is meant in two senses: first, as the poetical and a psychical fact that, in the present condition of the human being, his spiritual ignorance is equivalent to darkness and his discovery of God is equivalent to light; second, as the scientific fact that has verified in its findings that all physical matter ultimately reduces itself to waves of light, and since God has made the universe out of His own substance, the light-waves are ultimately divine.(P)

76

The Light is World-Mind's active and creative force.

77

The Light of the World-Mind is the Source of the physical universe; the Love of the World-Mind is its structural basis.(P)

78

All the forces of the physical world are derived from a single source—the solar energy.(P)

79

This energy which is within the cosmos, from which it is drawn by man, this Life-Force, may be called "bio-electric" for it shows itself on one level as light, on another as the whole spectrum of colours.

80

Biology does not know or explain Life-Power, only its manifestations.

81

What the scientist formerly called "radiant light" became the stuff of which worlds are made; what the mystic visionary called "the body of God" and actually saw as a mysterious light, is still present in the world *and hence in man.*

82

If we seek an origin for the consciousness, however small finite and limited it may be, that a man possesses, none other can be found except the universal consciousness which informs the entire universe and guides its development.

83

All the different kinds of consciousness come from this Universal Mind. All the highest ideals and virtues of human consciousness come from it too. Even simple religious faith indirectly has its rise there.

84

It is the mysterious essence of all things and of nothing, the infinite presence that is everywhere and yet nowhere. Above all, it is at the very root of man's inward being.

85

Our roots are in the World-Mind. In that sense, our whole life is born and grows from it—physical and non-physical alike. There is our true Parent.

WORLD-MIND AND "CREATION"

How

How does God "create" the universe? Since in the beginning God alone is, there is no second substance that can be used for such "creation." God is forced to use his own substance for the purpose. God is Infinite Mind, so he uses mental power—Imagination—working on mental substance—Thought—to produce the result which appears to us as the universe.(P)

2

Can anything be derived from something that is essentially different from it? This is impossible. Therefore existence cannot be derived from non-existence. If the universe exists today, then its essence must have existed when the universe itself had not been formed. This essence needed no "creation" for it was God, World-Mind, Itself.(P)

3

The universe is the World-Mind coming out of itself and therefore making its manifestation out of its own substance—that is, Mind—just as the spider spins out a web from itself.

4

The visible cosmos has come into being out of the invisible absolute by a process of emanation. That is why the relation between them is not only pantheistic but also transcendent.(P)

5

The creation is inseparable from its creator; indeed, they are but two names for one and the same thing, for God has objectified part of his own being as the universe which we see.

6

"I called the whole world His dream: I looked again, and lo! His dream was Himself."—fifteenth-century Persian mystic Sayyid Nimatullah

7

The World-Mind, limiting itself, shutting down its focus, produces what we know as the physical universe.

8

The fact that the cosmic existence is a beginningless and endless one eliminates the need of finding a Creator. It is itself a manifestation of an eternal principle, which is its own divine soul and not a second and separate thing.

9

When Prospero says, in Shakespeare's play, "We are such stuff as dreams are made on," he implies the existence of some greater Mind in which we are the dreams.

10

Any hypnotist may invent a seeming world for you but it will be gone in a few minutes or hours. Only the World-Mind can invent one that will last and outlast the whole human race.

11

Will the cosmic dream come to an end? If his personal life is a dream for man, is the universe a dream for God? The answer is that the World-Mind *controls* its dream, man does not.

12

Mind is the first and last Real, the Doer Maker and Destroyer. It imagines the world even as it creates it.

13

Philosophers devoid of reason find
This world a mere idea of the mind;
'Tis an idea—but they fail to see
The great Idealist who looms behind.
—Jami

14

The universe is the imaginative construction of the World-Mind.

15

"The core and the surface of life are essentially the same," wrote wise old Lao Tzu.

16

Every form of existence can be reduced to a form of consciousness. The final essence of all these consciousnesses is God.

17

The tree of material objects and the tree of mental ideas rise from a common but unknown root—Brahman.

18

He who knows Brahman as the root and the universe as the branch of the tree of life fears not death, says an old Indian text.

19

The act of creative meditation which brings the universe into being is performed by the World-Mind. We, insofar as we experience the world, are participating in this act unconsciously. It is a thought-world and we are thought-beings.

20

Somehow, this infinite life germinates an infinite variety of minds and puts them through an infinite variety of experiences. However real they may seem through its mysterious working, they are all appearances only.

21

This play of mind upon mind will reach its end with the last act, and the world-dream will then begin to dissolve.

22

World-Mind is doing its works by providing the basic materials and necessary energies.

23

The One Mind appears both as the millions of little minds and as the mental images of things, creatures, or events which they come to know, see, or experience.

24

In the end all things finally come from World-Mind and for us come from mind, which itself comes from the same source.

25

The World-Mind is expressing through an infinite number of minds its own infinitude multiplied by infinity an infinite number of times.

26

Spinoza arrived at this truth by clear mathematical reflection, that "each particular thing is expressed by infinite ideas in infinite ways in the infinite understanding of God."(P)

27

In all these studies the principal concept should be returned to again and again: the entire universe, everything—objects and creatures—is in Mind. I hold all the objects of my experience in *my* consciousness but I myself am held, along with them, in an incredibly greater consciousness, the World-Mind's.(P)

28

The notion propounded by certain celebrated theologians and mystics that "God has need of me just as I have need of him" is a fantasy, a self-constructed opinion based upon an egoism which is unwilling and unable to let go of its own importance.

29
God does his own work. He needs no partner, no associate, no helper.

30
Eckhart's assertion that "Without man God would not know he existed" requires explanation.

31
It is not that God, the Unique, needs a second thing, a cosmos, in order to be Itself, but that our human thought about God is incapacitated by the utter void in which God dwells.

32
God needs no partner and has no enemy. For the power of God is not only above that of all other entities but it is the source whence they themselves derive.

33
It is the *presence* of the World-Mind which makes things happen according to the World-Idea: the former does not need to put forward each particular activity.(P)

34
No engineer can form an engine merely by throwing together all the necessary pieces of metal, not even by throwing together all the finished parts. His mind and will must be brought to bear upon them. It is exactly the same with the universe itself. A universal intelligence, a World-Mind and its willed activity, must be active behind it, too.

35
Mind is not the final Reality, but a basic aspect of it. Will is another.

Why

36
The self-sufficing World-Mind has nothing to gain for itself by this universal activity.

37
What could the Supreme Power gain by bringing the world into existence? It is not like the humans who have desires to be satisfied or limitations to be removed.

38
Those who point to the marvellous pattern of the universe as a proof of the existence of Deity, do well; but when they begin to render account of the reasons which induced Deity to turn Himself into myriad souls and to blind their divine sight by involving them into this material universe, it is time to put on our shoes and walk away. For no philosopher and no

theologian, no occultist and no mystic has yet solved this supreme riddle in a truly satisfying manner.

39

World-Mind imagines and objectifies things and happenings, and man is within this space-time net. God is within the universe but unbound by its limitations. God is free in a sense in which no human being is free. For the conflict of motives which precedes every act of human freedom is entirely absent from the acts of God, which are truly spontaneous.

40

No one knows *why* the Infinite Power must go on incarnating something of Itself in the universe; everyone can in the end only accept the fact, for the question is answerless.

41

Why do I reiterate, "All is Opinion"? Because *no one was or could have been present at creation*—hence all theories of creation *and of God* are guesses only. Moreover, God is utterly incomprehensible to finite man.

42

All those who pretend to give answer to the purpose of life, and why the universe was created, may be answered with the words of India's oldest known book, the *Rig-Veda*: "Who knows exactly, and who shall in this world declare, whence and why this creation took place? The gods are subsequent to the production of this world: then who can know whence it proceeded? He who in the highest heaven is the ruler of this universe—he knows or does not know!"

43

The World-Mind is forever attempting to reflect its qualities and attributes in the universe but its success is forever only a very limited one.

44

When I say that God did not bring forth the universe by first arriving at the decision to "create" it and then deliberately carrying out this decision, but rather by inherent Nature and inner necessity, I mean that the universe is already and eternally within God. No decision was needed nor could there have been one, any more than a man may decide to be masculine. Bringing the universe out of Itself is a function, quality, or attribute— none of these terms is quite correct but a better is hard to find—an obedience to the law of God's own being.

45

The movement which brings the universe into being out of the World-Mind's stillness is a spontaneous, not a deliberate, one. It just happens because it is the very nature of the World-Mind to make this movement.

46

It is an inner compulsion rather than an inner necessity that moves the World-Mind to bring about these repeated reincarnations of the universe.

47

What I termed in *The Wisdom of the Overself* "an inner necessity" as being responsible for this self-activity of World-Mind in bringing forth the universe needs, I now see, some clarification if it is not to be incorrectly understood. It is the nature of World-Mind to be passive by turns, just as it is the nature of animals and humans to be active on waking, at rest when sleeping. In this nature, there is imbedded a desire to express something of itself in the cosmos. But this desire is not for its own benefit, for the Perfect has nothing to gain. In all manifested creatures, desire seeks self-benefit, obvious or hidden; not so in the World-Mind. Its activity exists only for the benefit of this multitude of creatures.

48

It is exempt from evolution and retrogression and ever will be what it ever was. Consequently it can have no self-benefiting purposes in the cosmic process.

49

If we try to consider the inner necessity which makes the World-Mind manifest Itself to Itself through an other, a cosmos, we find ourselves on the threshold of a mystery. How could compulsion, limit, or desire arise in the desireless one? Human intellect can only formulate such a question, but cannot answer it.

50

The moment we assert that this infinite Power has a motive in making the cosmos, a purpose in creating the world, in that moment we limit it and ascribe need or want or lack to it.

51

The World-Mind has the power of vigorous creativeness as an essential attribute of its nature. It will stop its work of sustaining the universe when it stops being what it is. There is no other purpose behind creation than that of continuing its own existence. To understand this is to understand that the question as to purpose is not at all applicable to the World-Mind but only to an imagined and inferior being, one which could start or discontinue.

Distinguishing World-Mind and Mind

52

It is not enough to know what World-Mind has put forth in this universe by its presence. We must also know, intellectually at least, what it is in itself.

53

Out of this vast void comes the universe. What then must be the ineffable and incredible Mystery hidden behind it from our sightless eyes?

54

Take the beginning and the end of the Greek alphabet and suppose that the first letter, Alpha, is the first faint stirrings of the universe. And take the last letter, Omega, to be the last vanishing trace of that universe. Imagine that Alpha is the reincarnation of the previous Omega, and you will have a key to what is really happening. But what is this mysterious invisible intangible source whence all this is derived and into which all this passes?

55

The notion of a Personal God includes a truth and an error. So far as there is a World-Mind, manifesting along with a world itself, the notion is true. But so far as there is only the Unique, the One without a Second, both are appearances, phenomena out of the Noumenon. In the case of the world, it appears in time out of the Timeless; but in the case of the World-Mind, all times are embraced in its Duration. Yet it too withdraws into its other aspect, Mind—only.

56

There has been so much friction and clash between the different religions because of this idea: whether God is personal or impersonal—so much persecution, even hatred, so unnecessarily. I say unnecessarily because the difference between the two conceptions is only an apparent one. Mind is the source of all; this is Mind inactive. Mind as World-Mind-in-manifestation is the personal God. Between essence and manifestation the only difference is that essence is hidden and manifestation is known. World-Mind is personal (in the sense of being what the Hindus call "Ishvara"); Mind is totally impersonal. Basically, the two are one.(P)

57

On the two views of God—transcendence and immanence: One view conditions your conception of God, the other sets limits to him. But if you simultaneously affirm both one and the other point of view, you will be exempt from error.

58

As Mind, it is beyond all the relativities of this world, beyond time and space, human thought and human imagination. As World-Mind it is immanent in the world itself, the Lord of the All, the God whom men worship, yet cyclic in Its existences.

59

The World-Mind, however, has a double life. As Mind, it is eternally free but as the World-Mind, it is eternally crucified, as Plato said, on the cross of the world's body.(P)

60

Manifestation implies the necessity of manifesting. But it might be objected that any sort of necessity existing in the divine equally implies its insufficiency. The answer is that the number One may become aware of itself as being one only by becoming aware of the presence of Two—itself and another. But the figure Nought is under no compulsion. Here we have a mathematical hint towards understanding the riddle of manifestation. Mind as Void is the supreme inconceivable unmanifesting ultimate whereas the World-Mind is forever throwing forth the universe-series as a second, an "other" wherein it becomes self-aware.(P)

61

God-active, the Unseen Power, is (for us humans) the World-Mind. God-in-repose is Mind.(P)

62

The creative power or energy which comes from World-Mind is not the ultimate essence-consciousness which *is* God.

63

It is needful to point out the difference between the divine essence and the divine energies. The latter may be several and varied, but the former is always single.

64

It is the difference between Mind as it is in itself, and Mind as it expresses through the cosmos.

65

It would, however, be a mistake to consider the World-Mind as one entity and Mind as another separate from it. It would be truer to consider World-Mind as the active function of Mind. Mind cannot be separated from its powers. The two are one. In its quiescent state it is simply Mind. In its active state it is World-Mind. Mind in its inmost transcendent nature is the inscrutable mystery of Mysteries but when expressing itself in act and immanent in the universe, it is the World-Mind. We may find in the attributes of the manifested God—that is, the World-Mind—the only indications of the quality, existence, and character of the unmanifest Godhead that it is possible for man to comprehend. All this is a mystery which is and perhaps forever will remain an incomprehensible paradox.(P)

66

Mind active and mind in quiescence are not two separate beings, but two aspects of one and the same being as they appear to human inquiry. Mind active expresses itself in the heart of man as his higher self and in the universe as the World-Mind.

67

The World-Mind is a radiation of the forever incomprehensible Mind. It is the essence of all things and all beings, from the smallest to the largest.(P)

68

Mind is the Real; matter is the appearance it takes on. The universe comes by degrees out of the ultimate Being, beyond which nothing is or could possibly be. It is Mind, measureless, with a Power equally measureless. World-Mind is this power in operation, creating, maintaining, and in the end destroying what it has brought forth.

69

If it be true that absolute divine Mind knows nothing of the universe, nothing of mortal man, then it is also true that the World-Mind, which is its other aspect, does know them.(P)

Part 4:
THE ALONE

The Real stands alone. It is without any kind of support, and needs none. It is without any kind of dependence or dependent relationship.

The emptiness of space is a symbol. The universe spread out in that space is also a symbol. Both speak of the Real that is in them, but each in a different way. Yes, within every localized point, every timed instant, That which Is proclaims Itself as the unique Fact outside relationship and beyond change.

1

ABSOLUTE MIND

Mind alone Is

All he needs to take him through intricate problems of metaphysics is this single masterly conception: Mind alone is.

2

In the last summation, there is only a single infinite thing, but it expresses itself brokenly through infinitely varied forms.

3

Philosophy defines God as pure Mind from the human standpoint and perfect Reality from the cosmic one. The time has indeed come for us to rise to meditate upon the supreme Mind. It is the source of all appearances, the explanation of all existences. It is the only reality, the only thing which is, was, and shall be unalterably the same. Mind itself is ineffable and indestructible. We never see it as it is in itself but only the things which are its passing phases.

4

The ultimate reality is one and the same, no matter what it is called; to the Chinese mystic it is TAO, that is, the Significance; to the Christian mystic it is GOD; to the Chinese philosopher it is T'AI CHI, that is, The Great Extreme; to the Hindu philosopher it is TAT, that is, Absolute Existence. It has its own independent, everlasting, invisible, and infinite existence, while all worldly things and creatures are but fragmentary and fleeting expressions of IT on a lower sphere altogether. It lies deeply concealed as their innermost substance, and persists through their changes of form.

5

Before the personal ego came into being, Being was. "Before Abraham was I am," announced Jesus. Before thoughts, Thought! In its timelessness, Mind is the One without a Second; "in its timed manifestation it is all things."

6

The REAL is always there: we live in it.

7

Mind is primary being. It is mysteriously as still as it is self-active.

8

Absolute mind is the actuality of human life and the plenitude of universal existence. Apart from Mind they could not even come into existence, and separated from it they could not continue to exist. Their truth and being are in It. But it would be utterly wrong to imagine the Absolute as the sum total of all finite beings and individual beings. The absolute is not the integral of all its visible aspects. It is the unlimited, the boundless void within which millions of universes may appear and disappear ceaselessly and unendingly but yet leave It unaffected. The latter do not exhaust even one millionth of its being.(P)

9

The Great Mind—invisible and untouchable; the host of little minds visible and pseudoconscious; the words incessantly poured out until the Silence descends. The Great Mind again! Yet it was always there but men looked elsewhere.

10

With every thought we break the divine stillness. Yet behind all thoughts is Mind. Behind all things that give rise to thoughts is Mind.

11

The One Infinite Life-Power is the ultimate of all things and all consciousness. There is no thing and no mind beyond it.

12

Within and without the universe there is only a single absolute power, a single uncreated essence, a single primary reality.

13

The ultimate metaphysical principle of Mind behind all this ordered activity is the same as the ultimate religious principle worshipped as God.

14

This is the mysterious element which hides as the unknown quantity— the algebraic x—of the universe.

15

That which is at the heart of all existence—the world's and yours—must be real, if anything can be. The world may be an illusion, your ego a fiction, but the ultimate essence cannot be either. Reality must be here or nowhere.

16

Mind is the essence in man and the power in the universe.

17

It is always there, the only reality in a mind-made world.

18

It is in here and out there, the fundament upon which all universes are structured, the substance of which they are composed, yet it is nowhere to be seen microscopically or measured geometrically. When all else is extinct it remains, indestructible and unique.

19

There is a principle of life which is conscious in its own unique way, which is the essential being of all entities and the essential reality behind all substances.

20

The Infinite Being is there and will be there whether universes exist or not.

21

The essence of all these finite forms is an infinite one.

22

No one can see the Real yet everyone may see the things which come from it. Although it is itself untouchable, whatever we touch enshrines its presence.

23

There is but One God, One Life, One infinite Power, one all-knowing Mind. Each man individualizes it but does not multiply it. He brings it to a point, the Overself, but does not alter its unity or change its character.(P)

24

The One Mind is experiencing itself in us, less in the ego-shadow and fully in the Overself, hardly aware in that shadow and self-realized in the light that casts it.(P)

25

The term nonduality remains a sound in the air when heard, a visual image when read. Without the key of mentalism it remains just that. How many Vedanta students and, be it said, teachers interpret it aright? And that is to understand there are no two separate entities—a thing and also the thought of it. The thing is in mind, is a projection of mind as the thought. This is nonduality, for mind is not apart from what comes from and goes back into it. As with things, so with bodies and worlds. All appear along with the ultimately cosmic but immediately individual thought of them.(P)

26

The teaching of nonduality is that *all* things are within one and the same element—Consciousness. Hence there are no two or three or three million things and entities: there is in reality only the One Consciousness.

27

Duality exists, but only within nonduality, which has the last word.

28

If we could raise ourselves to the ultimate point of view, we would see all forms in one spirit, one essence in all atoms, and hence no difference between one world and another, one thing and another, one man and another.

29

Just as a larger circle may contain a smaller one within it, yet the one need not contradict the other, so the ever-being of Mind may contain the ever-changing incredibly numerous forms of Nature without any contradiction.

30

The universal reality is neither a unit nor a cipher. Were it a cipher we could never know it, could not even think of it, for then we would not be thinking. Were it a unit it could not stand alone but would mask a host of other units, thus making a plurality of realities. For it can be proved mathematically that the existence of one always implies the existence of a whole series of figures, from two upwards. What is it then? The answer, be it said to their credit, was discovered by old Indian sages. It is nonduality.

31

The notion of the One belongs to the realms of instruction for beginners; in reality it is as illusory as the Many, because it presupposes the truth of the latter; the reality of number one implies the reality of number two, and so forth. Hence Monism is not our doctrine, but rather Nonduality. There is a vast difference between the two terms.

32

Nonduality simply means that there is nothing other than the unseen Power, nothing else, no universe, no creature.(P)

33

This is Absolute Being, where duality does not exist and multiplicity cannot.

34

In the end, when truth is seen and its relativities are transcended, there is only this: nonduality, nonorigination, and noncausality.

35

Everything exists in opposing pairs, that is, in twos. Hence the Origin, the Ultimate, is called by Hindu sages "the Not-TWO" (*Advaita*).

36

All distinctions between this and that, here and there, before and after, are dissolved in the Absolute.

37

In the highest Sanskrit texts, the universe is pointed to as "This" and the final reality as "That."

38

In *The Hidden Teaching Beyond Yoga* and *The Wisdom of the Overself* I unveiled that portion of the hidden teaching which negated materialism and showed the world to be immaterial and spiritual. In this book I unveil the remaining portion which shows that the person himself is devoid of real existence, that the ego is a fiction, and that there is only the One Universal Mind.(P)

39

There is only the One inexhaustible Source out of which all this vast complex of universal existence emerges. It alone always *is*; the rest is an ever-changing picture.

40

Just as the dreamer's mind appears to split itself up into the various figures and persons of his dream, so the One has never really split itself up into the many, but it has *appeared* to do so.

Levels, phases, functions of Mind

41

When Mind concentrates itself into the World-Mind, it establishes a focus. However vast, it goes out of its own unlimited condition, it passes from the true Infinite to the pseudo-Infinite. Consequently the World-Mind, being occupied with its cosmos, cannot be regarded as possessed of the absolute character of Pure Mind. For what is its work but a movement of imagination? And where in the ineffable absolute is there room for either work or imagination? The one would break its eternal stillness, the other would veil its unchangeable reality. This of course it can never do, for Being can never become Non-Being. But it can send forth an emanation from itself. Such an emanation is the World-Mind. Through its prolonged contemplation of the cosmos Mind thus becomes a fragment of itself, bereft of its own undifferentiated unbroken unity. Nevertheless the World-Mind, through its deputy the Overself, is still for humans the highest possible goal.(P)

42

Because of Mind's presence, that which men call God arises, creates, and dissolves entire worlds, kingdoms of Nature; yet Mind itself never moves, never acts, is forever still, is the ultimate of all ultimates, forever the only Unpassing, the only Unconditioned, the untouchable Mystery.

43

Mind is the essence of all manifested things as World-Mind and the Mystery behind unmanifest Nothing.(P)

44

The distinguishing quality of Mind is a continuous stillness, whereas that of World-Mind is a continuous activity. In the one there is absolutely nothing whereas in the other there is an infinite array of universes.

45

Mind is the essence of all conscious beings. Their consciousness is derivative, borrowed from it; they could know nothing of their own power; whereas Mind alone knows all things and itself. When it knows them in time, it is World-Mind; when it knows itself alone, it is the unknown to man and unknowable Godhead.(P)

46

The World-Mind pervades the cosmos; Mind extends beyond it.

47

Among all numbers, it is the lowest one—1—which is the foundation as well as the constituent of the entire series. But the empty number—nought—is even more important and significant because it symbolizes the inexpressible, ineffable, and inconceivable Power behind all powers.

48

The term *Tao*, as used by Lao Tzu, does not refer to the World-Mind, that which is responsible for the manifested universe, but to the pure, essential being of Mind-in-itself. What I have called the World-Mind, he calls *Teh*.

49

When Eckhart uses the term God he means the maker and governor of the world. By Godhead he means Mind, the absolute, beyond even the gods.

50

Whether we see its presence in the untiring activity of the universe or in the complete quiet of the Void, we do not see two different things but rather two phases of a single thing.

51

World-Mind is only a function of Mind. It is not a separate entity. There is only one Life-Power, not two. Hence it is wrong to say that World-Mind *arises* within Mind, as I said in *The Wisdom of the Overself*. Similarly of the Overself; it too is a different *function* of the same Mind.

52

The Mind's first expression is the Void. The second and succeeding is the Light, that is, the World-Mind. This is followed by the third, the World-Idea. Finally comes the fourth, manifestation of the world itself.(P)

53

The Supreme Godhead is unindividualized. The World-Mind is individuated (but not personalized) into emanated Overselves. The Overself is an individual, but not a person. The ego is personal.(P)

54

What is the meaning of the words "the Holy Trinity"? The Father is the absolute and ineffable Godhead, Mind in its ultimate being. The Son is the soul of the universe, that is, the World-Mind. The Holy Ghost is the soul of each individual, that is, the Overself. The Godhead is one and indivisible and not multiform and can never divide itself up into three personalities.(P)

55

What is the Holy Trinity? How could it be three Gods? No—It is the Good, the Beautiful, and the True—three aspects of the One, only God.

56

The holy trinity is truth, goodness, and beauty. For they are leading attributes of the divine soul in man.

57

Mind in itself stays always in absolute repose: there is then no operation whatever, no movement or manifestation, no creation or communication or revelation; it is forever inaccessible and unknown. This is the "Divine Darkness" of early Christian Fathers, the Godhead of medieval Christian theologians.

58

The idea of Mind in utter repose, absolutely still, unmanifested in any way whatsoever, is the farthest limit of human finite thought about the Deity.

59

Mind as such is unconcerned with any world. It is without any limits and could not be confined in any form.

On knowing Why

60

We are constantly faced by the hoariest of all problems, which is "Why did the Universe arise out of the depth and darkness of the Absolute Spirit?" The Seer can offer us a picture of the way in which this Spirit has involved itself into matter and is evolving itself back to self-knowledge. That is only the *How* and not the *Why* of the world. The truth is not only that nobody has ever known, that nobody knows, and that nobody will ever know the final and fundamental purpose of creation, but that God himself does not even know—for God too has arisen out of the Absolute no less than the universe, has found himself emanated from the primeval darkness and utter silence. Even God must be content to watch the flow and not wonder why, for both God and man must merge and be absorbed when they face the Absolute for the last time. (In the symbolic language of the Bible, "For man cannot meet God face to face and live.")(P)

61

That which *IS* can be none other than Final Being itself, not dependent on anything or anyone, mysteriously self-sufficient without a shape, yet all shaped things and creatures have emerged from elements which trace back to it. Forever alone, there was none to witness the Beginning.

62

As Mind the Real is static, as World-Mind it is dynamic. As Godhead It alone *is* in the stillness of being; but as God it is the source, substance, and power of the universe. As Mind there is no second thing, no second intelligence to ask the question why it stirred and breathed forth World-Mind, hence why the whole world-process exists. Only man asks this question and it returns unanswered.(P)

63

For all of us, for the witless and for the wise, there are unanswerable questions in life and we must learn to live with them. None of us is a full and finalized encyclopaedia, for however far we may penetrate into the meaning of things we are always confronted in the end by the Unknowable Mystery. We do not know why the whole process of involution and evolution ever started at all: because we find that there is in the deepest metaphysical sense no becoming and process at all, there is only the Real.

64

At the ultimate level there is neither purpose nor plan because there is no creation.

65

Mind, which forever is, can undergo no change in itself and no multiplication of itself. If it could, it would not be what it is—the Ultimate, the Absolute, the Unconditioned, and the Unique. Nor, being perfect, complete, could it have desire, purpose, aim, or motive for itself. Therefore it could not have projected the universe on account of any benefit sought or gain needed. There is no answer to the question why the universe was sent forth.

66

It is to impose human limitation upon the transcendental Godhead to say that It has any eternal purpose to fulfil for Itself in the cosmos, whether that purpose be the establishment of a perfect society on earth or the training of individuals to enter into fellowship with It and participate in Its creative work. Purpose implies a movement in time whereas the Godhead is also the Timeless. Neither this earth nor the societies upon it can be necessary to God's serenely self-sufficient being. Yet these fallacies are still taught by the theology of theistic orthodoxy.

67

We know as much, and as little, about the Primal Mind as we know why there was a beginning of the universe—that is, precisely nothing.

Real as self-existent, transcendent, unique

68

There is That which abides in itself, sufficient to itself, unique, the Consciousness, the Finality. There is nothing beyond it. Before That one must bow in utmost reverence, humbled to the ground.

69

This is the only thing which is able to subsist entirely by itself, which is independent of and beyond all relations with any other thing. This, considered absolutely, is God.

70

In the beginning was Being—Mind; the principle of being, living, was inseparable from the principle of Knowing, Consciousness. It was transcendental and eternal. It is only we humans who are compelled to talk of beginnings although there was no such thing. This is why the Absolute is unapproachable, ineffable.

71

The world is not self-existent but MIND is.

72

Because it is utterly independent of all other things and entities, it is the Absolute.

73

It is in Sanskrit *Aja*, "the UNBORN," the only thing which had no beginning in time and which can have no ending for it is BEING itself.

74

There were those among the ancient Greek sages who taught with reverence about "THAT WHICH REALLY IS."

75

It is Self-existent, all-pervading, and boundless in every way.

76

The huge paradox of life becomes plainer as one becomes older. Nothing stands alone, all things come in couples. But stay!—there is one which is exempt from this law. No law can hold it for it holds them all itself.

77

Mind is the ever-free, bound by no authority, chained to no law, not even the law of cause and effect.

78

This is what Lao Tzu called "being-by-itself" but others called "Nonbeing." These are simply two descriptions of the same thing—one positive, the other negative.

79

Every other entity or thing cannot not be, but not the Supreme Principle, for it is Be-ing itself.

80

That which exists through itself is MIND.

81

This infinite being has the power to support itself—nothing else has.

82

The Infinite Power can never become exhausted. It is self-sustaining.(P)

83

This is the ultimate Being beyond which there is nothing.

84

We are dependent on and dwell in Mind but Mind on the contrary is self-sustained and dwells in itself.

85

If we say, "God is a Mind," we err greatly. If we say, "God is Mind" we speak more rightly. The introduction of this shortest of short words falsifies our idea of God because it separates, personalizes, and differentiates the Absolute.

86

Mind, alone, has the right to say, "I AM!" But then, it is forever silent. All others can only say, "I am me," indicating a person.

87

"Before Abraham was I am!" These words are an expression of the higher mentalism. Note carefully that Jesus did not say "I was." This means that he as the non-personal unindividuated Mind existed before the birth of Abraham. "I am" points to the eternal One where no individual entity ever was, is, or shall be.

88

Philosophy raises the question of Reality and pursues it until an answer can be found. That answer asserts there is something unique which alone can be the Real, which ever was, is, and shall be.

89

Philosophy's fundamental postulate is that there is but one ultimate Power, one sublime Reality, one transcendent Being. It is invisible to all, since it is the power that makes the world visible. It is without form, since it is the Substance out of which all forms are made.

90

The Real is unique—the *only* undivided, unsplit being beyond which there is nothing else.

91

There is nothing else either beyond it or besides it.

92

It is the unique not only because of what IT is but also because two statements concerning IT can be quite contradictory, yet each can still be correct!(P)

93

One transcends all categories.

94

Since the Real is unique, the One without a second and not the One which is related to the Many that spring out of it, it cannot correctly be set up in opposition to the Unreal, the Illusory, the Appearance. They are not on the same level.

95

That which both Greek Plato and Indian Vedantin called "the One" did not refer to the beginning figure of a series, but to "One-without-a-Second."(P)

96

It is unique. There is nothing to which it can be justly likened, or with which it can be compared. This must be so since it goes beyond and transcends *all* things without any exception. It is inexpressible. Whatever is said of it will only succeed in describing an idea in the mind of the sayer, and this goes beyond and transcends all ideas, again without any exception.

97

You can compare one being or one thing with another but not This, not This!

98

There is a Mind which is self-existent, unique, unlike anything else, unbegotten.

99

The universal Mind is also unique in that, while comprehending all things, it is itself incomprehensible.

100

It stands alone, unique, unseen and untouchable. Yet from it emerge all the gods of all the planets which they govern, all the ethical injunctions which men need and must have in the end.

Real as unchangeable

101

The Real is forever and unalterably the same, whether it be the unmanifest Void or the manifested world. It has never been born and consequently can never die. It cannot divide itself into different "realities" with different space-time levels or multiply itself beyond its own primal oneness. It cannot evolve or diminish, improve or deteriorate. Whereas everything else exists in dependence upon Mind and exists for a limited time, however prolonged, and therefore has only a relative existence, Mind is the absolute, the unique, the ultimate reality because with all its innumerable manifestations in the universe it has never at any moment ceased to be itself. Only its appearances suffer change because they are in time and space, never itself, which is out of time and space. The divisions of time into past present and future are meaningless here; we may speak only of its "everness." The truth about it is timeless, as no scientific truth could ever be, in the sense that whatever fate the universe undergoes its own ultimate significance remains unchanged. If the Absolute appears *to us* as the first in the time-series, as the First Cause of the Universe, this is only true from our limited standpoint. It is in fact only our human idea. The human mind can take into itself the truth of transcendental being only by taking out of itself the screens of time space and person. For being eternally self-existence, reality is utterly timeless. Space divisions are equally unmeaning in its "Be-ness." The Absolute is both everywhere and nowhere. It cannot be considered in spatial terms. Even the word "infinite" is really such a term. If it is used here because no other is available, let it be clearly understood, then, that it is used merely as a suggestive metaphor. If the infinite did not include the finite then it would be less than infinite. It is erroneous to make them both mutually exclusive. The finite alone must exclude the infinite from its experience but not vice versa. In the same way the infinite Duration does not exclude finite time.(P)

102

What is Reality? In *The Hidden Teaching Beyond Yoga*, I defined it as that unique entity which is not subject to change. But we can look at it from another standpoint and define it as that which would alone remain if every other entity in the universe and the universe itself disappeared.

103

That which always remains the same, never changes, that is reality.

104

THAT is real being which is faultless and partless, and without a single one of the characteristic properties belonging to this physical world. It never varies whereas that world is constantly changing. Such everlasting being is incomparable, unique, and beyond human picturization. THAT is the essence of all things, the base whence, eventually, the universe is projected.

105

That is the Real which not only is not subject to any change but also would still abide even if the entire universe vanished. Everything and everyone else must come out of some prior element which traces itself down even to the first and original element, but the Real alone is self-abiding and self-existing. It has its own independent Being.

106

There is no period so far off in the future, no time so distant in the past, no area anywhere in space, that will be or has been without Being. If men can find it today, they will find it then as they found it in antiquity. If they commune with it on this earth, or enter into some relationship with it here, they can do likewise on other planets. Moreover it remains ever the Same, the Unchanged and Unchangeable.

107

Reality being what it is, a gigantic fact which is utterly impregnable against time and change, even the total disappearance of the exponents of that truth which points to it could not alter its own status.

108

We must never forget that the entire dynamic movement occurs insep-
arably within a static blessed repose. Becoming is not apart from Being. Its
kinetic movement takes place in the eternal stillness. World-Mind is forever working in the universe whereas Mind is forever at rest and its still
motionlessness paradoxically makes all activity and motion possible. The
infinite unconditioned Essence could never become confined within or
subject to the finite limited world-form. The one dwells in a transcendental
timelessness whereas the other exists in a continuous time. There cannot
be two eternal principles, two ultimate realities, for each will limit the
other's existence and thus deprive it of its absolute character. There is only
the One, which is beyond all phenomena and yet includes them. The
manifestation of the cosmic order, filled with countless objects and entities
though it be, does not in any way or to any extent alter the character of the
absolute Reality in which it appears. That character is unvarying—is never
reduced to a lower form, never confined in a limited one, never modified
by conditions, never deprived of a single iota of its being, substance,
amplitude, or quality. It always is what it was. It is the ultimate origin of
everything and everyone in this universe, yet it remains as unchanged by
their death as by their birth, by their absence as by their presence. Everything in the universe is liable to changes, because it was born and must die.
We venerate God because He is not liable to change, being ever-existent
and self-subsisting, birthless and deathless.(P)

109

Considered from its own standpoint, the infinite can never manifest as
the finite, the Real can never alter its nature and evolve into the unreal;
hence the pictures of creation or evolution belong to the realm of dream
and illusion. The grand verity is that the Universal self has never incarnated into matter, nor ever shall. It remains what it was, is, must forever
be—the Unchanged and Unchangeable.

110

The infinite has never, can never, become the finite.

111

The Real is neither the Many nor the Changing but THAT from which
these are both derived.

112

Such a truth will never need to be replaced by a newer one: it will hold
its place, and satisfy the searching mind, in a thousand years' time as much
as it does today.

113

Bradley's errors are: (a) to turn the Absolute into a system or a process,
and (b) to identify the Absolute with its contents.

Real as Void

114

If Mind is to be regarded aright, we must put out of our thought even the notion of the cosmic Ever-Becoming. But to do this is to enter a virtual Void? Precisely. When we take away all the forms of external physical existence and all the differences of internal mental existence, what we get is an utter emptiness of being which can hardly be differentiated after we have taken away its features and individualities, its finite times and finite distances. There is then nothing but a great void. What is the nature of this void? It is pure Thought. It is out of this empty Thought that the fullness of the universe has paradoxically evolved. Hence it is said that the world's reality is secondary whereas Mind's reality is primary. In the Void the hidden oneness of things is disengaged from the things themselves. Silence therefore is not merely the negation of sound but rather the element in which, as Carlyle said, great things fashion themselves. It is the supreme storehouse of power.(P)

115

There is here no form to be perceived, no image born of the senses to be worshipped, no oracular utterance to be listened for, and no emotional ecstasy to be revelled in. Hence the Chinese sage, Lao Tzu, said: "In eternal non-existence I look for the spirituality of things!" The philosopher perceives that there is no such thing as creation out of nothing for the simple reason that Mind is eternally and universally present. "Nothing" is merely an appearance. Here indeed there is neither time nor space. It is like a great silent boundless circle wherein no life seems to stir, no consciousness seems to be at work, and no activity is in sway. Yet the seer will know by a pure insight which will grip his consciousness as it has never been gripped before, that here indeed is the root of all life, all consciousness, and all activity. But how it is so is as inexplicable intellectually as what its nature is. With the Mind the last word of human comprehension is uttered. With the Mind the last world of possible being is explored. But whereas the utterance is comprehensible by his consciousness, the speaker is not. It is a Silence which speaks but what it says is only that it IS; more than that none can hear.(P)

116

"The Godhead is as void as though it were not," said Eckhart. "Pass from the station of 'I' and 'We' and choose for thy home Non-entity. For when thou hast done the like of this, thou shalt reach the supreme felicity," wrote Qurratulayn, a Persian poetess, nearly a century ago. We may begin to grasp the meaning of such statements by grasping the conception that

Infinite Mind is the formless, matterless, Void, Spirit. Mortal error is mistaking forms for final realities instead of penetrating to their essence, Mind. Whatever can be said about the unnameable "Void" will be not enough at least and merely symbolic at most. The mystic's last Word is the Freemason's lost Word. It can never be spoken for it can never be heard. It is the one idea which can never be transferred to another mind, the one meaning which can never get through any pen or any lip. Yet it is there—the supreme Fact behind all the myriad facts of universal existence. To elevate any form by an external worship or an internal meditation which should be given only to the formless Void is to elevate an idol in the place of God. Muhammed is reported to have once said that the worship of any one other than the great Allah, i.e., "the Beginningless, the Endless," was the first of major sins. Yet to honour the sublime No-thing by thought or rite is hard for the unmetaphysical. And it requires much metaphysical insight to perceive its truth. The cold impersonality of this idea is at first repelled by us with something like horror. A change in this attitude can come about only gradually at most. But if we perseveringly pursue our quest of truth we shall overcome our aversion in the end. If it be true that Truth is not something we can utter, that the Nameless cannot fitly be represented by any name, we may however continue to use any word we like, provided we keep its limitations clearly in our understanding of it. After all, although the thinking intellect creates its own image of truth, it is the Overself that starts the creative process working. But in the end we shall have to reserve our best worship not for a particular manifestation in time but for the Timeless itself, not for a historical personage but for the impersonal Infinite.(P)

117

Suzuki says "Suchness" is the Godhead of Eckhart, the Emptiness.

118

It would be completely false to regard the Void as being a nothing and containing nothing. It is Being itself, and contains reality behind all things. Nor is it a kind of inertia, of paralysis. All action springs out of it, all the world-forces derive from it.(P)

119

The Void is not a nothing-at-all-ness in the absolute sense, or how could the whole cosmos come forth out of it, how could I myself be released by it, how could the very intellect which thinks this concept appear from it into activity and produce thoughts?

120

Is this not the greatest of Paradoxes that the origin of all things is seeming Nothingness?

121

Within that seeming Void lie the vanished planets of yesterday and the evolving worlds of tomorrow.

122

Since all things are limited in some way or other, or conditioned by some circumstance or other, THAT which is unlimited and unconditioned, which does not exist as they do, cannot rightly be called a thing. It is no-thing, the Void.

123

There is no other, no thing, no experience of an object for it. It is alone in the Void.

Real as Consciousness

124

IT is the Principle behind both consciousness and unconsciousness, making the first possible and the second significant. Yet neither consciousness nor unconsciousness, *as we humans know them, resembles it.*(P)

125

There is a single Consciousness without beginning or end, ever the same in itself, beyond and behind which there is nothing else.

126

Consciousness-in-itself, its own pure formless being, is incorruptible; but viewed from our side, our relation to it, universal and collective, we, individual entities, emerge from it and eventually fall back into it. This applies to all who take on an existence, however tiny it be in dimension or however immense in time, however feeble in power or however majestic in rulership.

127

Although the Absolute is the Unknowable to us, it must be able to know and understand its own being and its own nature.

128

Consciousness untouched by any thought, picture, or name—this has yet to be studied by our Western psychologists.

129

Ultimate reality does not lie in this world, nor in that which perceives it, but in that which perceives the perceiver.

130

Consciousness can exist apart from the world, from the things and creatures in it, and even from the ego, but the world exists only as a projection of consciousness. In this sense the world has no lasting reality but, by contrast, the consciousness has.

131

What is Spirit? It is that which is the essence of mind and therefore mind in its pure state divested of all thoughts, all personal emotions, and all personal egoism. Therefore, it transcends the human concept of individual being. To ascribe human qualities to it is to falsify it and yet, because it is the essence of the mind, it is the essence of every human being.

132

The intellect can never understand this point until it understands that the conception of individuality and the conception of existence are separate and different from each other. Individuality may go but existence may remain.

133

Beyond all forms which consciousness can take is its very essence, consciousness in itself, alone and unique. It can never be transformed or changed and it can never disintegrate.

134

Pure consciousness is not a mental state, but Mind-in-itself, the Mind when gathered entirely into itself. The mental states are brought about by some kind of mental activity, but not here.

135

Consciousness-in-itself is something apart from its objects, which are thoughts, feelings, imaginations, things, bodies—in short, experience.

136

Consciousness stripped of thoughts and pictures becomes bare Being.

137

Consciousness-in-itself does not vary, but its phases and states do.

138

It is Mind which not only lights up its own existence but also all other existence.

139

There are various kinds of consciousness but there is only a single pure Consciousness, one where nothing is put into it—no thoughts, emotions, or objects, even no ego.

2

OUR RELATION TO THE ABSOLUTE

Inadequacy of human symbolization

We may argue about everything except Truth. Even the very best argument can produce only another thought at the end. For Truth can be expressed in words, spoken or written, only by bringing it down to the level of intellect, whereas on its own level as being knowledge of the Real it transcends intellect. Any thought of the Real merely makes an object of it, one among a multitude of other objects, and hence fails to arrive at it.

2

It is impossible to think of the Pure Self without making it an idea, that is, an object, and therefore without missing it.

3

God is neither to be looked upon with human eyes nor comprehended with human intellect. For the eyes see only things and the intellect takes hold only of thoughts.

4

Absolute Being is neither analysable nor measurable, neither imaginable nor weighable.

5

If the Real is unique, if it has no duplicate, nothing inferior to it can make it an object of experience. The ego, the self which sets out to do so, cannot come closer than getting its own personal reactions, however rarefied these may be and however uncommon these mystic experiences are.

6

What the Godhead is we do not know. The nature and the structure of the Grand Mystery are beyond all human investigation. We cannot describe it correctly or name it accurately. We can only observe some of its workings and effects in our individual selves and in the universe.

7

The Infinite Reality cannot be reasoned with, but only reasoned about. It cannot even be adequately symbolized, for regarding it as a mental image, a pictured thought, is only a more refined form of idol-worship. It can only be designated. The true Godhead is unconditioned, formless, not picturable. No individual worship can reach what is utterly beyond all individual existence. No name can be given that will properly stand for what is without attributes and without limitations. In the ultimate reality there are and can be no distinctions and no differences, no grades and no change.

8

The utter incomprehensibility of the ultimate Source makes it impossible for any religion to offer more than its own symbols to the human mind. From them man creates his own mental pictures. But he does not and cannot touch the Untouchable.

9

God is unpicturable by human imagination, truth is unattainable by human thinking. There is a grand mystery at the heart of things. Why then degrade the Unique by confounding its symbols or traditions (in all religions) with its reality?

10

If, remembering the infinitude of the Ultimate Reality, we refuse to personify it and refuse to worship such a personification, we lift ourselves from the exclusively religious to the integrally religio-mystical-philosophic standpoint.

11

In ancient Mexico, the Highest Godhead was "the Idea that could not be reproduced" and no personification or representation of it of any kind was allowed. But this was doctrine only for the upper classes and the intellectually cultivated. The masses were given a God who was visible and comprehensible.

12

The ultimate reality cannot be represented with any fidelity nor can the ultimate truth be communicated with any accuracy.

13

Let no one confuse this grand concept of the Absolute, the Unbounded, the Timeless, with the lesser concept of a God made in a semi-human image.

14

We may not personalize the Absolute except at the terrible cost of utterly deceiving ourselves.

15

Just as Islam allows no portrait, no graven image to represent the man Muhammed; just as Buddha forbade any figure of himself to be made or used (a prohibition disobeyed after a century or two); just as the Jews were willing to be executed rather than to allow Caesarian deificatory effigies newly brought to Jerusalem to be displayed, so philosophy holds that no words can ever describe, no concept ever express, no human leader ever incarnate the ineffable truth, and that all assertions to the contrary merely defile truth. IT cannot be confined.

16

It is totally incommunicable, but *thoughts* about it *can* be communicated in words or formed into pictures.

17

So far as truth can appear in words, this is so. But on the ultimate level, this is but an echo of an echo infinitely multiplied.

18

It is merely a statement *about* reality, but it is not reality itself. It is a sound in the air (if voiced) or a mark on paper (if printed) but not truth.

19

Nothing that words could say could give any proper description of That Which Is, for it belongs to a totally different dimension. So this is God, or more correctly, as near as man can get to God.

20

No one can describe the Absolute, or speak on its behalf, for that would impose his human consciousness upon it and merely create a private imagination about it.

21

The Real cannot be put under any label or classification because it is what it is of itself. Yet it pervades all things.

22

We must separate, in our human thought, Mind as passive reality (the void) from Mind as active being (World-Mind). All our understanding and interpretation of such words as are affixed to this state, be they Over-self, Divine Being, Absolute, or Reality, is inevitably drawn from, and associated with, our experience in the world of time-space and relativity. It is what these words mean for *our* minds, not what they mean in themselves, that constitutes our use of them. We easily fall into self-deception about them, for the meaning given them is what we *imagine*, not what we know.

23

Being especially above all relationships and contrasts that the intellect can make or the imagination can create, it cannot rightly be called "The One" as it so often has been, for that implies that a second or a third entity of the same kind could be added to it, which is false. The intellect may attempt the task during its highest flights, but in the end what does it produce? Only more thoughts!

24

This is the Godhead, of which, in nearly all the ancient religious Mysteries, lawfully man may make no image and to which he may give no name.

25

Why is it that Lao Tzu wrote the Tao cannot be named? Simply because all names attached to it and all descriptions made of it cannot help being incomplete.

26

Each word which can be used for the first goal tells of some particular aspect, be it knowledge, awakening, or enlightenment. Beyond that incomplete description words cannot go, except negatively.

27

The last thought that intelligence can make is about this divine mystery which lies beyond everything thinkable: but it will necessarily have to be a negative thought, that is, it can only say what the Godhead is not, deny any and every affirmation about it, unknow all that it has previously known about God.

28

Every attempt at understanding the Great Mystery, and very much more at representing it, merely leads to self-deception.

29

It is not only the Uncontradictable, but also the Unapproachable.

30

We may ascribe no attributes to Mind nor confine it within any limitations.

31

The great mysterious emptiness—that is all man can know of God.

32

Although nothing can be written about IT that is truly descriptive, everything can be written about what leads up to the revelation of IT; that can be written with precision and luminosity. The inside must forever elude words, but the outside need not. The greatest of questions, "What is Truth?" is answered best by Silence; this answer is inherent in the question. Metaphysics and poetry may provide a medium for clues and hints, symbols and images.

33

To say what the Absolute is not, to describe it in negatives, is correct so far as it goes but is not so satisfactory. The terms Void or Space, being more positive, are even better.

34

Space is a good metaphor for Mind. In one aspect it is bounded, in another it is infinite. Mind also is static and dynamic, still and active, within universes yet transcending them all.

35

What Tibetan Buddhism used as a symbol of the Infinite Being, medieval Christian theology used for the same idea—the circle.

36

Where is the man who has ever known the unknowable and indescribable Supreme Godhead? For all men came into existence after it already was there. But whoever receives knowledge by tradition, investigation, or intuition, by meditation, revelation, or even by science leading into metaphysics, by art or poetry or literature, may acquire the tremendous certitude that it *is* there. More—it must always have been there.

37

That which transcends even the highest of the gods, even World-Mind, is unthinkable and unimaginable. Therefore is it without name or form, beyond all contact with the senses, beginningless and endless, neither growing nor diminishing, indestructible, free from any relations or comparisons—this is the Undefinable Mystery of Mysteries. Let no one seek it, for he cannot find IT. But he can know that it is there and, through its manifestations, the Gods, worship IT.

38

All human explanation of the nature of Mind, as all human expositions of the working of the World-Mind, are limited forms of language. This cannot be helped, for "that which can be named is not the Tao," as a Chinese sage affirmed. It is outside time in a Now beyond the successive character of human thinking and incomprehensible to it. Yet intellect, though it cannot enter this Grand Mystery, can at its most brilliant perception infer that it is.

39

Try as it might, the finite thinking mind cannot break through this sound-barrier of mystery which surrounds the Unique Being, That which is ever the same. All thoughts simply pile up, leaving the last one unanswered, if not unanswerable, or else ending in an involved labyrinth from which there is no outlet. IT cannot be investigated, but the fact of its necessary existence can be stated more emphatically than can any other of the innumerable or observable facts.

40

In the end he will have to confess, as the English hermit Richard Rolle confessed six hundred years ago, despite his deep mystical experiences, that it is not possible to know what God is but only *that* he is.

41

When the last words have been uttered, the final sentences written down; when the sermons, books, and articles have exhausted all that human intellect and human intuition can explain, suggest, or hint; when the profoundest mystical experience has yielded all that it could reveal, there will still remain an awed feeling before the Grand Mystery that is God, a tremendous humility before Its unknowableness.

42

Because there is nothing quite like it in human experience and because there is no opposite in the entire cosmos from which it can be differentiated, the Absolute Being remains utterly incomprehensible to the human intellect.

43

The mystery of That Which Is baffles not only the comprehension of the ordinary mind but also that of the philosophic mind.

44

There is an abyss which no human can cross, a mystery which remains utterly impenetrable to him. This is the transcendent Godhead.

45

We can know as much, and as little, of God as the wave dashing against the Californian coastline can know of the immense ocean stretching so many thousand miles to the Australian shore: such is human insignificance in relation to that activity of God which is directed to this universe. But in relation to that non-activity which is God-in-itself, at rest, we can know absolutely nothing. For here is Being without end, Mind without individualization of any kind, and Life without any bottom or top to it.

46

The Unfathomable Mystery of Mind will always remain.

47

Despite all the absurd claims to the contrary, no one has ever interpreted to us the great Mystery of mysteries, the Godhead behind the God active in the universe.

48

The absoluteness of the Godhead is complete and basic. It is not categorically identical with man any more than the ray is with the sun; they are different although not more fundamentally different than the ray from the sun. Hence there can be no direct communication and no positive relationship between them. A profound impenetrability, an existence beyond comprehension, is the first characteristic of the Godhead, when gazed at by human sight.(P)

49

The Godhead as he is, and God as he appears; God in the vacuous repose of Nothingness, and God in the continuous activity of a cosmos; God forever hidden in his own being and forever unknown to mortals, and God revealed in relation to man; THAT which is not perceptible to human thinking as opposed to HE who is experienceable by intuition—these differences seem to imply an inherent contradiction. Those attractive and positive attributes which we always associate with the very name God—justice, goodness, and the like—cannot be associated with the Godhead for the reason that nobody, not the greatest of mystics, knows or ever can know the Godhead.

50

If man is made in the image of God, then this God is something other than the Ultimate Principle, for THAT has no likeness with anything else; it is a void, a no-thing, and so utterly beyond human perception that it is destined to remain forever unknown.

51

Neither the practice of yoga nor the reflection of metaphysics is alone adequate to comprehend the Real. Neither can inner peace affirm it nor can intellect negate it.

52

Not for the finite mind is there to be knowledge of *Ein Soph*, the Hebrew philosopher's idea of the Infinite, what he terms "the Most Hidden of the Hidden."

53

Leave God alone! Why must men forever bleat and whimper, praise and glorify That of which they know nothing and imagine everything! Why don't they write and fight, argue and quarrel about those things which they can touch or know, see or examine?

54

There is no discernible sign, form, or clue by which the Absolute, the

Unmanifest, may be known. It is wrapped in blackness, which is why the Manifested World is symbolized by light, why its colour is white when contrasted with the other.

55

The great Mystery remains where it always has been—untouched by man's feelings and undefined by his thoughts.

56

Human mentality cannot comprehend the real nature of this mysterious substratum of all existence. Human understanding cannot assimilate that which utterly transcends it.

57

It is not a testable truth; it must be left the mystery that it is.

Reporting, nonetheless, has value

58

If, out of the Silent Mind, words come forth to affirm the consciousness of Consciousness, let it be known that the truth never dies but springs back to life again. We should be glad, enormously happy, that it is so.

59

Philosophy understands sympathetically but does not agree practically with the Buddha's consistent refusal to explain the ultimate realization. His counsel to disciples was: "What word is there to be sent from a region where the chariot of speech finds no track on which to go? Therefore to their questionings offer them silence only."

It is certainly hard to capture this transcendental indefinable experience in prosaic pen-and-ink notes. But is it really so impossible for the initiate to break his silence and voice his knowledge in some dim finited adumbration of the Infinite? To confess that intellectually we know nothing and can know nothing about the Absolute is understandable. But to say that therefore we should leave its existence entirely out of our intellectual world-view, is not. For although the exact definition and direct explanation of words are unable to catch the whole of this subtle experience within their receiving range because they are turned into ordinary human intellectual emotional and physical experience, they may nevertheless evoke an intuitive recognition of its beauty; they may suggest to sensitive minds a hint of its worth and they may arouse the first aspiration towards its attainment for oneself.

Why if this state transcends thinking, whether in words or pictures, have so many mystics nevertheless written so much about it? That they have protested at the same time the impossibility of describing the highest levels of their experience does not alter this curious fact. The answer to our question is that to have kept completely silent and not to have revealed that such a unique experience is possible and that such a supreme reality is existent would have been to have left their less fortunate fellow men in utter ignorance of an immensely important truth about human life and destiny. But to have left some record behind them, even if it would only hint at what it could not adequately describe, would be to have left some light in the darkness. And even though an intellectual statement of a super-intellectual fact is only like an indirect and reflected light, nevertheless it is better than having no light at all.

So long as men feel the need to converse with other men on this subject, so long as masters seek to instruct disciples in it, and so long as fortunate seers recognize the duty to leave some record—even if it be an imperfect one—of their enlightenment behind them for unfortunate humanity, so long will the silence have to be broken, despite Buddha, and the lost word uttered anew.(P)

60

It is the topic most worth writing about yet least understood. Whoever has entered into a partial understanding—it would be too much to demand more—of it, bears some responsibility. He must communicate with his fellows.

61

There was one question which Jesus left unanswered. It was Pontius Pilate's "What is truth?" There was one question which Buddha heard several times but always refused to answer. It was "What is Reality?" Since truth is the knowledge of reality, both amount to the same.

62

The poverty and limitation of human language in this matter, however rich in most other references, makes it necessary to warn the users and readers of words to be careful here. There can only be clues, hints, traces.

63

What can a writer do when confronted with the work of describing the Transcendental except make allusions to it, provide clues which must be followed up by the reader himself, and affirm that it IS?

64

The mystic who tries to give utterance, which is an intellectual act, to that which is itself unutterable, because it transcends intellect, must be understood suggestively and not literally.

65

Because the Real is beyond the thinking intellect's grasp, it cannot be formulated into ideas. Yet because we need signposts and a goal to give guidance and direction, we must tentatively and provisionally formulate it.

66

When the Chinese sages were confronted with the need of telling others what their insight revealed, they said that anything communicated could be affirmed in one way or negated in another, and that therefore it would be quite incorrect. For behind Nature, or as they called it "at the Head," was Mystery beyond all knowing, all thinking, all describing, absolute Being beyond all relativity, that was also Non-Being.

67

All evaluative theories, opinions, judgements, interpretations are as-semblages of thoughts. Insofar as religious theories depart from or lack direct insight into the Real, into what is, they are mere thoughts. Where these thoughts enter into the recording, or the communication, of the result of such insight they colour it, add to it, adulterate it. It is when the person attempts to report the Impersonal that this danger exists.

68

Do not attempt to describe what God is, for whatever you say would limit God, who would then become something inferior to God. This is why Hebrew and Hindu bible alike say he is the Nameless One. But you may describe what God is not, you may draw illustrations from human mind, capacity, and character to suggest what some aspect of God may be like in a quite different degree and way.

69

Once, when the Buddha was at Savatthi, a Brahmin came into the presence of the Exalted One, exchanged greetings, and spake thus: "What think you, Bho Gotama—Everything is?" "Everything is, that Brahmin, is the chief world superstition." "Then indeed, Bho Gotama, nothing is?" "Nothing is, that Brahmin, is the second world superstition." "What think you, Bho Gotama—Everything is a unity?" "Everything is a unity, that Brahmin, is the third world superstition." "Then, indeed, Bho Gotama— everything is a plurality?" "Everything is a plurality, that Brahmin, is the fourth world superstition."

70

Some of the seers even call it blasphemy to proclaim or write down a description of the Supreme Divinity. By this they mean that the mind cannot bring Truth into any limited thought, so a description would be false. The most appropriate act is silent awestruck reverence.

71

Words circumscribe meaning, confine it by the very act of defining it. But the Real is infinite, outside all circumscription and beyond all inclusion. If you must express it, you may do so correctly only by silence. But it is essentially inexpressible.

72

Concepts, thoughts, and words would bring him down from the plane of Being to that of thinking, which would not only be a descent but also a falsification at worst, or a deformation at best.

73

The man who really believes that he can explain nothing of the highest truth to any other man ought to follow his theory into practice. He ought to write nothing and speak nothing about it, create nothing artistically to suggest it. In short, he ought to act as if it does not exist.

74

It is a fundamental error to turn the pure mind into an object of experience in an attempt to reach comprehension. Mind can know everything else and is the inescapable condition of every experience, for by its light every object and every event is revealed, but it cannot itself be known in the same way that we know everything else. Ordinarily there is a knower and a known, and mind would have to transcend such a relation were it to become aware of itself, which means that it would have to transcend thinking itself. Mind itself produces the categories of time, space, and cause which make world experience possible and knowable—that is, thinkable—which is why it cannot be grasped in the same way. The nature of mind is unique, and before its sublime verity speech trembles into silence.

75

In affirming that the One alone exists, they imply their own existence. The affirmation points to someone who affirms, so he must be added to the One, making Two. The more they prattle about the One, the more they proclaim, by inference, the Two.

76

We may perceive how the highest truth turns all lesser doctrines into illusions and yet admits their validity on their own level.

77

There is a beauty in the infinite reality which outshines whatever beauty there is in the imaginative phantasy.

78

"With the lamp of Word one must go beyond Word."—*Lankavatara Sutra*

Reality reveals itself through Overself

79

The chasm between the Real and man seems entirely impassable. The intellect is conditioned by its own finitude, by its particular set of space and time perceptions. It is unable to function where absolutes alone reign. The infinite eternal and absolute existence eludes the grasp of man's logical thought. He may form mental pictures of it but at best they will be as far off from it as a photograph is far off from flesh and blood. Idea-worship is idol-worship. Everything else is an object of knowledge, experienced in a certain way by ourself as the knower of it; but the Infinite Real cannot be an object of anyone's knowledge simply because it cannot be conditioned in any way whatsoever. It is absolute. If it is to be known to all it must therefore be in a totally different way from that of ordinary experience. It is as inaccessible to psychic experience as it is impenetrable by thought and feeling. But although we may not directly know Reality, we may know that it is, and that in some mysterious way the whole cosmic existence roots from it. Thus whichever way man turns he, the finite creature, finds the door closed upon his face. The Infinite and Absolute Essence is forever beyond his vision, unreachable by his knowing capacity and inaccessible to his experience, and will forever remain so. The point is so subtle that, unless its development is expressed with great care here, it is likely to be misunderstood. Although man must pause here and say, with Socrates, "None knoweth save God only"—for with this conception he has gone as far as human thought can grasp such mysteries—nevertheless he may know that the seers have not invented an imaginary Reality. He has neither been left alone in his mortality nor abandoned utterly to his finitude. The mysterious Godhead has provided a witness to its sacred existence, a Deputy to evidence its secret rulership. And that Witness and Deputy *can* be found for it sits imperishable in the very heart of man himself. It is indeed his true self, his immortal soul, his Overself. Although the ultimate principle is said to be inconceivable and unknowable, this is so only in relation to man's ordinary intellect and physical senses. It is not so in relation to a faculty in him which is still potential and unevolved—insight. If it be true that even no adept has ever seen the mysterious absolute, it is also true that he has seen the way it manifests its presence through something intimately emanated from it. If the nameless formless Void from which all things spring up and into which they go back is a world so subtle that it is not really intellectually understandable and so mysterious that it is not even mystically experienceable, we may however experience the strange atmosphere emanating from it, the unearthly aura signifying its hidden presence.(P)

80

Although God is inaccessible to man, man is not inaccessible to God. [Note attached to para reads, PB: Use above as the basic principle of Agnostic Mysticism in former class XIII.]

81

When we seek comprehension of that aspect of the Overself where there is no universe at all, no activity, no ideation, we seem to enter a great void, an utter no-thingness. The "I" cannot breathe in this rarefied atmosphere. And yet it would be the supreme illusion in a world of illusions to regard this void as the abode of unreality.

No object in the universe corresponds to the Overself; therefore we are forced to term it "The Void," but the existence of all objects is only explained by its own.

We may fittingly compare the Overself with any catalytic agent of chemistry which, unaltered itself, activates other substances by its presence. We may carry the comparison further and point out that just as the catalyst is ultimately a product of the same primal stuff as these substances, however different they appear to be, so the thoughts and things whose play constitutes the universe are ultimately of the same primal essence as the Overself.

82

This is passive Mind or pure Being, the First, the Unconditioned Origin of all, the Inconceivable and Unknowable. It is beyond the capacity of any individual entity to penetrate this mystery of mysteries and still remain an individual. A mediating principle is necessary. This exists in the Overself, in man's higher self, which is nothing less than a germ of that same infinite life. If this were not present in man, not only would mystical experience be impossible for him but all religious intuition would be mythical to him.

83

"I and the Father are One," said Jesus. The student asks why the individual should not therefore know the One as oneself? The saying of Jesus presuppposes duality and difference, which explains why the awareness such a student seeks does not exist; it can come only after *all* duality disappears—even that mystical monism which *seems* to have transcended duality but has not really. The theosophy of *The Secret Doctrine* does not reach the height of the doctrine of Nonduality. That is quite all right because it purported to be only a "fragment" of the truth. H.P.Blavatsky wrote that the Causeless Cause, as she termed it, the Absolute, was unknowable and that seekers could reach only to the Logos. Dr. Brunton does not teach that. If all else but the Absolute is illusory (including the Logos) then the path is not worthwhile because truth is unattainable. This philosophy says that Truth *is* attainable and the so-called Absolute *can* be realized by man. Some theosophic studies will help in the understanding of the teachings of this path, while others will bring the student's mind into direct conflict with them. He will have to decide for himself whether to give his loyalty to the one or the other, but this doctrine cannot be mixed with any other save at the risk of diluting its truth. This path is based solely on the appeal to reason, never to belief, whereas there are many items of theosophy which no one can *prove*.

84

Wang Yang-ming and Chou Tun-Yi taught a metaphysic which made "Principle" the Real, the Unique and the Absolute, the ground of all being and existence: they taught that man's nature was aligned with Principle but he had to find his way to this consciousness: they taught that he has the capacity but must realize it, to think and live in goodness, sincerity; finally that the truth, being innate in him, could be found by intuiting it.

85

To say that the ultimate Reality is utterly unknowable is quite correct from the standpoint of the actual human situation involving ordinary and familiar instruments of knowledge, namely, the body's senses and the mind's reasonings. But it is not quite correct from the standpoint of possible human attainment. What neither sense nor intellect can find, a third and higher faculty, now latent, may find. This is the faculty of insight.

86

This is the wordless and pictureless discovery that insight reveals and intelligence confirms. This is the beautiful source of all life and unfailing sustainer of all beings.

87

It is a wisdom-knowledge which is no mere intellectual abstraction but a truly living, deeply felt, and mystically experienced evolution discovery or event—call it as you wish.

88

They are all aware of relative truths concerning this realm of human affairs, but very few are aware of the relativity itself which limits them. The basis of unchanging verities can only be *gnosis*, the deepest kind of perception, the final awareness of mind's absolute experience which swallows up the knower himself by carrying him outside time. This is rarely taught in religion.

89

The inability of little man to enter into the knowledge of transcendent God does not doom him to perpetual ignorance. For God, being present in all things, is present in him too. The flame is still in the spark. Here is his hope and chance. Just as he knows his own personal identity, so God knows God in him as the Overself. This divine knowing *is continually going on, whether he is awake or asleep, whether he is an atheist or a saint.* He can share in it too, but only by consenting to submit his intellect to his intuition. This is not an arbitrary condition imposed by theocratic whim but one which inheres in the very nature of the knowing processes. By accepting it, he may put the whole matter to the test and learn for himself, in due time, his other nonpersonal identity.(P)

90

The divine essence is Unknowable to the finite intellect, but knowable, in a certain sense, by the deepest intuition. And this sense can arise to the man previously prepared by instruction and purification, or by studied knowledge and purification, if he puts away thoughts, even those about the essence, or lets them lapse of their own accord, and awaits its self-disclosure patiently, reverently, lovingly—three conditions of high importance.(P)

91

The Godhead is too far beyond man's conception, experience, and knowledge; the Absolute cannot be comprehended by his finite capacity. It is indeed *the Unknowable.* Now metaphysical ideas must be metaphysically understood. If they are understood sensuously or physically, or if an eternal principle is replaced by a historical person, truth is turned to idolatry. Those who are able to hold such a lofty conception of its fleshly appearance as an Incarnation cannot cramp it into the little box of human individuality. Any prophet who makes such a claim repeatedly is merely emphasizing his person at the cost of his Overself, is glorifying his little self rather than the Infinite whose messenger he claims to be. The man who understands his own limitations and the Absolute's lack of them will never claim equality with it. Such a man will never ask others to show him the reverence which they ought to show to the pure spirit nor to give him the allegiance which they ought to give to God. Whereas nearly all popular religions set up as an intermediary between It and us "The Divinely Incarnate Prophet" or else "The Son of God," philosophy depersonalizes it and sets up instead the true self, the divine soul in man. For even the prophets and avatars whom the divine Godhead sends down to mankind are sent not only to teach them that this Absolute exists but also to direct them towards the realization of their own true inner self. The true self will then reflect as much of the divine as it is able to, but it can never exhaust it. It is the Overself and, through the threefold path, is *Knowable*. In the Unique Godhead, ever mysterious in its unmanifested self-existence, there rises and sets, like the sun's light, the manifested World-Mind, in which—in its turn—there rises and sets all this wonderful cosmos of which it is the very soul. The first is forever beyond man but the second is always accessible to man as the Overself within him.

92

We cannot know it as it is but only can know that the creative God could not have been there if IT had not been there first. We cannot give it any name for no picture, no concept, no thinkable nature is within our apprehension concerning IT. At the enunciation of its mere possibility we are hushed into silence, struck dumb. Let us retreat, then, into territory where a contact is possible, where GOD and MAN may meet.

93

This is the Great Aloneness, where no other living creature may intrude—no matter who—where man and God mingle.

94

When we, human beings, through our most enlightened representatives, look for the highest principle of being, life, existence, consciousness—the Supreme Power, the Origin of all Substance, the ultimate Deity, in fact—we find It is one and the same thing looked at from different human standpoints. It is nameless but we may call it, Mind. There is no point where we can come into contact with It for It transcends everything, every human capacity. When we look for It in relation to the universe which includes us, we may call It World-Mind, or in religious terminology, God. Here there is real possibility of a contact, for in our innermost self the connection is already there.

95

Let us not deceive ourselves and dishonour the Supreme Being by thinking that we know anything at all about IT. We know nothing. The intellect may formulate conceptions, the intuition may give glimpses, but these are our human reactions to IT. Even the sage, who has attained a harmony with his Overself, has found only the godlike *within himself*. Yes, it is certainly the Light, but it is so *for him*, for the human being. He still stands as much outside the divine Mystery as everyone else. The difference is that whereas they stand in darkness he stands in this Light.(P)

96

Philosophic meditation will show him that his own existence is rooted in that of a higher power, while philosophic study will explain some of the laws governing his experiences from birth to death. But at the bottom of existence and experience is ineffable incomprehensible Mystery.(P)

97

Neither the senses nor the intellect can tell us anything about the intrinsic nature of this Infinite Mind. Nevertheless we are not left in total ignorance about it. From its manifestation, the cosmos, we may catch a hint of its Intelligence. From its emanation, the soul, we may catch more than a hint of its Beneficence. "More than," I say, because the emanation may be felt within us as our very being whereas the manifestation is outside us and is apart.(P)

98

After the last sermon has been preached, the last book written, Mind remains the Mystery behind all mysteries. Thought cannot conceive It, imagination picture It, nor language express It. The greatest mystic's experience is only his own personal reaction to Its atmosphere, as from a distance. Even this blows him to pieces like a bomb, but the fact that he can collect them together again afterwards shows that it must have been present in some inexplicable supernormal way and was not lost, both to continue existence and to remember the event.(P)

Meditations on Mind

99

The topic with which all such metaphysical thinking should end after it has pondered on mentalism is that out of which the thinking principle itself arises—Mind—and it should be considered under its aspect as the one reality. When this intellectual understanding is brought within one's own experience as fact, when it is made as much one's own as a bodily pain, then it becomes direct insight. Such thinking is the most profitable and resultful in which he can engage, for it brings the student to the very portal of Mind where it stops activity by itself and where the differentiation of ideas disappears. As the mental muscles strain after this concept of the Absolute, the Ineffable and Infinite, they lose their materialist rigidity and become more sensitive to intimations from the Overself. When thinking is able to reach such a profound depth that it attains utter impersonality and calm universality, it is able to approach the fundamental principle of its own being. When hard thinking reaches a culminating point, it then voluntarily destroys itself. Such an attainment of course can take place deep within the innermost recesses of the individual's consciousness alone.(P)

100

He will arrive at the firm unshakeable conviction that there is an inward reality behind all existence. If he wishes he may go farther still and seek to translate the intellectual idea of this reality into a conscious fact. In that case the comprehension that in the quest of pure Mind he is in quest of that which is alone the Supreme Reality in this entire universe, must possess him. The mystery of Mind is a theme upon which no aspirant can ever reflect enough: first, because of its importance, and second, because of its capacity to unfold his latent spirituality. He will doubtless feel cold on these lofty peaks of thought, but in the end he will find a heavenly reward whilst still on earth. We are not saying that something of the nature of mind as we humans know it is the supreme reality of the universe, but only that it is more like that reality than anything else we know of and certainly more like it than what we usually call by the name of "matter." The simplest way to express this is to say that Reality is of the nature of our mind rather than of our body, although it is Mind transcending the familiar phases and raised to infinity. It is the ultimate being the highest state. This is the Principle which forever remains what it was and will be. It is in the universe and yet the universe is in it too. It never evolves, for it is outside time. It has no shape, for it is outside space. It is beyond man's consciousness, for it is beyond both his thoughts and sense-experience, yet all consciousness springs mysteriously out of it. Nevertheless man may enter into its knowledge, may enter into its Void, so soon as he can drop his thoughts, let go his sense-experience, but keep his sense of being. Then he may understand what Jesus meant when saying: "He that loseth his life shall find it." Such an accomplishment may appear too spectral to be of any use to his matter-of-fact generation. What is their madness will be his sanity. He will know there is reality where they think there is nothingness.(P)

101

To keep this origin always at the back of one's mind because it is also the end of all things, is a necessary practice. But this can only be done if one cultivates reactionlessness to the happenings of every day. This does not mean showing no outward reaction, but it does mean that deep down indifference has been achieved—not an empty indifference, but one based on seeing the Divine essence in all things, all creatures, and a Divine meaning in all happenings.(P)

102

There is only this one Mind. All else is a seeming show on its surface. To forget the ego and think of this infinite and unending reality is the highest kind of meditation.

103

First, remember that It is appearing as ego; then remember to think that *you* are It; finally cease to think *of* It so you may be free of thoughts to be It!(P)

104

To attach oneself to a guru, an avatar, one religion, one creed, is to see the stars only. To put one's faith in the Infinite Being and in its presence within the heart, is to see the vast empty sky itself. The stars will come and go, will disintegrate and vanish, but the sky remains.(P)

105

In a world of constantly changing scenes, fortunes, health, and relation-ships, a precious possession is the knowledge that there is the unseen Unchanging Real. Still more precious is awareness within oneself of ITS ever-presence.

106

In the moment that there dawns on his understanding the fact of Mind's beginninglessness and deathlessness, he gains the second illumination, the first being that of the ego's illusoriness and transiency.(P)

107

Not to find the Energy of the Spirit but the Spirit itself is the ultimate goal—not its power or effects or qualities or attributes but the actuality of pure being. The aspirant is not to stop short with any of these but to push on.

108

He will have gone far intellectually when he can understand the state-ment that mind is the seeker but Mind is the sought.(P)

109

He who puts his mind on the Unlimited instead of on the little parts, who does not deal with fractions but with the all-absorbing Whole, gains some of Its power.

110

What we need to grasp is that although our apprehension of the Real is gradual, the Real is nonetheless with us at every moment in all its radiant totality. Modern science has filled our heads with the false notion that reality is in a state of evolution, whereas it is only our mental concept of reality which is in a state of evolution.(P)

111

Thinking can, ordinarily, only produce more thoughts. Even thinking about truth, about reality, however correct it be, shares this limitation. But if properly instructed it will know its place and understand the situation, with the consequence that at the proper moment it will make no further effort, and will seek to merge into meditation. When the merger is successfully completed, a holy silence will pervade the consciousness which remains. Truth will then be revealed of its own accord.(P)

112

When all thoughts are gone, when all vibration, movement, or activity of the thinking faculty has ceased, then is the self-revealing possible of Mind-in-itself, of Consciousness without its states.

113

Where the intellect is active it creates a double result—the thought and the thinker. Where the enlightened man goes into the Stillness this duality does not appear but Consciousness remains. It contains nothing created by him. It is the Alone.

114

Every creature, from the most primitive amoeba up to the most intellectual man, has some kind and degree of awareness; but only the Illuminate has that toward which awareness itself is striving to attain—Consciousness.

115

The "Void" means void of all mental activity and productivity. It means that the notions and images of the mind have been emptied out, that all perceptions of the body and conceptions of the brain have gone.(P)

116

Master Huang Po: "This Mind is here, now. But as soon as any thought arises you miss it. It is like space . . . unthinkable."

117

What Lao Tzu calls "the great Emptiness" is the Ultimate Being, without form, Matterless and Motionless, ineffable, and undescribable except by statements of what it is not. Those whose study can lead them to this high level must then let go of words, abandon images, representations, symbols, numberings, divisions, and dualities; must be ready to enter the Stillness.

118

This is what Lao Tzu meant when he advised: "Attain to the utmost Vacuity. Cling single-heartedly to Quietude."

119

Mentalism is the study of Mind and its product, thoughts. To separate the two, to disentangle them, is to become aware of Awareness itself. This achievement comes not by any process of intellectual activity but by the very opposite—suspending such activity. And it comes not as another idea but as extremely vivid, powerfully compelling insight.(P)

120

Nothing that the mind can think into mental existence is IT.

121

Mind in its most unlimited sense is reality. A man can know it only by the intuitive process of *being* it, in the same manner in which he knows his name, which is not an intellectual process but an immediate one.

122

We shall never grasp that totality of being with our intellect, but we shall grasp it with the only thing capable of holding it, with Consciousness.

123

The *awareness* of It as being It is something other, and more, than the mere emptiness of mind.

124

God is unfathomable and unknowable. Every idea of Him is a false idea, created to satisfy our little human mental need but also sharing our finite human limitations. That is, the idea describes something about man, nothing about God. We prefer to delude ourselves with such images and idols, rather than to take off our shoes at the very remembrance of God and enter the mosque of the Silenced Mind. Here, at least, we get no untrue concepts which have to be discarded in the end. Here the awakened faint or strong intuition may get intimations godlike in quality, of THAT which must always remain incomprehensible to the intellect.

125

Those who look to God as a healer, or as a mother, or as a father, or as a teacher are still looking for God within the ego. They are thinking of God only in relation to themselves because their first interest is in themselves. But those who look to God in the Void, and not in any relationship or under any image or idea, really find God. Therefore they really find "the peace which passeth understanding."

126

All attempts to explain the inexplicable, to describe the inscrutable, to communicate the ineffable must end in failure if they begin and end in words. For then it is merely intellect talking to intellect. But let the attempts be made in the stillness, let "heart speak to heart," and the Real may reveal itself.

127

All talk of things being inside or outside the mind is submission to the spell of a vicious spatial metaphor. All language is applicable to things and thoughts, but not to the august infinity of mind. Here every word can be at best symbolic and at worst irrelevant, while remaining always as remote from definable meaning as unseen and unseeable universes are from our own. We have lived in illusions long enough. Let us not yield the last grand hope of man to the deceptive sway of profane words. Here there must and shall be SILENCE—serene, profound, mysterious, yet satisfying beyond all earthly satisfactions.

128

It is not possible for a finite human being to grasp the infinite significance of the Infinite Being, nor to gather any true idea about such Being. He can only think what It is not: otherwise he must retreat into utter silence, not merely of speech alone but also of mental imaginative and passional activity.

129

(a) Awareness alone *is* whatever it turns its attention to, seems to exist at the time: only that. If to Void then there is nothing else. If to world, then world assumes reality. (b) What is it that is aware? The thought of a point of awareness creates, gives reality at the lowest level to ego, and at the highest to Higher Self but when the thought itself is dropped there is only the One Existence, Being, in the divine Emptiness. It is therefore the Source of all life, intelligence, form. (c) The idea held becomes direct experience for the personality, the awareness becomes direct perception.(P)

130

Awareness is the very nature of one's being: it *is* the Self.(P)

131

Every man credits himself with having consciousness during the wakeful state. He never questions or disputes the fact. He does not need anyone else to tell it to him, nor does he tell it to himself. It is the surest part of his knowledge. Yet this is not a knowing which he brings into the field of awareness. It is known differently from the way other facts are known by him. This difference is that the ego is absent from the knowledge—the fact is not actually perceived.(P)

132

Reason tells us that pure Thought cannot know itself because that would set up a duality which would be false if pure thought is the only real existence. But this is only reason's inability to measure what transcends itself. Although all ordinary experience confirms it, extraordinary experience refutes it.(P)

133

Consciousness is the best witness to its own existence.

134

When we experience Mind through the senses we call it *matter*. When we experience it through imagination or thinking we call it *idea*. When we experience it as it is in its own pure being, we call it Spirit, or better, Overself.

The ultimate "experience"

135

In grammar, sentences are built up basically from three things: a subject, a verb, and an object, with the subject acting upon the object through the verb. A sentence is not considered complete unless it has these three things, this relationship between the subject and the object. In metaphysics, every experience also requires a subject and an object—a person or a thing who is affected by or produces an action on a second entity. All statements about human experiences must include this subject-object relationship. Thus, in the relationship between a man and his thoughts, the man is the subject and the thoughts are the objects. In Oriental metaphysics, a similar relationship holds good—except that the subject is there called the seer, the object is called the seen, and seeing describes the relationship between the two. All existence in the time-space order as experienced by a human being necessarily has these three elements within it. There is no subject without an object, no seer without a seen plus the relationship or the action between them. They are always linked together. If however we look beyond this existence to the timeless spaceless Reality, it is obvious that there can be no such relationship therein, for it is completely nondual, the Reality which never changes, which has no second thing. We learn from mentalism that this Reality is Mind. If we are ever to find it we know that it cannot be found as if it were a second thing, with us as subject and it as object. In that sense we can never find it, but only substitutes which themselves are in duality. We have indeed to set up a search for the kind of consciousness where there is no object to be experienced and therefore where there is no subject-ego to receive the experience. Such is the unified consciousness which is none other than Mind itself. We can use this criterion not only with reference to our experiences of the world but also with reference to our inner mystical experiences and check from this on what level they really are.

136

Mind has no second thing to know and experience, no world. Nor can anyone know and experience Mind and yet remain an individual, a person.(P)

137

When thought of the little self vanishes, even gloating thought of its spiritual rapture, and That which is behind or beyond it in utter stillness is alone felt and known, then he is said to experience "the touch of the Untouchable," as ancient sages called it.

138

Asparsa Yoga: The literal meaning is "non-touching" or, possibly, "touching the Untouchable." Everything is either related to, or in contact with, something else, that is, in touch with it. But in the state of *Asparsa* there is no such possibility because the nondual Brahman is alone acknowledged, THAT which is uncontacted by anything.

139

If you believe that you have had the ultimate experience, it is more likely that you had an emotional, or mental, or mystic one. The authentic thing does not *enter* consciousness. You do not know that it has transpired. You discover it is already here only by looking back at what you were and contrasting it with what you now are; or when others recognize it in you and draw attention to it; or when a situation arises which throws up your real status. It is a permanent fact, not a brief mystic "glimpse."(P)

140

The true union, completely authentic and completely beatific, where mind melts into Mind without the admixture of personal wish or traditional suggestion, cannot be properly described in words. For he who experiences it may know its onset or its end because of the enormous contrast with his ordinary self, but he will not know its full height simply because he will not even know that he is experiencing it. *For to do so would be to re-introduce the ego again and thus fall away from the purity of the union.* There would then be admixture—which is the fate of most unions.(P)

141

All teachings which try to inform us what the Real is like can only honestly do so if they use negative terms: they can only say what it is not like. For where is the individual who can continue to exist in its discovery and note its nature or attributes? His limited consciousness has dissolved in the larger one. Only afterwards, when looking back at the experience, dare he say that the *experience* itself was ineffable but what it concerned was incomprehensible; it was luminous, but that which shone was an unseen power.

142

The actual experience alone can settle this argument. This is what I found: The ego vanished; the everyday "I" which the world knew and which knew the world, was no longer there. But a new and diviner individuality appeared in its place, a consciousness which could say "I AM" and which I recognized to have been my real self all along. It was not lost, merged, or dissolved: it was fully and vividly conscious that it was a point *in* universal Mind and so not apart from that Mind itself. Only the lower self, the false self, was gone but that was a loss for which to be immeasurably grateful.(P)

143

When you speak of "an experience" you imply that first, there is an experiencer and second, there is an object of which he has an experience. That is, you refer to the realm of duality. It may be lofty, inspiring, unusual, but it is an event with a beginning and an ending; it is inside time, however variously the sense of time changes. It is not to be identified with the Real.

144

The ordinary person is quite incapable of penetrating the absolute. The extraordinary person—the genius—may get flashes of intuition which reflect some truths that lift him above the little self. But no one really attains the absoluteness without getting dissolved in it, without knowing and remembering nothing of it. Those who claim these "unions with God" are really describing something quite different. Too often they are overwhelmed by their experience and quite naturally take it to be outside relativity when it is in fact a higher degree of it.

145

The question of "I" and of self-consciousness in any form, whether universal or personal, vanishes when the truth is known because there is none then to mark out selfhood of any kind. When it is understood that the mind cannot become an object to itself, it will be understood that everything one may say about it will merely impose an illusory limitation upon it. There are not two thoughts, the ego and the universal self, to enter into relationship in the final stage.

146

The ocean of infinite impersonal being closes over the man's ego, and he is forever submerged in anonymity, never again to see or be seen.

147

The final grade of inner experience, the deepest phase of contemplation, is one where the experiencer himself disappears, the meditator vanishes, the knower no longer has an object—not even the Overself—to know for duality collapses. Because this grade is beyond the supreme "Light" experience where the Overself reveals its presence visually as a dazzling mass, shaft, ball, or ray of unearthly radiance which is seen whether the bodily eyes are open or closed, it has been called the divine darkness.(P)

148

He can find the nothingness within himself only after he has evaluated the nothingness of himself. The mystery of the Great Void does not disclose itself to the smugly satisfied or the arrogantly proud or the intellectually conceited.(P)

149

The truth becomes self-evident on this highest level and needs no endorsement from anything or anyone outside. It puts the searching intellect and the aspiring emotions back in their place as mere channels for its use.

150

Here is the most private experience anyone can have—to be alone with the Alone!

151

To return to the Source is to hold on until you immerse yourself in the threefold being of Time, Space, and Mind which together make the One, the Source of God.

152

What the Sage Plotinus called the First Principle, the One, is as high as enlightenment can bring the seeker.

153

In this astonishing revelation, he discovers that he himself is the seeker, the teacher, and the sought-for goal.

154

Without keeping steadily in view this original mentalness of things and hence their original oneness with self and Mind, the mystic must naturally get confused if not deceived by what he takes to be the opposition of Spirit and Matter. The mystic looks within, to self; the materialist looks without, to world. And each misses what the other finds. But to the philosopher neither of these is primary. He looks to that Mind of which both self and world are but manifestations and in which he finds the manifestations also. It is not enough for him to receive, as the mystic receives, fitful and occasional illuminations from periodic meditation. He relates this intellectual understanding to his further discovery got during mystical self-absorption in the Void that the reality of his own self is Mind. Back in the world once more he studies it again under this further light, confirms that the manifold world consists ultimately of mental images, conjoins with his full metaphysical understanding that it is simply Mind in manifestation, and thus comes to comprehend that it is essentially one with the same Mind which he experiences in self-absorption. Thus his insight actualizes, experiences, this Mind-in-itself as and not apart from the sensuous world whereas the mystic divides them. With insight, the sense of oneness does not destroy the sense of difference but both remain strangely present, whereas with the ordinary mystical perception each cancels the other. The myriad forms which make up the picture of this world will not disappear as an essential characteristic of reality nor will his awareness of them or his traffic with them be affected. Hence he possesses a firm and final attainment wherein he will permanently possess the insight into pure Mind even in the midst of physical sensations. He sees everything in this multitudinous world as being but the Mind itself as easily as he can see nothing, the imageless Void, as being but the Mind itself, whenever he cares to turn aside into self-absorption. He sees both the outer faces of all men and the inner depths of his own self as being but the Mind itself. Thus he experiences the unity of all existence; not intermittently but at every moment he knows the Mind as ultimate. This is the philosophic or final realization. It is as permanent as the mystic's is transient. Whatever he does or refrains from doing, whatever he experiences or fails to experience, he gives up all discriminations between reality and appearance, between truth and illusion, and lets his insight function freely as his thoughts select and cling to nothing. He experiences the miracle of undifferentiated being, the wonder of undifferenced unity. The artificial man-made frontiers melt away. He sees his fellow men as inescapably and inherently divine as they are, not merely as the mundane creatures they believe they are, so that any traces of an ascetical holier-than-thou attitude fall completely away from him.(P)

155

Only after he has worked his way through different degrees of comprehension of the world whose passing his own development requires, and even after he has penetrated the mystery beyond it, does he come to the unexpected insight and attitude which frees him from both. In other words he is neither in the Void, the One, or the Many yet nor is he not in them. Truth thus becomes a triple paradox!(P)

156

In the highest level there are utterly unalterable truths. They are not got by logic, worked out by intellect, or discovered by observation. They are announced. No one can know their mysterious source in the sense that we know anything else. It is unique, indescribable, and hence unnameable, unimaginable, and beyond all the forms of worship given to all other gods—nowhere to be found in place or time, history or commentary. It is more honest to let the Mystery of Mysteries remain as it is than to repeat ancient portrayals or create new ones—all the labour of the human ego's trivial or even misleading ideation. Within that silent *seeming* void, which is as near as most are likely to come, they may be pacified, content, perhaps even dissolved during those utterly surrendered lapses.

Index for Part 1

Entries are listed by chapter number followed by "para" number. For example, 1.77 means chapter 1, para 77, and 2.126, 141 means chapter 2, paras 126 and 141. Chapter listings are separated by a semicolon. Please note also that, for the reader's convenience, the first number in the right-hand running heads throughout the text indicates chapter number.

Index for Parts 2, 3, 4

Entries for this composite index are listed by category *and* chapter number followed by "para" number. For example, 28:1.4 means category 28 (*The Alone*), chapter 1, para 4, and 26:4.245, 260 means category 26 (*World-Idea*), chapter 4, paras 245 and 260. Category-and-chapter listings are separated by a semicolon. Please note also that, for the reader's convenience, the first number in the right-hand running heads throughout the text indicates chapter number.

oppositions in 26:3.18, 23, 29, 38,
  48, 54, 61, 63
and World-Idea 26:1.14; 26:4.213;
  27:1.28
necessity 26:1.76; 27:3.60
Nepalese-Tibetan esotericism 27:2.9
New Testament 26:1.71; 27:2.4
Nietzsche, Friedrich
  Wilhelm 26:3.123
Non-being 28:1.78
noncausality 28:1.34
nonduality 26:3.8; 26:4.260;
  28:1.25–36; 28:2.83, 135; *see also*
  duality
Nothing 26:1.197; 27:2.68; 28:1.43,
  115–116
Nothingness 28:1.120; 28:2.148
nought 27:3.60; 28:1.47
Noumenon 27:3.55
Nous (Mind) 26:1.81
Now 26:1.89; 28:2.38
number 26:1.103, 106, 108; 27:2.55;
  28:1.47
  two 27:3.60; 28:1.31; 28:2.75
  see also nought; One

O

One 27:2.69; 28:2.155
  implies reality of two 27:3.60;
    28:1.30; 28:2.23, 75, 83
  and Many 28:1.31, 40
  number 27:3.60; 28:1.31, 47
  see also number
One Base 26:1.220
One Infinite Life-Power 27:1.48;
  28:1.11
One Infinite Mind 27:2.26
One Reality 26:4.160
opposites 26:3.8, 10, 17, 146;
  27:2.48
Oriental religions 26:3.18
Ouspensky, P.D. 26:3.122
Overself 26:4.44, 105, 123, 128–129,
  213, 254, 265; 27:1.29; 27:2.40;

28:1.23–24, 53–54, 116; 28:2.22,
  134, 147
  awareness of 26:4.43
  consciousness of 26:4.255
  as Deputy 28:1.41; 28:2.79
  and ego 26:4.86, 249, 256–257,
    264
  as function of Mind 28:1.51
  as germ of infinite life 28:2.82
  I-ness 26:4.234
  as infinite absolute principle of
    mind 26:4.178
  as revealing Reality 28:2.79–98

P

pantheism 27:3.4
paradox 26:1.197; 26:3.1–7, 79;
  27:3.65; 28:1.76, 120; 28:2.155
path, threefold 28:2.91
Pavese, Cesare 26:3.49
Persia 26:3.18
philosopher 27:1.52; 28:1.115;
  28:2.154
  and government 26:4.231
  and knowledge of World-
    Idea 26:1.47
philosophic truth, God of 27:1.1
philosophic meditation and
  study 28:2.96
philosophic realization 28:2.154
philosophy 26:1.2, 166; 26:2.24;
  26:4.123, 186, 260; 27:2.2; 28:1.3,
  88–89; 28:2.15, 59, 83, 91
  on evolution 26:4.20, 257
physics 26:2.26; 26:3.115
Pilate, Pontius 28:2.61
piranha 26:1.32; 26:3.48
Planck, Max 26:1.165
planets 26:1.19, 128; 27:2.7
  other and waves of life 26:4.235–
    237
  visitation from higher 26:1.153
  see also earth, and planets

T

T'ai Chi 26:3.8; 28:1.4
Tao 27:2.58; 28:1.4, 48; 28:2.25, 38
Tao Teh Ching 26:3.3
TAT 28:1.4
teacher 28:2.153
Teh 28:1.48
theologians 27:3.28
theosophic studies 28:2.83
thinking 26:3.33; 27:1.56; 28:2.99
  and meditation on Mind 28:2.111–113
Thought 27:3.1
and thoughts 26:1.210; 28:1.5
thought 26:1.65; 26:4.37, 72;
  27:2.36; 28:2.154
thought-world 27:3.19
time 26:4.123 199, 249; 28:2.74, 100
  as moving image of
    eternity 26:1.237
  and World-Idea 26:1.8, 66, 88–91,
    94–98
  and World-Mind 27:2.34, 39
time and space 26:3.22; 27:1.48;
  27:2.30, 40, 46; 28:1.101; 28:2.22,
  135, 151
  beyond 27:3.58
Timeless 27:3.55; 28:1.108, 116
touch of the Untouchable 28:2.137–138
trance, and mineral
  consciousness 26:1.205
truth 26:1.184; 27:1.67; 28:1.34,
  116; 28:2.1, 32, 61, 76, 84, 111
  attainability of 28:2.83
  highest level of 28:2.156

U

ultimate, as Reality, *see* Reality, as
  Ultimate
ultimate experience 28:2.135–156

Unconditioned, revealing itself as
  Conditioned 26:1.196
unit of life 26:4.257
universal change, metaphysical view
  of 26:2.21–32
universal flux, spiral movement
  of 26:3.124–148
Universal Mind 26:1.78; 26:4.72,
  191; 27:1.18
universal reality, as neither unit nor
  cipher 28:1.30
universe 26:1.162; 26:4.78, 96;
  27:1.59; 27:2.2, 6, 37, 57; 28:1.60;
  28:2.81
  and appearance 26:1.157
  beauty of 26:1.200
  birth of 26:1.177
  creation of 26:1.148–177
  cyclic nature of 26:1.105, 170;
    26:3.83–123; 27:1.68
  divine order of, *see* Cat. 26, Ch. 1
  dualities of, *see* Cat. 26, Ch. 3
  as emanation of Reality 26:1.178–240
  first principle of 27:1.50
  in-breathing and out-breathing
    of 26:1.160; 26:3.22
  One and Many 27:2.74
  and opposites 26:3.20–82
  pulsation of 26:1.152–153 27:2.60
  vs. Reality 28:2.100
  repeated reincarnations of 26:3.22,
    46
  rhythm of 26:3.101–120
  as symbol 26:1.188–195
  symbols of structure of 26:3.53
  and World-Mind 27:2.25
  see also cosmos; world
universes
  appearance and disappearance
    of 26:1.171; 26:2.26; 27:3.54
  infinite number of 26:1.163, 231,
    240
  numerous and wave of life 26:1.74

THE NOTEBOOKS OF PAUL BRUNTON: FIRST SERIES

The twenty-eight categories from the "Ideas" section of the personal notebooks Paul Brunton (1898–1981) reserved for posthumous publication are presented sequentially in sixteen volumes. The following list reproduces chapter titles and subheadings for each volume in the series, except for volume one, which is a representative survey of all twenty-eight categories.

continued next page

continued next page

    continued next page

        continued next page

continued next page

        continued next page

Humility is needed
Longing for freedom from ego
Knowledge is needed
Tracing ego to its source
"Dissolution" of ego
Grace is needed
Who is seeking?
Results of dethroning ego

PART 2: FROM BIRTH TO REBIRTH
1   DEATH, DYING, AND IMMORTALITY
    Continuity, transition, and immortality
    The event of death
    The aftermath of death
2   REBIRTH AND REINCARNATION
    The influence past tendencies
    Reincarnation and Mentalism
    Beliefs about reincarnation
    Reincarnation and the Overself
3   LAWS AND PATTERNS OF EXPERIENCE
    Defining karma, fate, and destiny
    Karma's role in human development
    Destiny turns the wheel
    Astrology, fate, and free will
    Karma, free will, and the Overself
4   FREE WILL, RESPONSIBILITY, AND THE WORLD-IDEA
    The limitations of free will
    The freedom we have to evolve
    Human will in the World-Idea

Volume Seven   (Contains categories 10 and 11)
PART 1: HEALING OF THE SELF
1   THE LAWS OF NATURE
    The spiritual importance of health
    Disease has hidden causes
    Physical mortality
    The Philosopher's body
2   THE UNIVERSAL LIFE-FORCE
    The vital body
    Nature's healing power
    Exercises and meditations
3   THE ORIGINS OF ILLNESS
    The karma of the body
    Mental states and physical conditions
    The importance of hygiene
    Dangers of drugs and alcohol
        continued next page

    continued next page

Volume Ten: The Orient (Contains category 15)

continued next page

Volume Twelve   (Contains categories 17 and 18)

PART 1: THE RELIGIOUS URGE
1   ORIGIN, PURPOSE OF RELIGIONS
    Introductory
    On evaluating religions
    Prophets and messengers
    Purpose of popular (mass) religion
    On diversity in religion
    On choosing one's religion
    Grading teaching to capacity
2   ORGANIZATION, CONTENT OF RELIGION
    Clergy
    Church and State
    Religious symbols
    Places of worship
    Ceremonies and rituals
    Relics
    Scriptures
    Conceptions of God
3   RELIGION AS PREPARATORY
    Doubt
    Inner worship is superior
    Mysticism and religion
4   PROBLEMS OF ORGANIZED RELIGION
    On criticism and scepticism
    Cycles of inspiration, decay
    Accretions, distortion, corruption
    Sectarianism
    Intolerance
    Superstition
    Dogma
    Institutionalism, exploitation
5   COMMENTS ON SPECIFIC RELIGIONS
    Ancient religions
    Bahaism
    Buddhism
    Christianity
    Hinduism
    Islam
    Jainism
    Judaism

continued next page

            continued next page

continued next page

         continued next page

        continued next page

continued next page

Master-disciple relationship, general
Master is symbol of Overself
True relationship is internal
Eventual graduation of disciple

PART 2: WORLD-IDEA
1   DIVINE ORDER OF THE UNIVERSE
    Meaning, purpose, intelligent order
    Ultimate "rightness" of events
    Nature of the World-Idea
    World-Idea is ultimate determinant
    Uniqueness, non-duplication
    On the "why" of "creation"
    Universe as emanation of Reality
2   CHANGE AS UNIVERSAL ACTIVITY
    Everything changes
    Metaphysical view of universal change
3   POLARITIES, COMPLEMENTARIES, DUALITIES OF THE UNIVERSE
    Paradox, duality, nonduality
    Opposites constitute universe
    Cyclic unfoldment, reversal
    Spiral movement of universal flux
4   TRUE IDEA OF MAN
    Man more than animal
    Divine essence of Man
    Purpose of human life
    Glimpsing the World-Idea
    Co-operating with the World-Idea
    World-Idea guides evolution
    Evolution's goal is not merger

PART 3: WORLD-MIND
1   WHAT IS GOD?
    Differing views of God
    Is God good, conscious?
    God beyond finite knowing
    The active God we worship
2   NATURE OF WORLD-MIND
    Attributes, characteristics, powers
    As source of all
3   WORLD-MIND AND "CREATION"
    How
    Why
    Distinguishing World-Mind and Mind
    continued next page